CLAMP

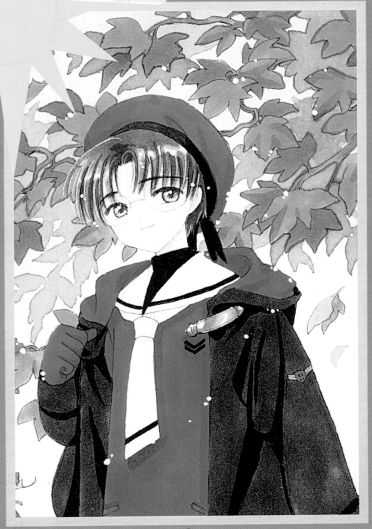

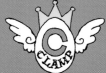

ALSO AVAILABLE FROM TOKYOPOP

MANGA

ANGELIC LAYER*
BABY BIRTH* (September 2003)
BATTLE ROYALE*
BRAIN POWERED* (June 2003)
BRIGADOON* (August 2003)
CARDCAPTOR SAKURA
CARDCAPTOR SAKURA: MASTER OF THE CLOW*
CLAMP SCHOOL DETECTIVES*
CHOBITS*
CHRONICLES OF THE CURSED SWORD (July 2003)
CLOVER
CONFIDENTIAL CONFESSIONS* (July 2003)
CORRECTOR YUI
COWBOY BEBOP*
COWBOY BEBOP: SHOOTING STAR* (June 2003)
DEMON DIARY (May 2003)
DIGIMON
DRAGON HUNTER (June 2003)
DRAGON KNIGHTS*
DUKLYON: CLAMP SCHOOL DEFENDERS* (September 2003)
ERIKA SAKURAZAWA* (May 2003)
ESCAFLOWNE* (July 2003)
FAKE*(May 2003)
FLCL* (September 2003).
FORBIDDEN DANCE* (August 2003)
GATE KEEPERS*
G-GUNDAM* (June 2003)
GRAVITATION* (June 2003)
GTO*
GUNDAM WING
GUNDAM WING: ENDLESS WALTZ*
GUNDAM: THE LAST OUTPOST*
HAPPY MANIA*
HARLEM BEAT
INITIAL D*
I.N.V.U.
ISLAND
JING: KING OF BANDITS* (June 2003)
JULINE
KARE KANO*
KINDAICHI CASE FILES* (June 2003)
KING OF HELL (June 2003)

KODOCHA*
LOVE HINA*
LUPIN III*
MAGIC KNIGHT RAYEARTH* (August 2003)
MAN OF MANY FACES* (May 2003)
MARMALADE BOY*
MARS*
MIRACLE GIRLS
MIYUKI-CHAN IN WONDERLAND* (October 2003)
MONSTERS, INC.
NIEA_7* (August 2003)
PARADISE KISS*
PARASYTE
PEACH GIRL
PEACH GIRL: CHANGE OF HEART*
PET SHOP OF HORRORS* (June 2003)
PLANET LADDER
PLANETS* (October 2003)
PRIEST
RAGNAROK
RAVE MASTER*
REAL BOUT HIGH SCHOOL*
REALITY CHECK
REBIRTH
REBOUND*
SABER MARIONETTE J* (July 2003)
SAILOR MOON
SAINT TAIL
SAMURAI DEEPER KYO* (June 2003)
SCRYED*
SHAOLIN SISTERS*
SHIRAHIME-SYO* (December 2003)
THE SKULL MAN*
SORCERER HUNTERS
TOKYO MEW MEW*
UNDER THE GLASS MOON (June 2003)
VAMPIRE GAME* (June 2003)
WILD ACT* (July 2003)
WISH*
X-DAY* (August 2003)
ZODIAC P.I.* (July 2003)

CINE-MANGA™

AKIRA*
CARDCAPTORS
JIMMY NEUTRON (COMING SOON)
KIM POSSIBLE
LIZZIE McGUIRE
SPONGEBOB SQUAREPANTS (COMING SOON)
SPY KIDS 2

NOVELS

SAILOR MOON
KARMA CLUB (COMING SOON)

TOKYOPOP KIDS

STRAY SHEEP (September 2003)

ART BOOKS

CARDCAPTOR SAKURA*
MAGIC KNIGHT RAYEARTH*

ANIME GUIDES

GUNDAM TECHNICAL MANUALS
COWBOY BEBOP
SAILOR MOON SCOUT GUIDES

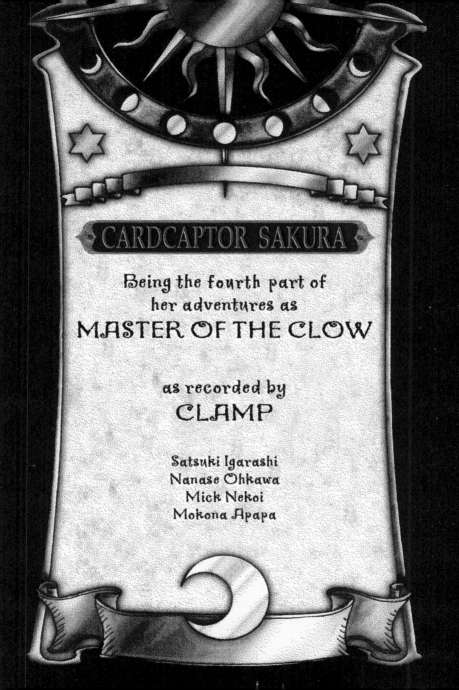

CARDCAPTOR SAKURA

Being the fourth part of
her adventures as
MASTER OF THE CLOW

as recorded by
CLAMP

Satsuki Igarashi
Nanase Ohkawa
Mick Nekoi
Mokona Apapa

Translator - Anita Sengupta
English Adaption - Carol Fox
Copy Editor - Jodi Bryson
Retouch & Lettering - Krystal Dawson
Cover Artist - Raymond Swanland
Cover Layout - Gary Shum

Senior Editor - Jake Forbes
Managing Editor - Jill Freshney
Production Coordinator - Antonio DePietro
Production Manager - Jennifer Miller
Art Director - Matthew Alford
Director of Editorial - Jeremy Ross
VP of Production & Manufacturing - Ron Klamert
President & C.O.O. - John Parker
Publisher - Stuart Levy

Email: editor@TOKYOPOP.com
Come visit us online at www.TOKYOPOP.com

A  Manga

TOKYOPOP® is an imprint of Mixx Entertainment, Inc.
5900 Wilshire Blvd. Suite 2000, Los Angeles, CA 90036

ISBN: 1-892213-78-8

First TOKYOPOP® printing: April 2003

10 9 8 7 6 5 4 3 2 1

Printed in the USA

I FEAR I MIGHT MAKE THINGS DIFFICULT FOR YOU, YOUNG SAKURA...

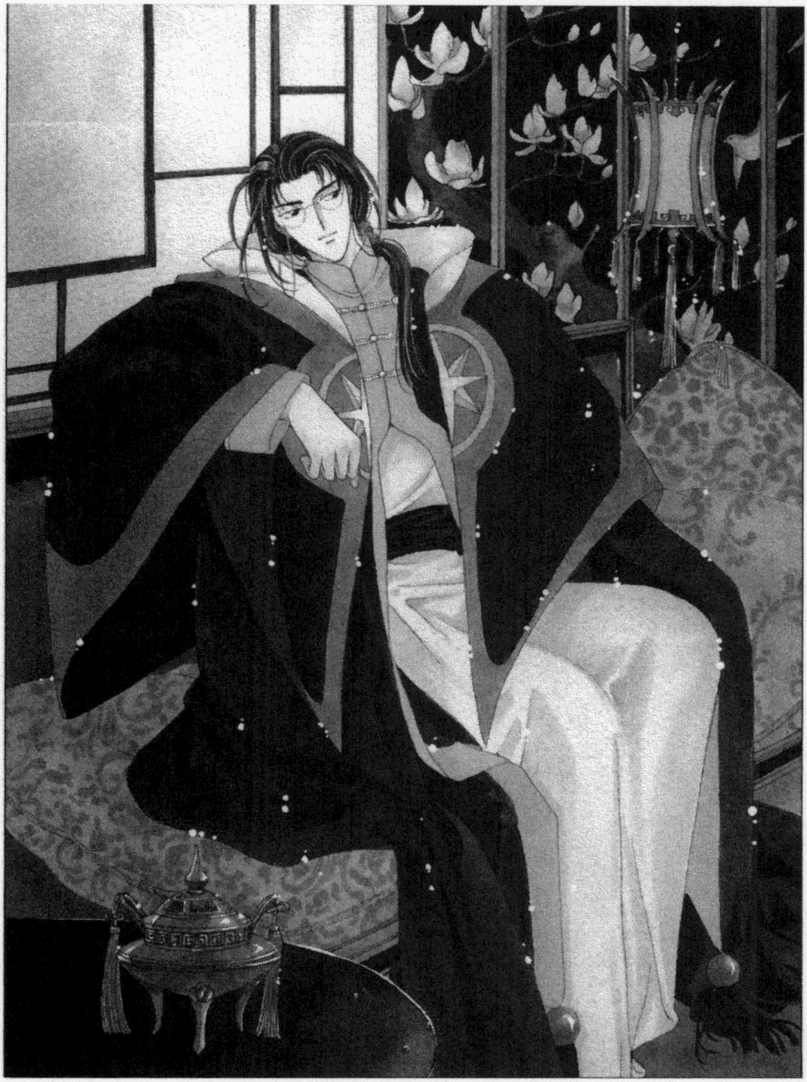

...BUT I'M SURE YOU'LL BE ALL RIGHT.

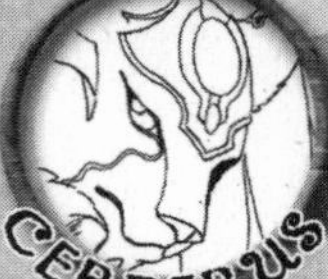

CERBERUS

Kero's true form is a lot... bigger. Unlike Yukito, Kero knows about his true form. His symbol of power is the sun.

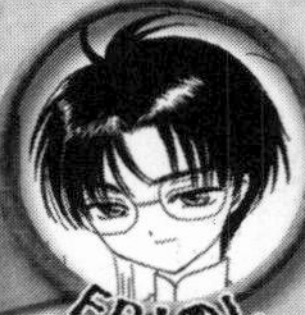

ERIOL

He just transferred into my class from England. Eriol is very polite and mature for his age. He seems to be very interested in me and my friends.

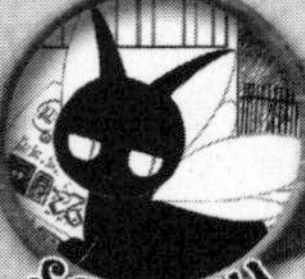

SOUPPY

He's a talking cat-like creature that lives with Eriol. He's very wise and likes his peace and quiet. I've never met him.

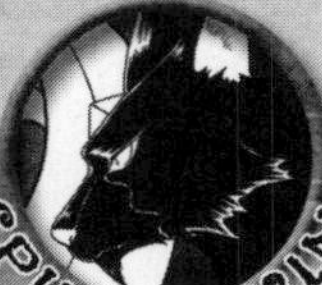

SPINNEL SUN

This fearsome winged panther appears in my dreams. [Sakura doesn't know this, but Spinnel Sun is Souppy's true form!]

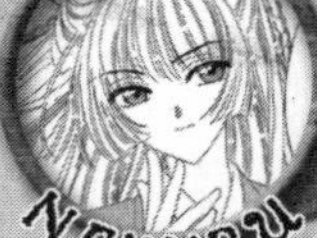

NAKURU

This obnoxious girl just transferred into Toya's class. I think she has a crush on him. She doesn't like Yukito at all. Talk about bad taste!

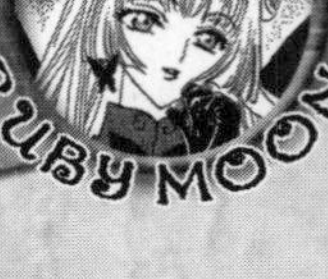

RUBY MOON

This beautiful woman with butterfly wings also keeps appearing in my dreams. [Actually, she's not male or female but is Nakuru's true form.]

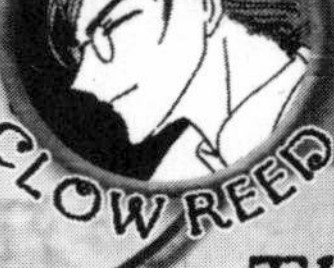

CLOW REED

He made the Clow Cards and created Kero and Yue. Even though he's been dead for many years, his presence is still hovering over Tomoeda.

THE STORY SO FAR...

What a bizarre year it's turning out to be! First, there was the incident with the Clow-endowed teddy bear that nearly trampled my house. Then, there was that weird hole in the park with all the plushie sheep that nearly swallowed me up! Kero and Yue don't know what's up, but Clow is definitely behind it. Speaking of Yue, I almost lost him...and Yukito, too! Since I don't have the power to support him and transform all the cards, he started to fade out of existence! The good news is he found another source of energy. The bad news is that the source of that power was my brother!

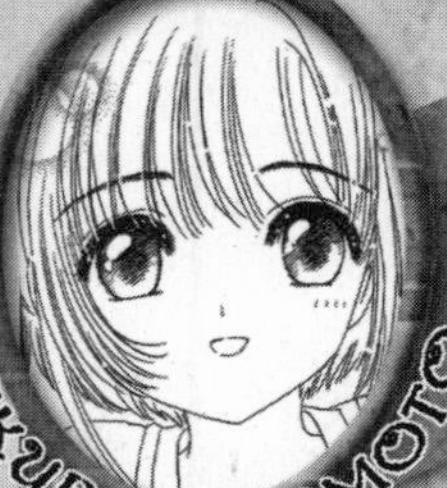

SAKURA KINOMOTO

I'm just your average fifth grader. I love P.E., I'm not too crazy about math (but I'm starting to get it), and... oh, yeah! I spent the last year collecting these magic Clow Cards. Now that I've found them all and passed the test, I'm Master of the Clow!

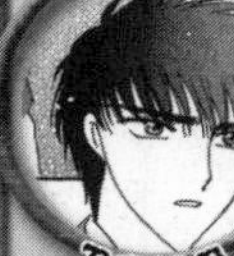

TOYA

He's my stupid brother. Even though he picks on me, I know he really cares. Magic must run in my family 'cuz people say Toya has a sixth sense.

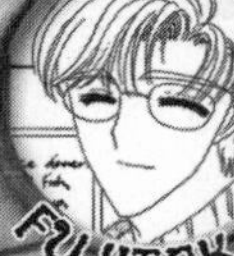

FUJITAKA

That's my dad. He teaches archaeology at the university, which means he's really smart. He's a good cook, too. I love him a lot.

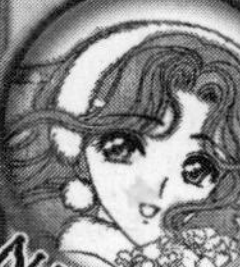

NADESHIKO

She's my mom. Isn't she pretty? She passed away when I was little, but it feels like she's still watching over us.

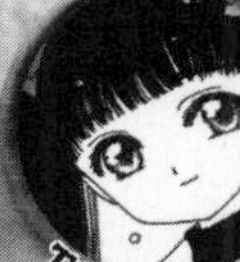

TOMOYO

She's my best friend. I don't know why, but she's always videotaping my battles. She also makes all of my costumes. Her mom and my mom were cousins.

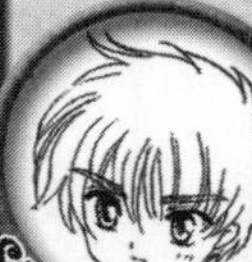

SYAORAN LI

Syaoran used to be my rival, but now we're good friends. He was going to go back to Hong Kong, but he ended up staying in Tomoeda for a while longer. He's been acting funny around me lately. I wonder why...

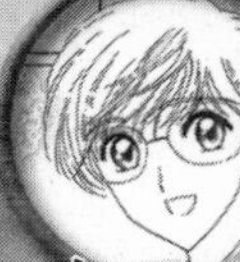

YUKITO

Isn't he just to die for! I don't know why he likes my brother so much, but I don't mind, 'cuz that means he comes over a lot. He's smart, kind, handsome, and he has a healthy appetite!

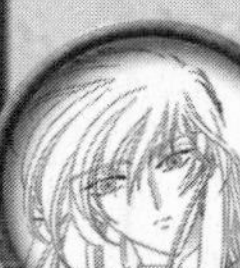

YUE

This is Yukito's true form. He's known as the Judge and his symbol of power is the moon. I'm a little scared of him, even though I'm kinda his boss.

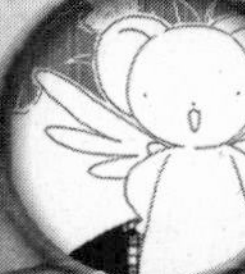

KERO

He may look like a plushie toy, but he's really the ancient, magical Guardian Beast. He gives me advice on all my adventures 'cuz he's really smart. Actually, he's more of a smart-aleck!

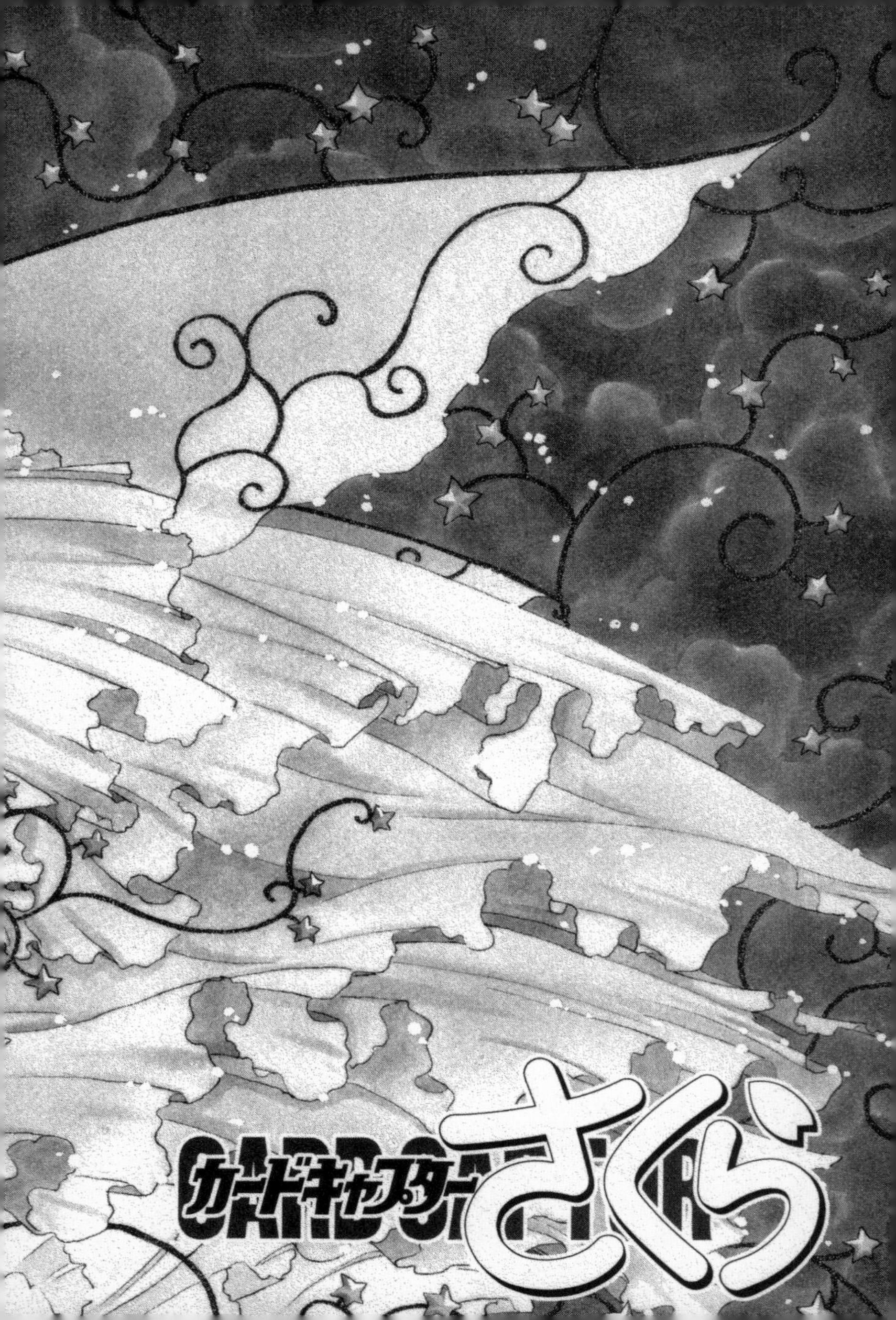
カードキャプター
さくら

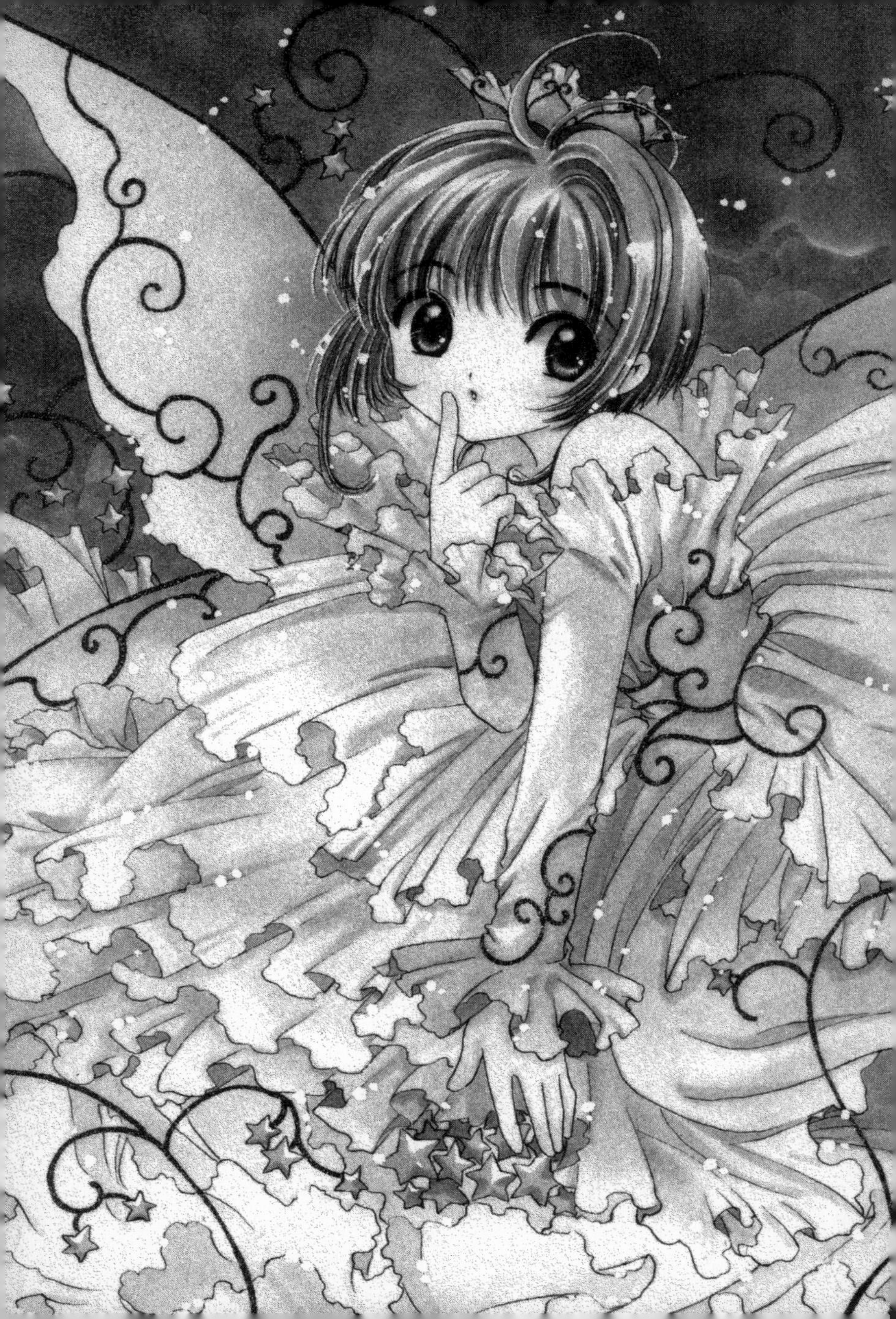

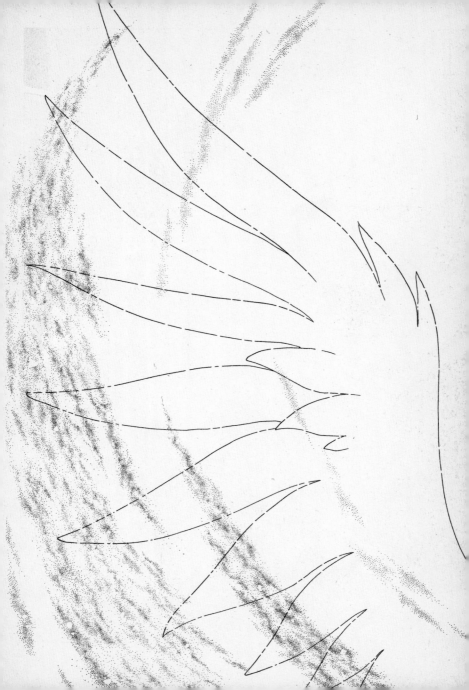

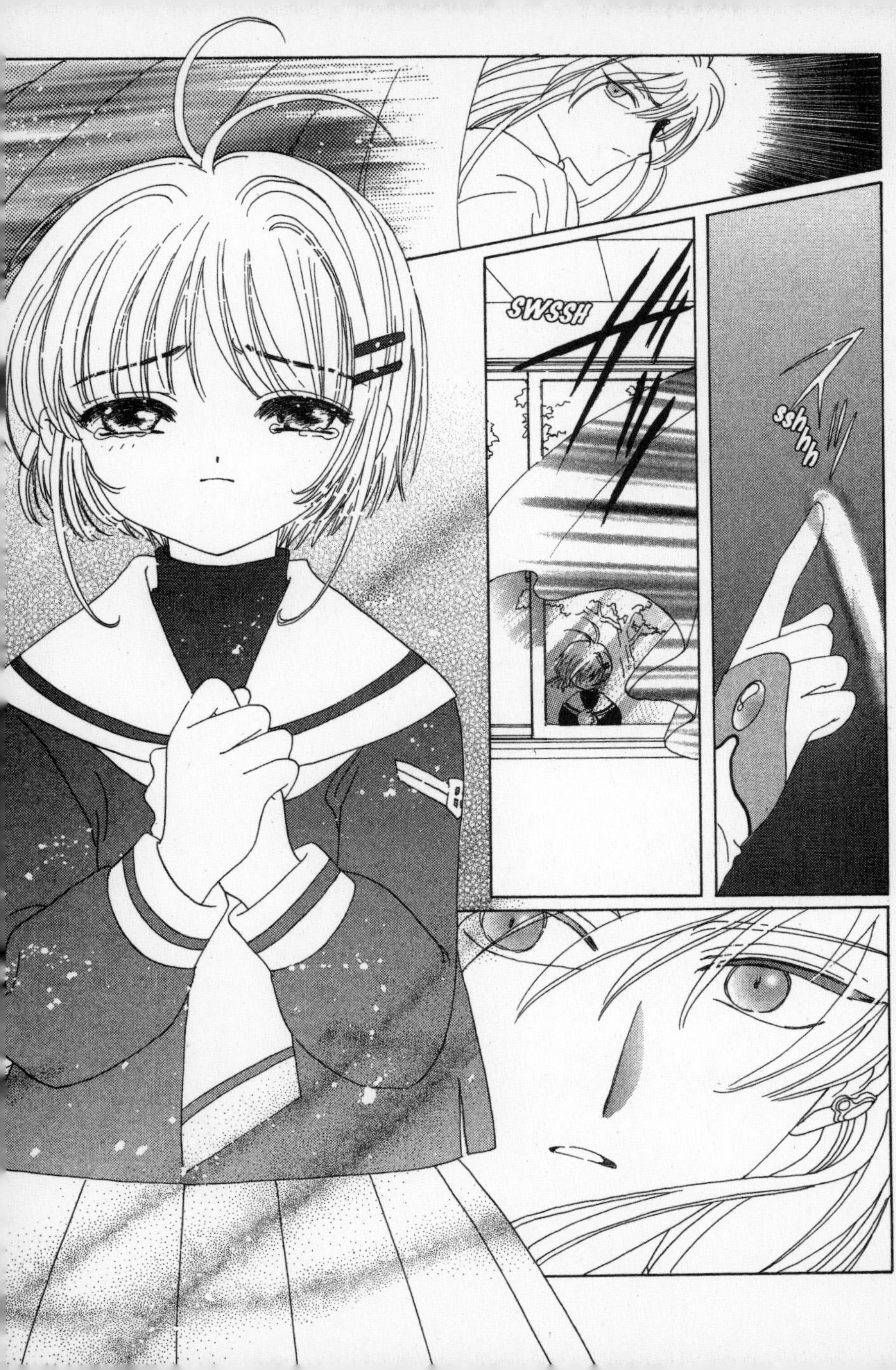
SWSSH
shhh

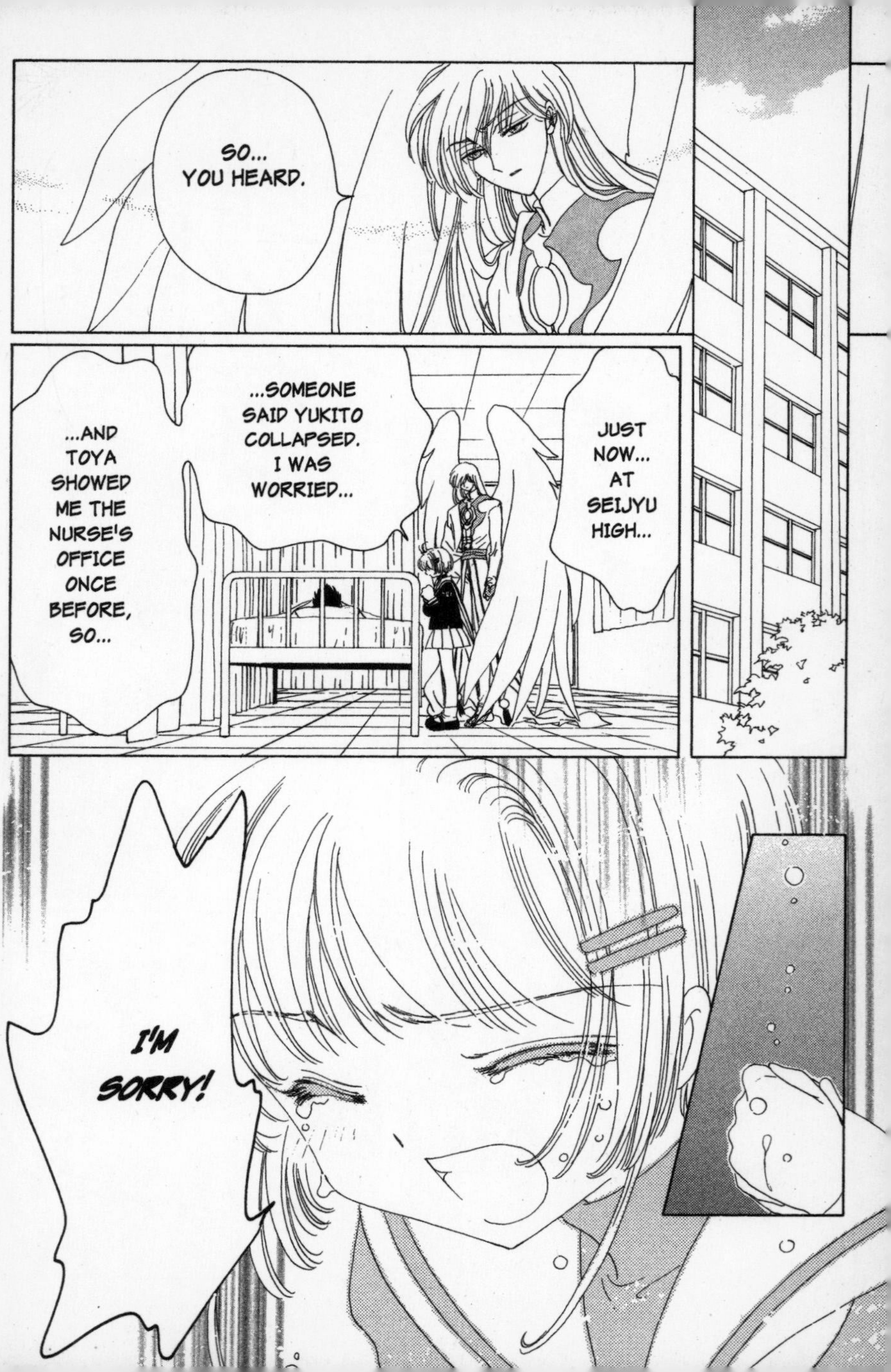
SO... YOU HEARD.
JUST NOW... AT SEIJYU HIGH...
...SOMEONE SAID YUKITO COLLAPSED. I WAS WORRIED...
...AND TOYA SHOWED ME THE NURSE'S OFFICE ONCE BEFORE, SO...
I'M SORRY!

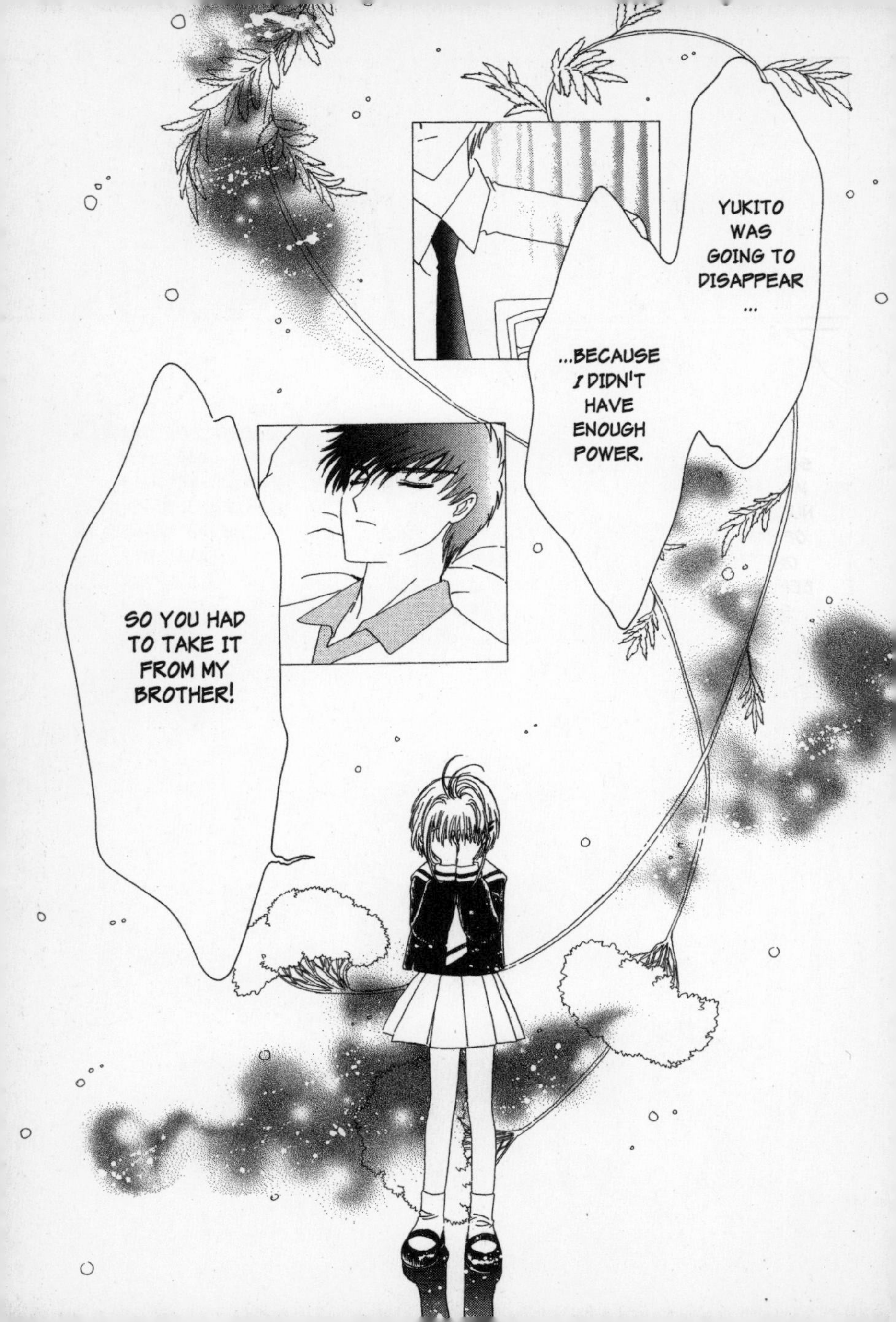
YUKITO WAS GOING TO DISAPPEAR ...
...BECAUSE I DIDN'T HAVE ENOUGH POWER.
SO YOU HAD TO TAKE IT FROM MY BROTHER!

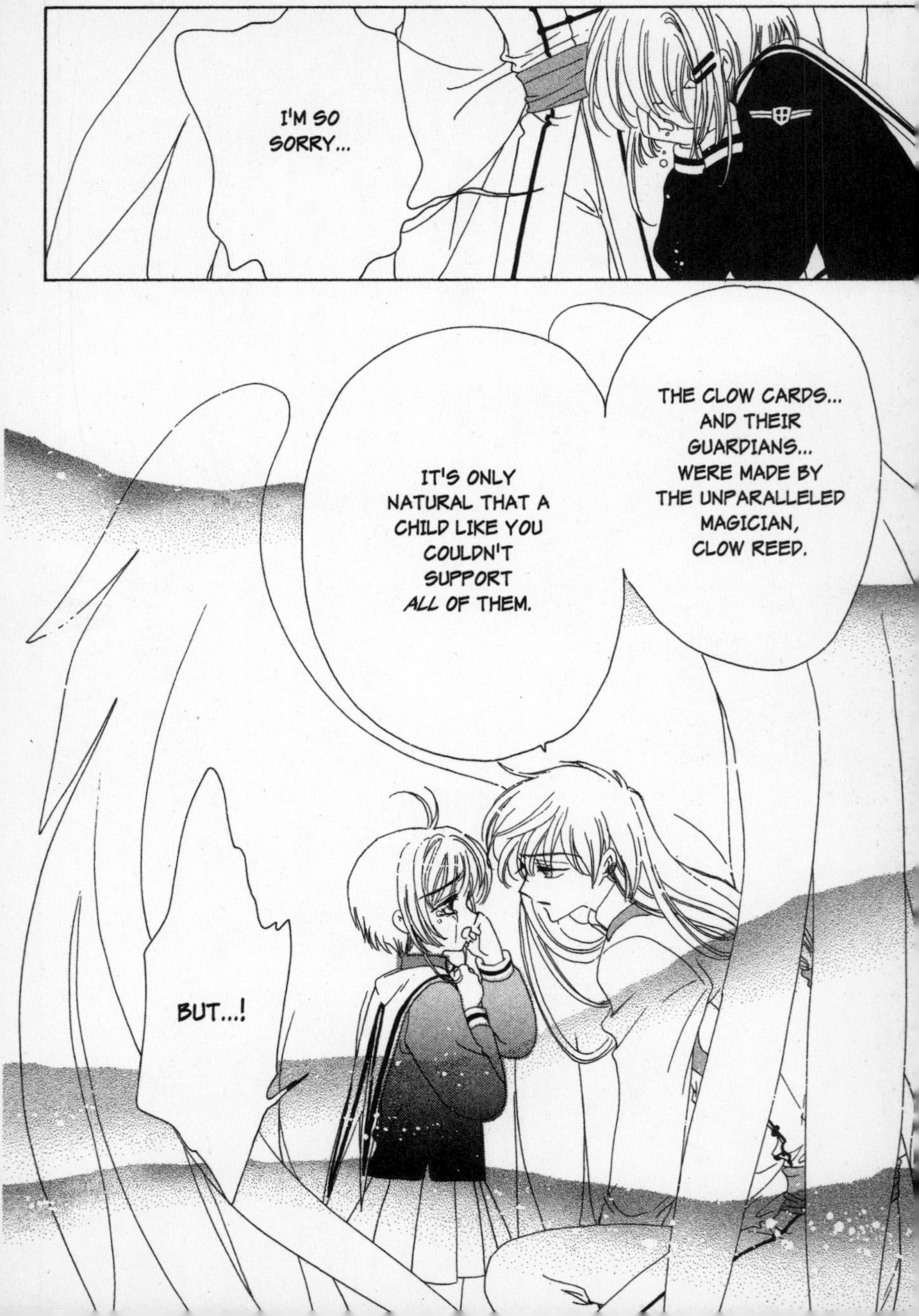
I'M SO SORRY...
THE CLOW CARDS... AND THEIR GUARDIANS... WERE MADE BY THE UNPARALLELED MAGICIAN, CLOW REED.
IT'S ONLY NATURAL THAT A CHILD LIKE YOU COULDN'T SUPPORT *ALL* OF THEM.
BUT...!

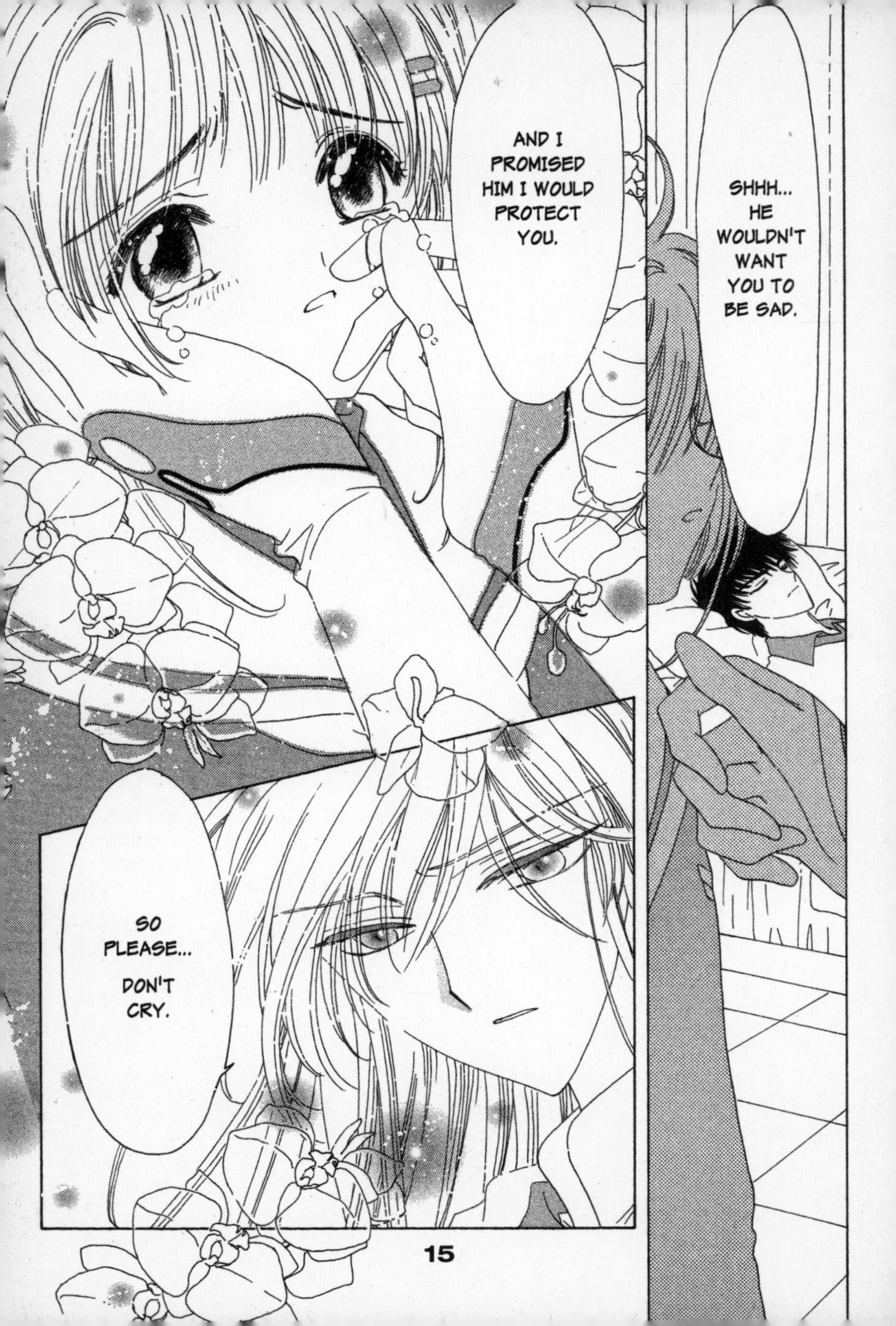
SHHH... HE WOULDN'T WANT YOU TO BE SAD.
AND I PROMISED HIM I WOULD PROTECT YOU.
SO PLEASE... DON'T CRY.

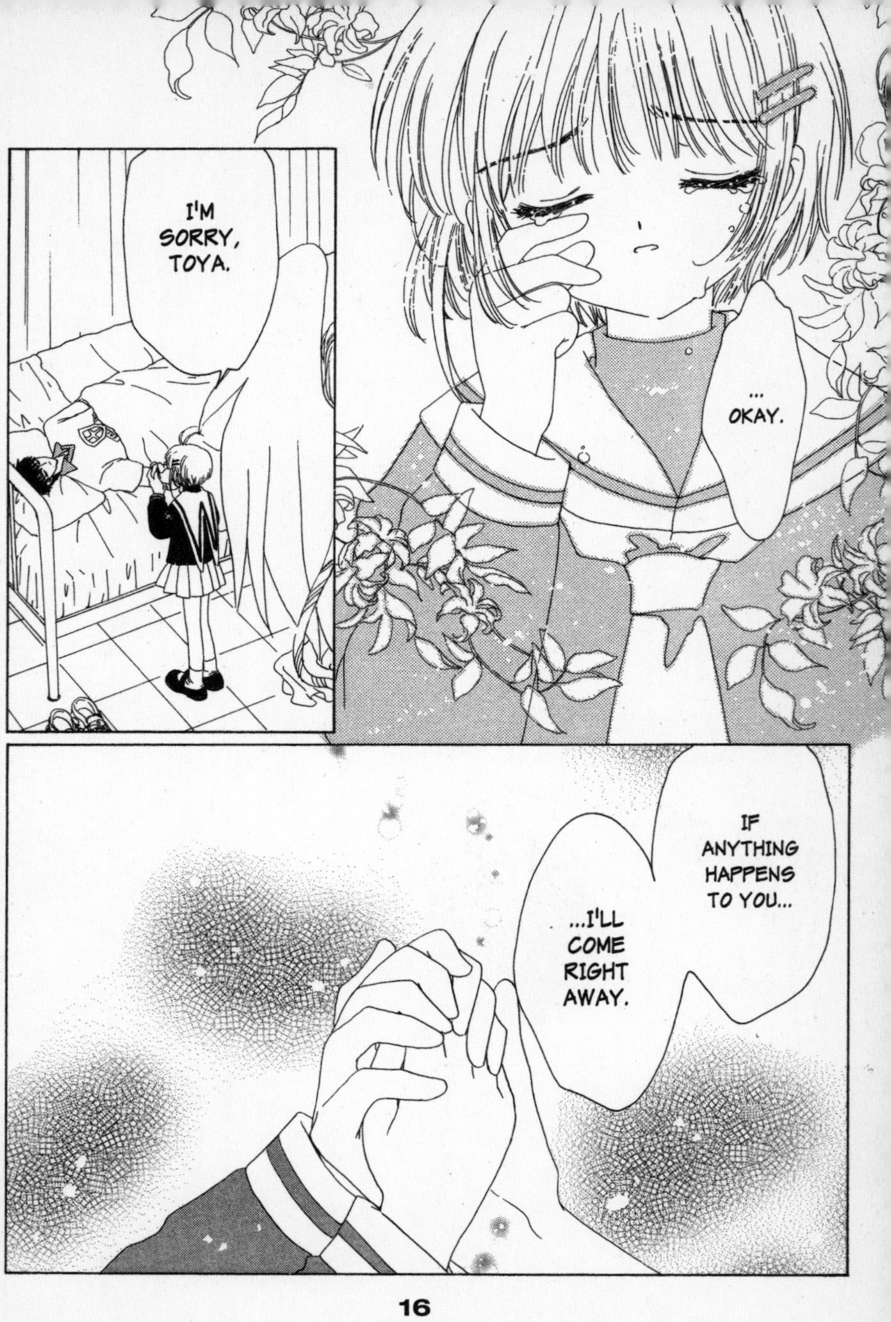
...OKAY.
I'M SORRY, TOYA.
IF ANYTHING HAPPENS TO YOU...
...I'LL COME RIGHT AWAY.

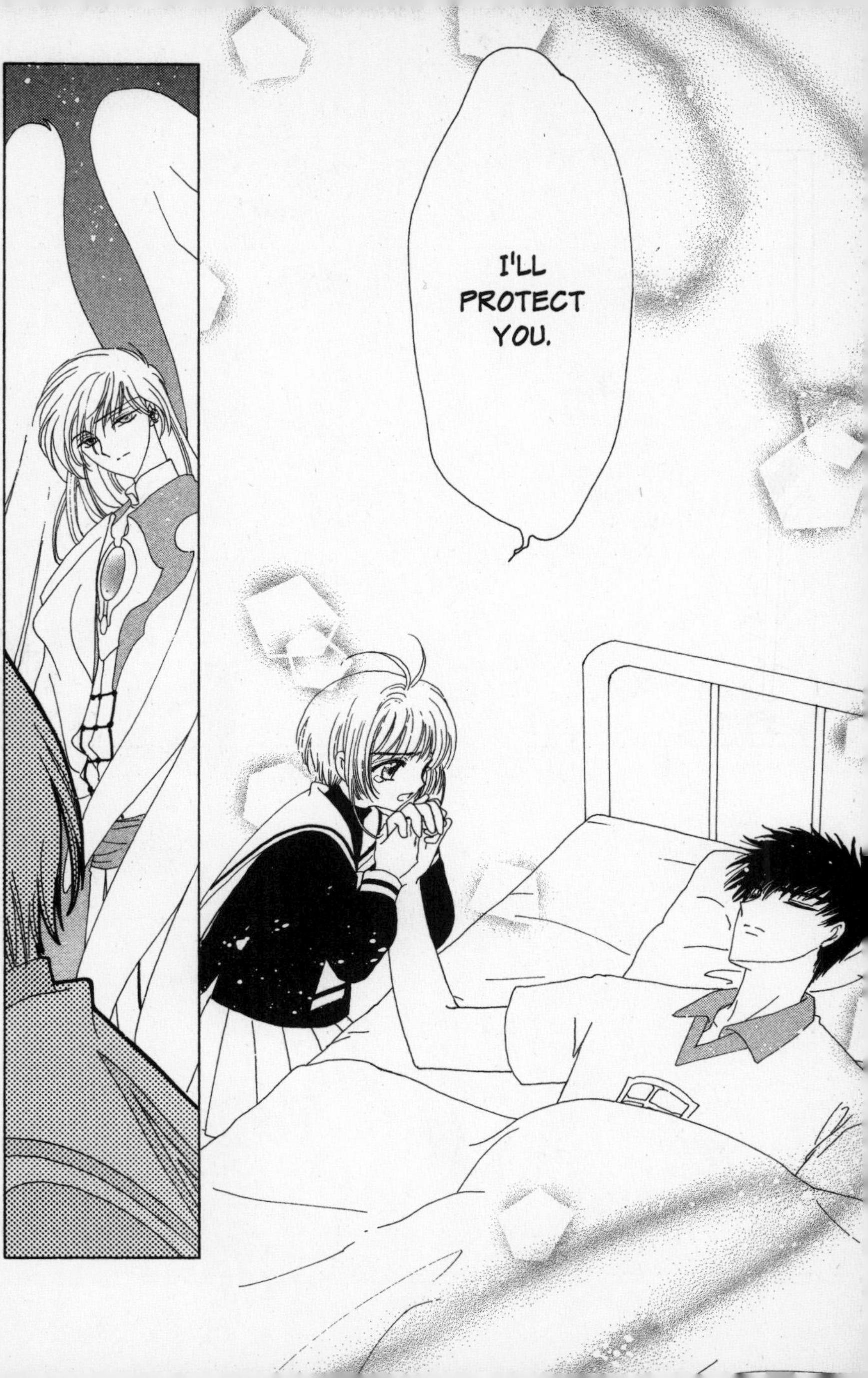
I'LL PROTECT YOU.

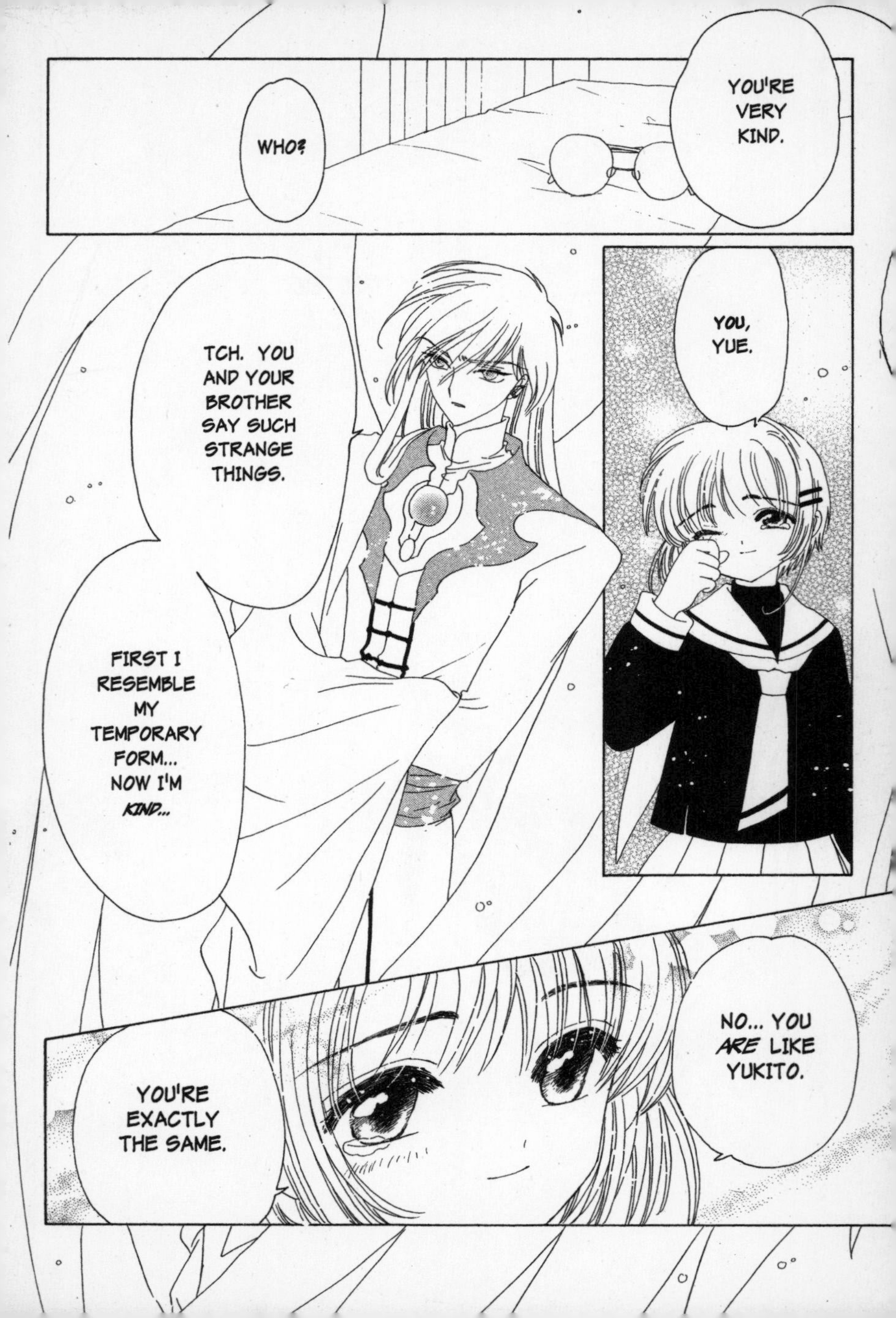
YOU'RE VERY KIND.
WHO?
YOU, YUE.
TCH. YOU AND YOUR BROTHER SAY SUCH STRANGE THINGS.
FIRST I RESEMBLE MY TEMPORARY FORM... NOW I'M *KIND*...
NO... YOU *ARE* LIKE YUKITO.
YOU'RE EXACTLY THE SAME.

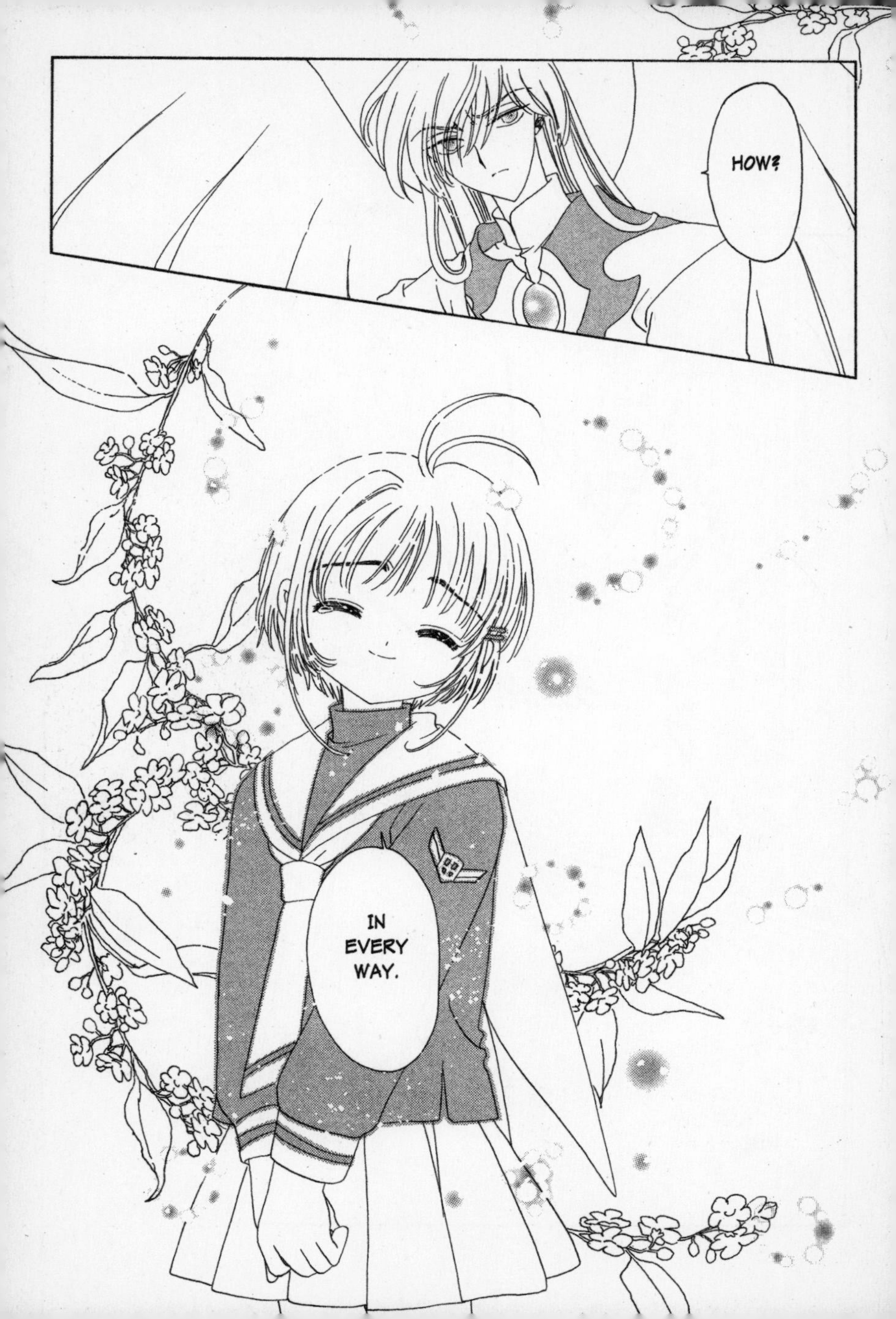
HOW?
IN EVERY WAY.

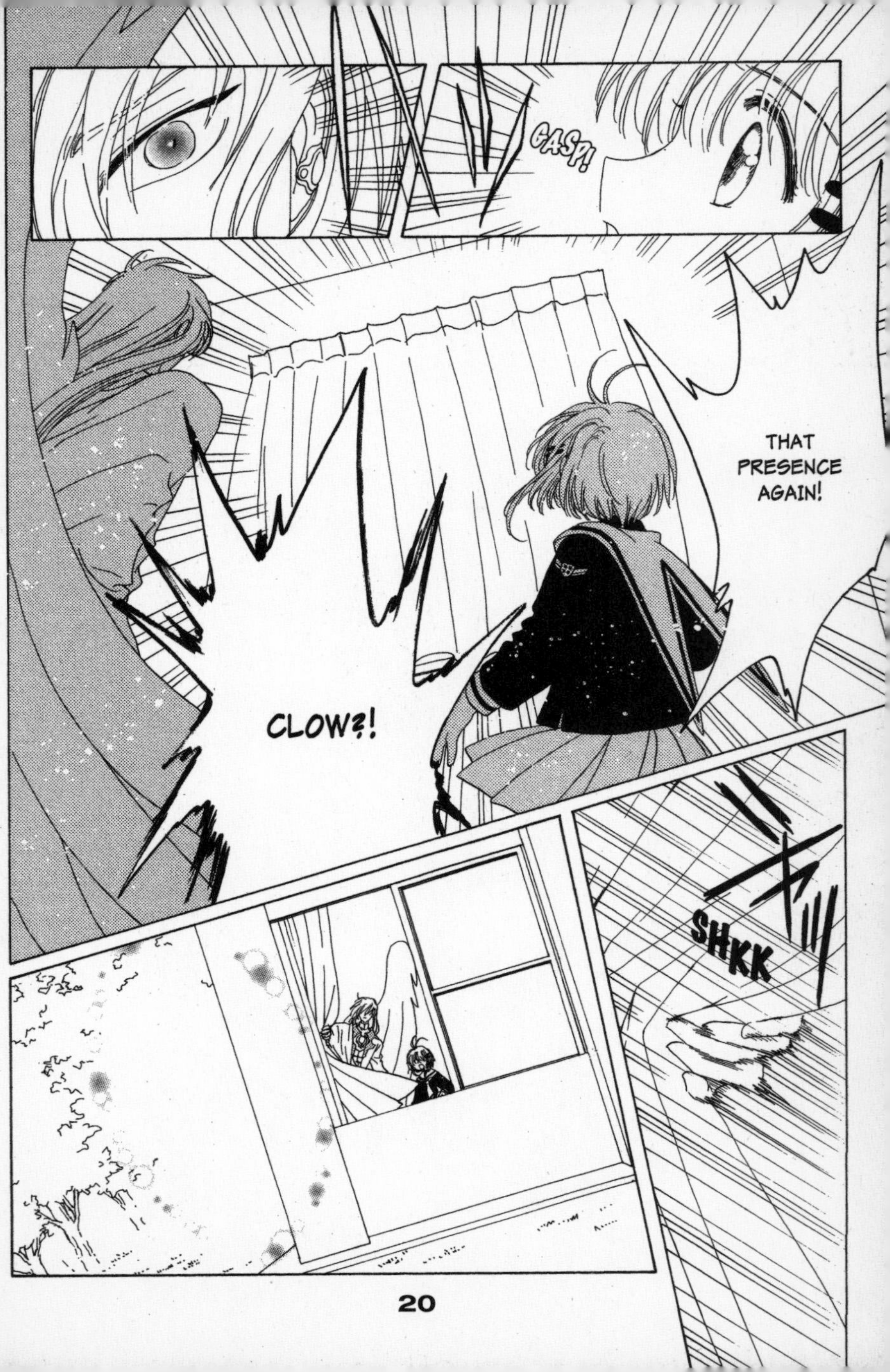
GASP!
THAT PRESENCE AGAIN!
CLOW?!
SHKK

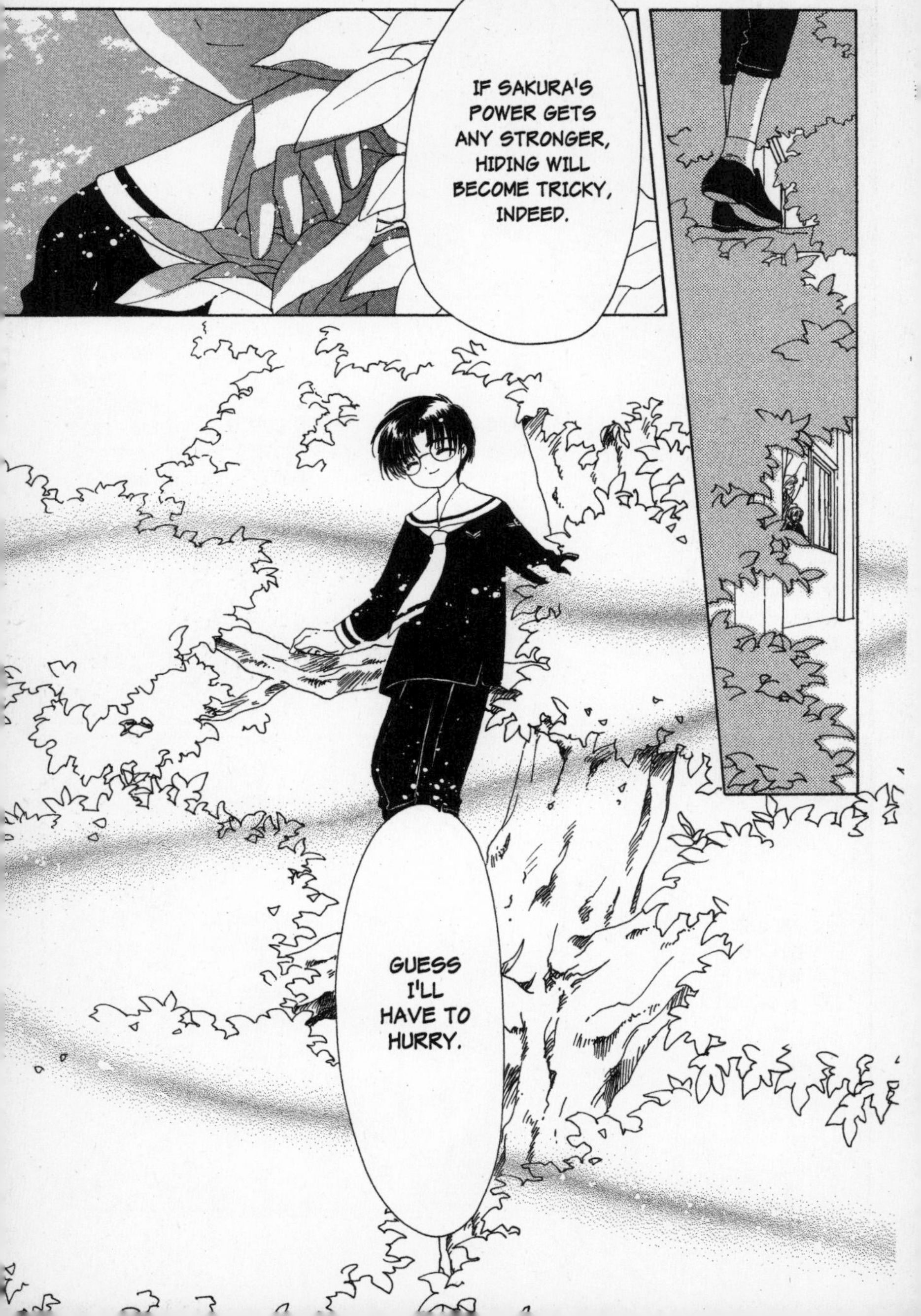
IF SAKURA'S POWER GETS ANY STRONGER, HIDING WILL BECOME TRICKY, INDEED.
GUESS I'LL HAVE TO HURRY.

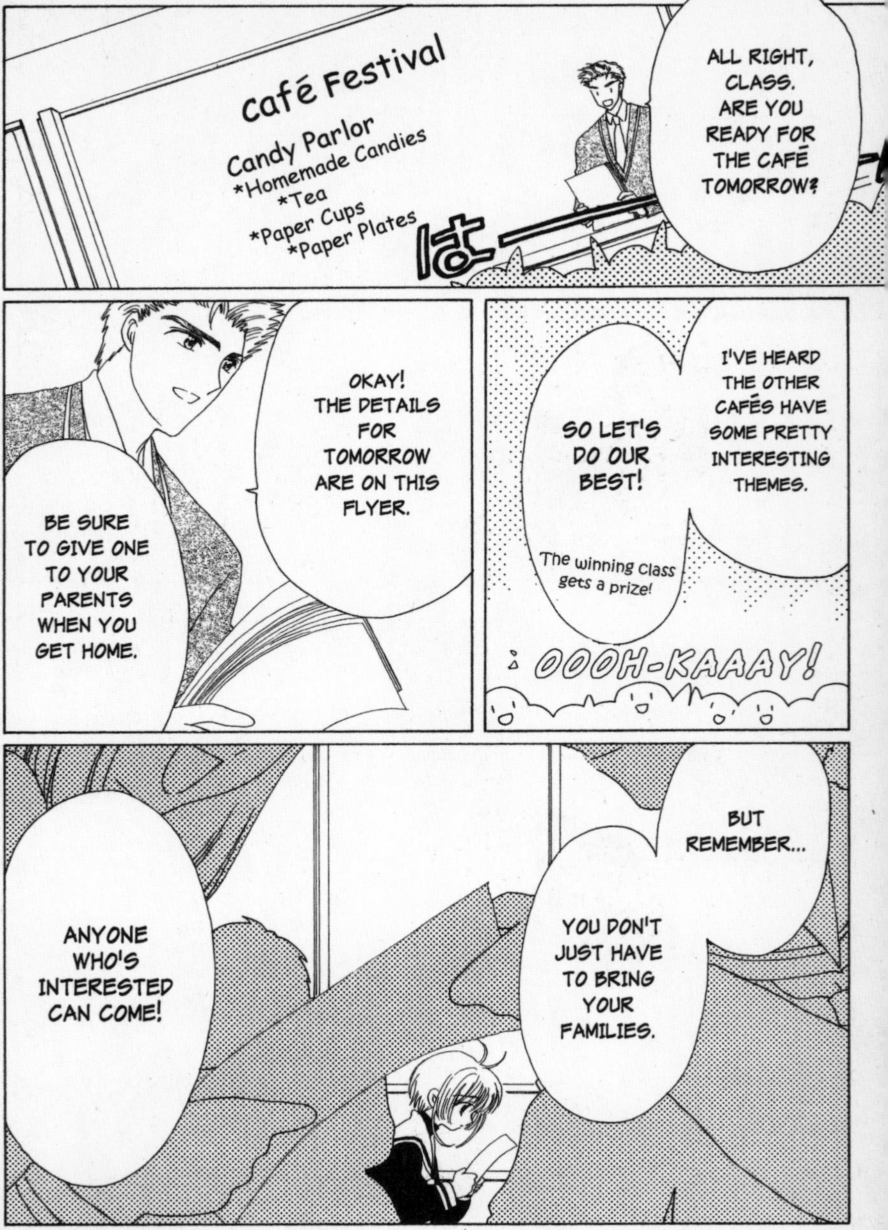
ALL RIGHT, CLASS. ARE YOU READY FOR THE CAFÉ TOMORROW?
Café Festival
Candy Parlor
*Homemade Candies
*Tea
*Paper Cups
*Paper Plates
は
I'VE HEARD THE OTHER CAFÉS HAVE SOME PRETTY INTERESTING THEMES.
SO LET'S DO OUR BEST!
The winning class gets a prize!
OOOH-KAAAY!
OKAY! THE DETAILS FOR TOMORROW ARE ON THIS FLYER.
BE SURE TO GIVE ONE TO YOUR PARENTS WHEN YOU GET HOME.
BUT REMEMBER...
YOU DON'T JUST HAVE TO BRING YOUR FAMILIES.
ANYONE WHO'S INTERESTED CAN COME!

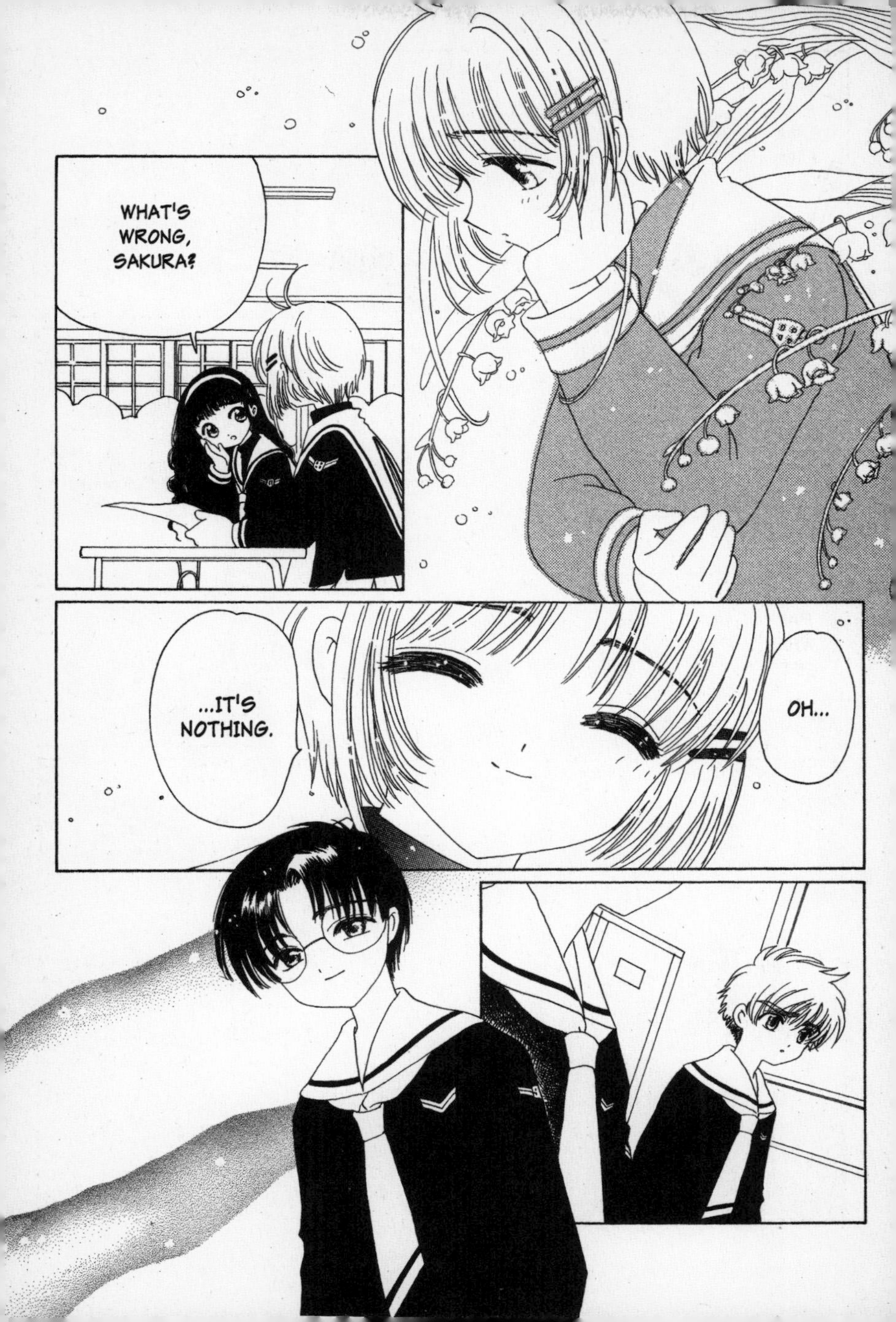
WHAT'S WRONG, SAKURA?
OH...
...IT'S NOTHING.

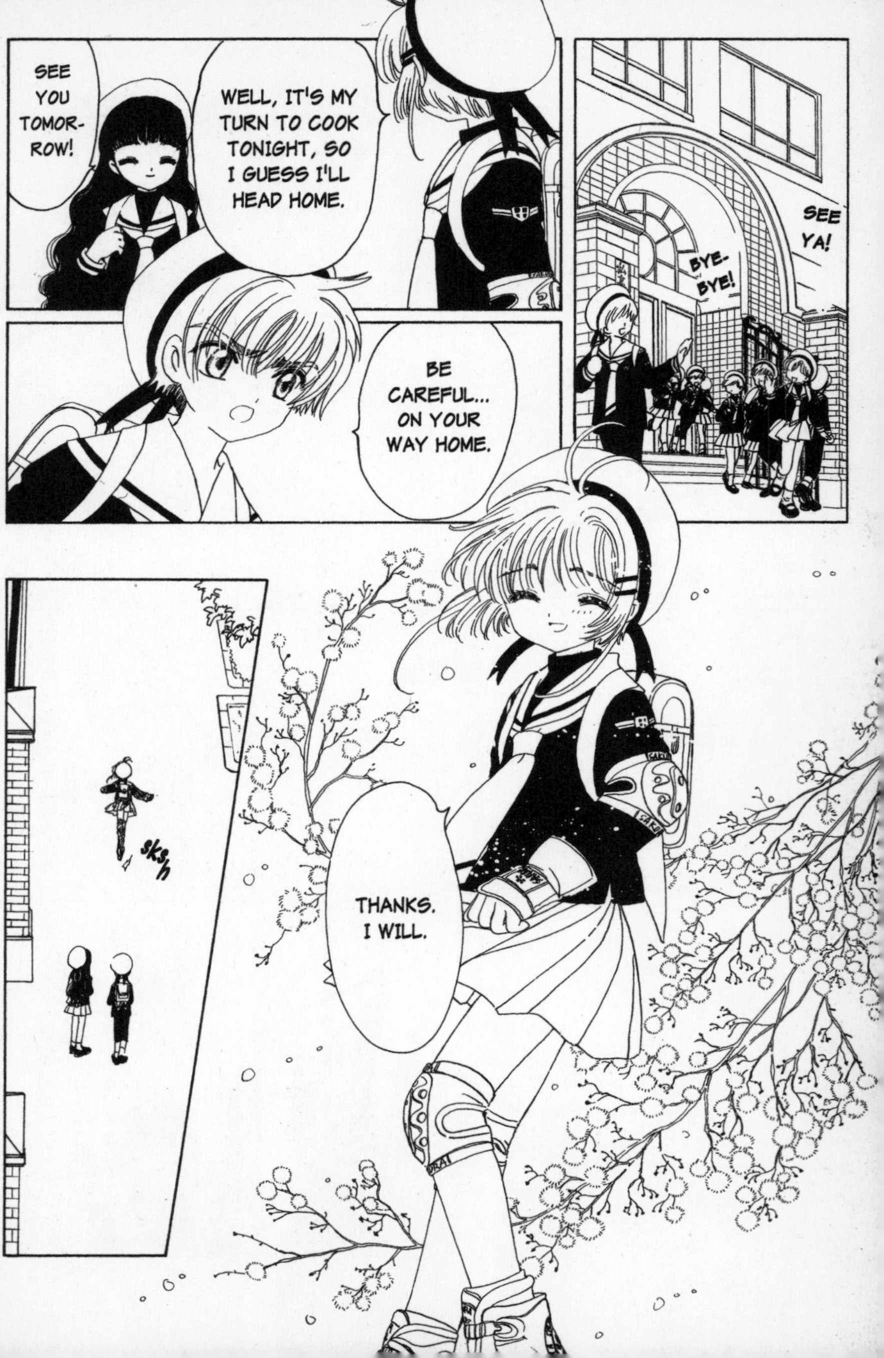
SEE YA!
BYE-BYE!
WELL, IT'S MY TURN TO COOK TONIGHT, SO I GUESS I'LL HEAD HOME.
SEE YOU TOMOR-ROW!
BE CAREFUL... ON YOUR WAY HOME.
THANKS. I WILL.
sksh

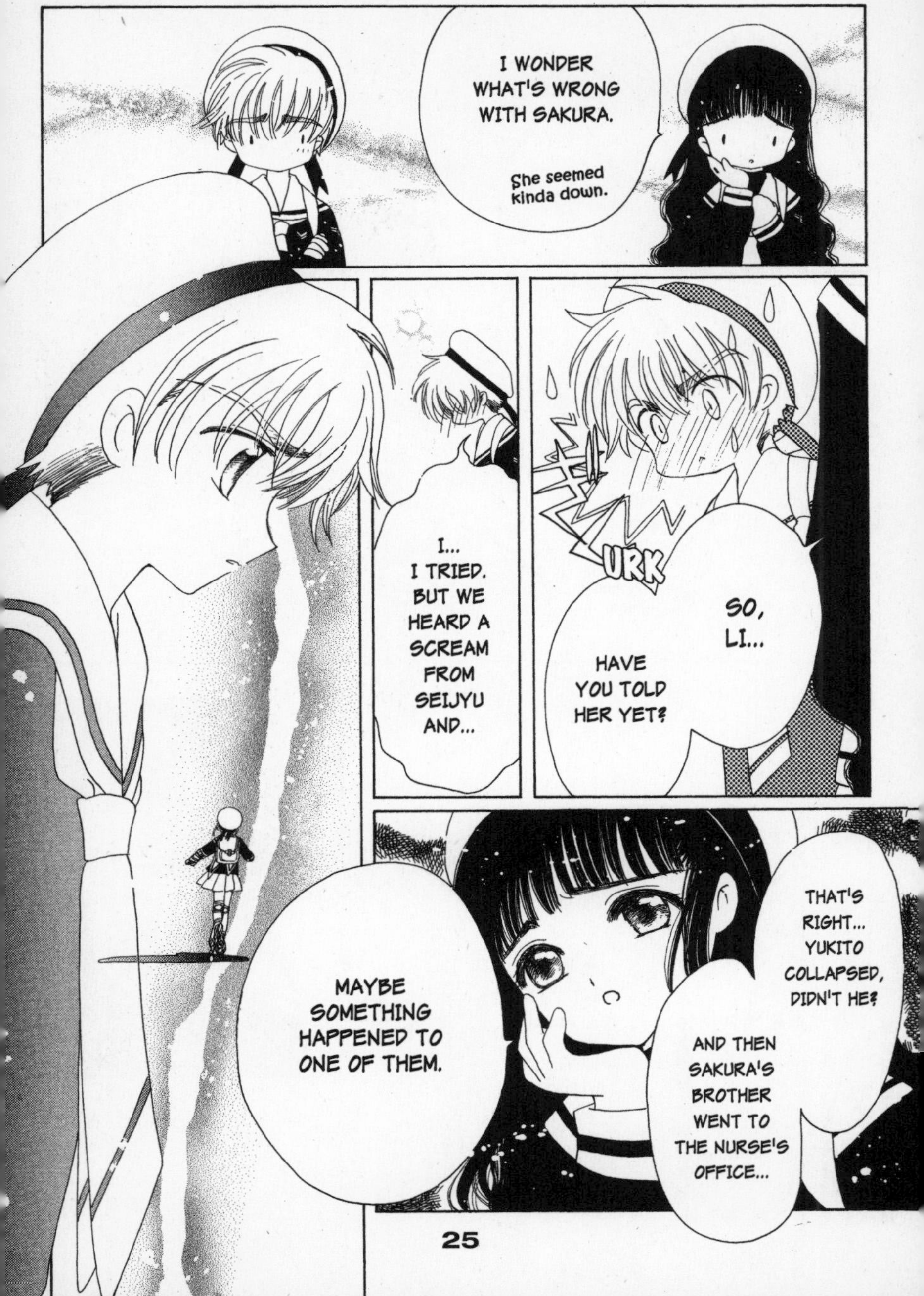
I WONDER WHAT'S WRONG WITH SAKURA.
She seemed kinda down.
SO, LI...
HAVE YOU TOLD HER YET?
URK
I... I TRIED. BUT WE HEARD A SCREAM FROM SEIJYU AND...
THAT'S RIGHT... YUKITO COLLAPSED, DIDN'T HE?
AND THEN SAKURA'S BROTHER WENT TO THE NURSE'S OFFICE...
MAYBE SOMETHING HAPPENED TO ONE OF THEM.

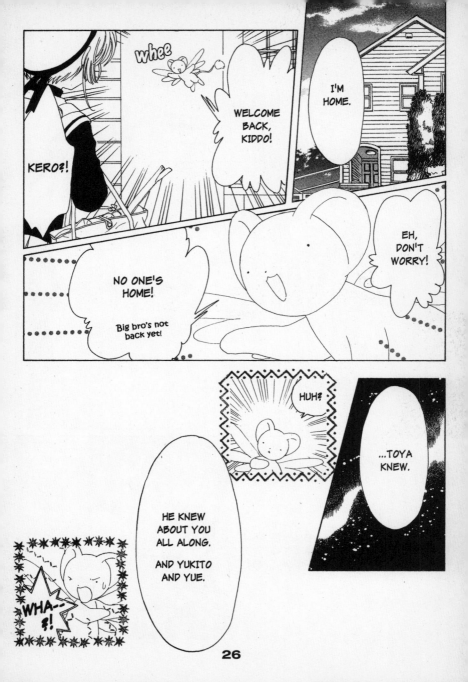

whee

KERO?!

WELCOME BACK, KIDDO!

I'M HOME.

NO ONE'S HOME!

Big bro's not back yet!

EH, DON'T WORRY!

HUH?

...TOYA KNEW.

HE KNEW ABOUT YOU ALL ALONG.

AND YUKITO AND YUE.

WHA--?!

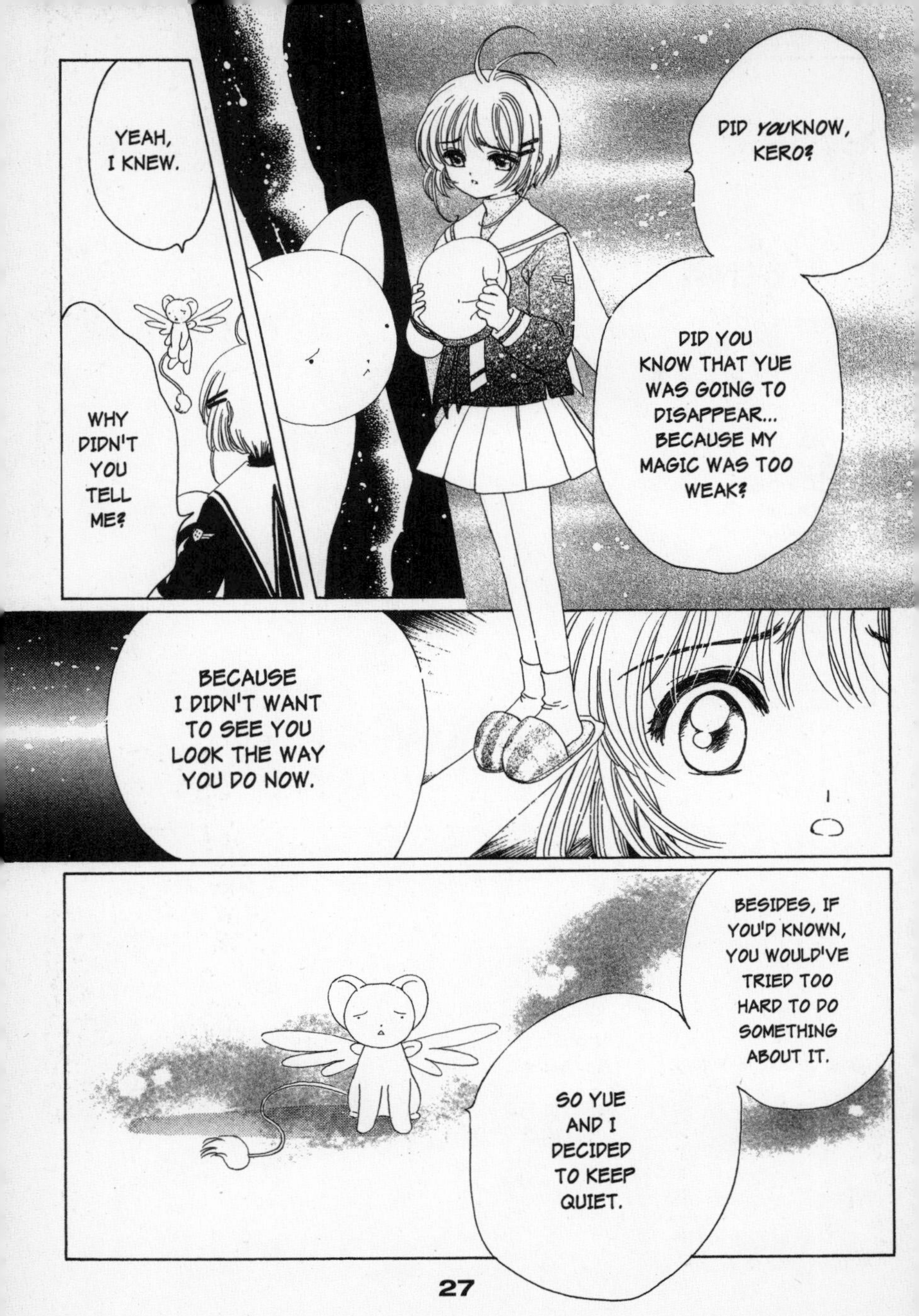
DID YOU KNOW, KERO?
DID YOU KNOW THAT YUE WAS GOING TO DISAPPEAR... BECAUSE MY MAGIC WAS TOO WEAK?
YEAH, I KNEW.
WHY DIDN'T YOU TELL ME?
BECAUSE I DIDN'T WANT TO SEE YOU LOOK THE WAY YOU DO NOW.
BESIDES, IF YOU'D KNOWN, YOU WOULD'VE TRIED TOO HARD TO DO SOMETHING ABOUT IT.
SO YUE AND I DECIDED TO KEEP QUIET.

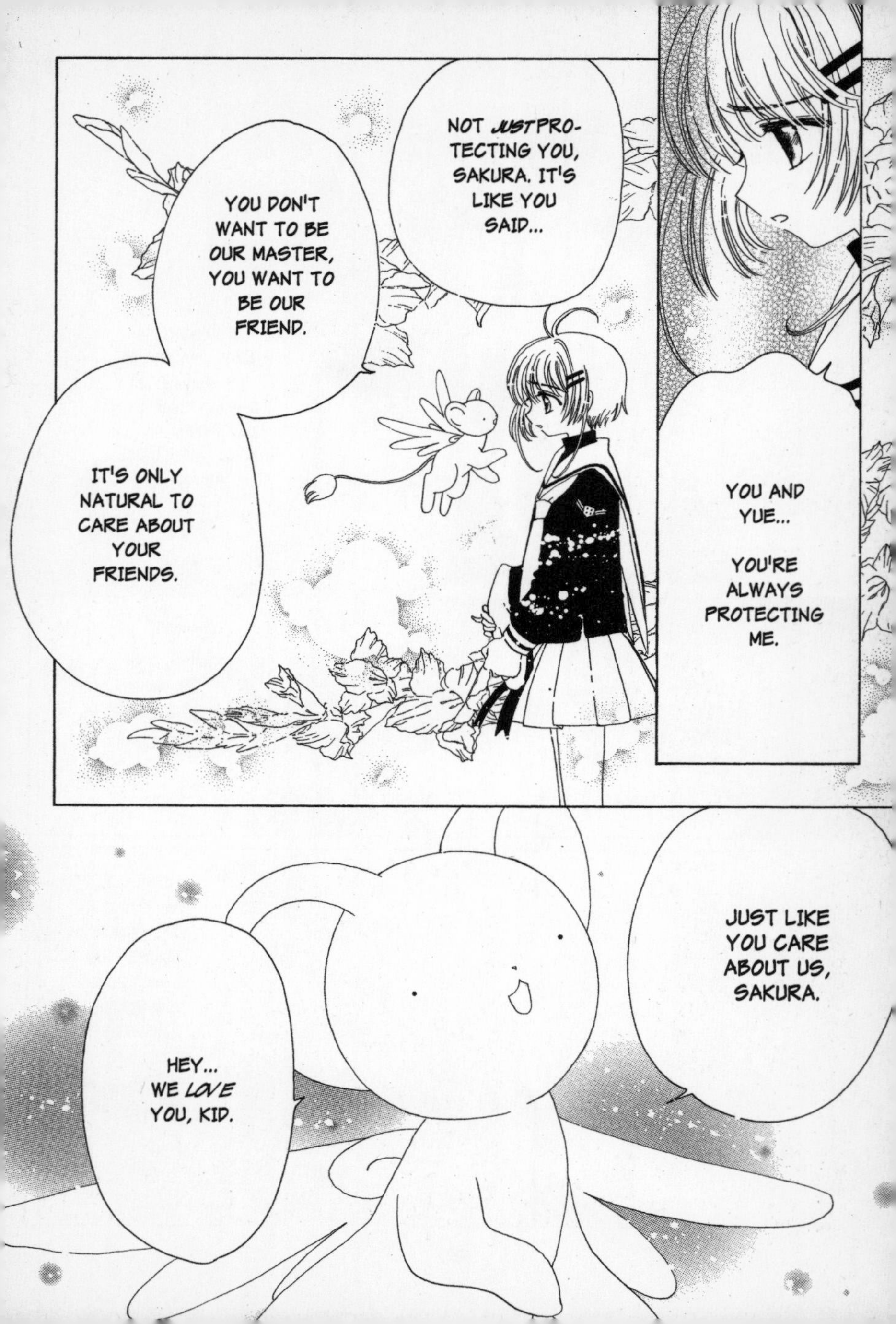
YOU AND YUE...
YOU'RE ALWAYS PROTECTING ME.
NOT *JUST* PRO-TECTING YOU, SAKURA. IT'S LIKE YOU SAID...
YOU DON'T WANT TO BE OUR MASTER, YOU WANT TO BE OUR FRIEND.
IT'S ONLY NATURAL TO CARE ABOUT YOUR FRIENDS.
JUST LIKE YOU CARE ABOUT US, SAKURA.
HEY... WE *LOVE* YOU, KID.

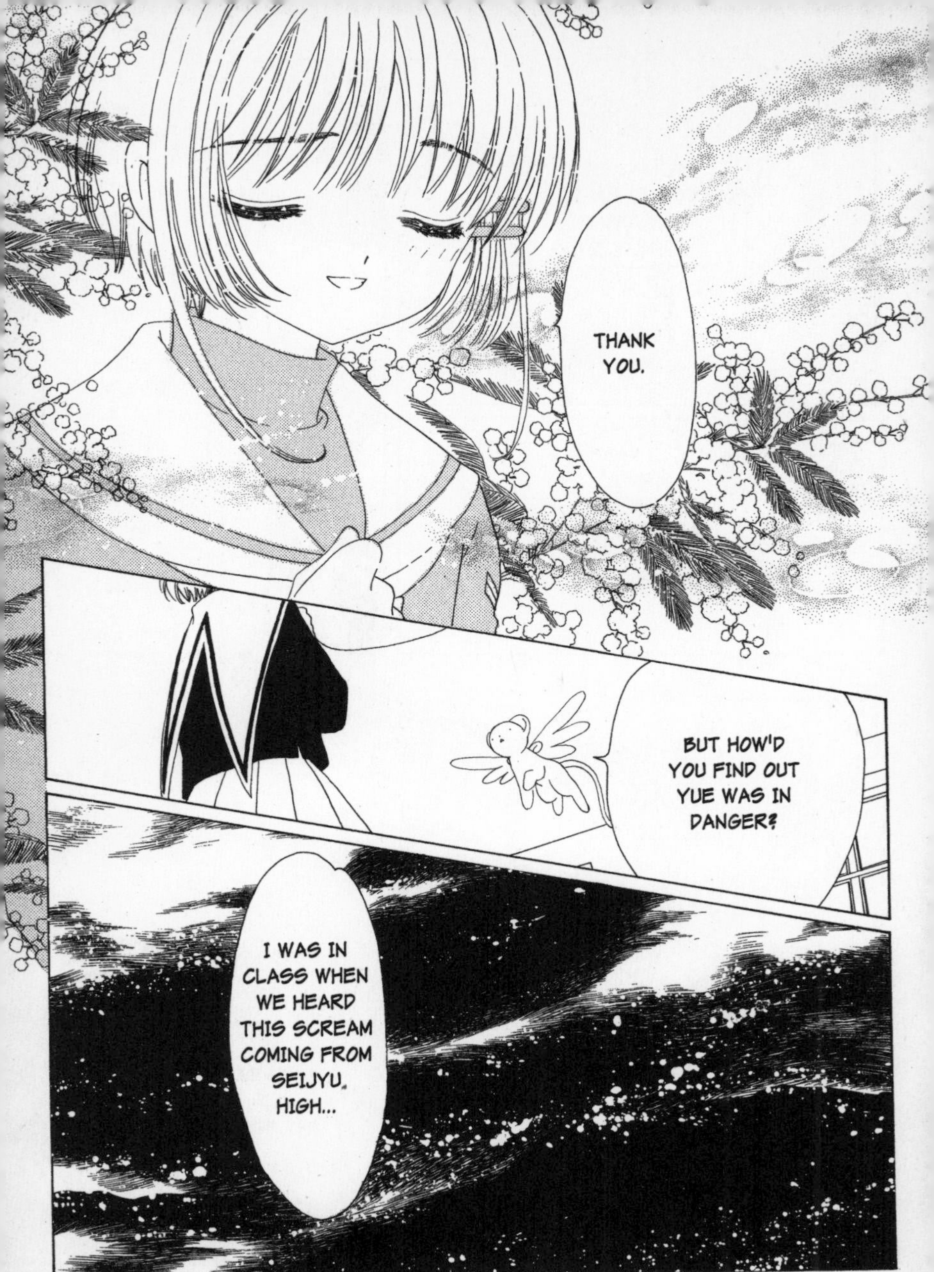
THANK YOU.
BUT HOW'D YOU FIND OUT YUE WAS IN DANGER?
I WAS IN CLASS WHEN WE HEARD THIS SCREAM COMING FROM SEIJYU HIGH...

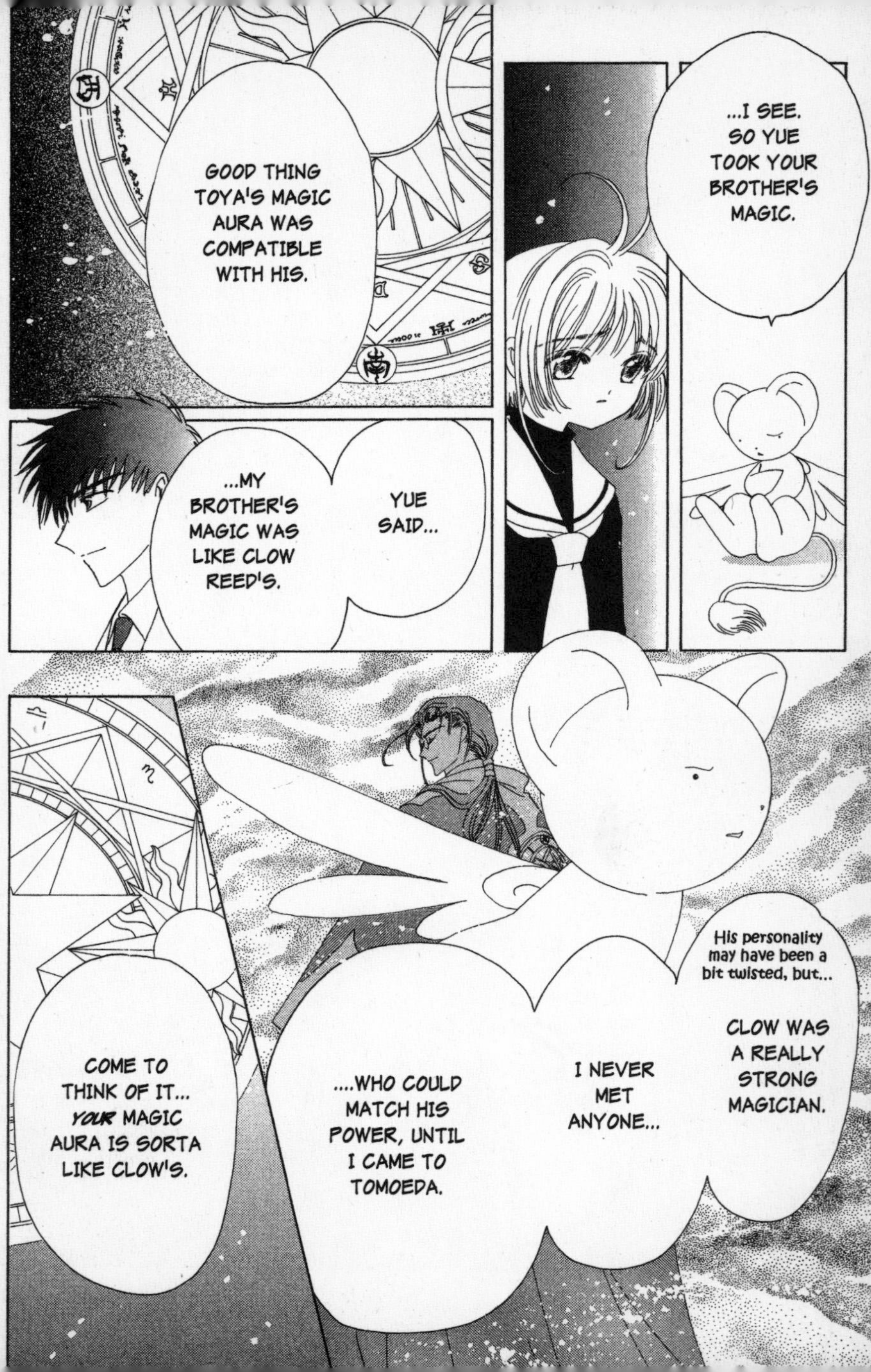
...I SEE. SO YUE TOOK YOUR BROTHER'S MAGIC.
GOOD THING TOYA'S MAGIC AURA WAS COMPATIBLE WITH HIS.
YUE SAID...
...MY BROTHER'S MAGIC WAS LIKE CLOW REED'S.
His personality may have been a bit twisted, but...
CLOW WAS A REALLY STRONG MAGICIAN.
I NEVER MET ANYONE...
....WHO COULD MATCH HIS POWER, UNTIL I CAME TO TOMOEDA.
COME TO THINK OF IT... *YOUR* MAGIC AURA IS SORTA LIKE CLOW'S.

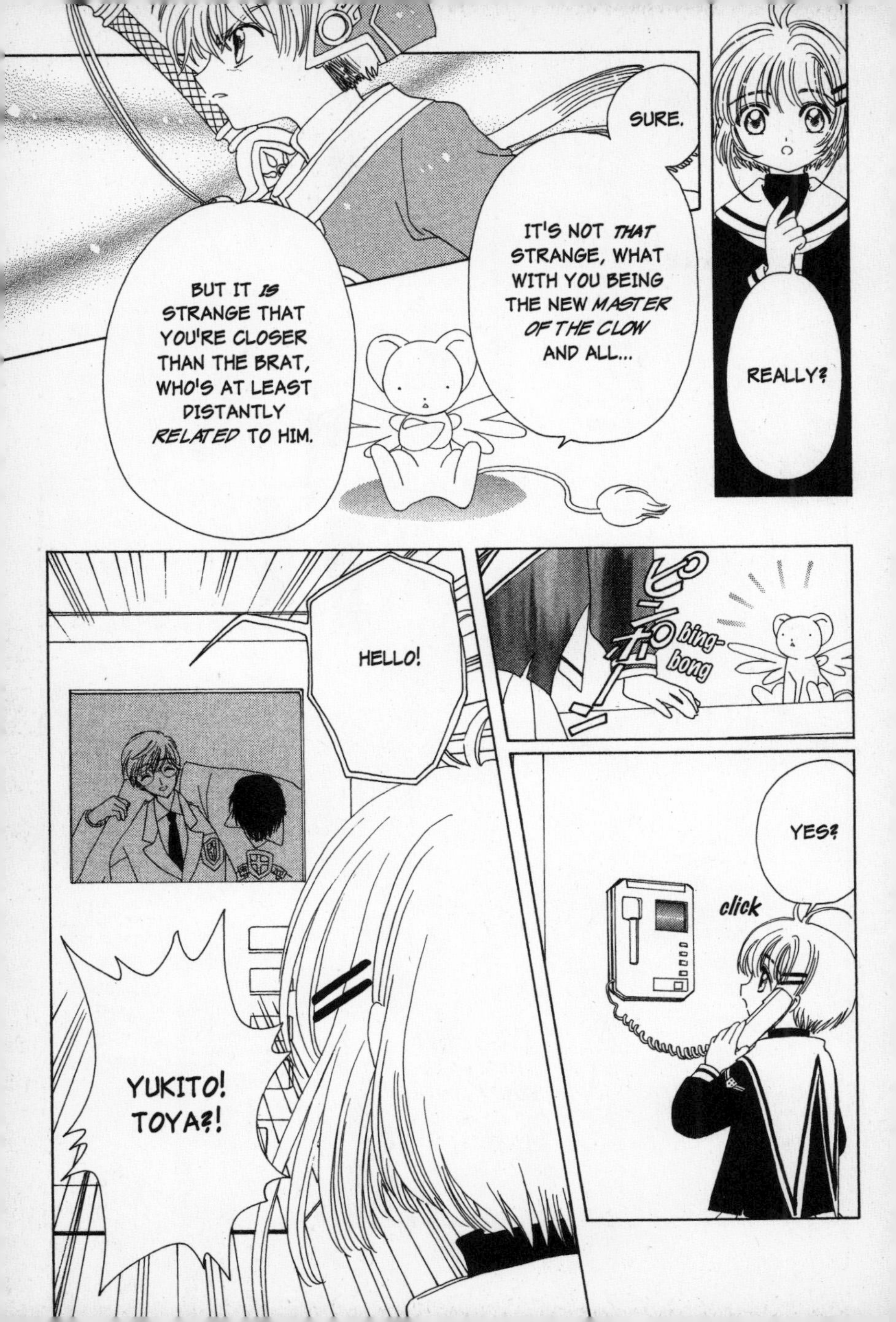
REALLY?
SURE.
IT'S NOT *THAT* STRANGE, WHAT WITH YOU BEING THE NEW *MASTER OF THE CLOW* AND ALL...
BUT IT *IS* STRANGE THAT YOU'RE CLOSER THAN THE BRAT, WHO'S AT LEAST DISTANTLY *RELATED* TO HIM.
ピーンポーン
bing-bong
YES?
click
HELLO!
YUKITO! TOYA?!

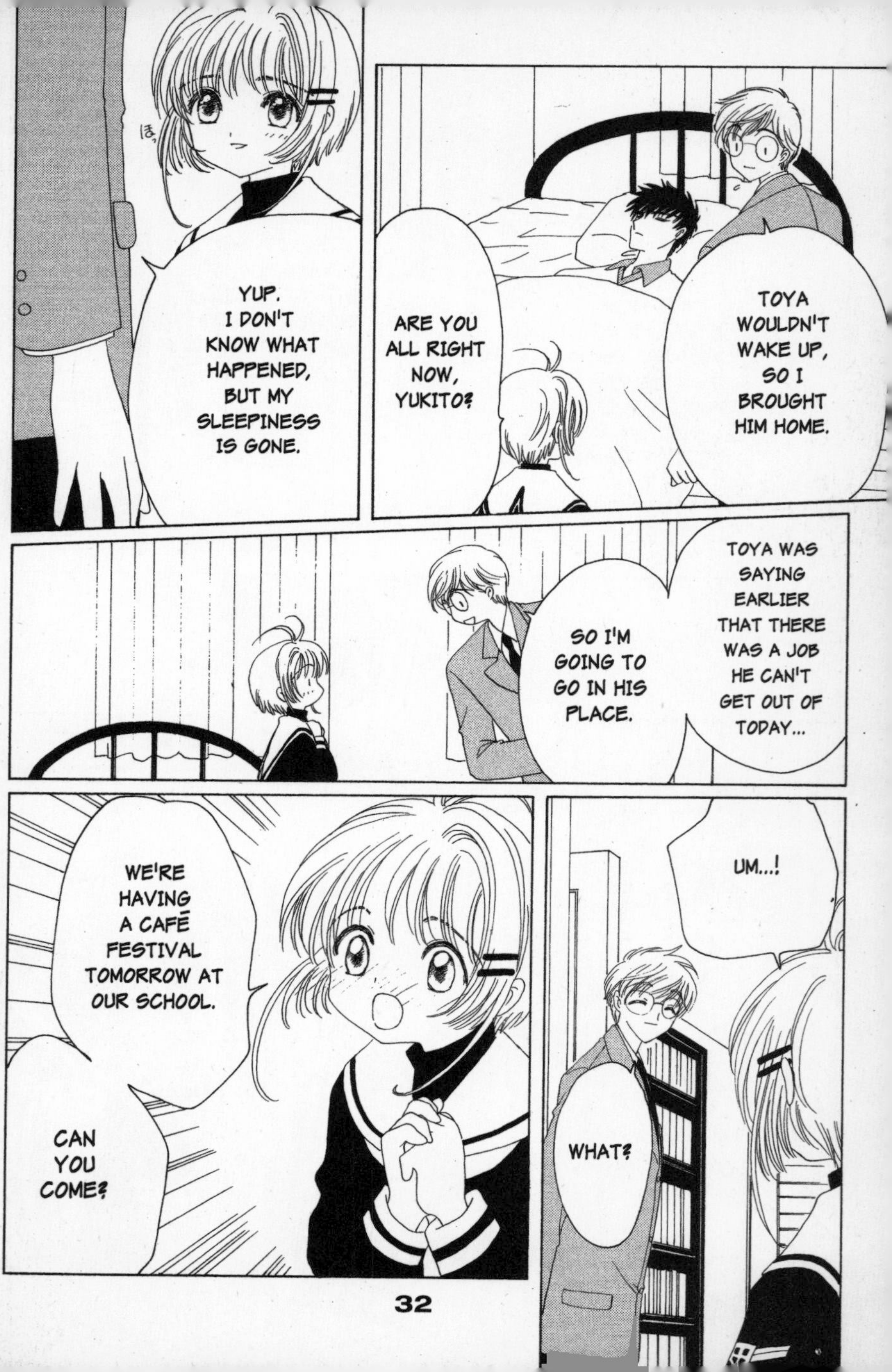
TOYA WOULDN'T WAKE UP, SO I BROUGHT HIM HOME.
ARE YOU ALL RIGHT NOW, YUKITO?
YUP. I DON'T KNOW WHAT HAPPENED, BUT MY SLEEPINESS IS GONE.
TOYA WAS SAYING EARLIER THAT THERE WAS A JOB HE CAN'T GET OUT OF TODAY...
SO I'M GOING TO GO IN HIS PLACE.
UM...!
WHAT?
WE'RE HAVING A CAFÉ FESTIVAL TOMORROW AT OUR SCHOOL.
CAN YOU COME?

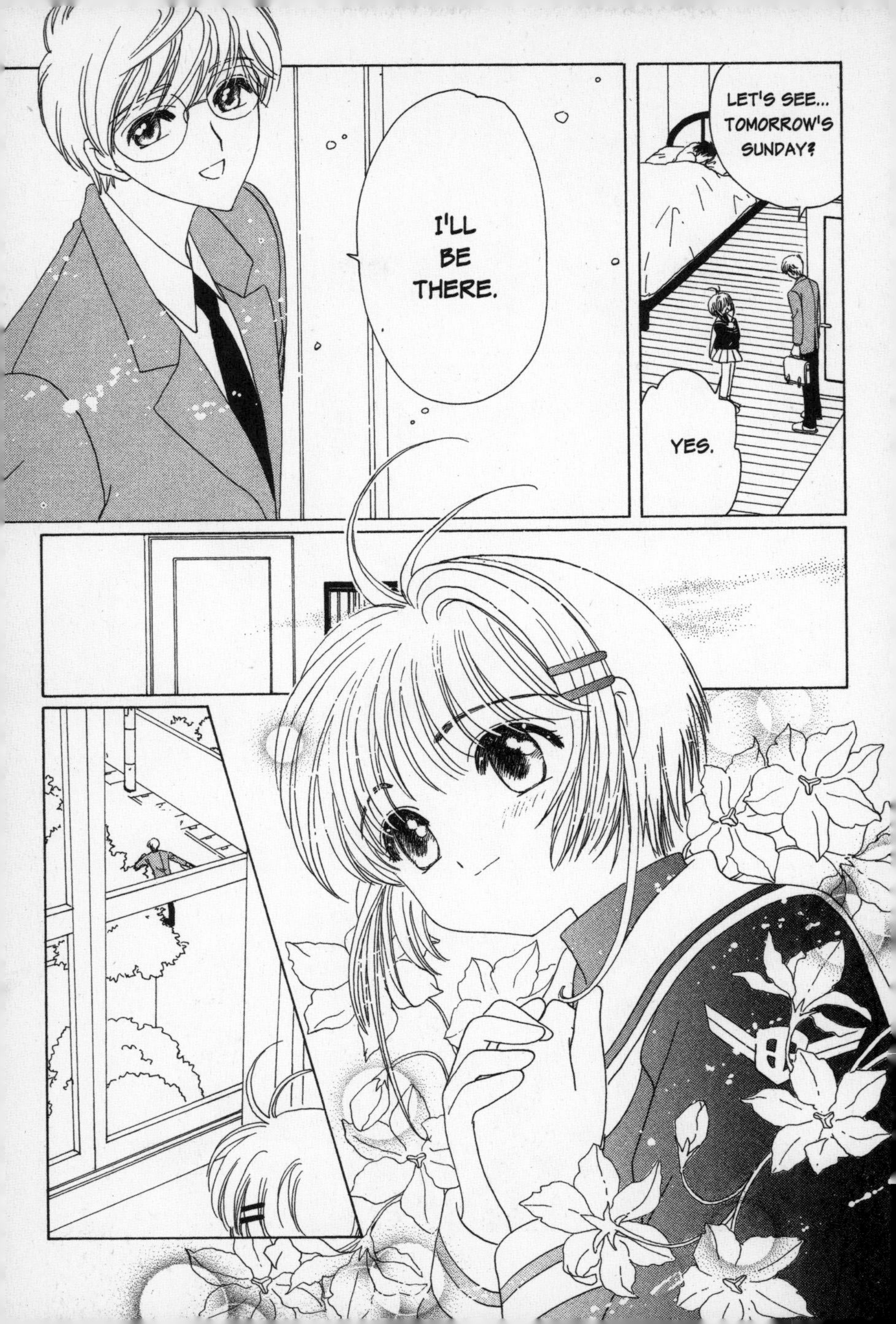
LET'S SEE... TOMORROW'S SUNDAY?
YES.
I'LL BE THERE.

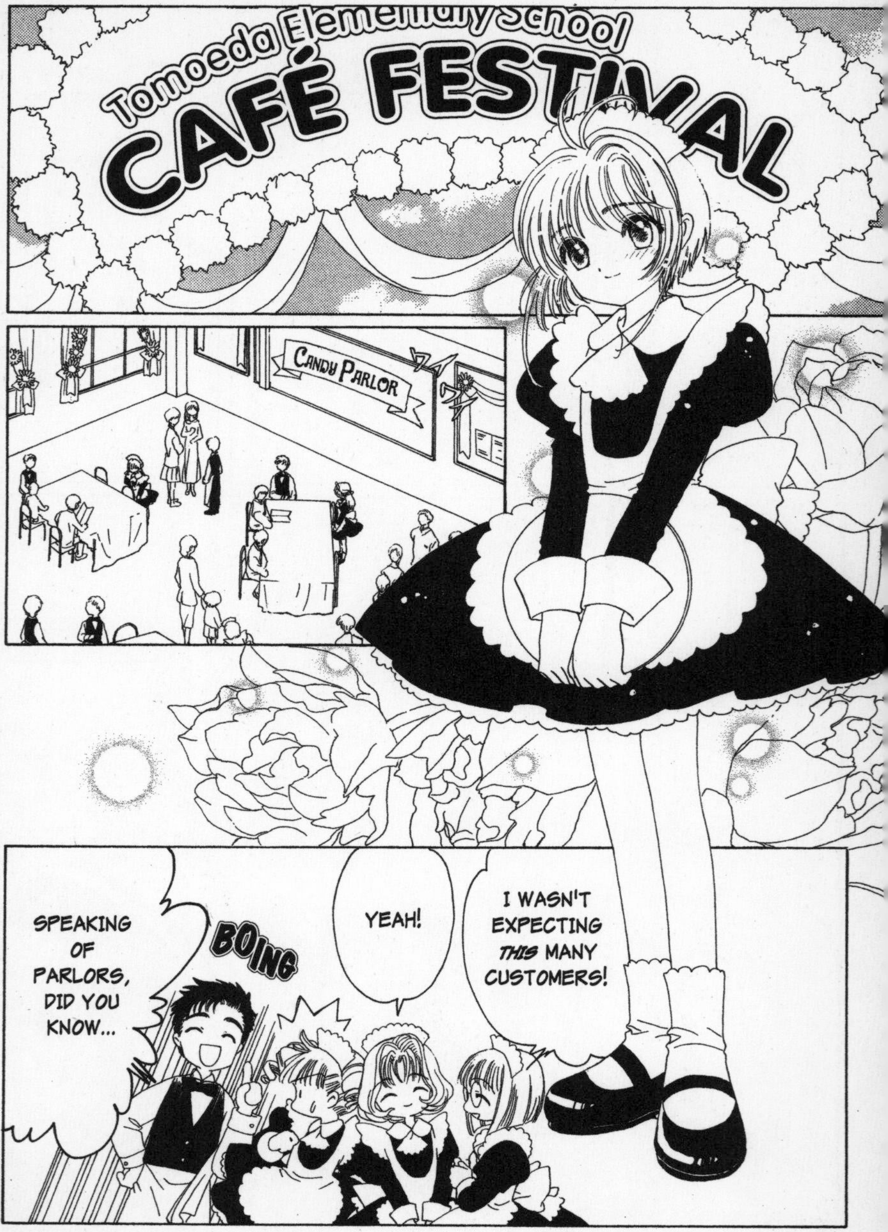
Tomoeda Elementary School
CAFÉ FESTIVAL
CANDY PARLOR
ワイワイ
I WASN'T EXPECTING *THIS* MANY CUSTOMERS!
YEAH!
BOING
SPEAKING OF PARLORS, DID YOU KNOW...

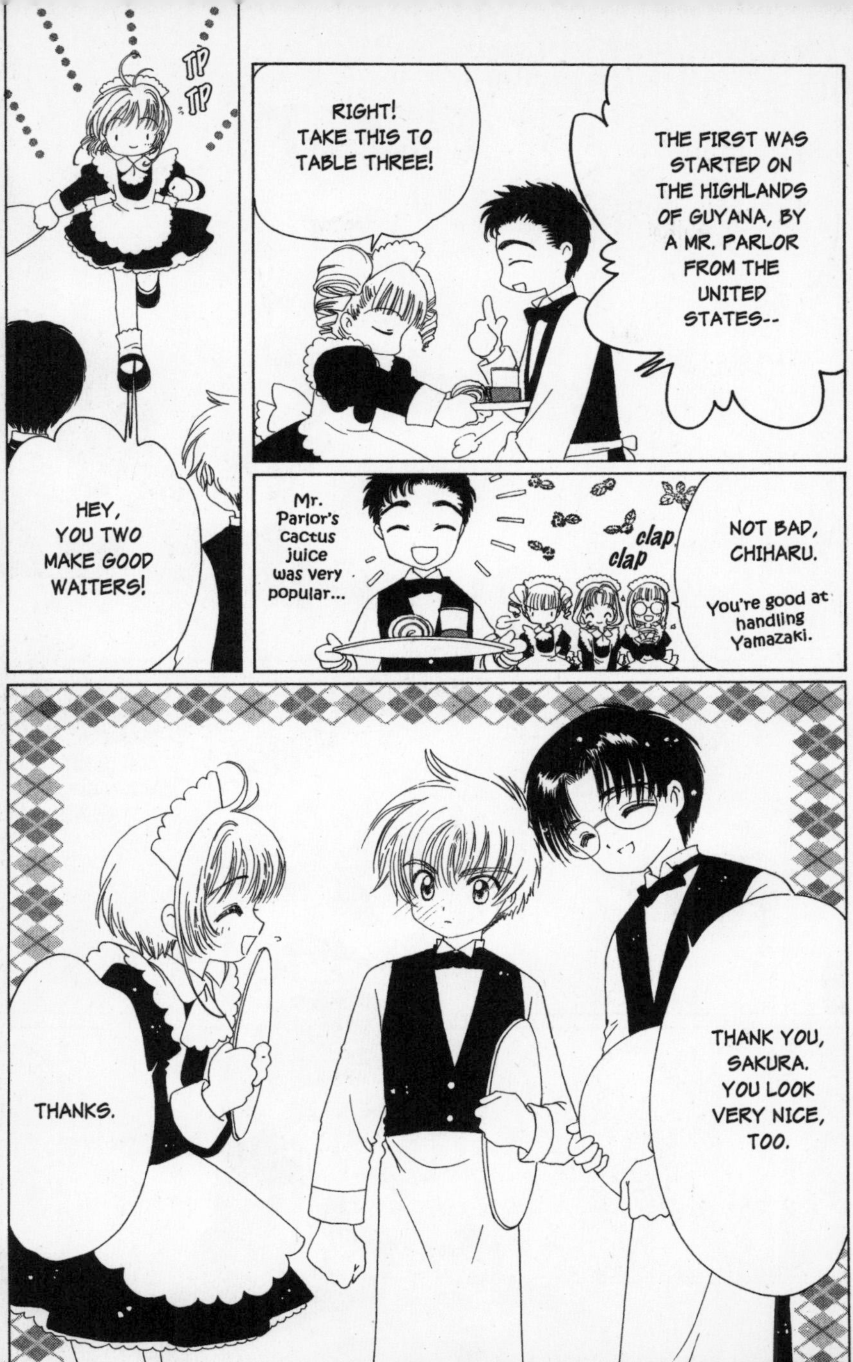
THE FIRST WAS STARTED ON THE HIGHLANDS OF GUYANA, BY A MR. PARLOR FROM THE UNITED STATES--
RIGHT! TAKE THIS TO TABLE THREE!
NOT BAD, CHIHARU.
You're good at handling Yamazaki.
clap clap
Mr. Parlor's cactus juice was very popular...
TP TP
HEY, YOU TWO MAKE GOOD WAITERS!
THANK YOU, SAKURA. YOU LOOK VERY NICE, TOO.
THANKS.

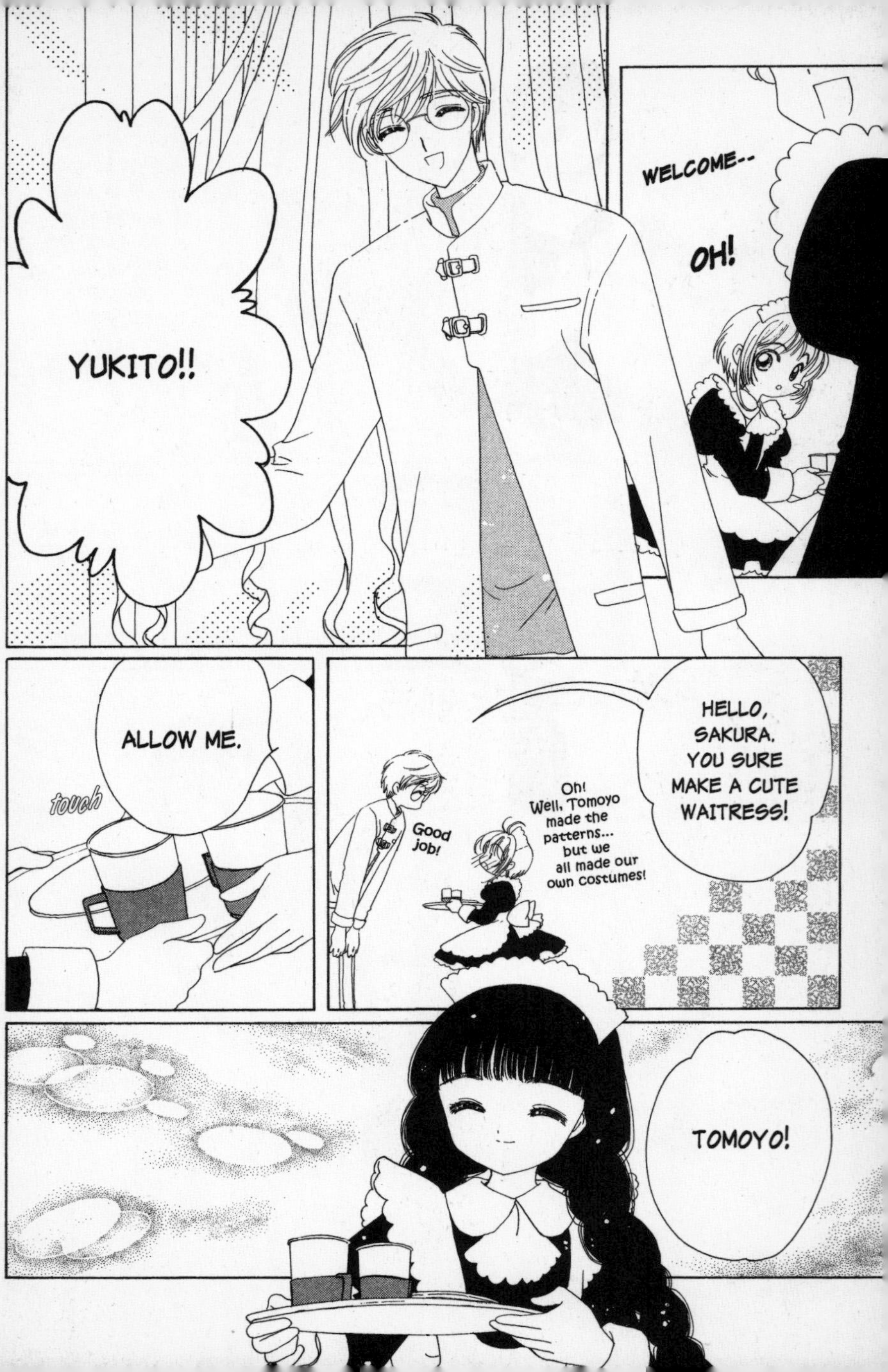
WELCOME--
OH!
YUKITO!!
HELLO, SAKURA. YOU SURE MAKE A CUTE WAITRESS!
Oh! Well, Tomoyo made the patterns... but we all made our own costumes!
Good job!
ALLOW ME.
touch
TOMOYO!

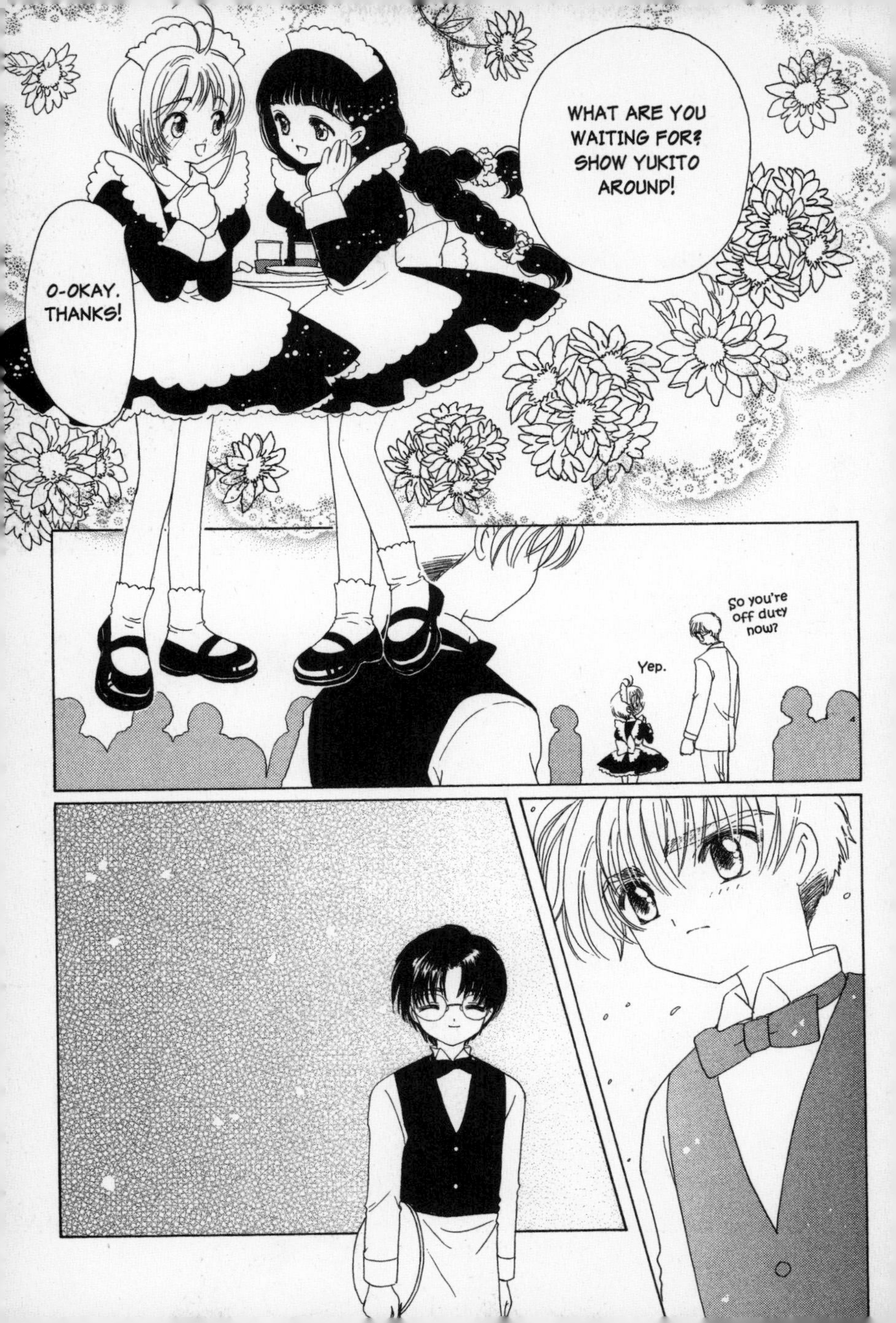
WHAT ARE YOU WAITING FOR? SHOW YUKITO AROUND!
O-OKAY. THANKS!
So you're off duty now?
Yep.

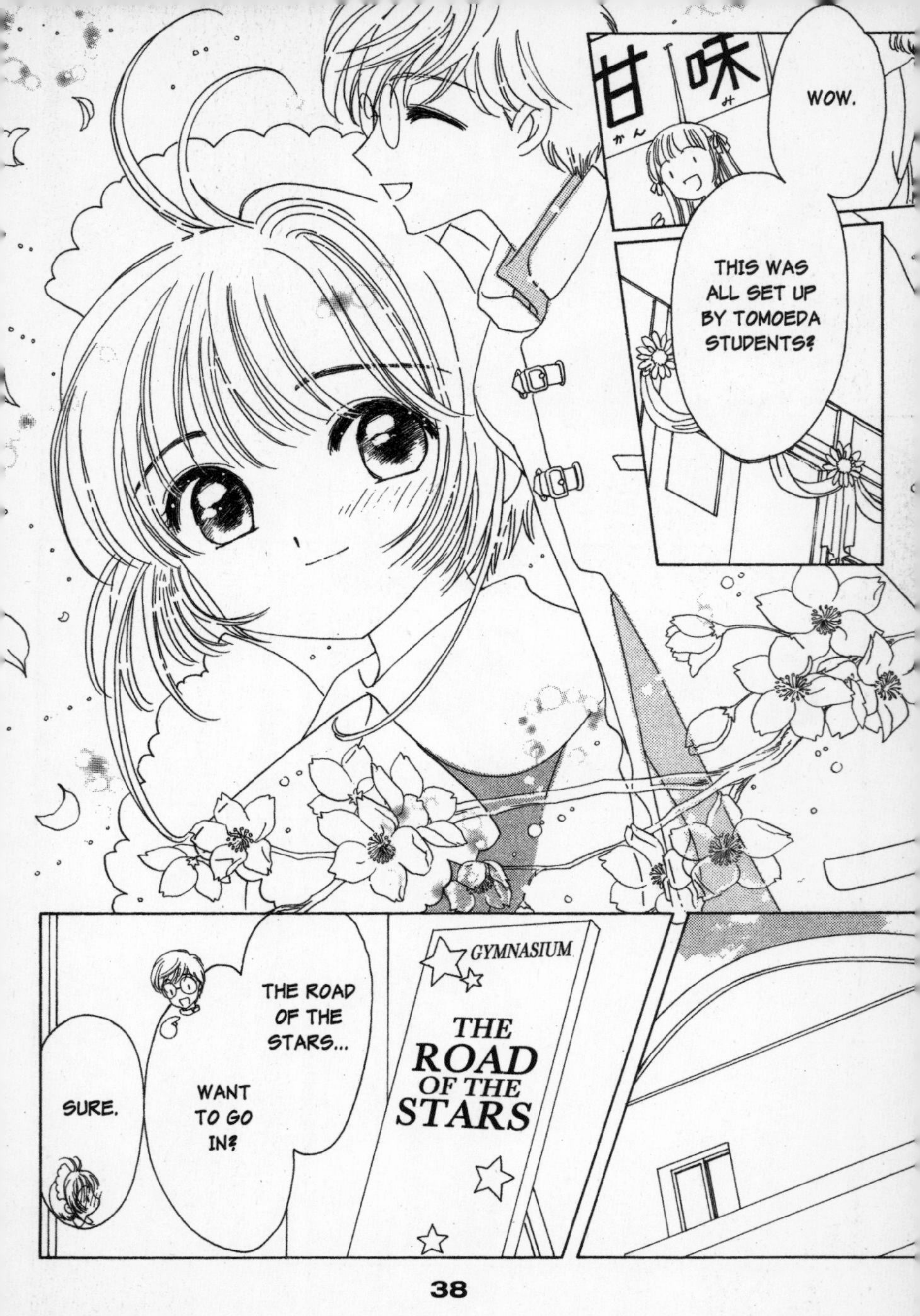
甘味
WOW.
THIS WAS ALL SET UP BY TOMOEDA STUDENTS?
GYMNASIUM
THE ROAD OF THE STARS
THE ROAD OF THE STARS...
WANT TO GO IN?
SURE.

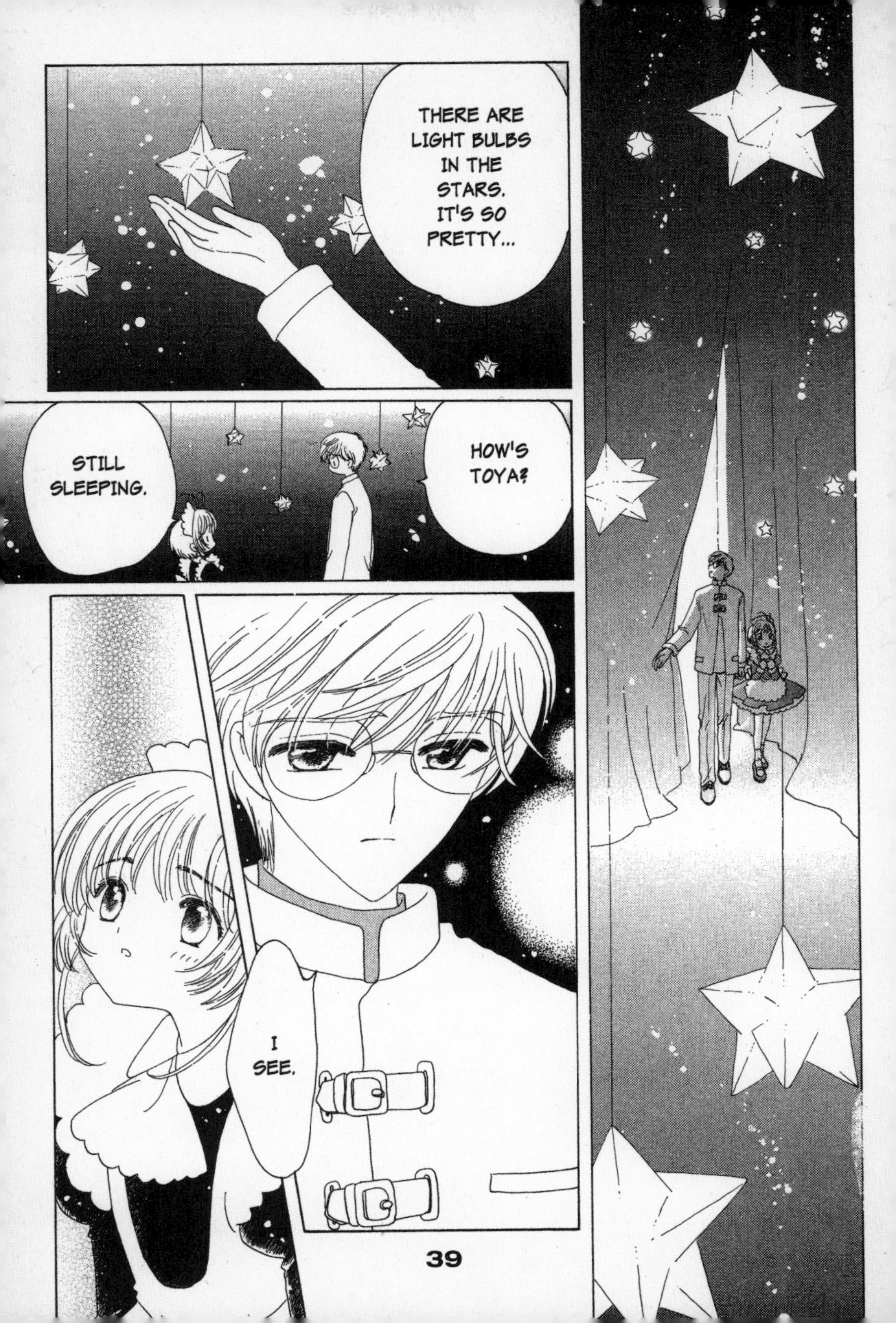
THERE ARE LIGHT BULBS IN THE STARS. IT'S SO PRETTY...
HOW'S TOYA?
STILL SLEEPING.
I SEE.

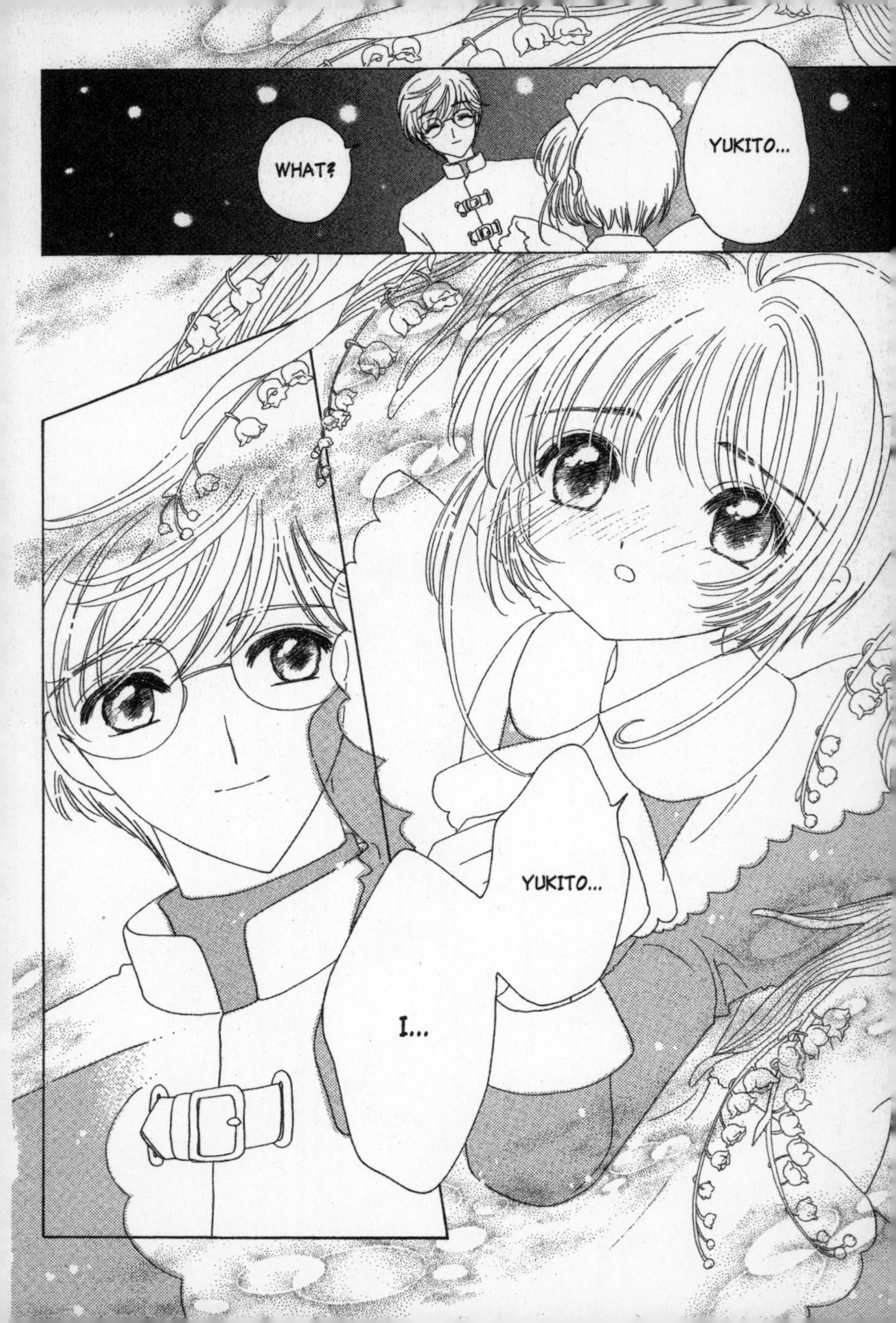
YUKITO...
WHAT?
YUKITO...
I...

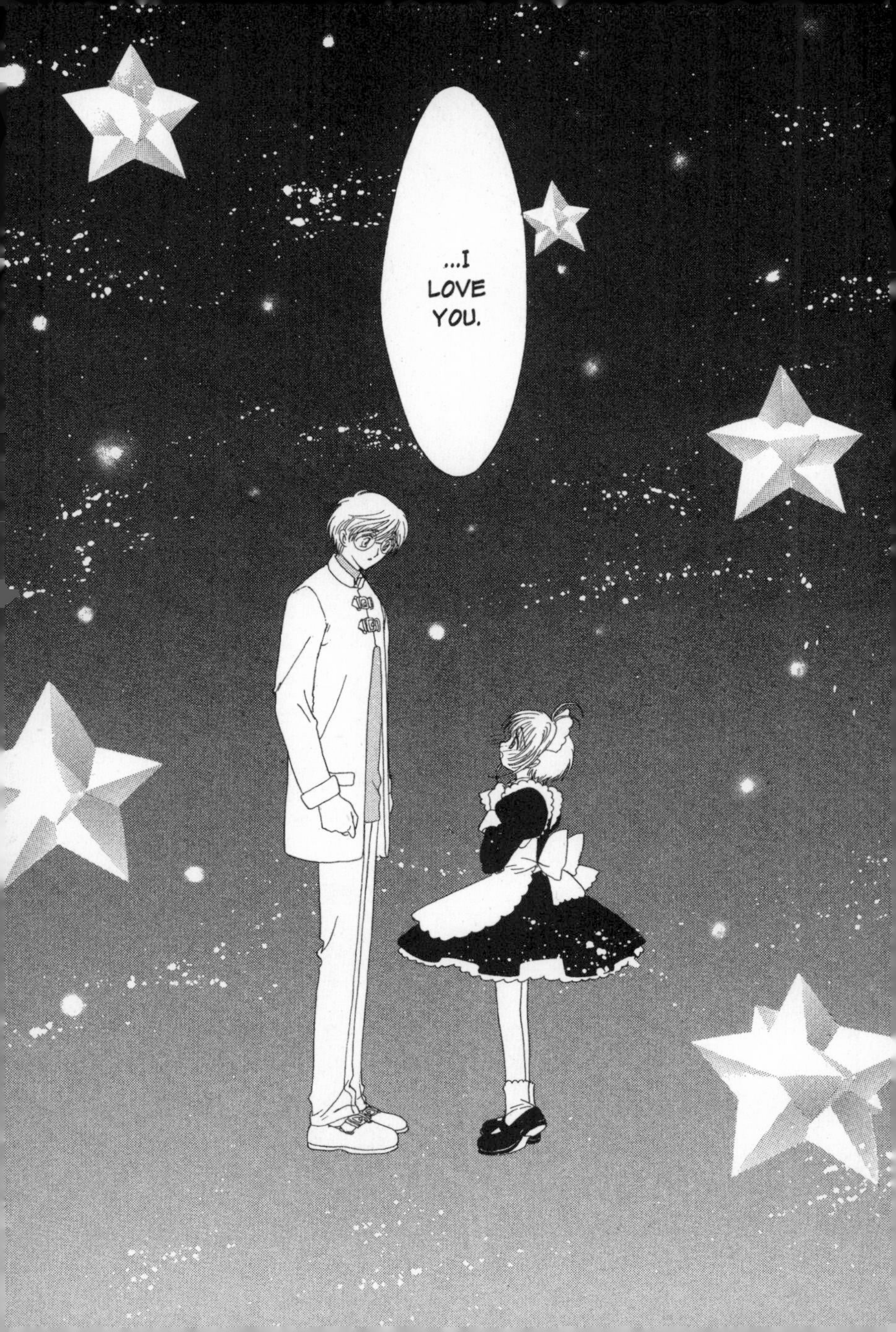
...I LOVE YOU.

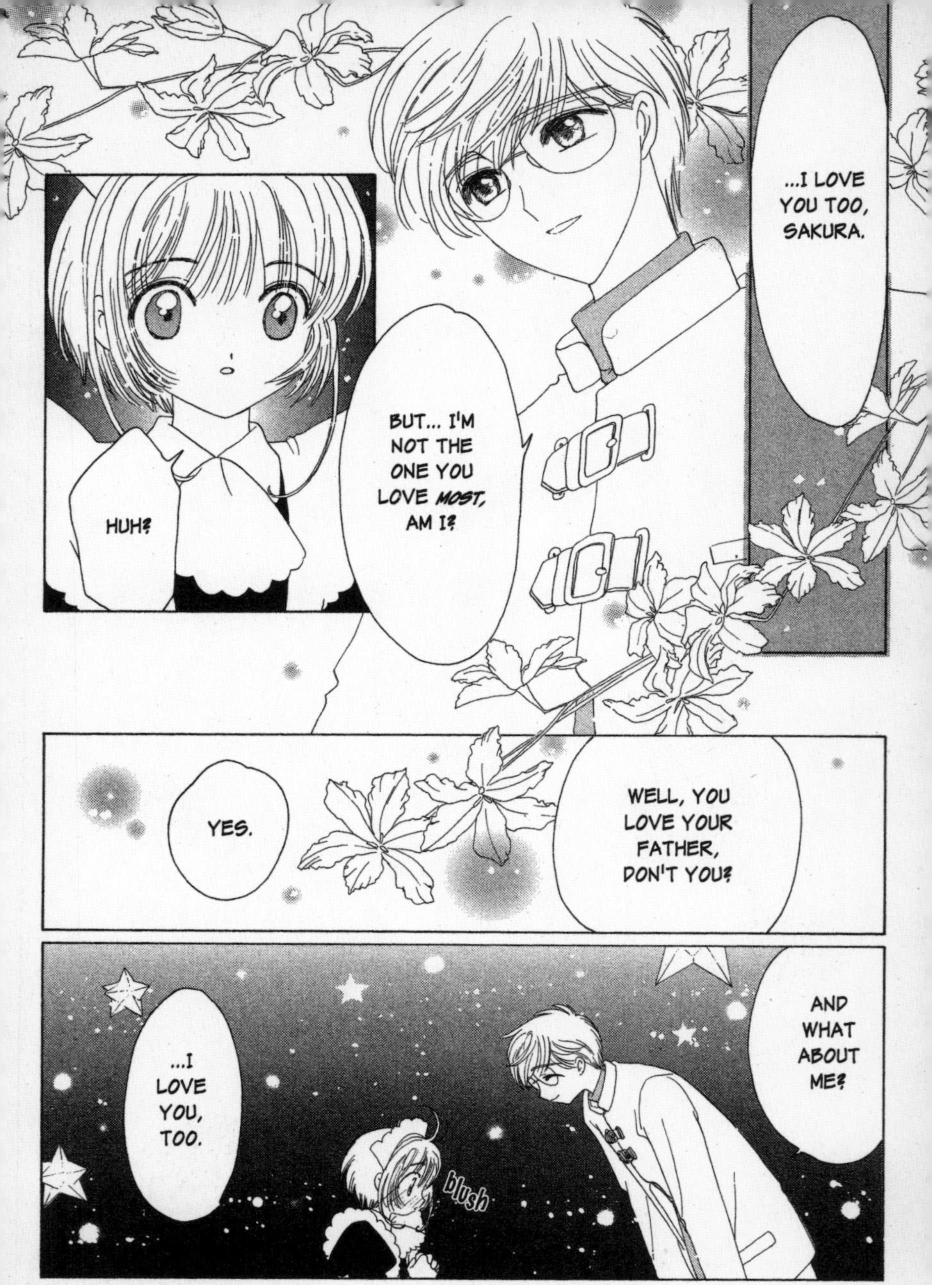
...I LOVE YOU TOO, SAKURA.
HUH?
BUT... I'M NOT THE ONE YOU LOVE *MOST,* AM I?
WELL, YOU LOVE YOUR FATHER, DON'T YOU?
YES.
AND WHAT ABOUT ME?
...I LOVE YOU, TOO.
blush

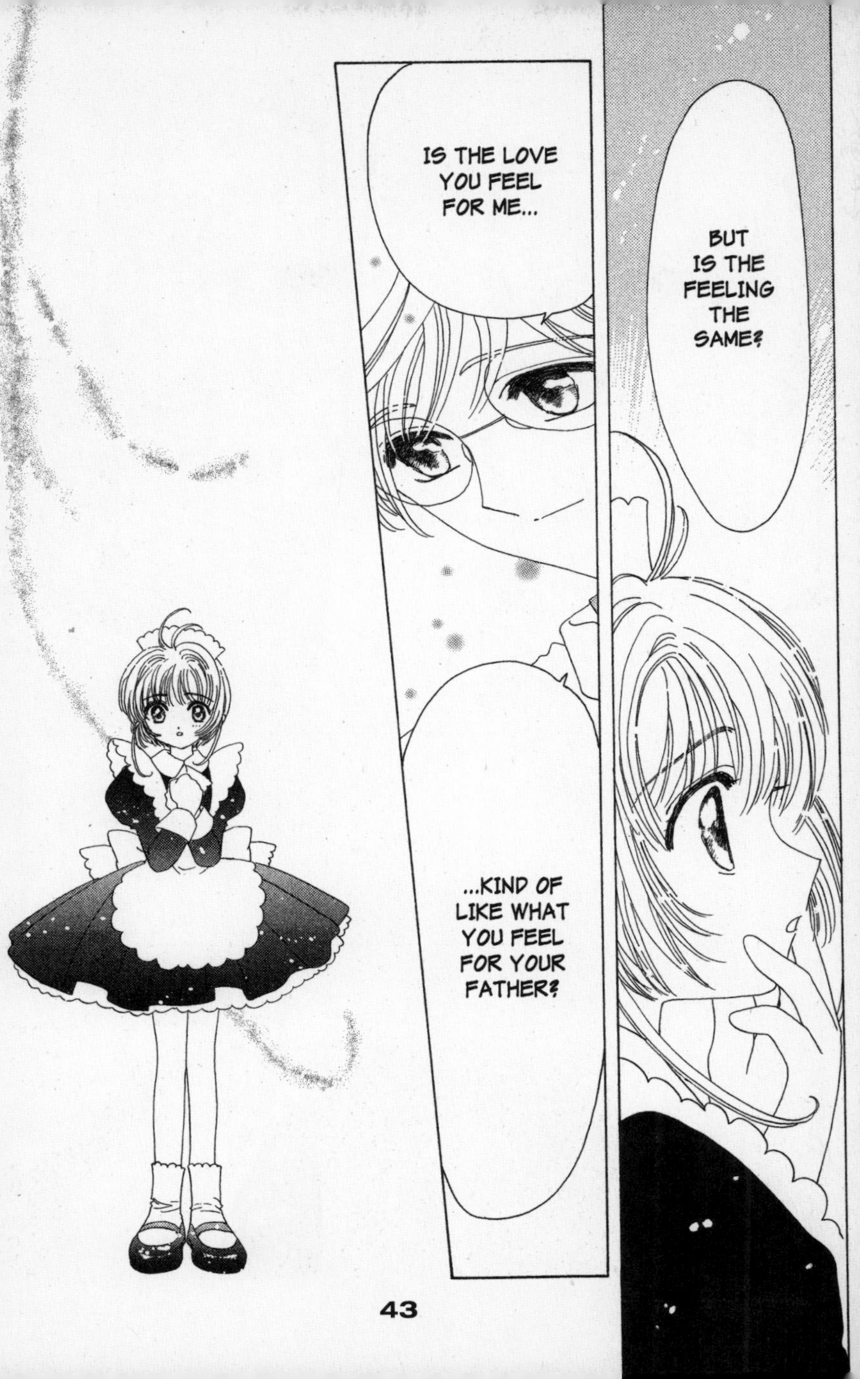
BUT IS THE FEELING THE SAME?
IS THE LOVE YOU FEEL FOR ME...
...KIND OF LIKE WHAT YOU FEEL FOR YOUR FATHER?

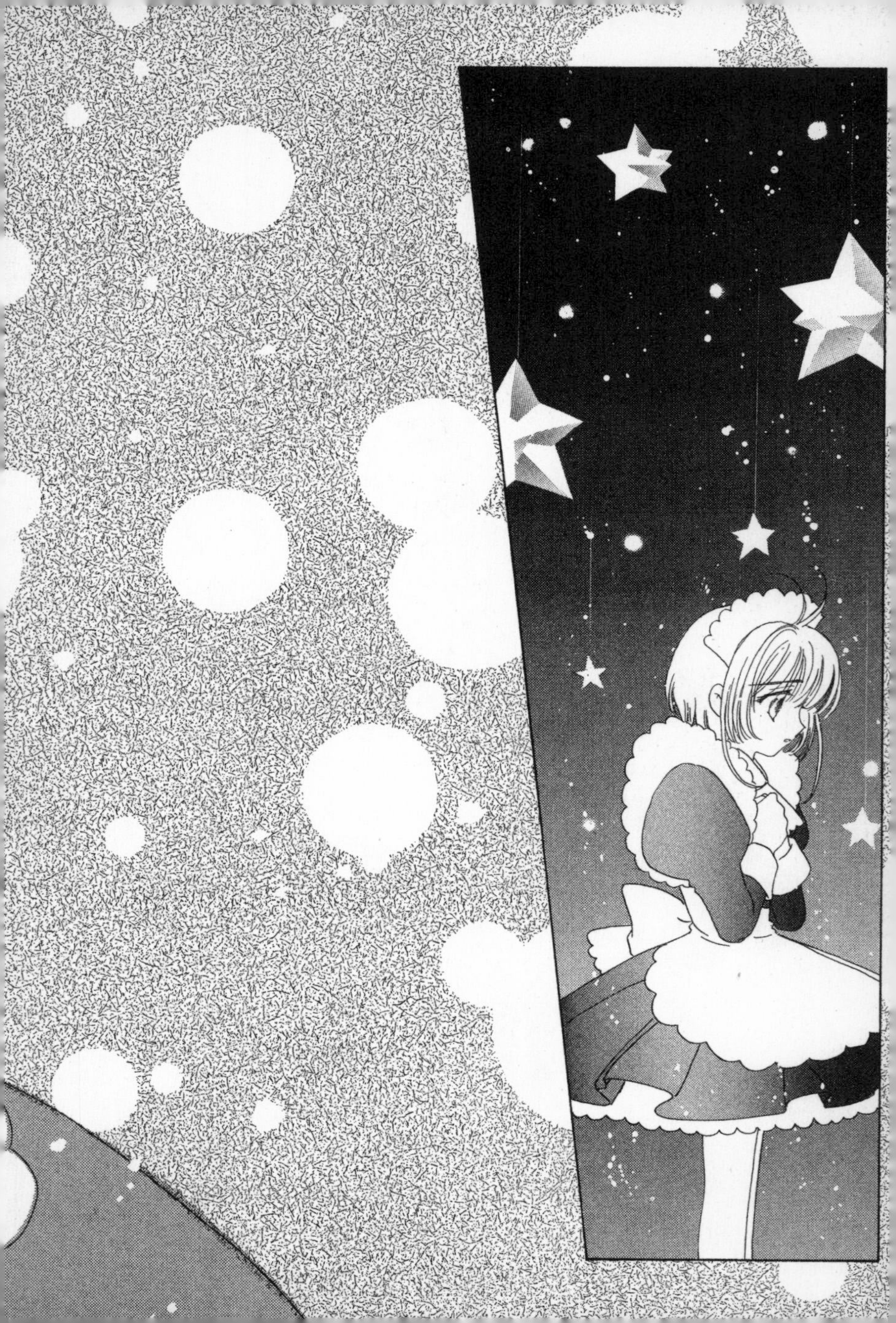

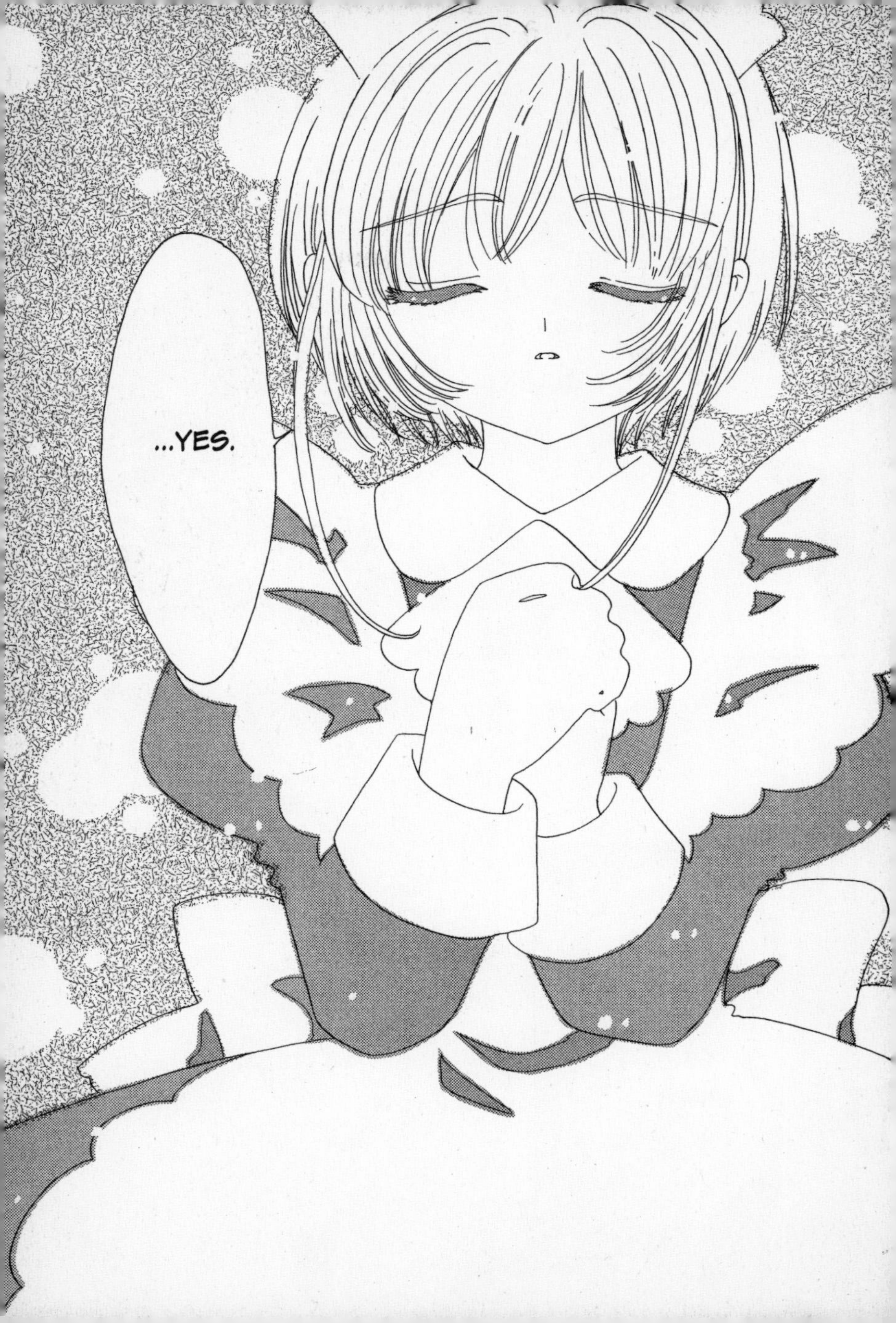
...YES.

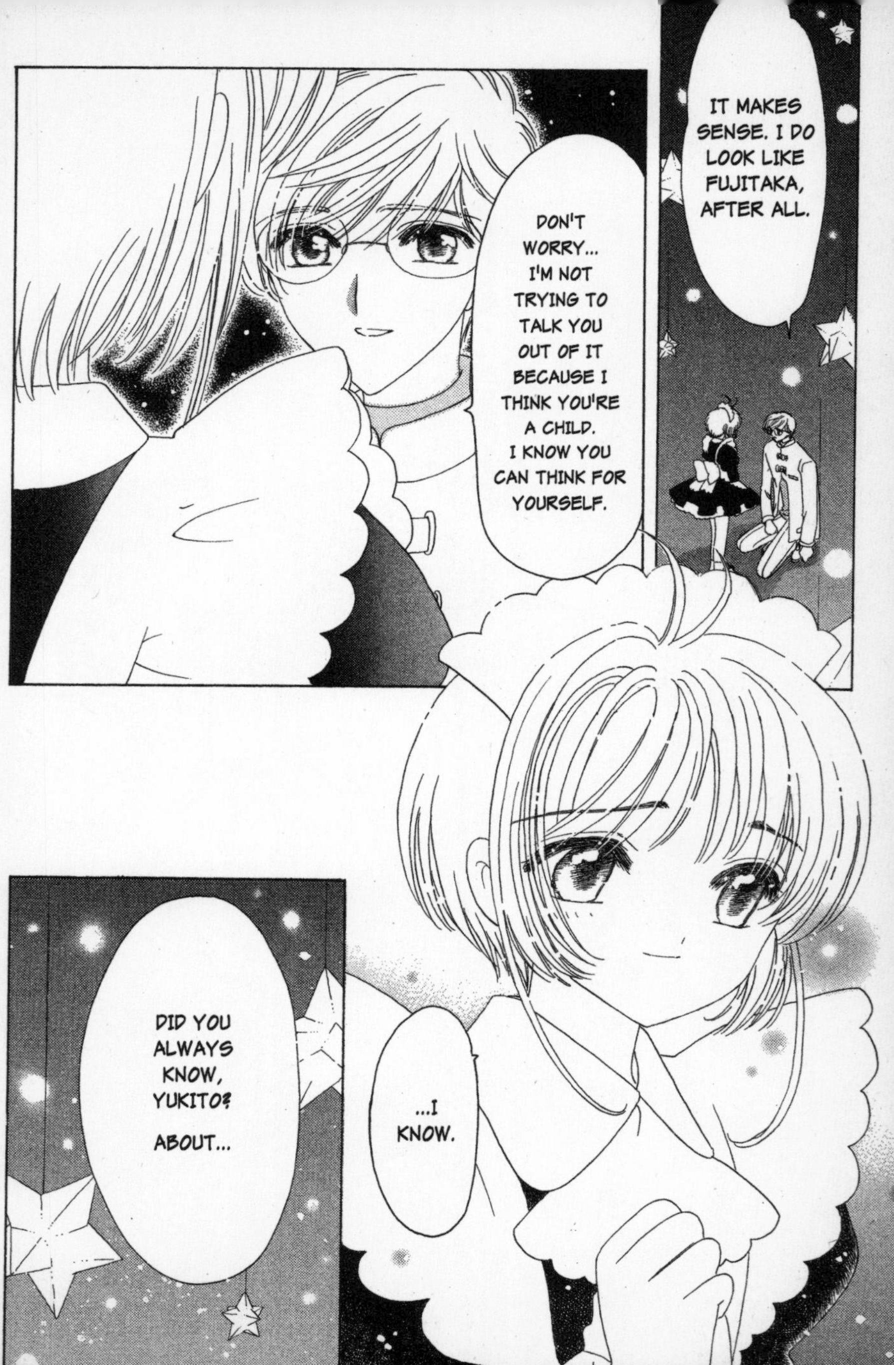
IT MAKES SENSE. I DO LOOK LIKE FUJITAKA, AFTER ALL.
DON'T WORRY... I'M NOT TRYING TO TALK YOU OUT OF IT BECAUSE I THINK YOU'RE A CHILD. I KNOW YOU CAN THINK FOR YOURSELF.
...I KNOW.
DID YOU ALWAYS KNOW, YUKITO?
ABOUT...

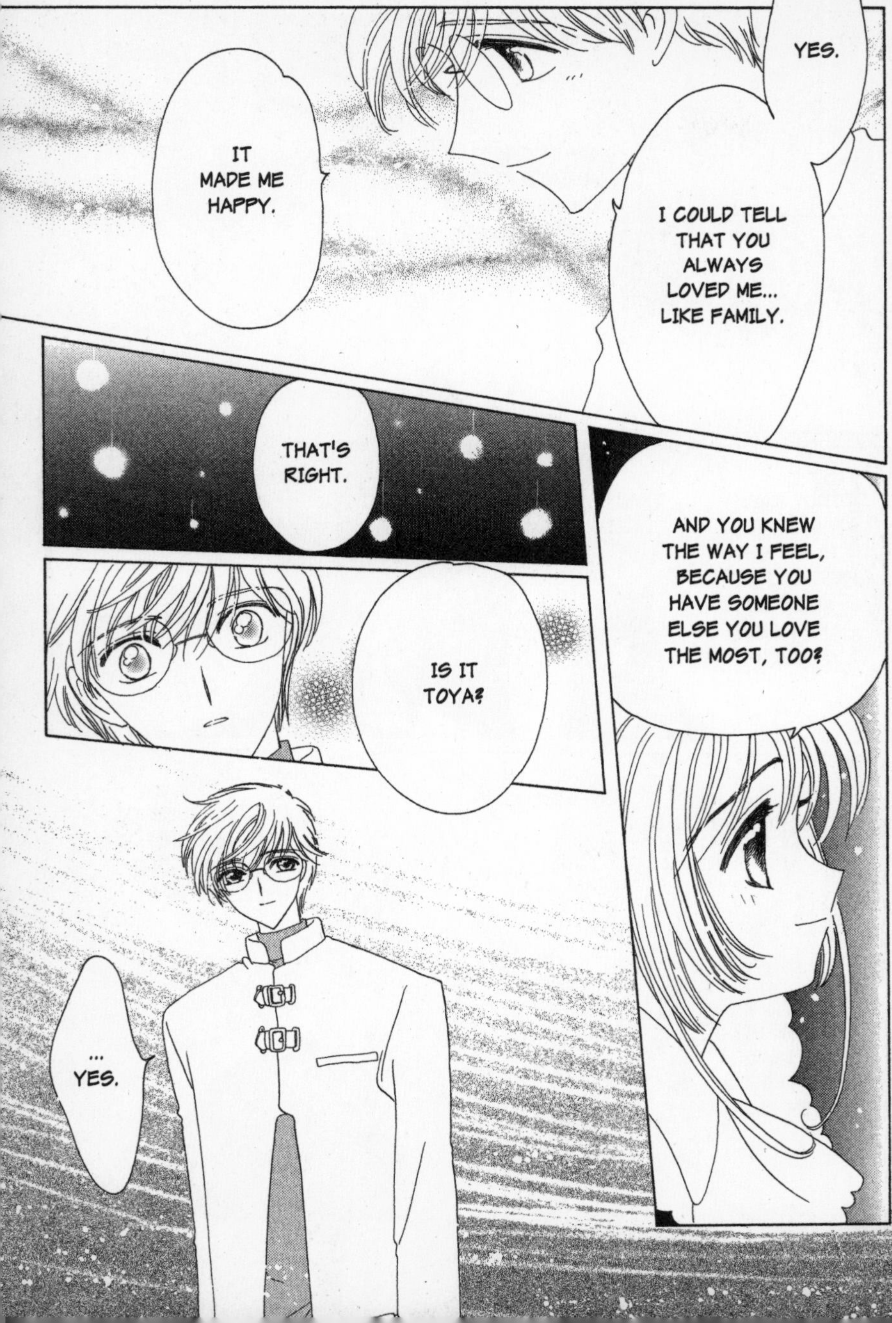
YES.
I COULD TELL THAT YOU ALWAYS LOVED ME... LIKE FAMILY.
IT MADE ME HAPPY.
AND YOU KNEW THE WAY I FEEL, BECAUSE YOU HAVE SOMEONE ELSE YOU LOVE THE MOST, TOO?
THAT'S RIGHT.
IS IT TOYA?
... YES.

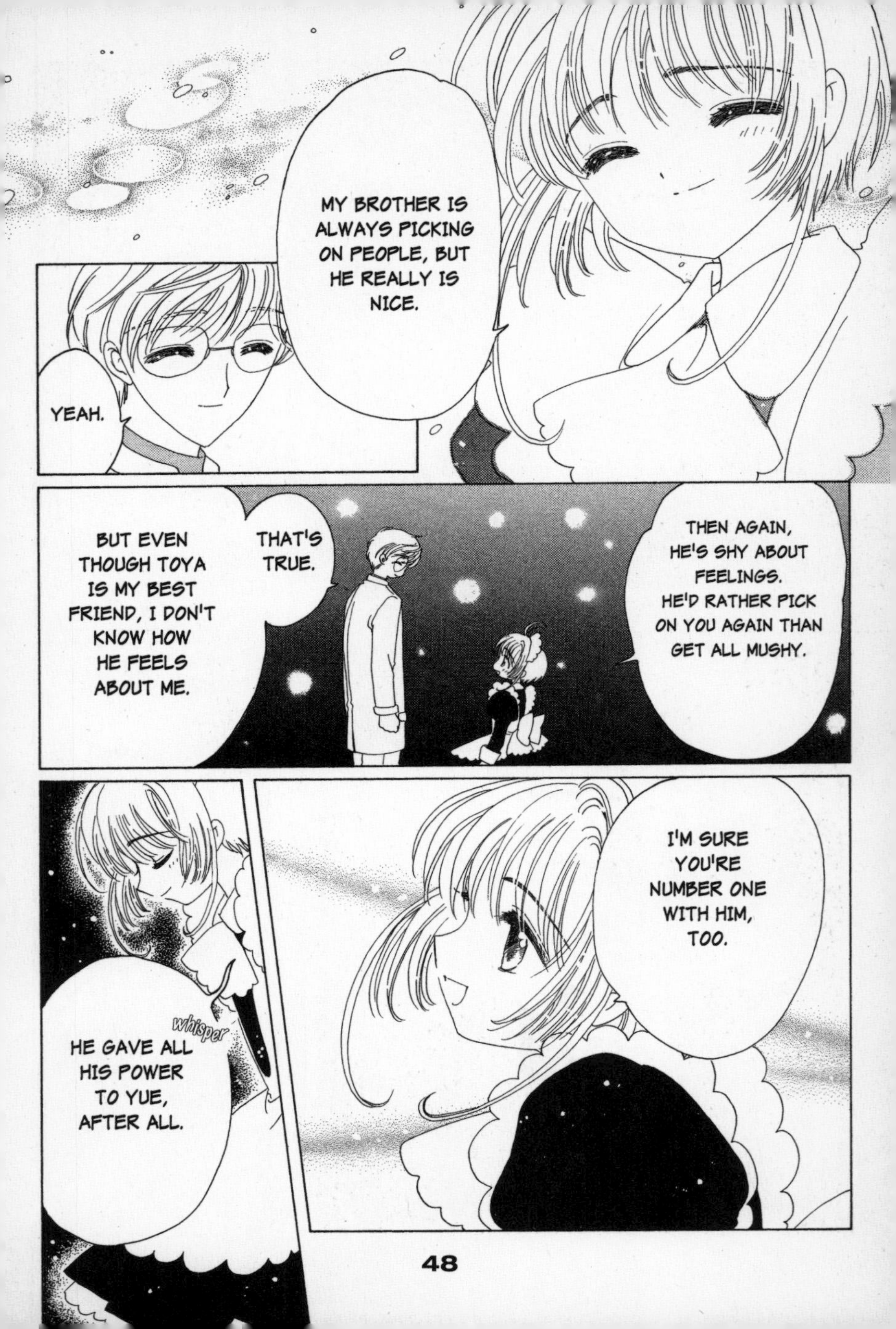
MY BROTHER IS ALWAYS PICKING ON PEOPLE, BUT HE REALLY IS NICE.
YEAH.
THAT'S TRUE.
BUT EVEN THOUGH TOYA IS MY BEST FRIEND, I DON'T KNOW HOW HE FEELS ABOUT ME.
THEN AGAIN, HE'S SHY ABOUT FEELINGS. HE'D RATHER PICK ON YOU AGAIN THAN GET ALL MUSHY.
I'M SURE YOU'RE NUMBER ONE WITH HIM, TOO.
whisper
HE GAVE ALL HIS POWER TO YUE, AFTER ALL.

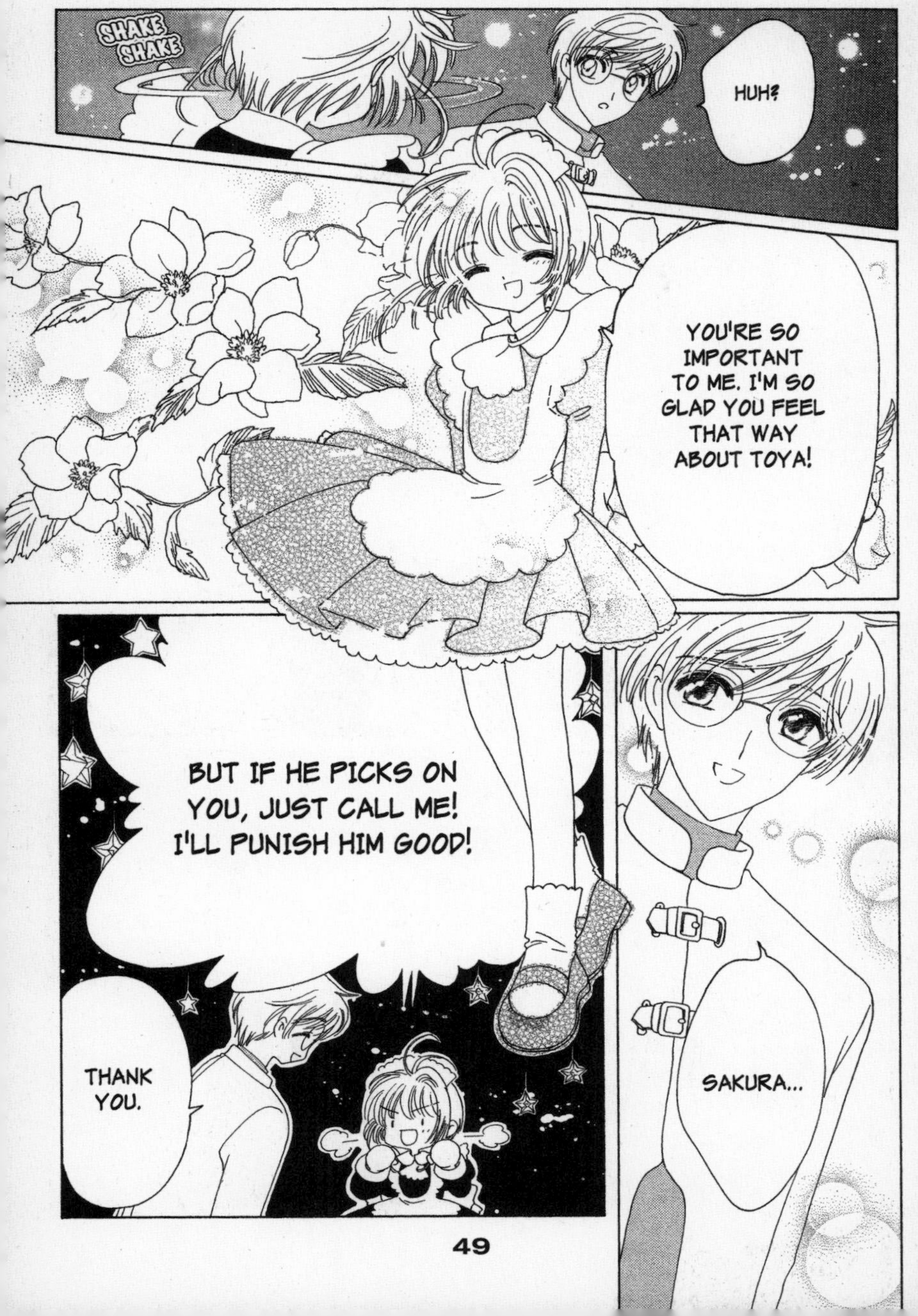
HUH?
SHAKE SHAKE
YOU'RE SO IMPORTANT TO ME. I'M SO GLAD YOU FEEL THAT WAY ABOUT TOYA!
SAKURA...
BUT IF HE PICKS ON YOU, JUST CALL ME! I'LL PUNISH HIM GOOD!
THANK YOU.

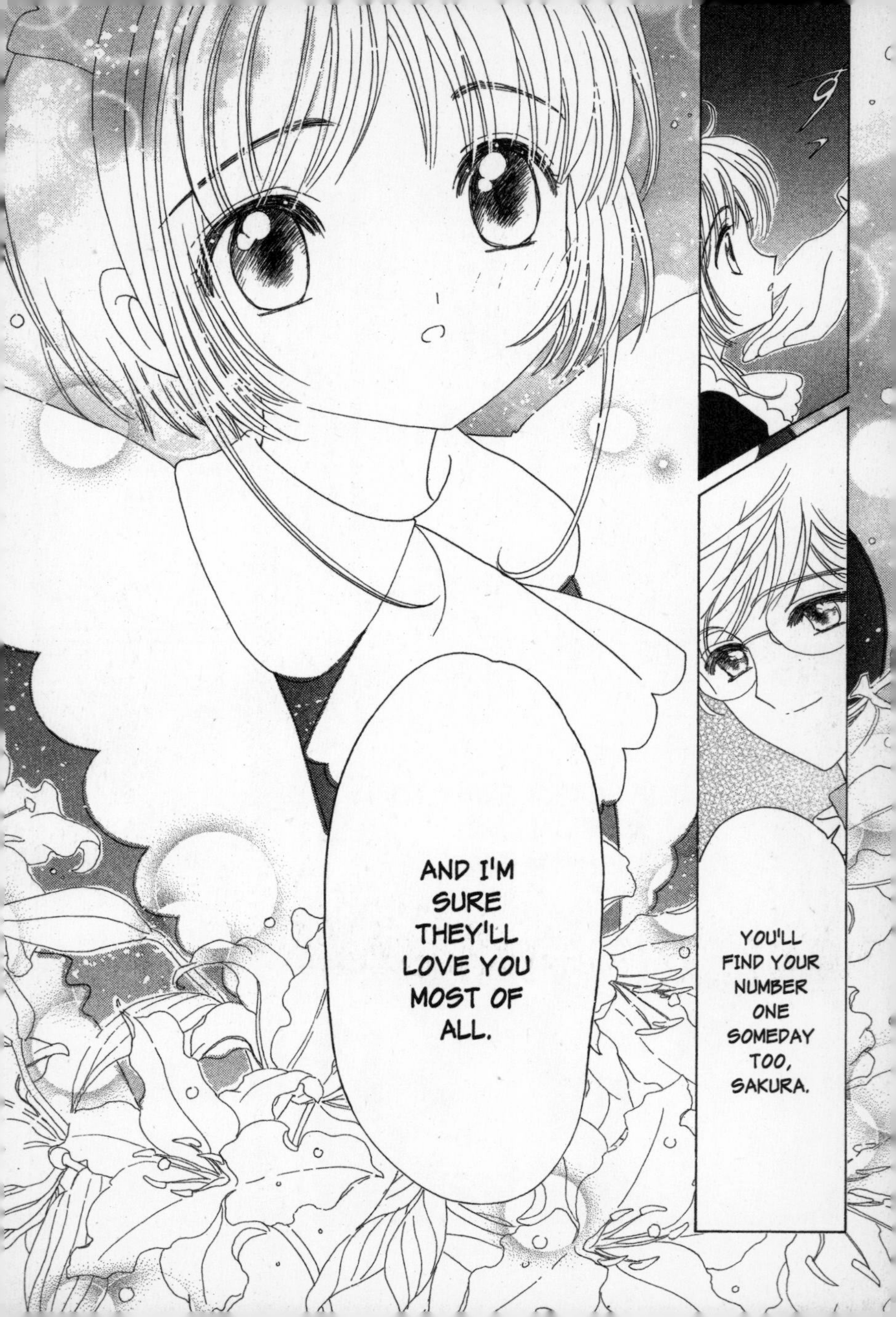
YOU'LL FIND YOUR NUMBER ONE SOMEDAY TOO, SAKURA.
AND I'M SURE THEY'LL LOVE YOU MOST OF ALL.

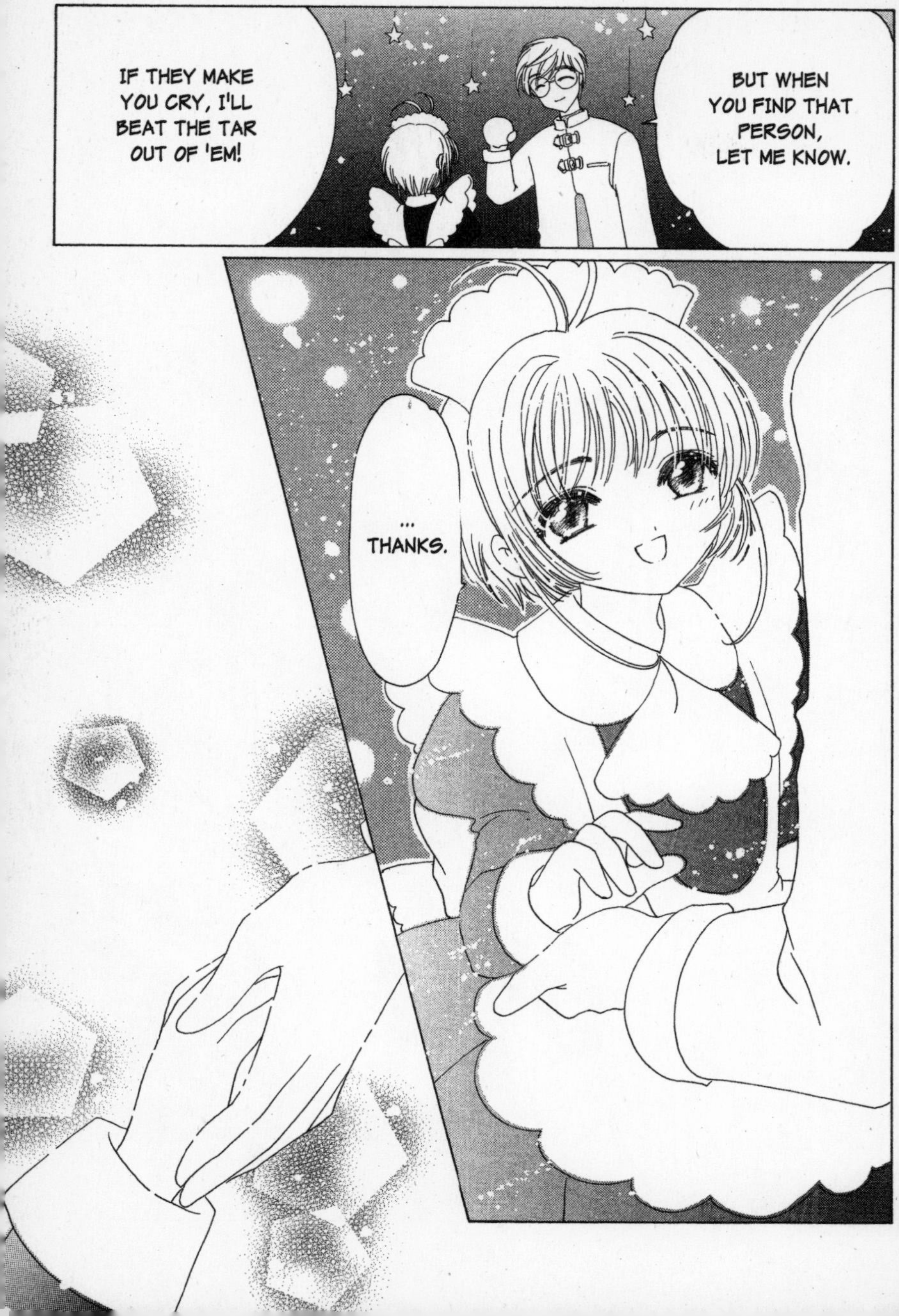

BUT WHEN YOU FIND THAT PERSON, LET ME KNOW.
IF THEY MAKE YOU CRY, I'LL BEAT THE TAR OUT OF 'EM!
... THANKS.

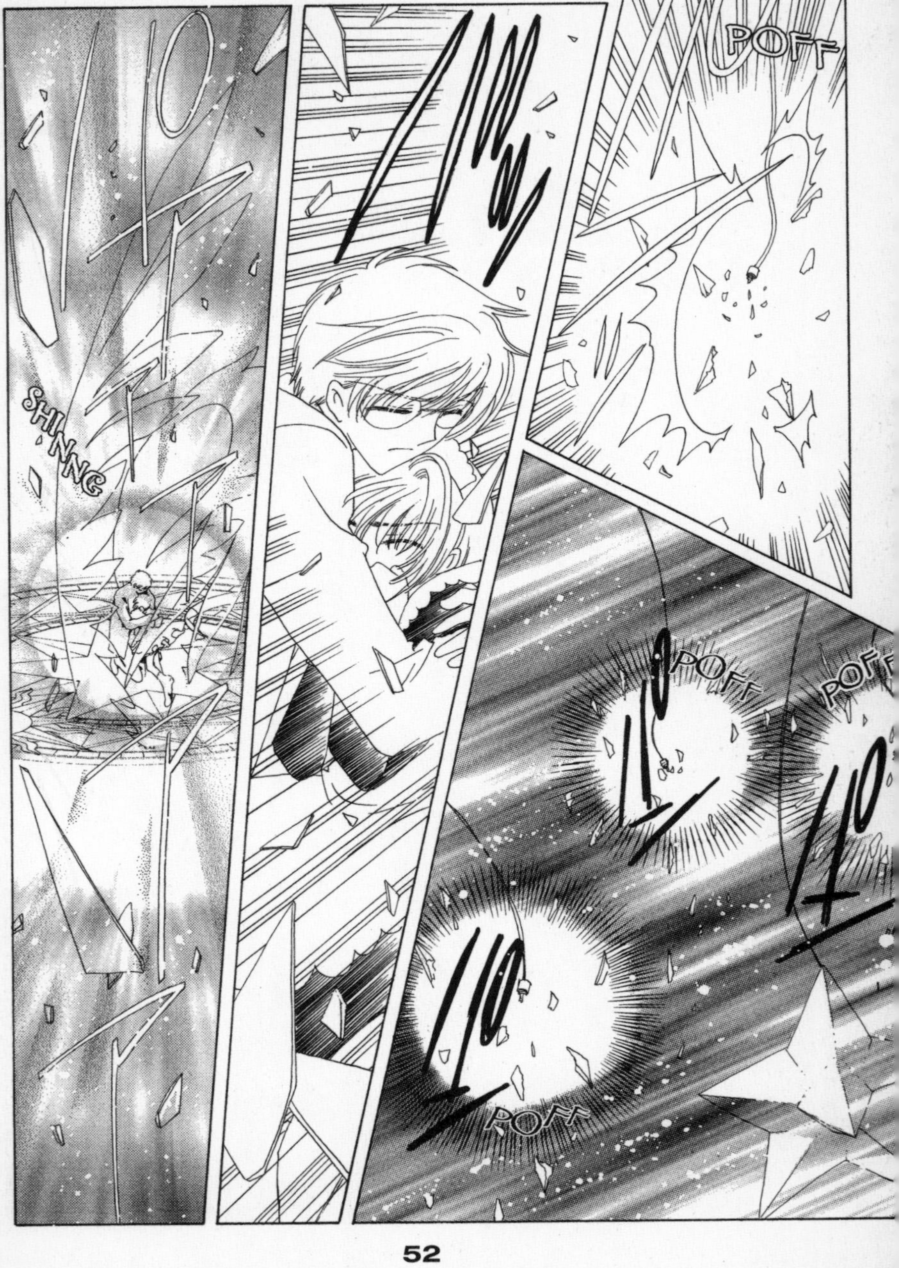
POFF
POF
POFF
POFF
SHINNG

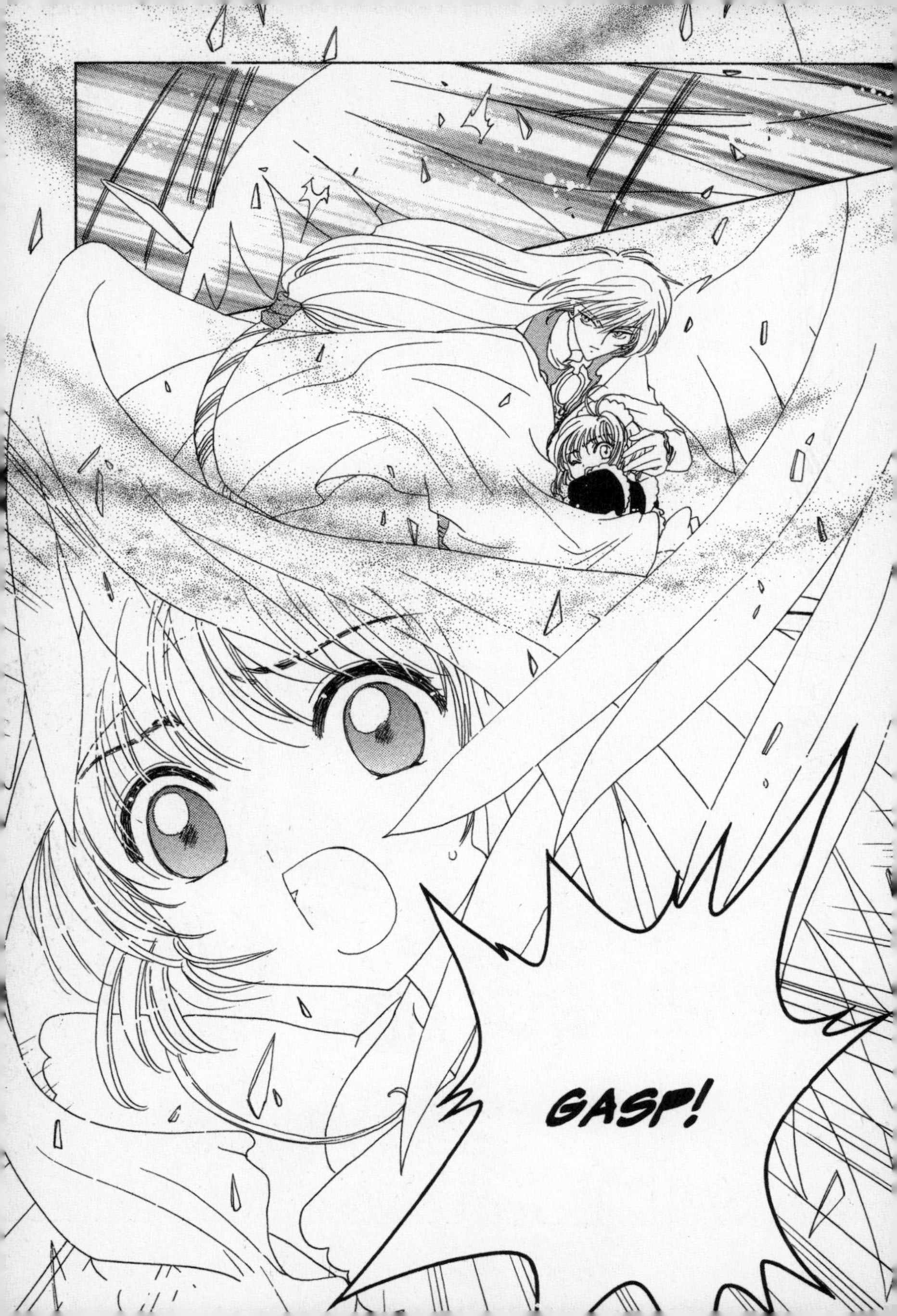
GASP!

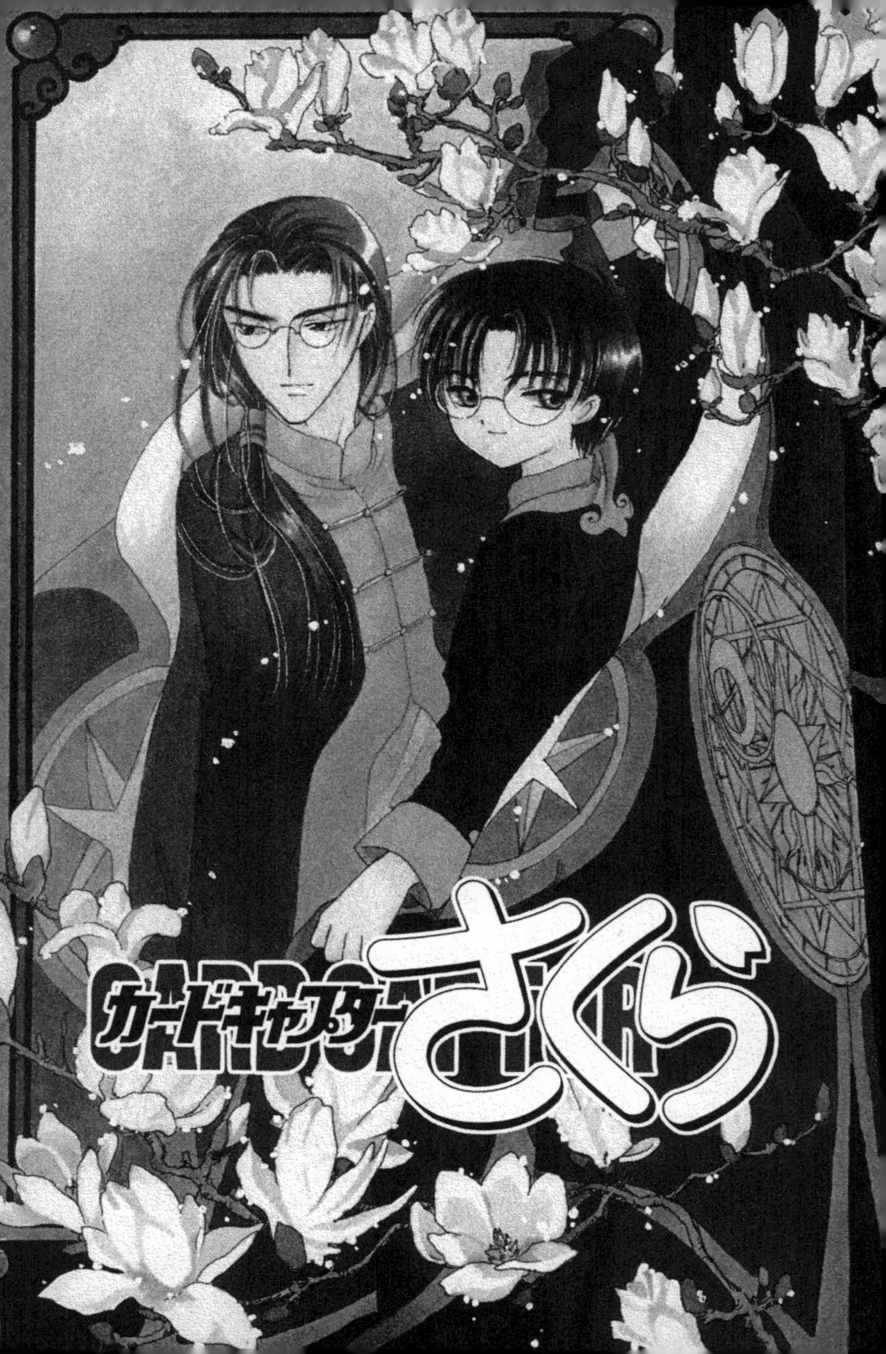
カードキャプターさくら

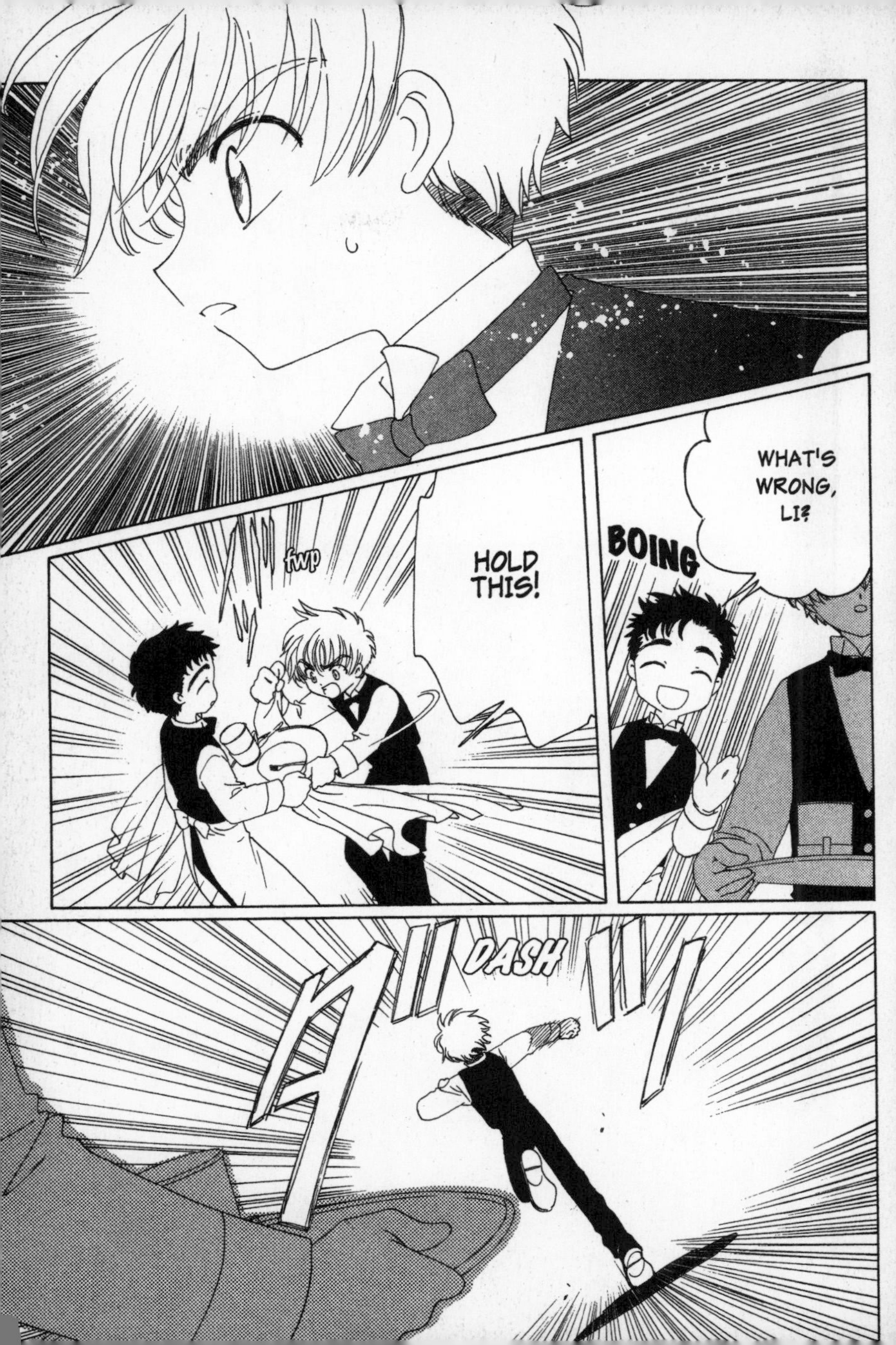
BOING
WHAT'S WRONG, LI?
fwp
HOLD THIS!
DASH

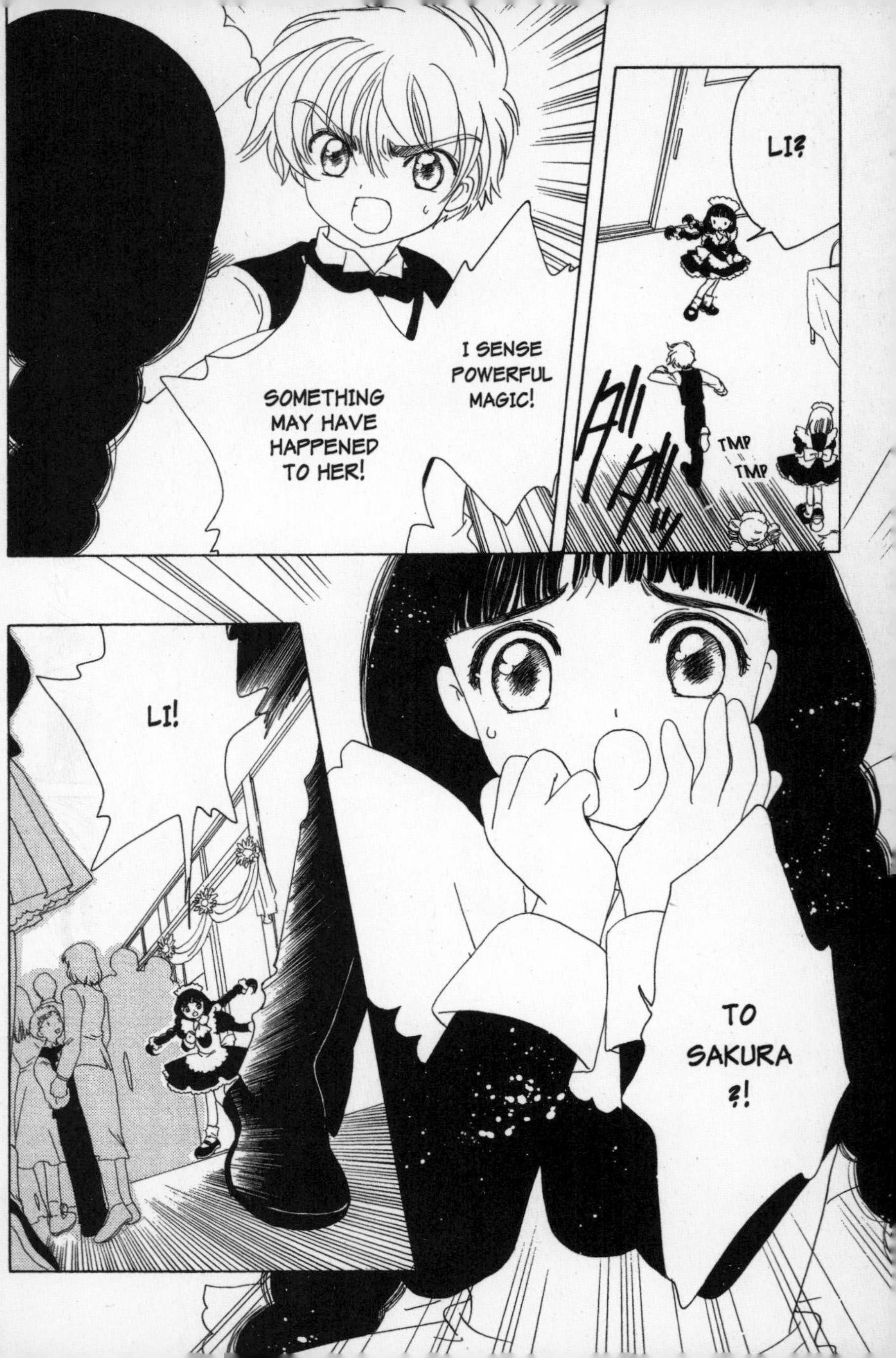
LI?
TMP
TMP
I SENSE POWERFUL MAGIC!
SOMETHING MAY HAVE HAPPENED TO HER!
TO SAKURA ?!
LI!

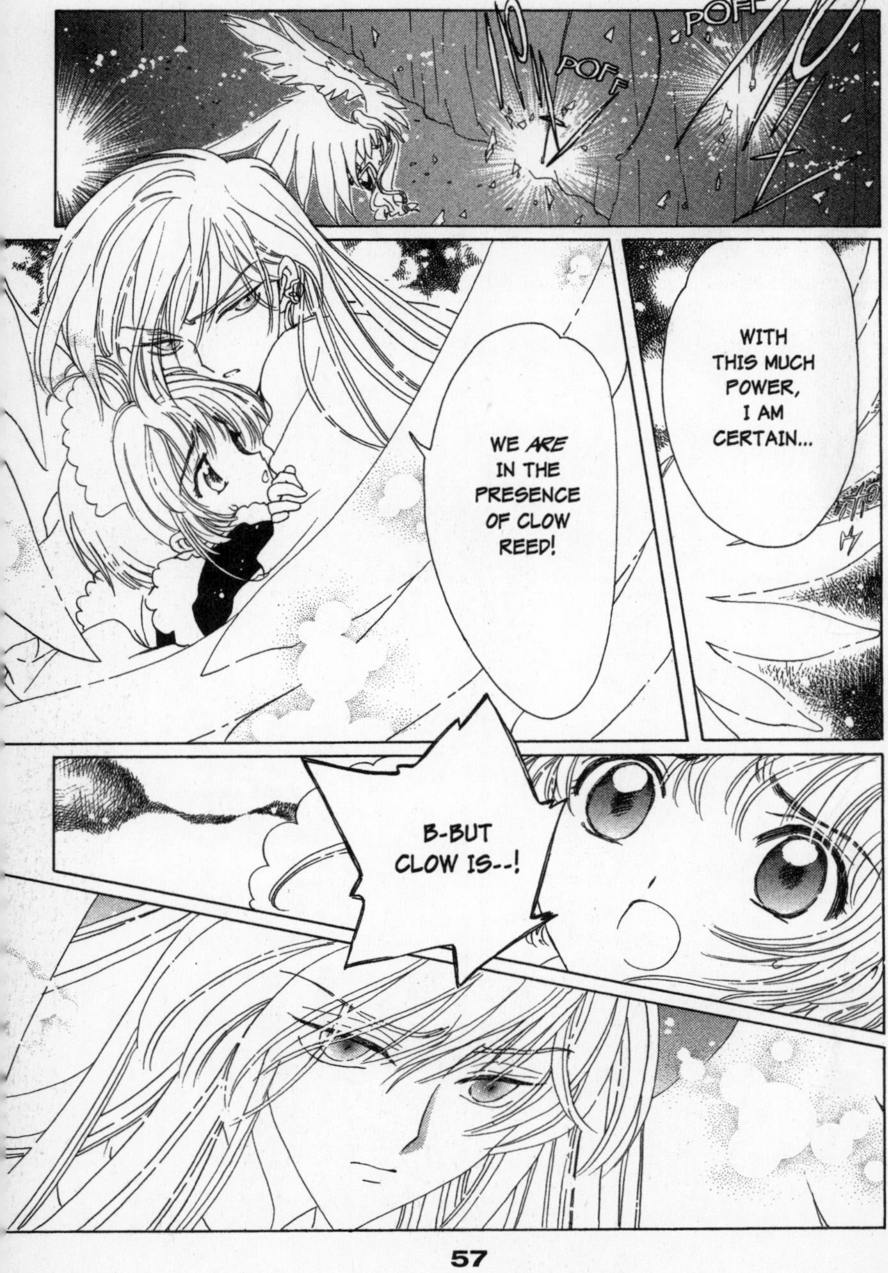
POFF
POFF
WITH THIS MUCH POWER, I AM CERTAIN...
WE *ARE* IN THE PRESENCE OF CLOW REED!
B-BUT CLOW IS--!

MUI MUI
ROAD OF THE STARS, HUH?
OOH, LET'S GO IN!
SOME-ONE'S COMING!
RELEASE!
SHINNNGG
迷
幻
ILLUSION

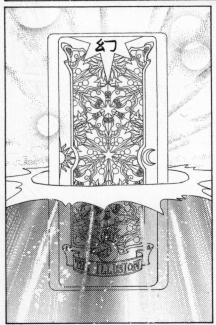

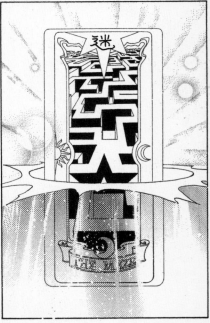

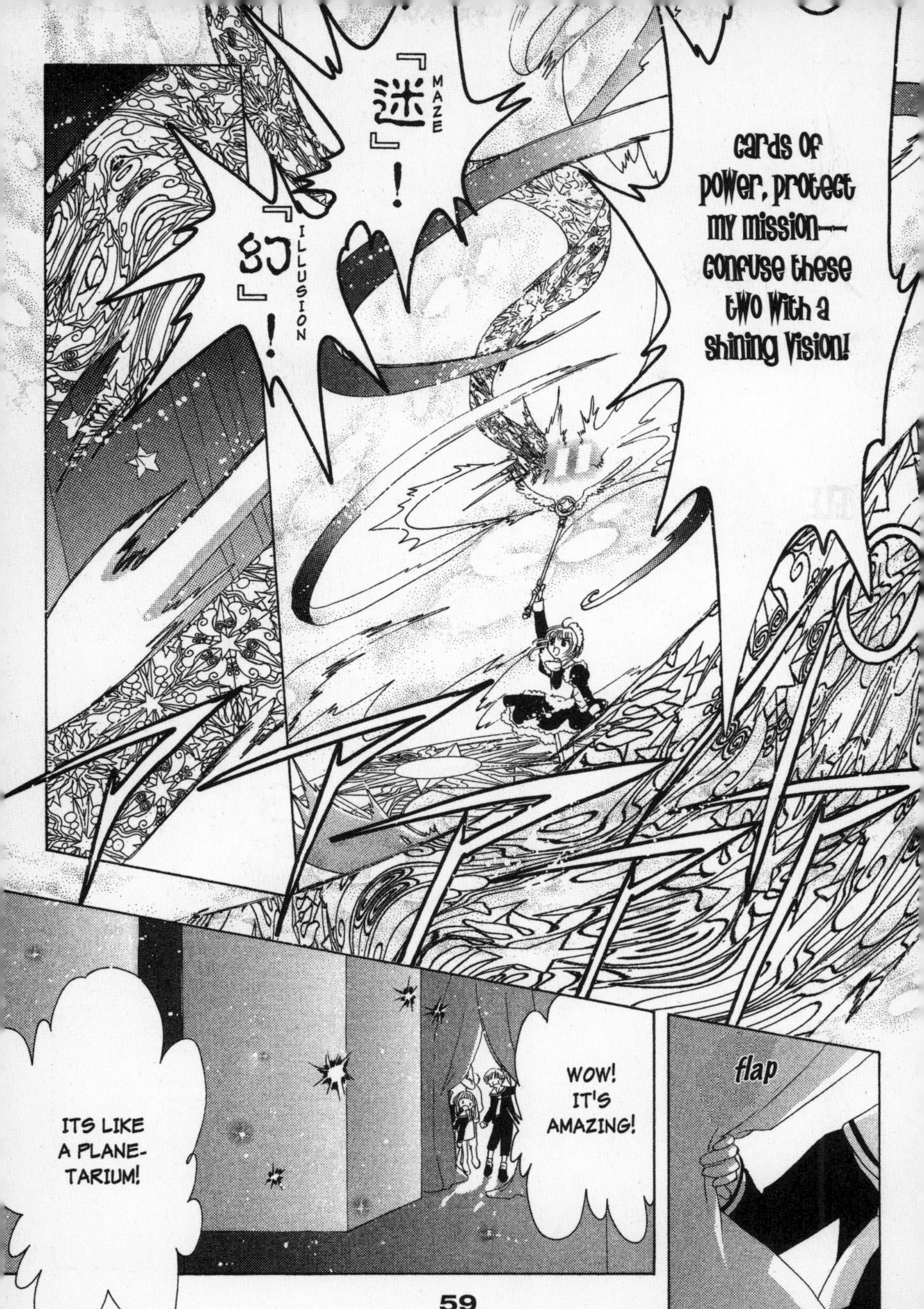

Cards of power, protect my mission— confuse these two with a shining vision!
『迷』! MAZE
『幻』! ILLUSION
flap
WOW! IT'S AMAZING!
ITS LIKE A PLANE-TARIUM!

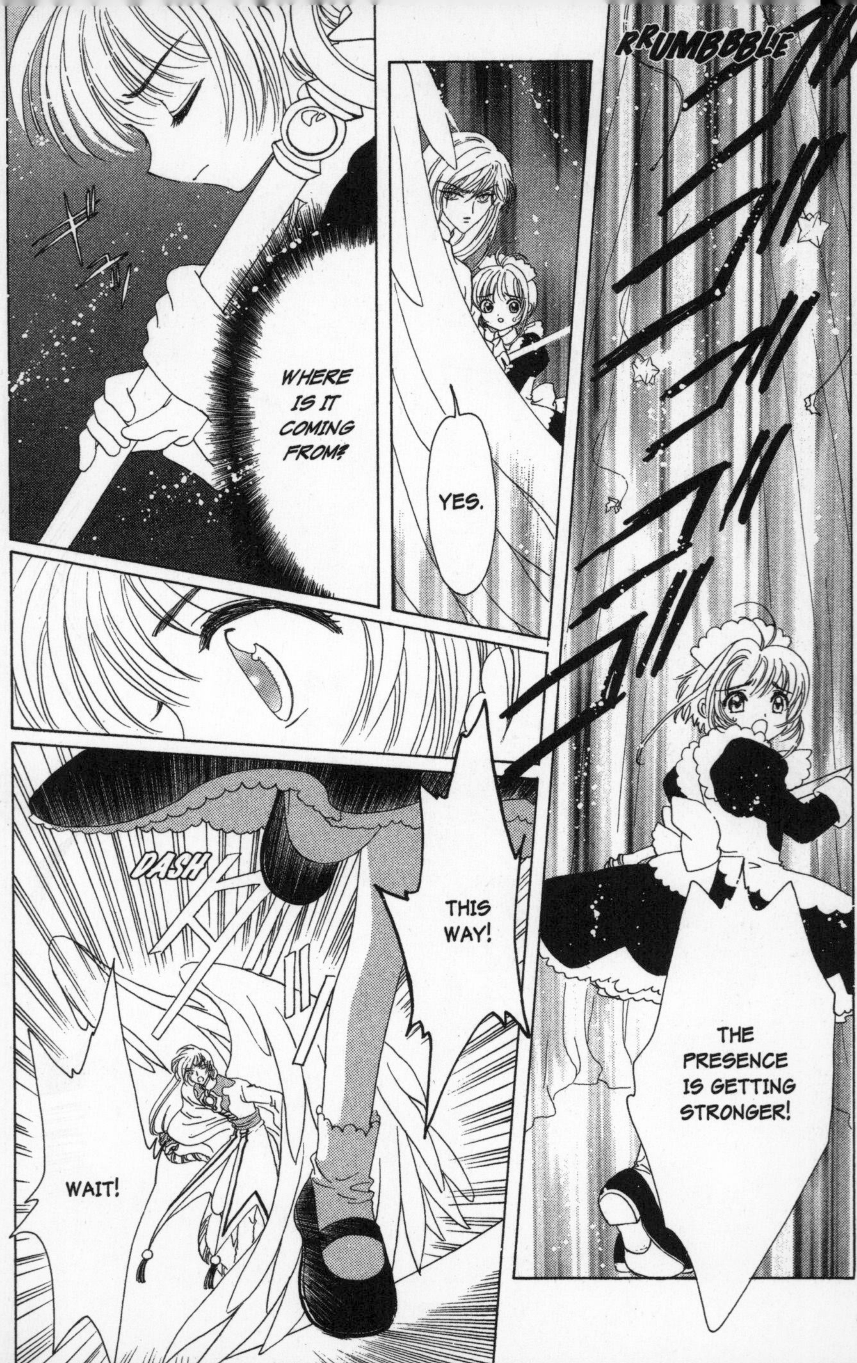
RRUMBBBLE
THE PRESENCE IS GETTING STRONGER!
YES.
WHERE IS IT COMING FROM?
DASH
THIS WAY!
WAIT!

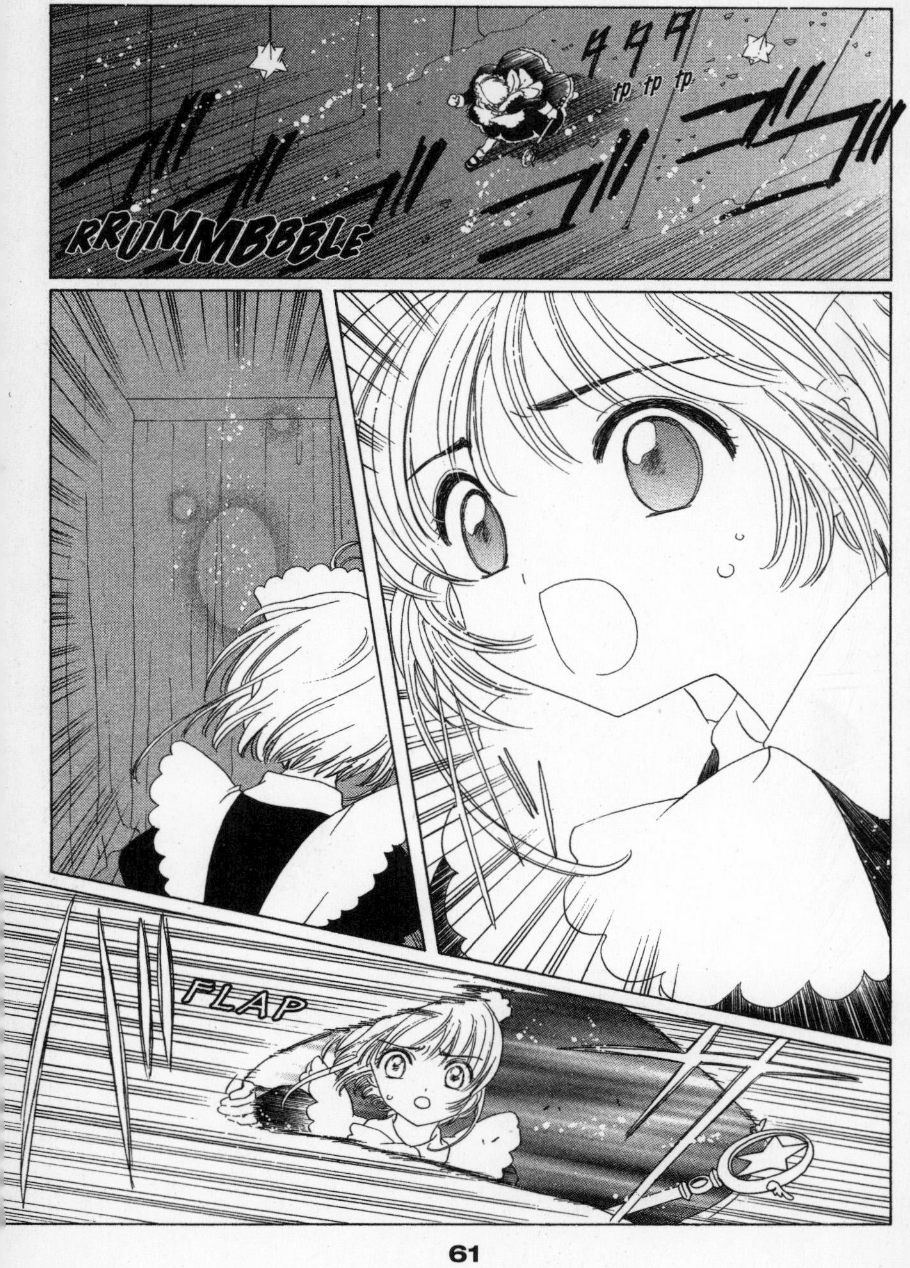
タタタ
tp tp tp
RRUMMBBBLE
FLAP

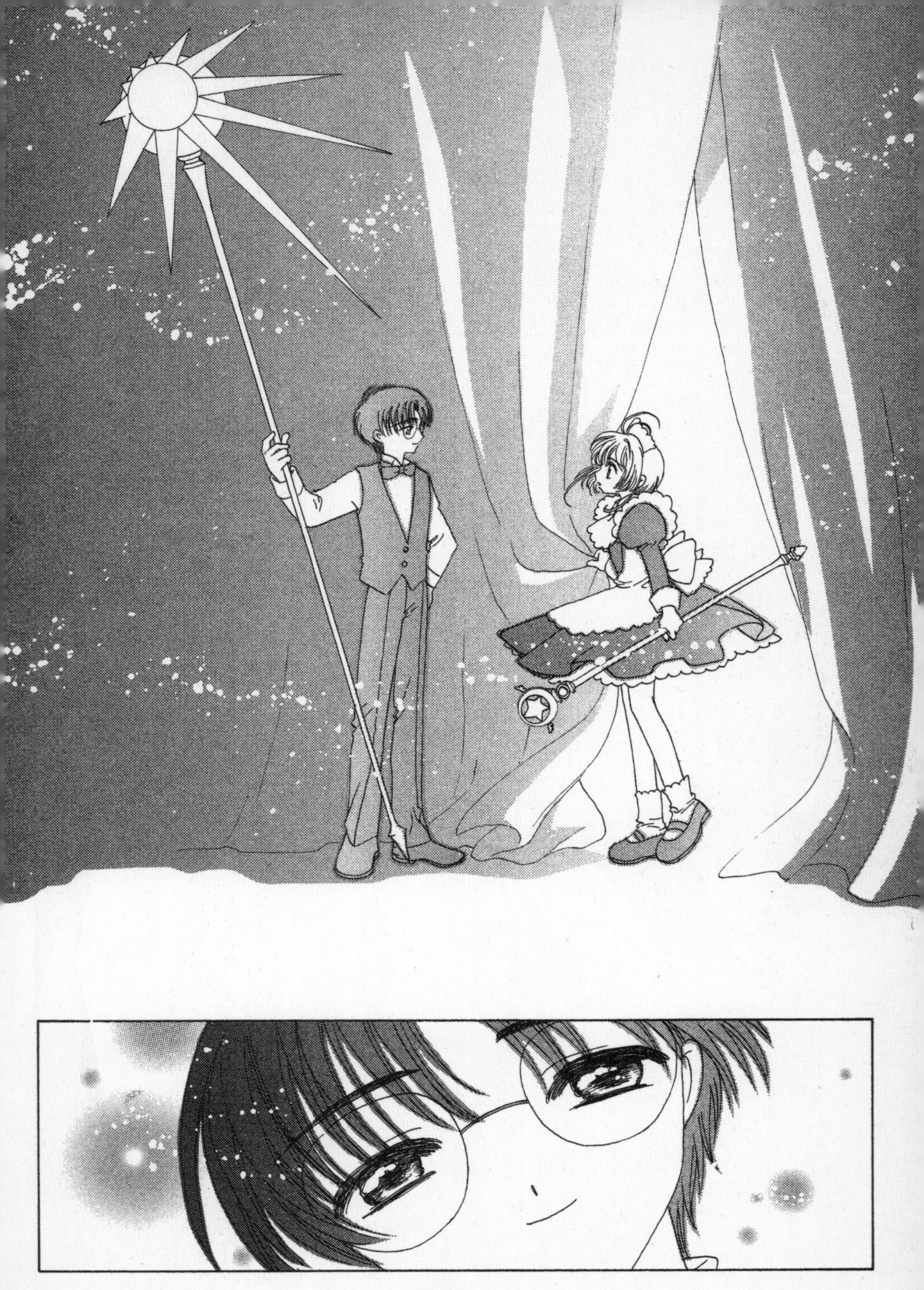

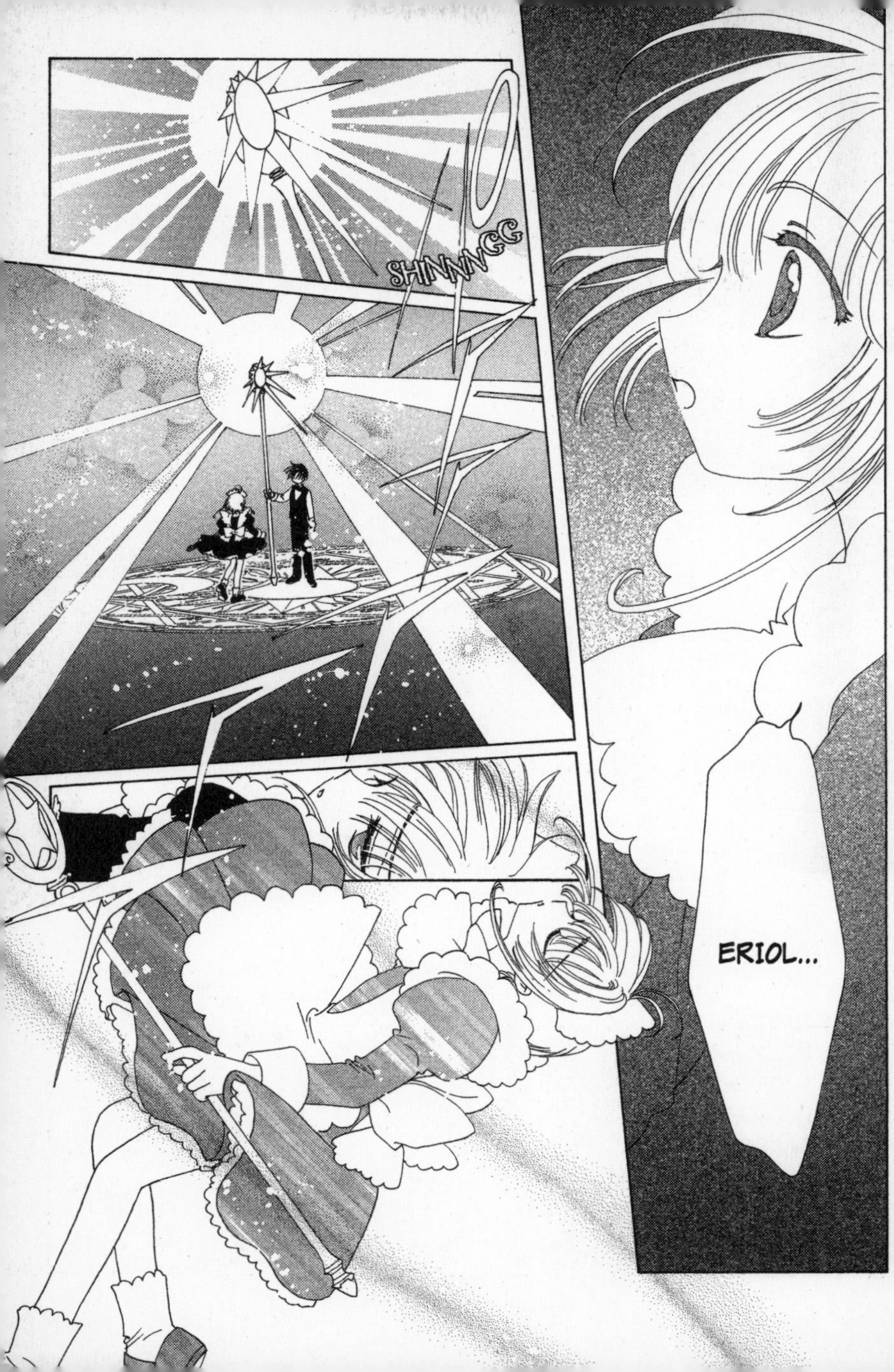
SHINNNGG
ERIOL...

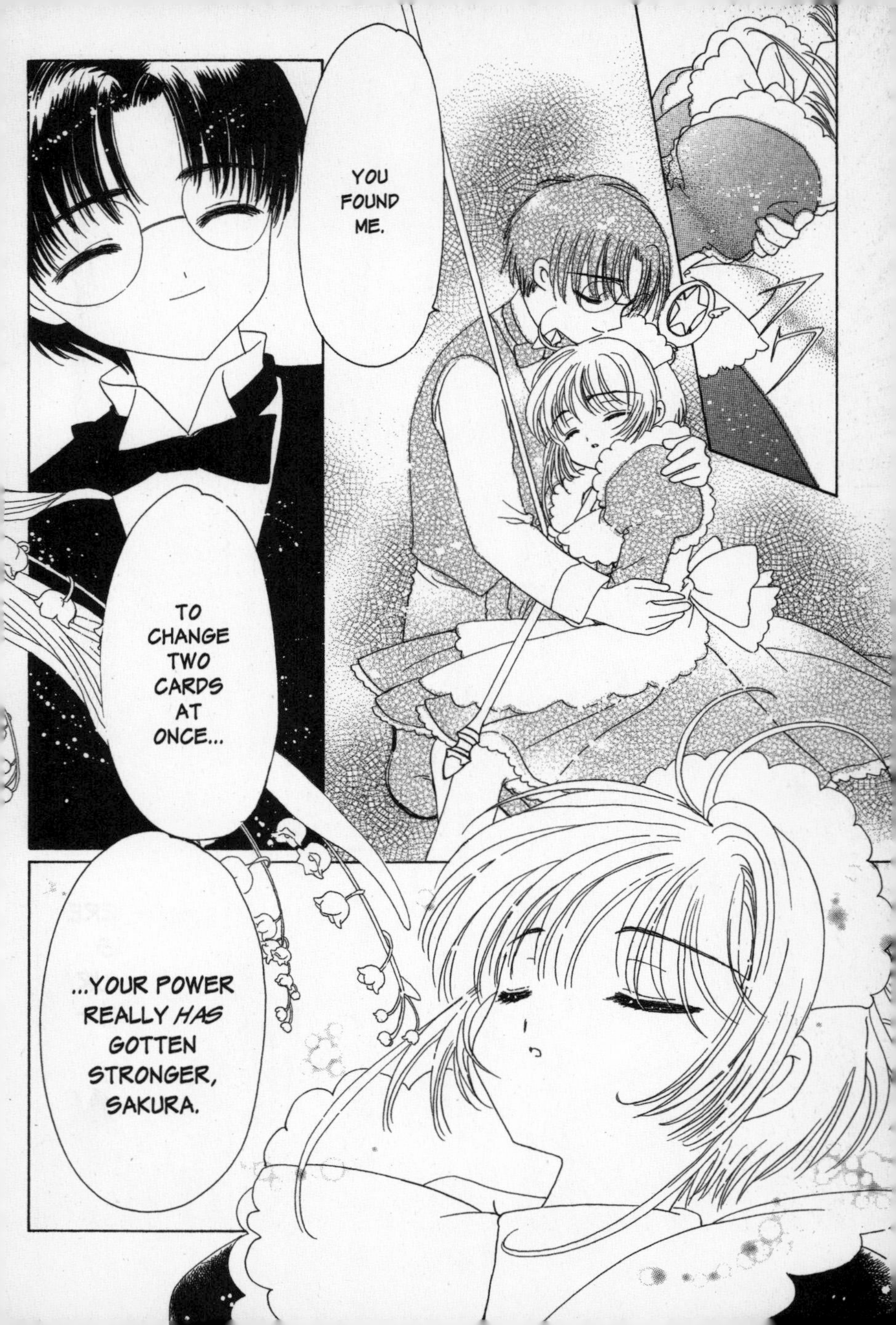
YOU FOUND ME.
TO CHANGE TWO CARDS AT ONCE...
...YOUR POWER REALLY *HAS* GOTTEN STRONGER, SAKURA.

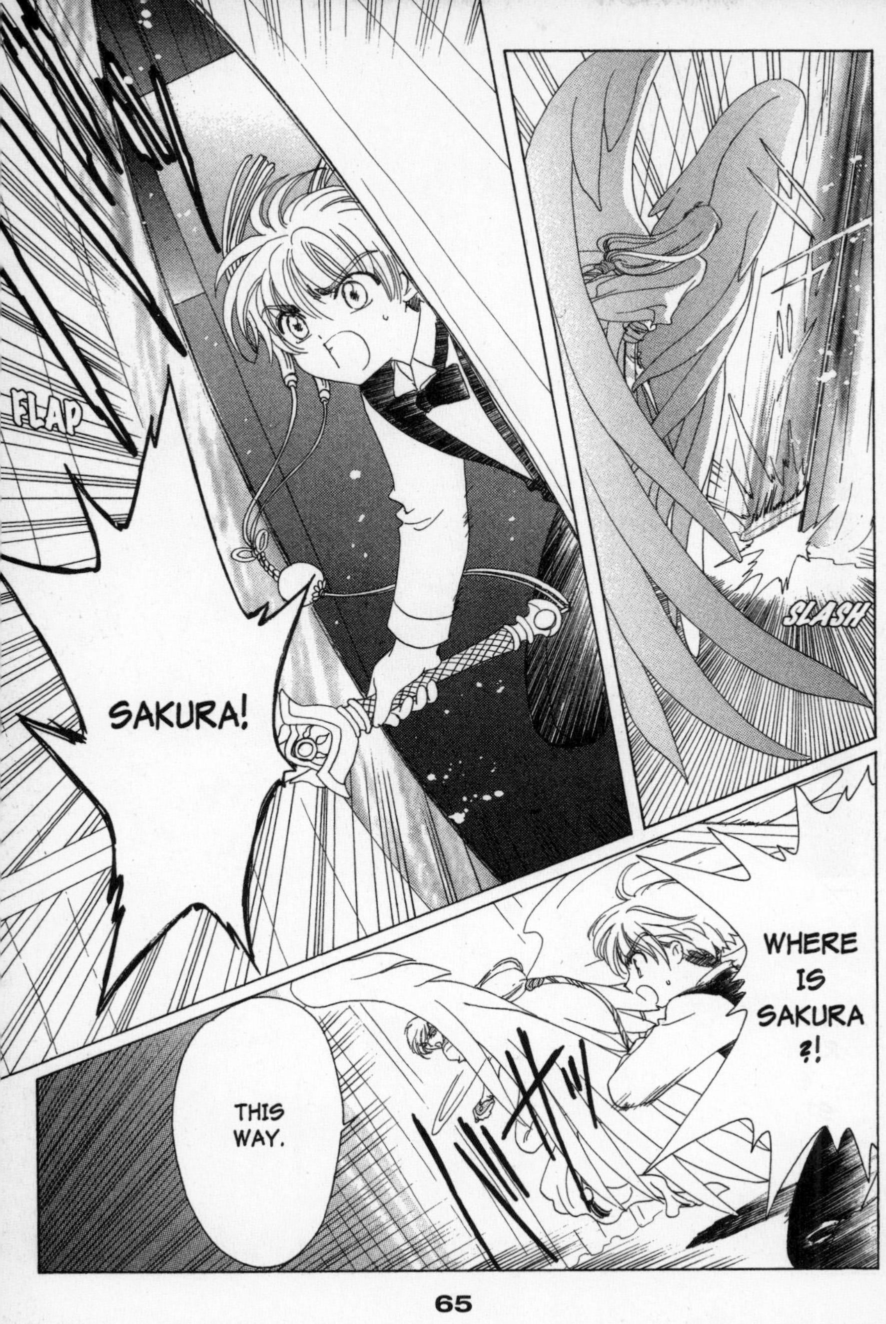
SLASH
FLAP
SAKURA!
WHERE IS SAKURA ?!
THIS WAY.

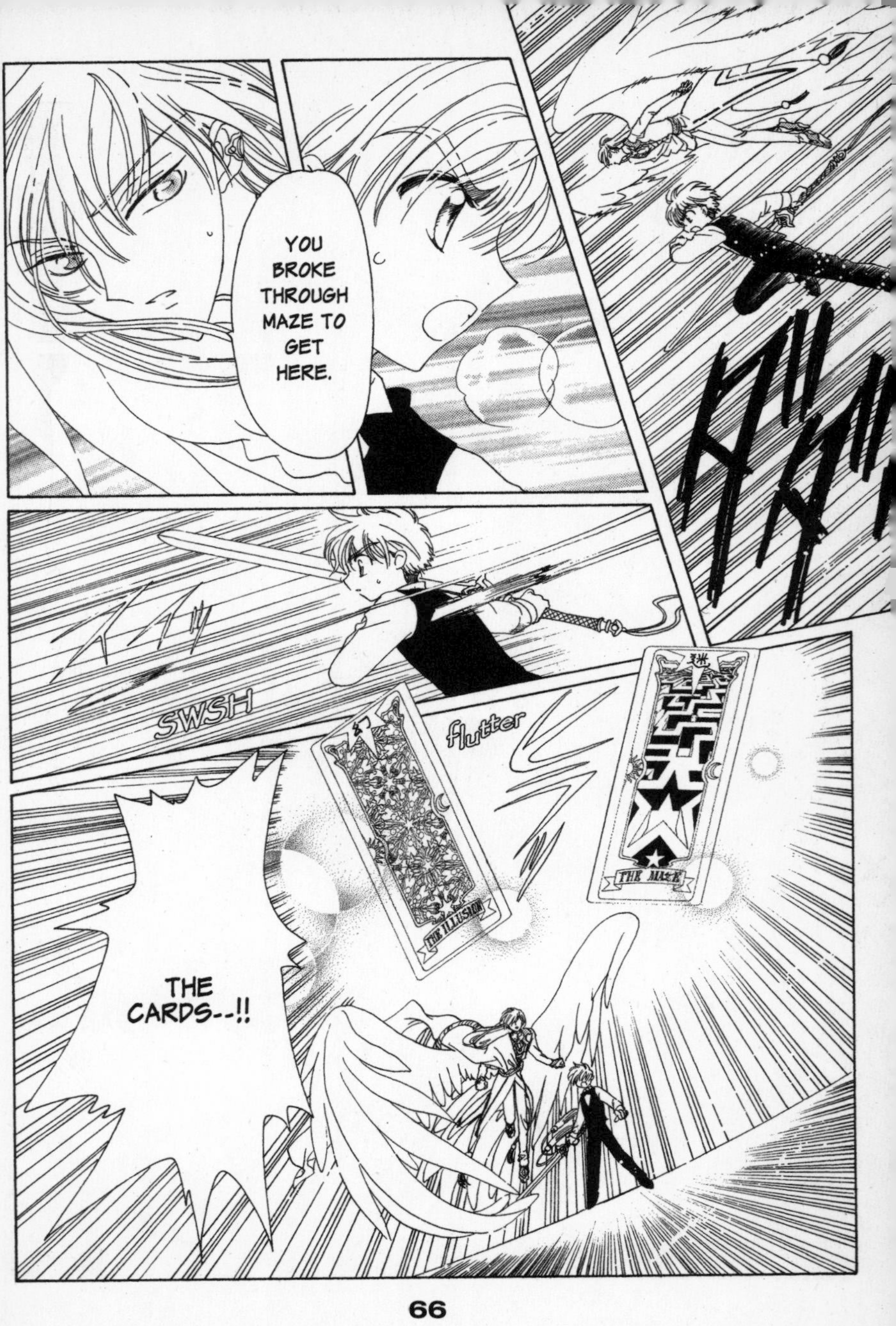

YOU BROKE THROUGH MAZE TO GET HERE.
SWSH
flutter
THE ILLUSION
THE CARDS--!!

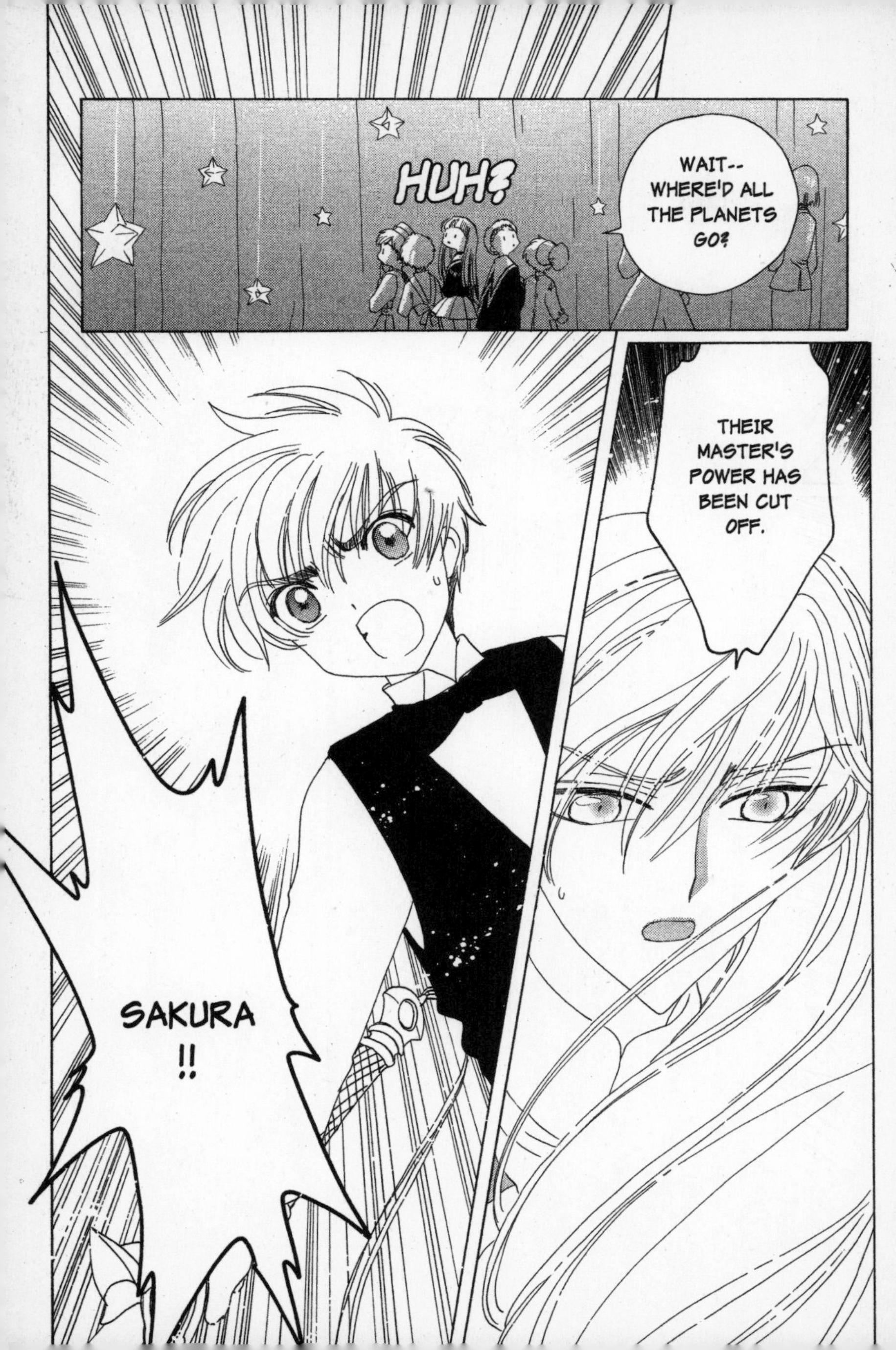
WAIT-- WHERE'D ALL THE PLANETS GO?
HUH?
THEIR MASTER'S POWER HAS BEEN CUT OFF.
SAKURA !!

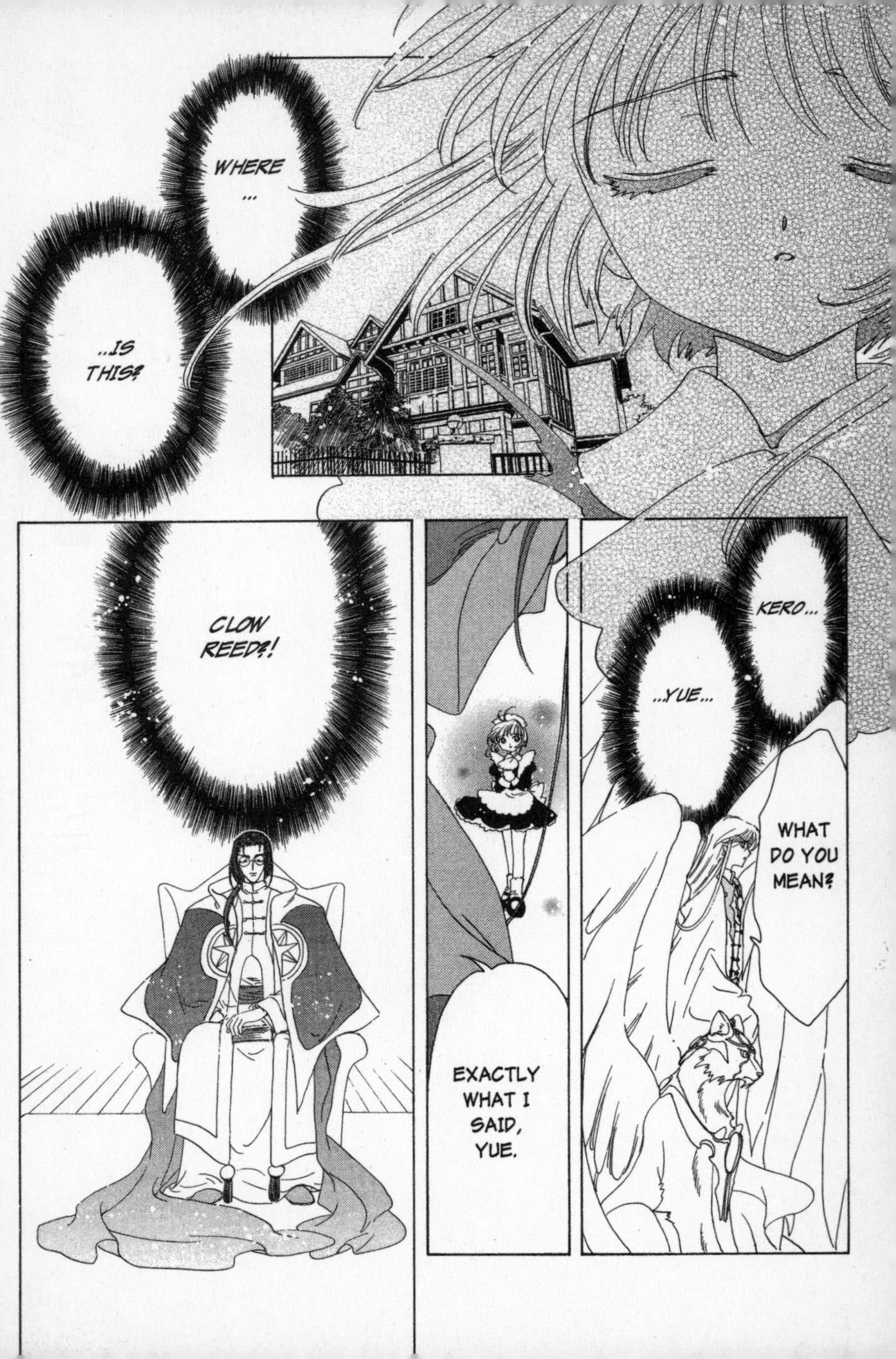
WHERE ...
...IS THIS?
KERO...
...YUE...
WHAT DO YOU MEAN?
EXACTLY WHAT I SAID, YUE.
CLOW REED?!

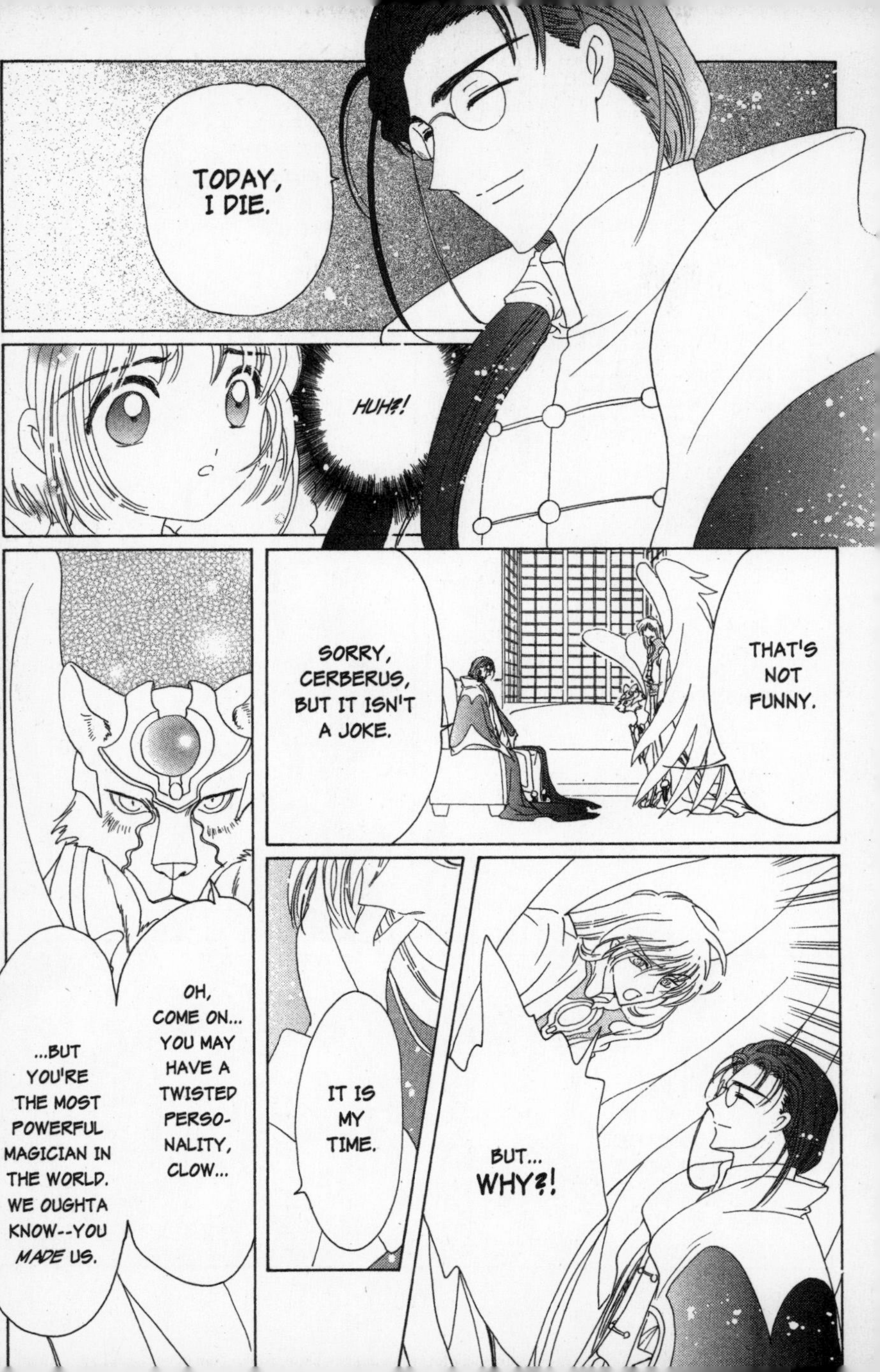
TODAY, I DIE.
HUH?!
THAT'S NOT FUNNY.
SORRY, CERBERUS, BUT IT ISN'T A JOKE.
BUT... WHY?!
IT IS MY TIME.
OH, COME ON... YOU MAY HAVE A TWISTED PERSO-NALITY, CLOW...
...BUT YOU'RE THE MOST POWERFUL MAGICIAN IN THE WORLD. WE OUGHTA KNOW--YOU *MADE* US.

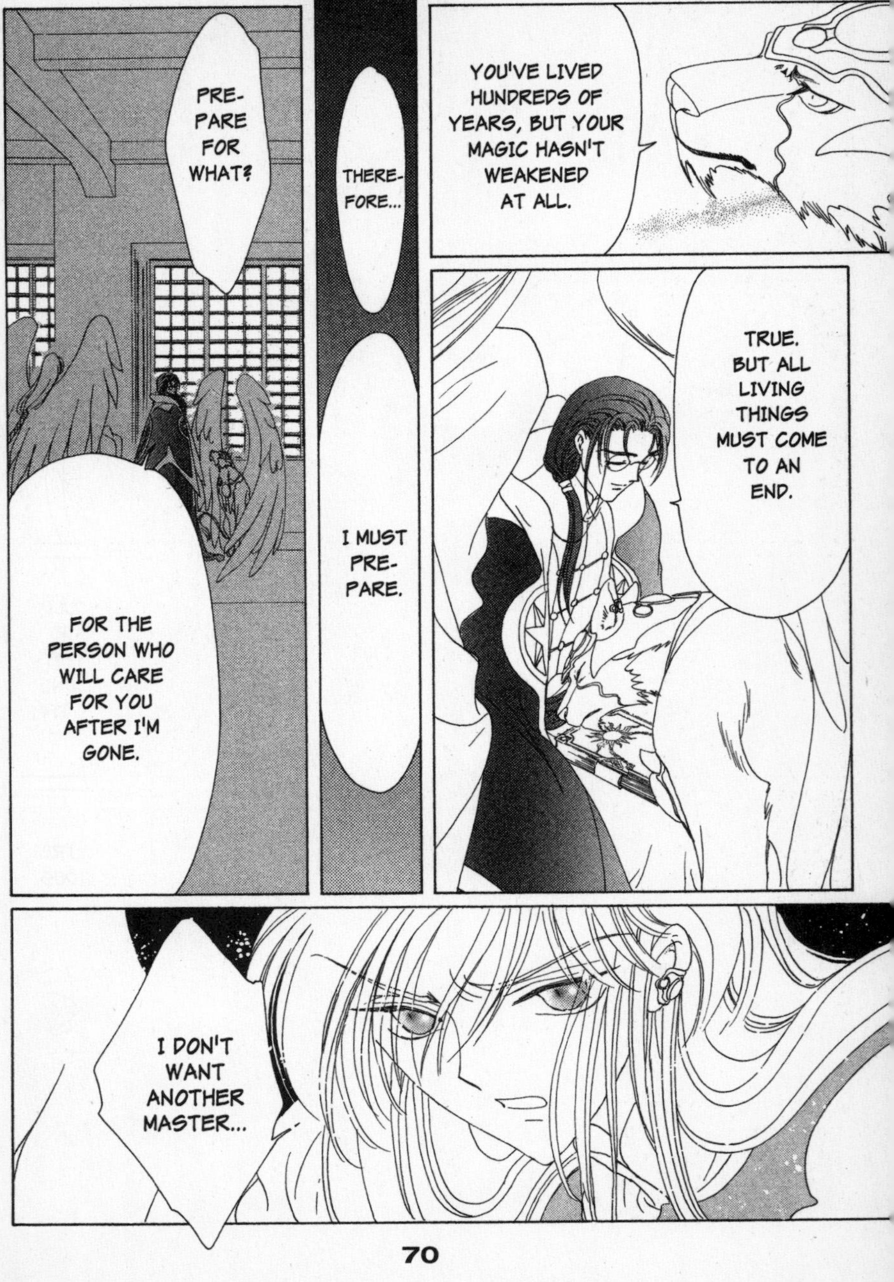
YOU'VE LIVED HUNDREDS OF YEARS, BUT YOUR MAGIC HASN'T WEAKENED AT ALL.
TRUE. BUT ALL LIVING THINGS MUST COME TO AN END.
THERE-FORE...
I MUST PRE-PARE.
PRE-PARE FOR WHAT?
FOR THE PERSON WHO WILL CARE FOR YOU AFTER I'M GONE.
I DON'T WANT ANOTHER MASTER...

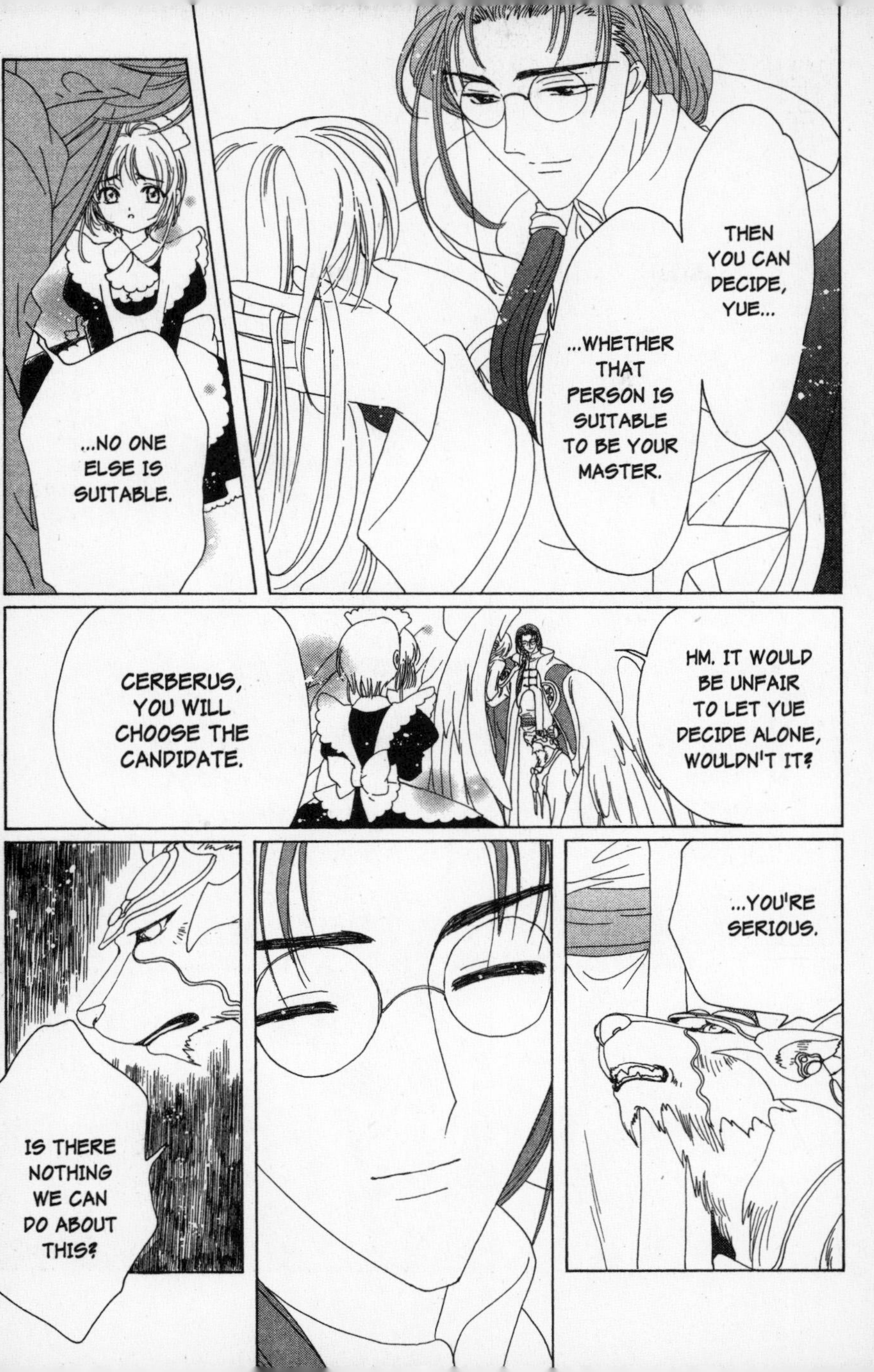
THEN YOU CAN DECIDE, YUE...
...WHETHER THAT PERSON IS SUITABLE TO BE YOUR MASTER.
...NO ONE ELSE IS SUITABLE.
HM. IT WOULD BE UNFAIR TO LET YUE DECIDE ALONE, WOULDN'T IT?
CERBERUS, YOU WILL CHOOSE THE CANDIDATE.
...YOU'RE SERIOUS.
IS THERE NOTHING WE CAN DO ABOUT THIS?

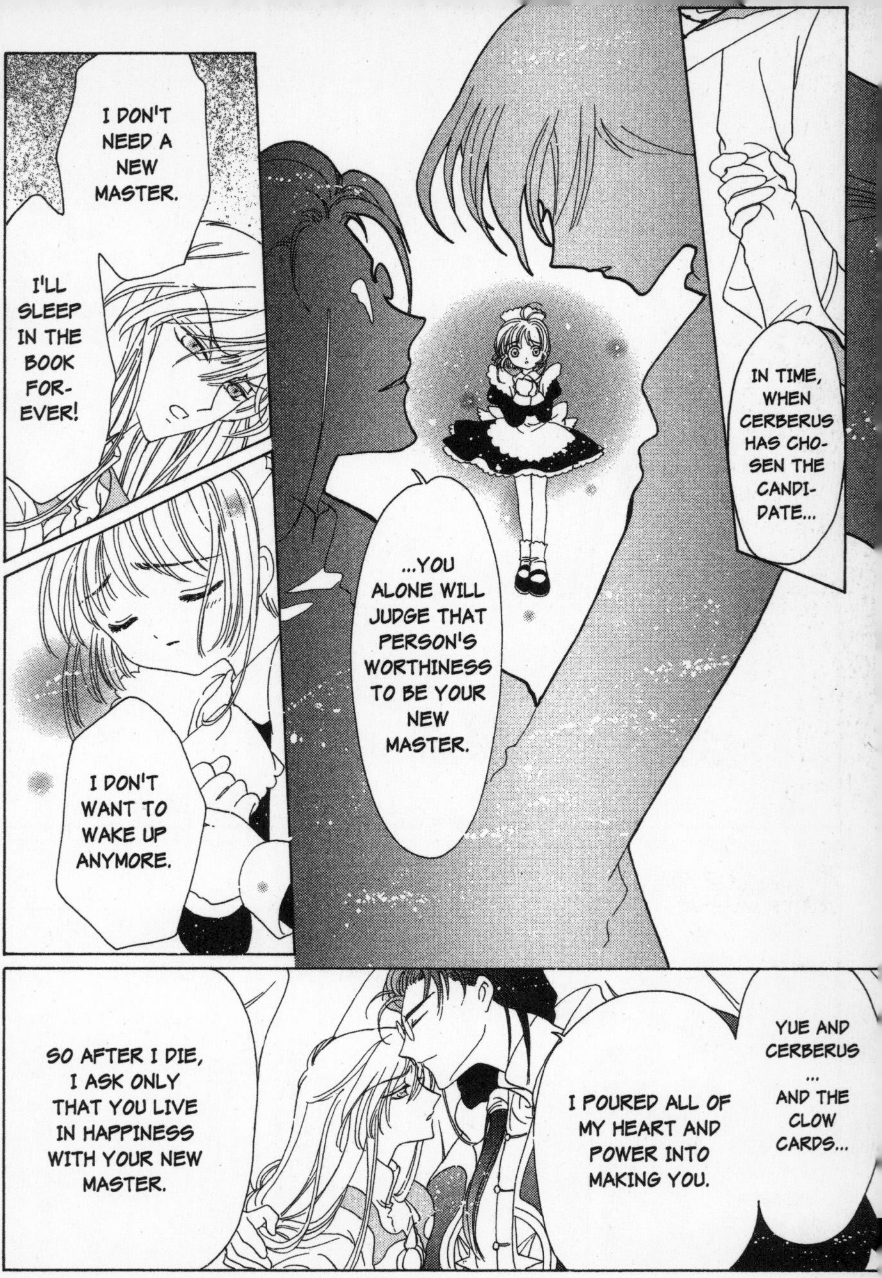
IN TIME, WHEN CERBERUS HAS CHOSEN THE CANDIDATE...
...YOU ALONE WILL JUDGE THAT PERSON'S WORTHINESS TO BE YOUR NEW MASTER.
I DON'T NEED A NEW MASTER.
I'LL SLEEP IN THE BOOK FOREVER!
I DON'T WANT TO WAKE UP ANYMORE.
YUE AND CERBERUS ... AND THE CLOW CARDS...
I POURED ALL OF MY HEART AND POWER INTO MAKING YOU.
SO AFTER I DIE, I ASK ONLY THAT YOU LIVE IN HAPPINESS WITH YOUR NEW MASTER.

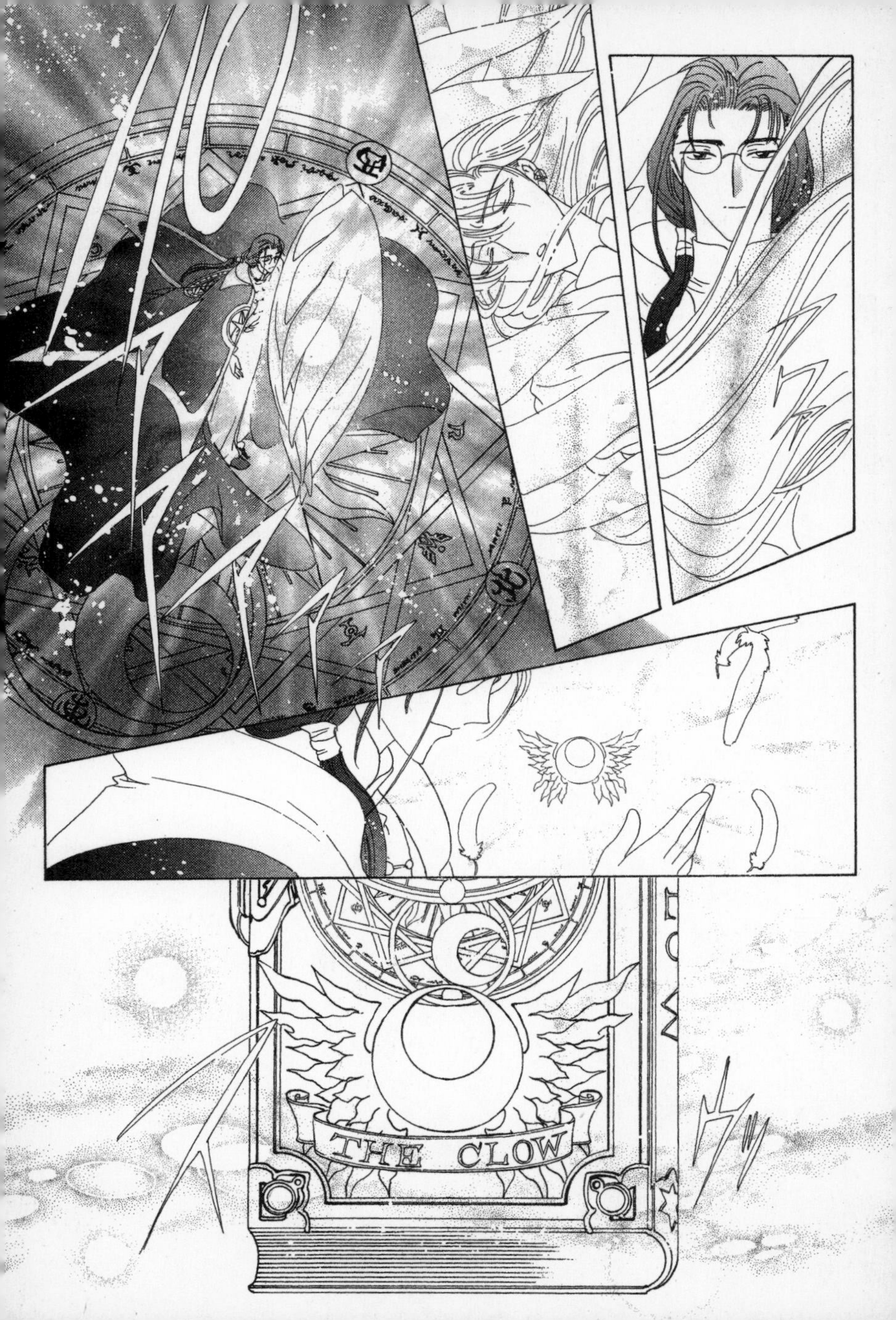
THE CLOW

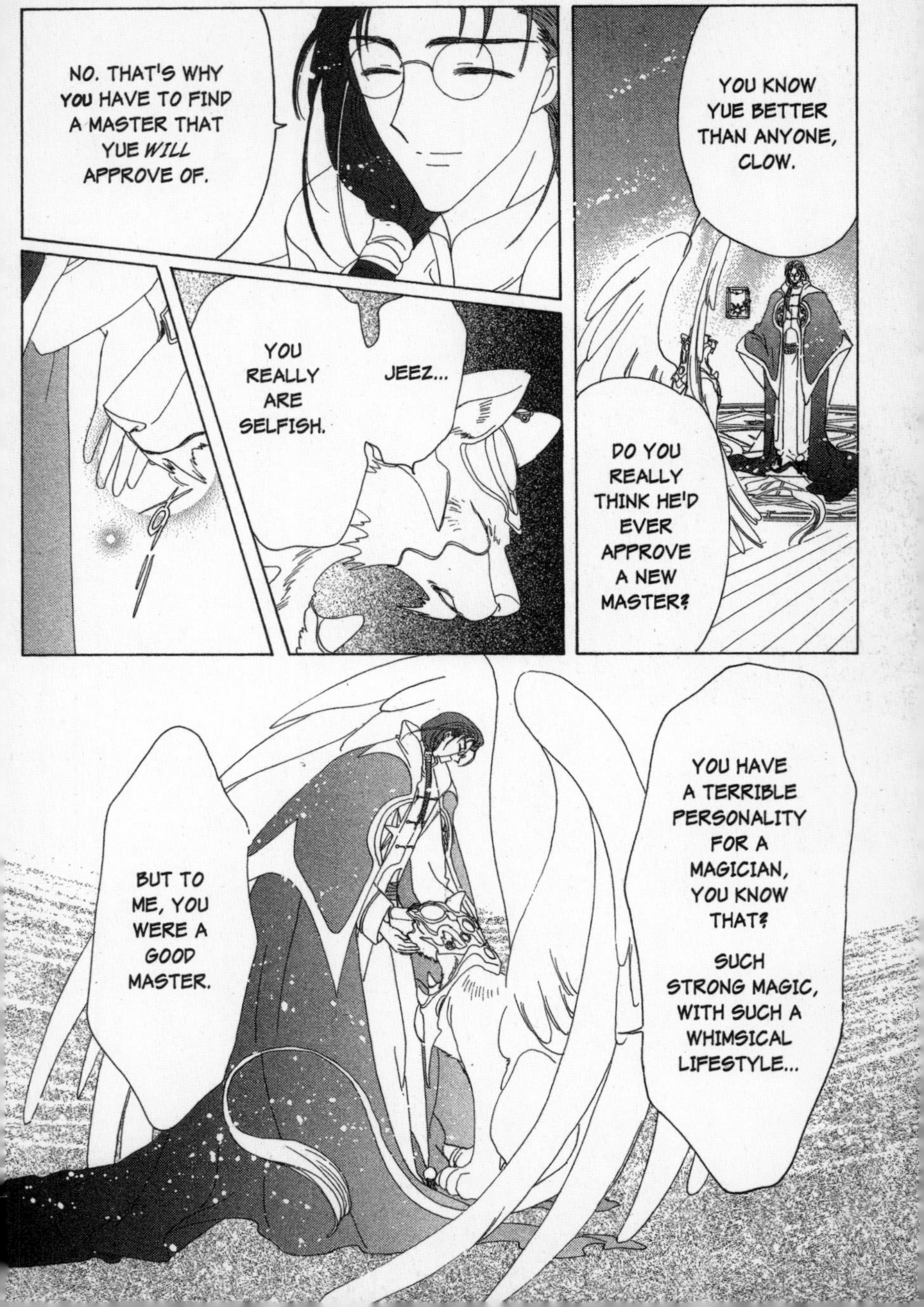
YOU KNOW YUE BETTER THAN ANYONE, CLOW.
DO YOU REALLY THINK HE'D EVER APPROVE A NEW MASTER?
NO. THAT'S WHY YOU HAVE TO FIND A MASTER THAT YUE *WILL* APPROVE OF.
JEEZ...
YOU REALLY ARE SELFISH.
YOU HAVE A TERRIBLE PERSONALITY FOR A MAGICIAN, YOU KNOW THAT?
SUCH STRONG MAGIC, WITH SUCH A WHIMSICAL LIFESTYLE...
BUT TO ME, YOU WERE A GOOD MASTER.

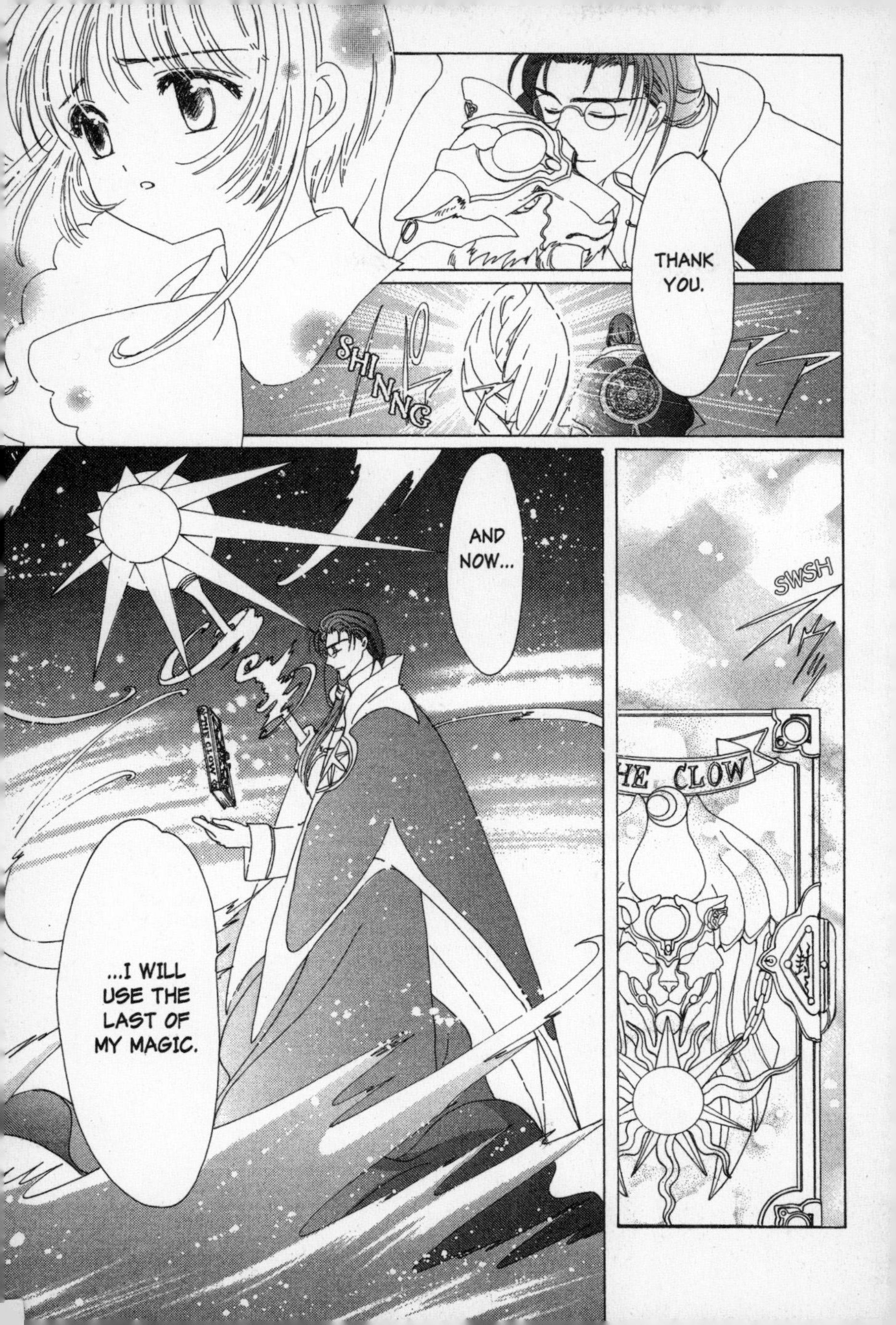
THANK YOU.
SHINNG
AND NOW...
...I WILL USE THE LAST OF MY MAGIC.
SWSH
THE CLOW
THE CLOW

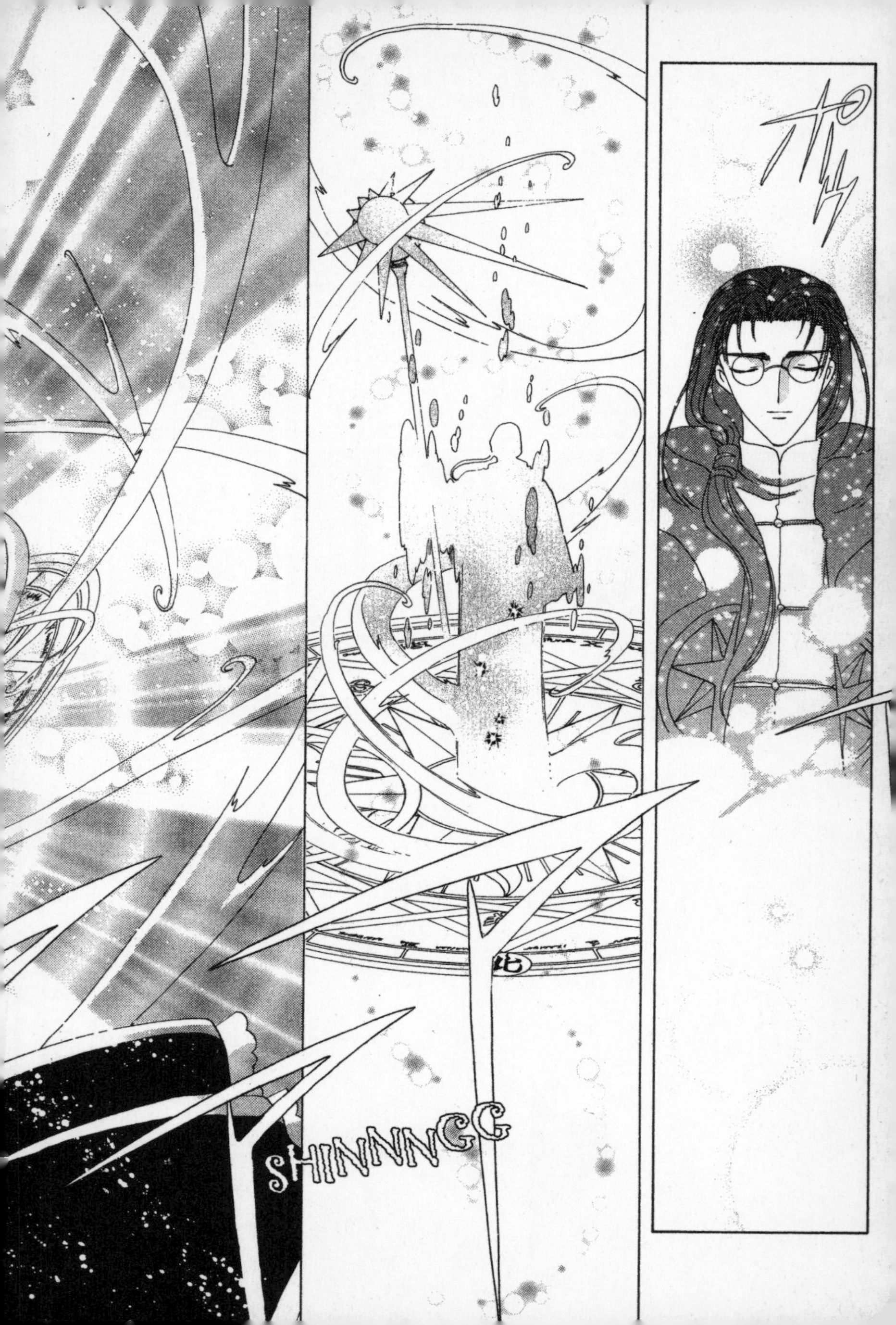
パッ
SHINNNGG

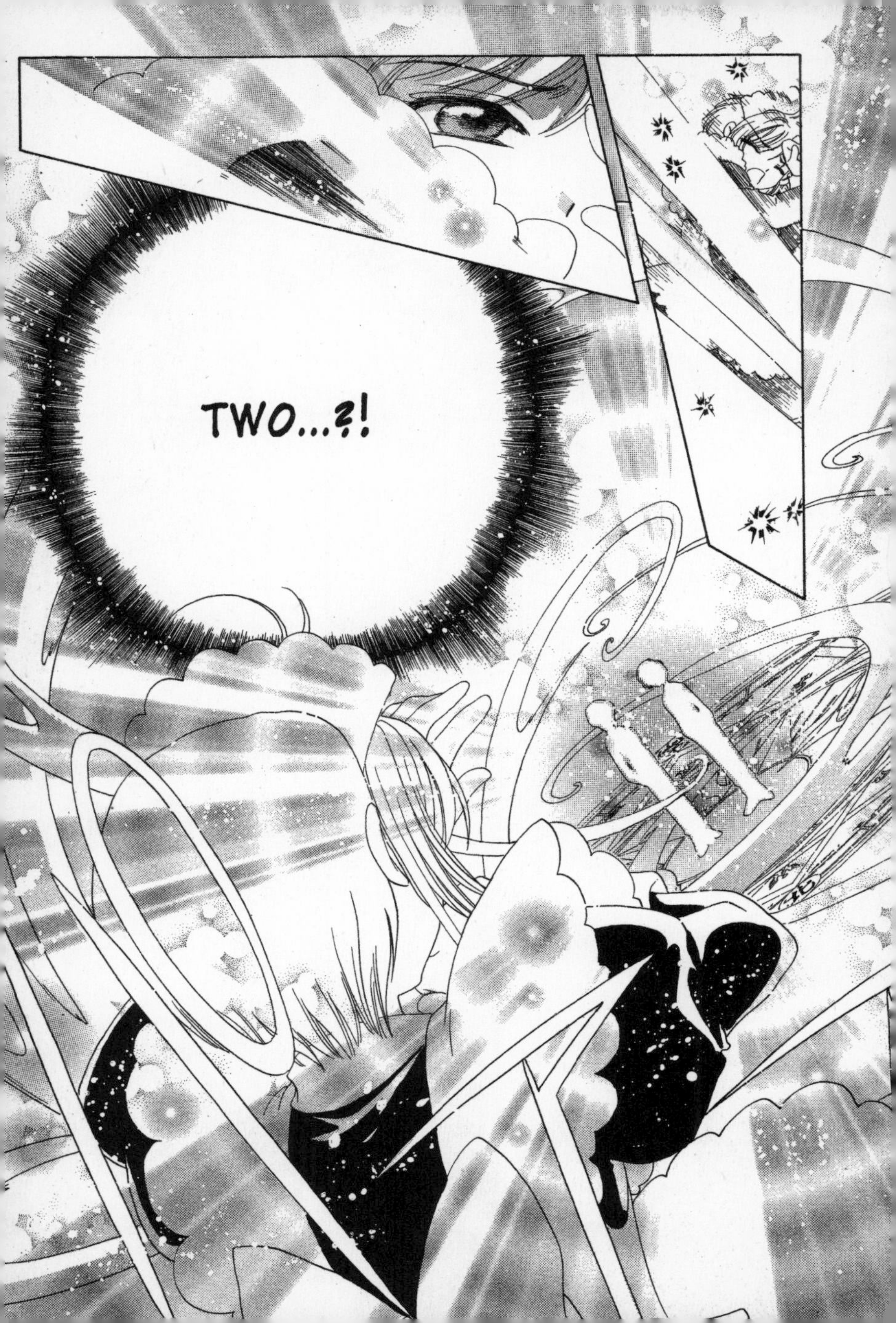
TWO...?!

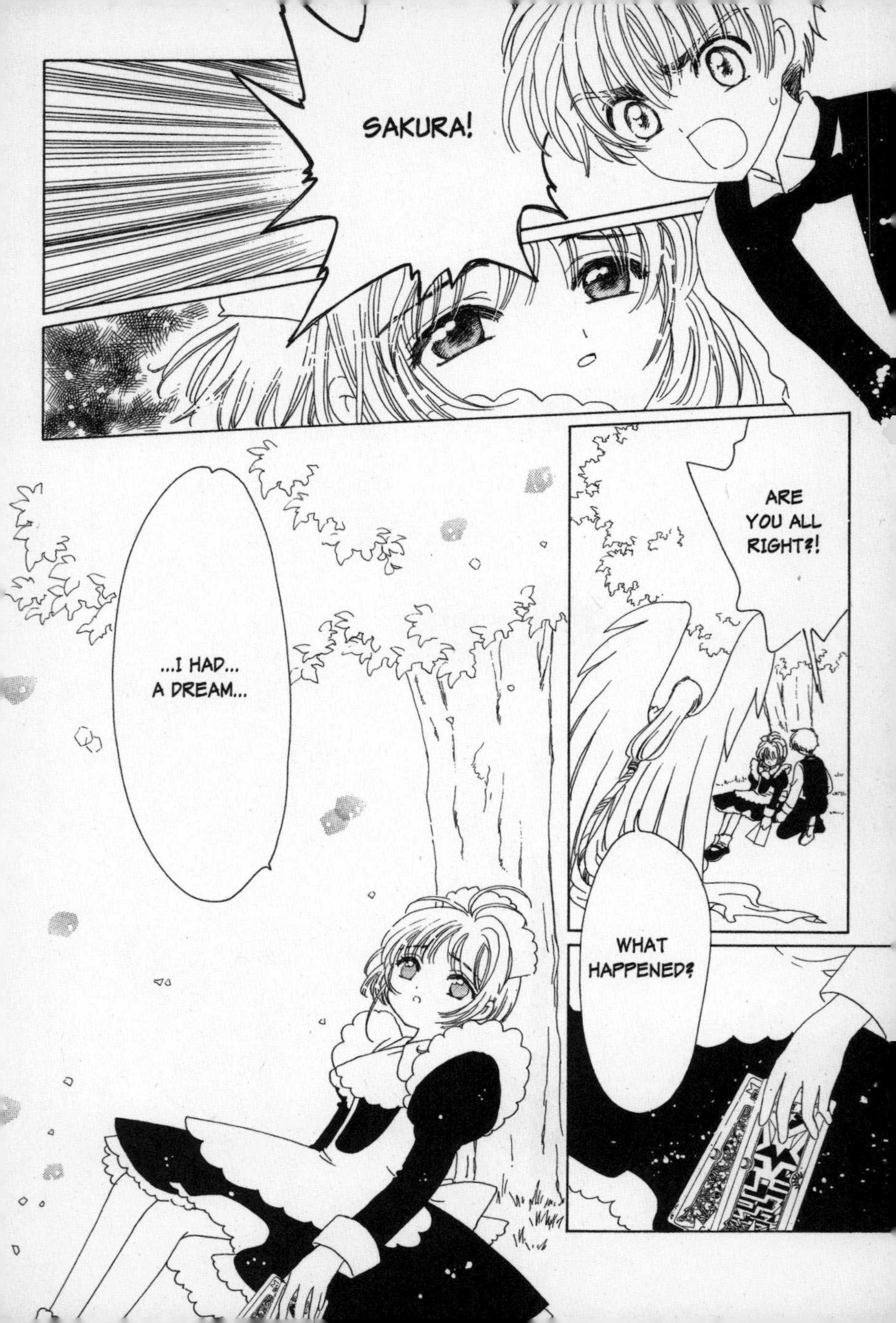
SAKURA!
ARE YOU ALL RIGHT?!
WHAT HAPPENED?
...I HAD... A DREAM...

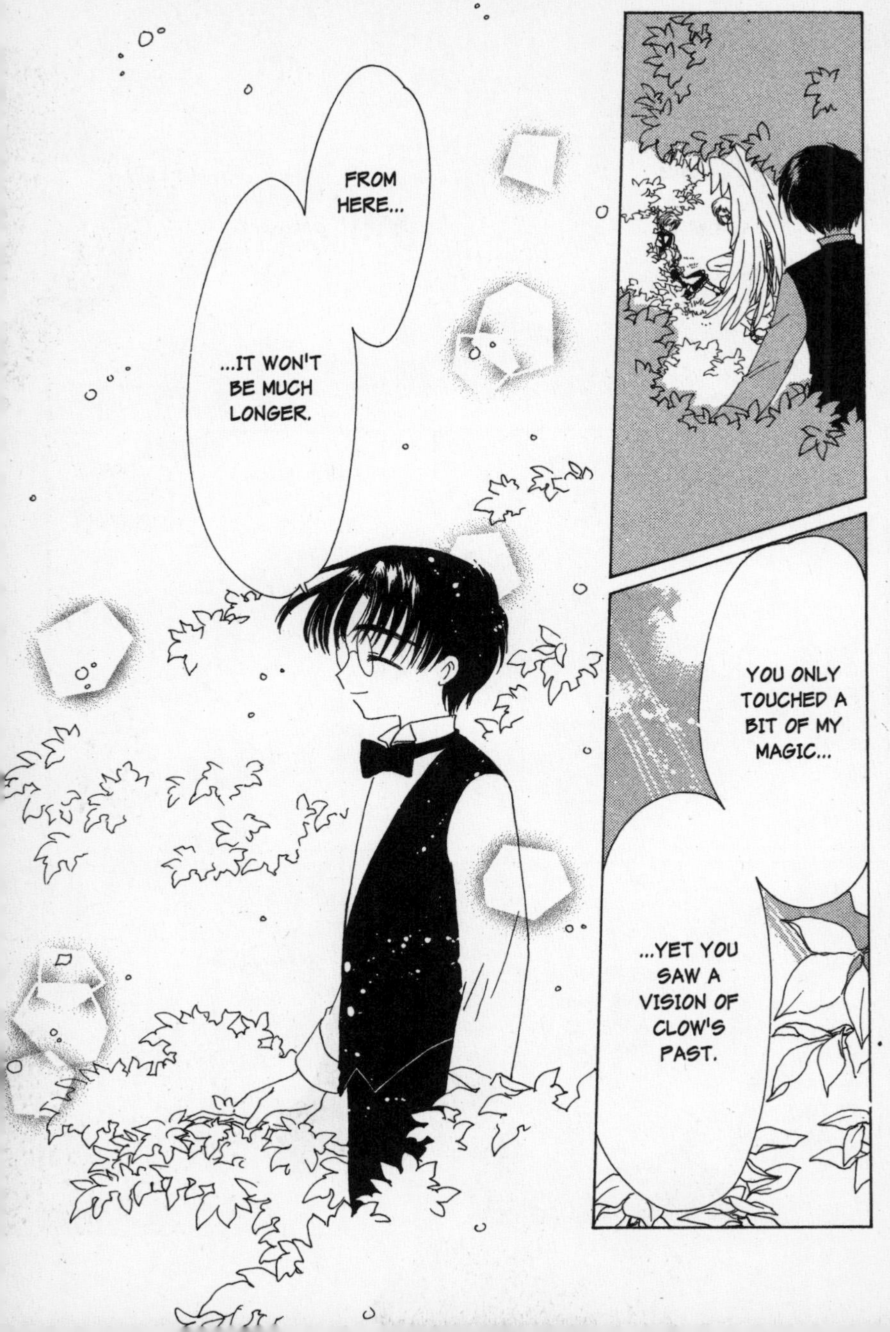
YOU ONLY TOUCHED A BIT OF MY MAGIC...
...YET YOU SAW A VISION OF CLOW'S PAST.
FROM HERE...
...IT WON'T BE MUCH LONGER.

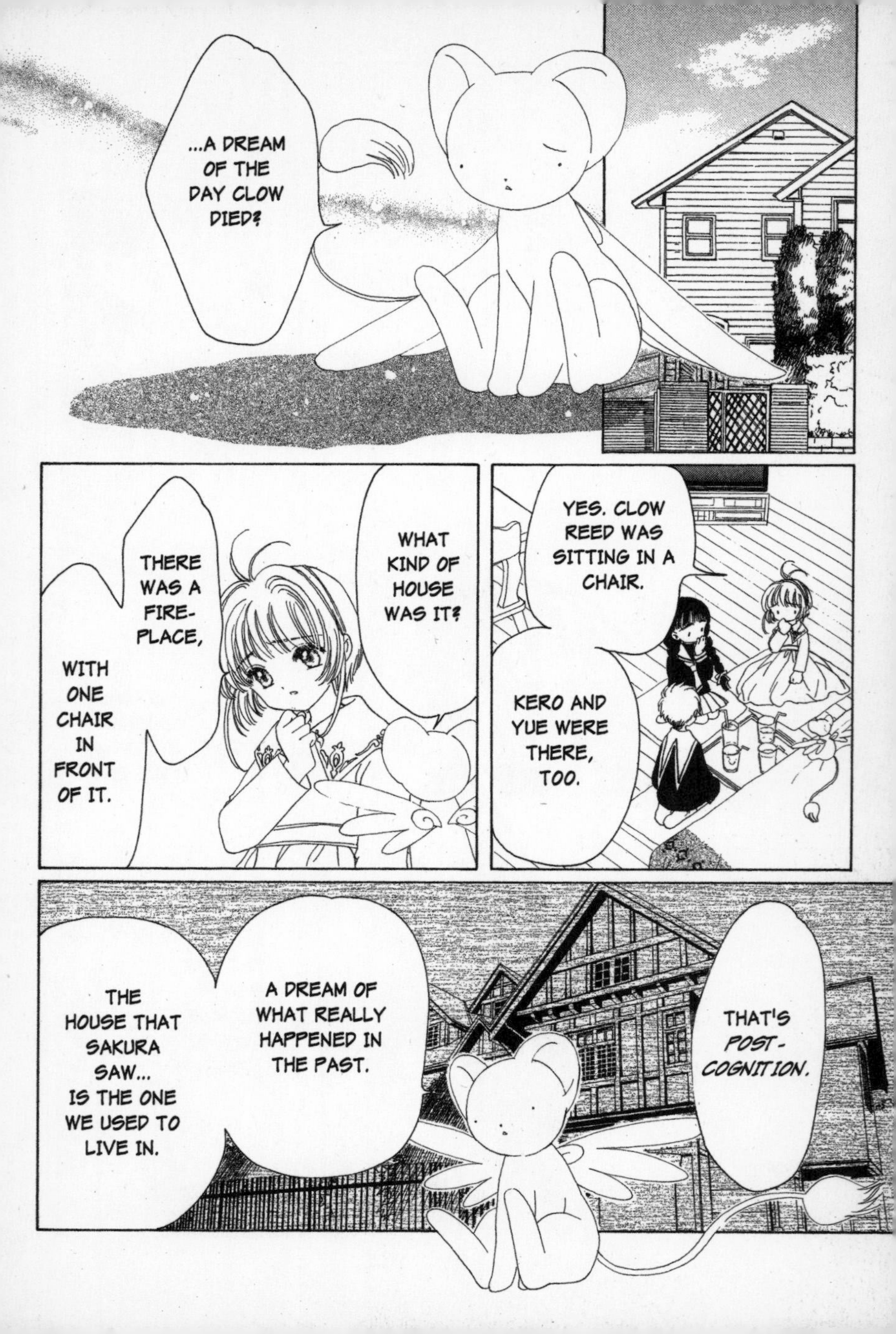
...A DREAM OF THE DAY CLOW DIED?
YES. CLOW REED WAS SITTING IN A CHAIR.
KERO AND YUE WERE THERE, TOO.
WHAT KIND OF HOUSE WAS IT?
THERE WAS A FIRE-PLACE,
WITH ONE CHAIR IN FRONT OF IT.
THAT'S *POST-COGNITION.*
A DREAM OF WHAT REALLY HAPPENED IN THE PAST.
THE HOUSE THAT SAKURA SAW... IS THE ONE WE USED TO LIVE IN.

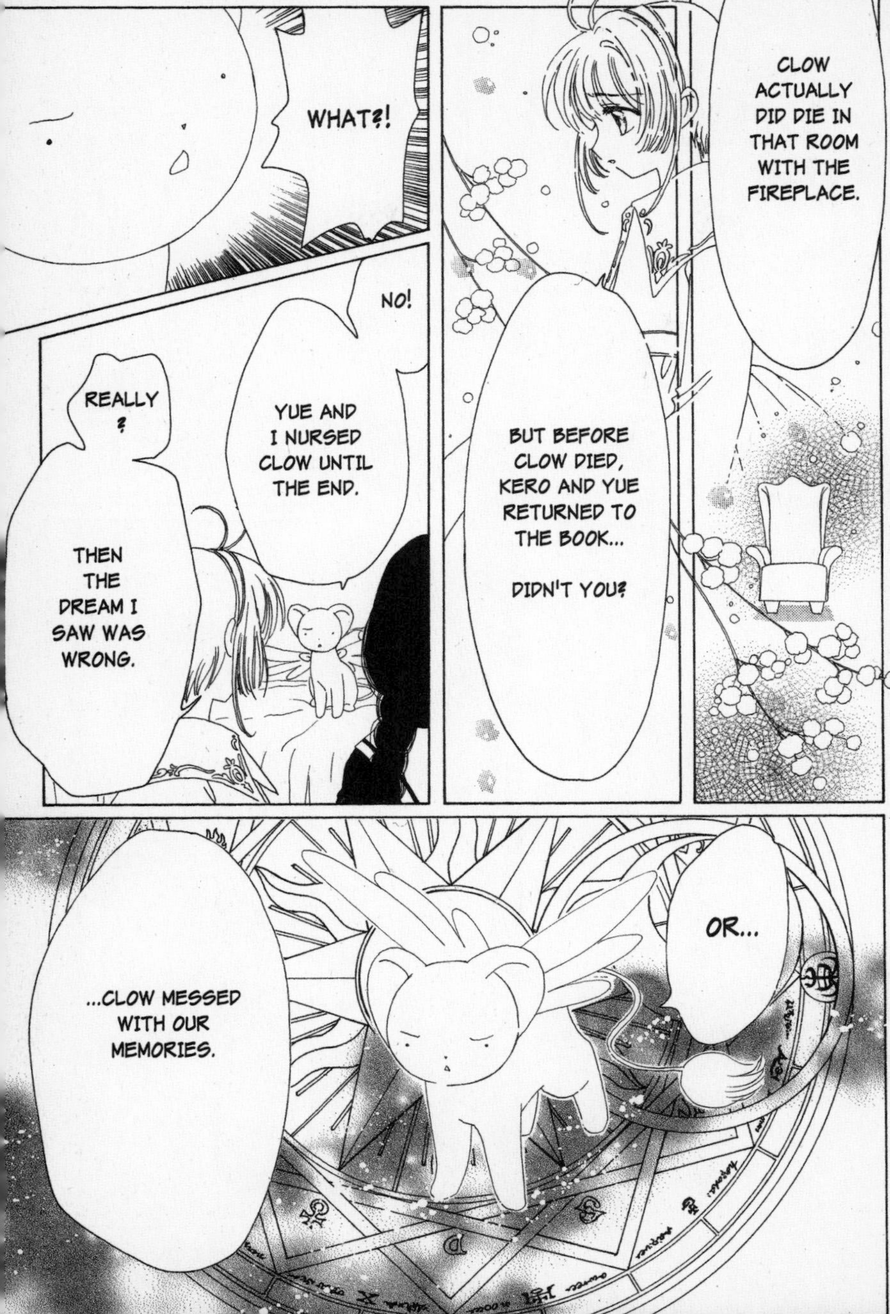
CLOW ACTUALLY DID DIE IN THAT ROOM WITH THE FIREPLACE.
BUT BEFORE CLOW DIED, KERO AND YUE RETURNED TO THE BOOK...
DIDN'T YOU?
WHAT?!
NO!
YUE AND I NURSED CLOW UNTIL THE END.
REALLY?
THEN THE DREAM I SAW WAS WRONG.
OR...
...CLOW MESSED WITH OUR MEMORIES.

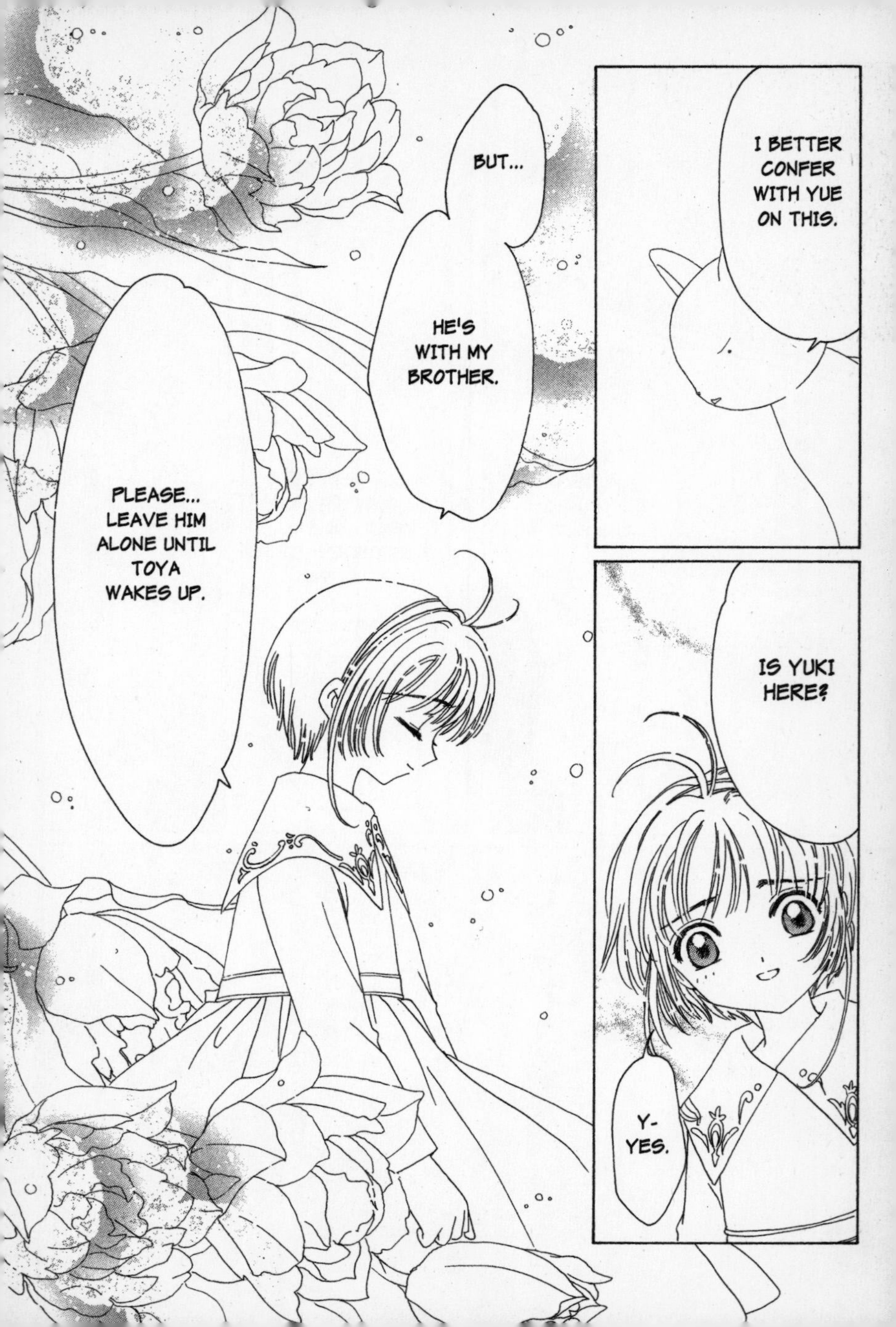
I BETTER CONFER WITH YUE ON THIS.
IS YUKI HERE?
Y-YES.
BUT...
HE'S WITH MY BROTHER.
PLEASE... LEAVE HIM ALONE UNTIL TOYA WAKES UP.

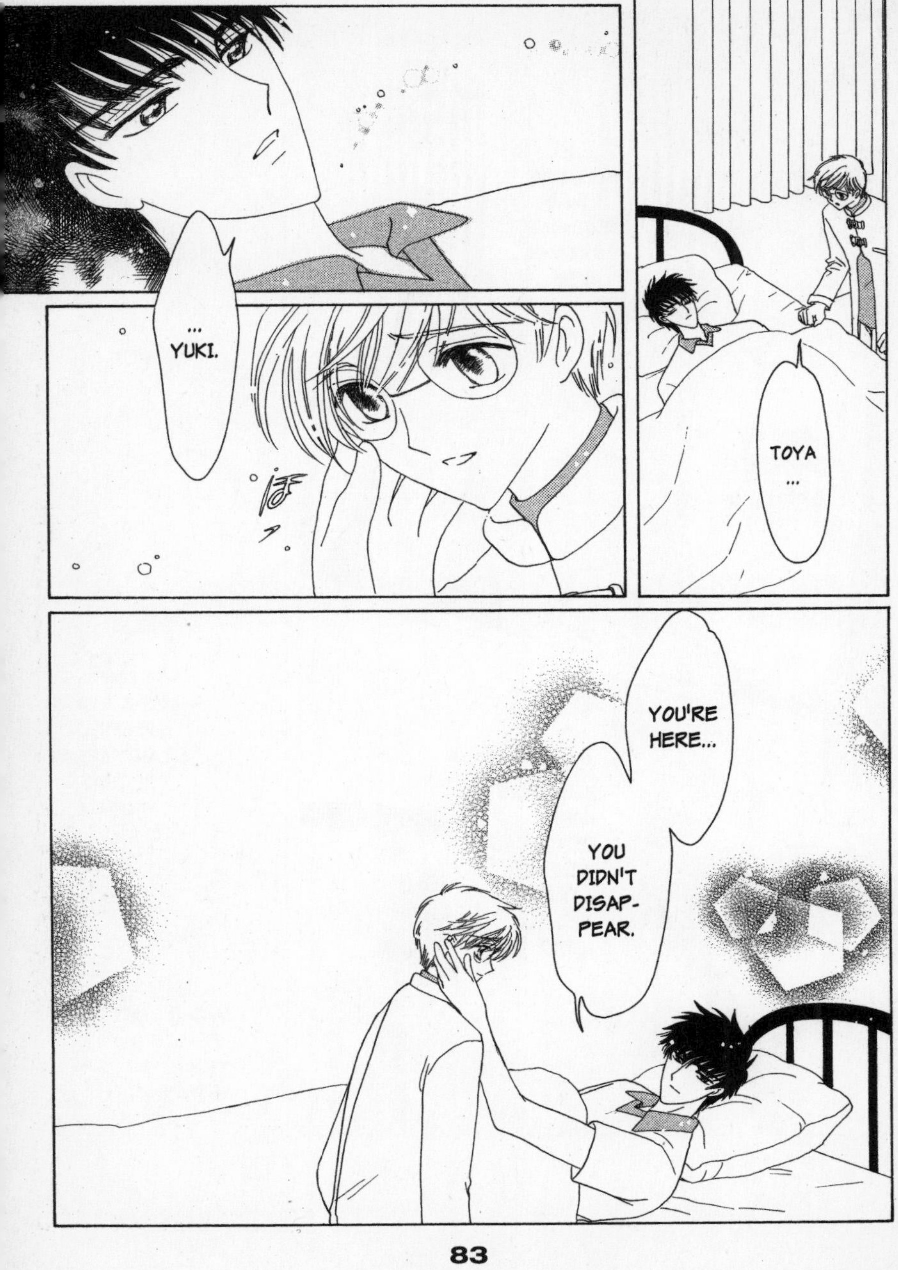
TOYA ...
... YUKI.
ぽ
YOU'RE HERE...
YOU DIDN'T DISAP-PEAR.

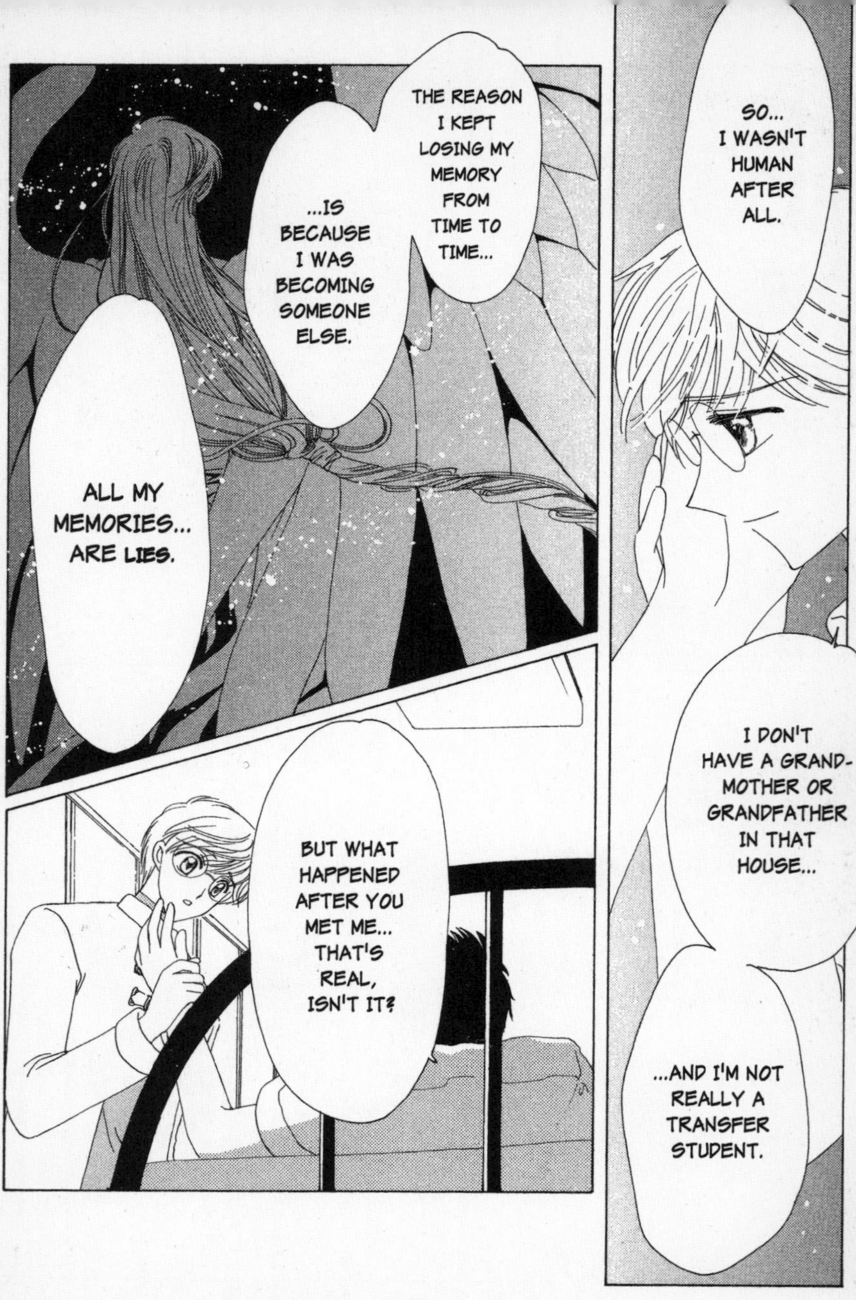
SO... I WASN'T HUMAN AFTER ALL.
I DON'T HAVE A GRAND-MOTHER OR GRANDFATHER IN THAT HOUSE...
...AND I'M NOT REALLY A TRANSFER STUDENT.
THE REASON I KEPT LOSING MY MEMORY FROM TIME TO TIME...
...IS BECAUSE I WAS BECOMING SOMEONE ELSE.
ALL MY MEMORIES... ARE LIES.
BUT WHAT HAPPENED AFTER YOU MET ME... THAT'S REAL, ISN'T IT?

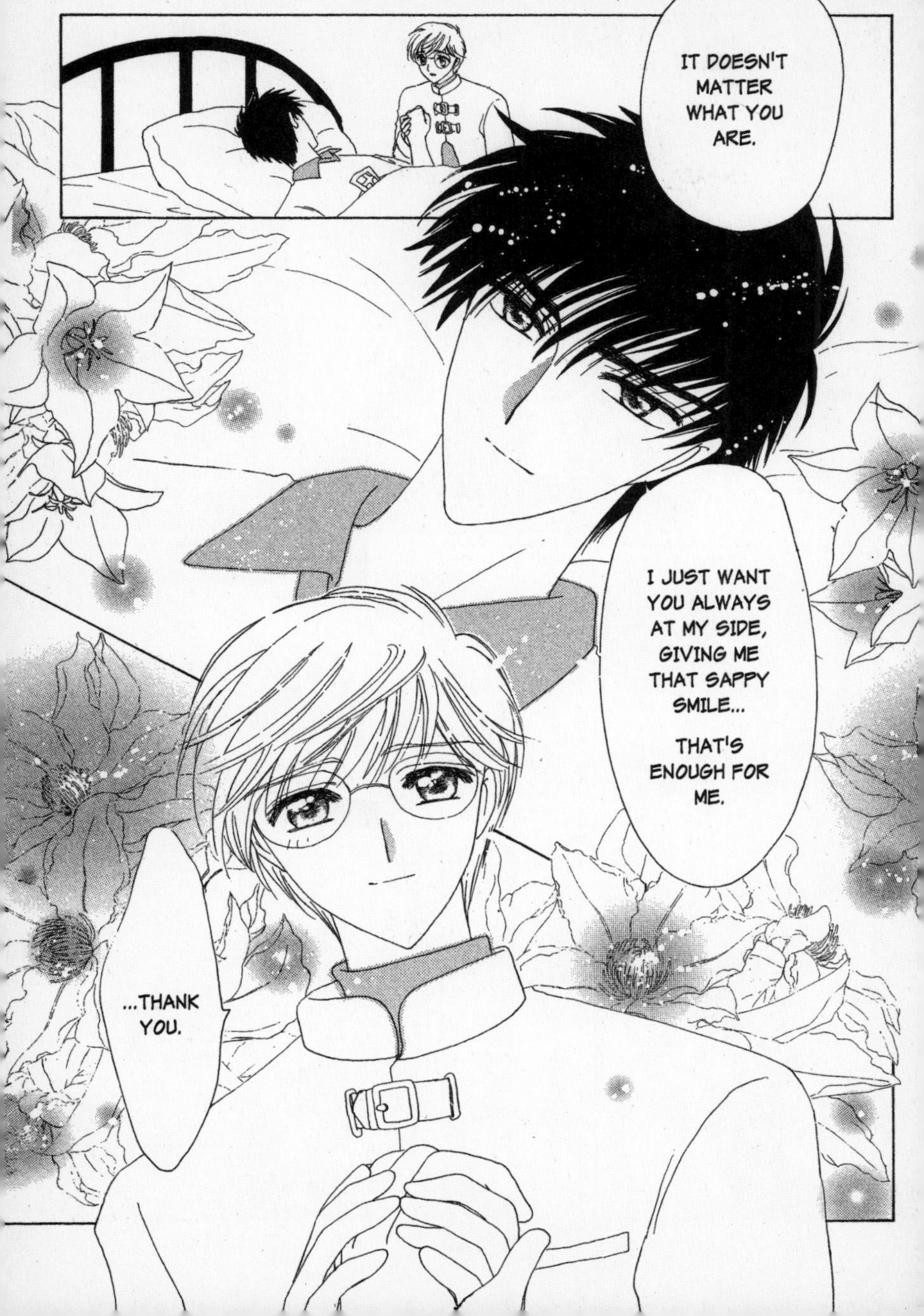
IT DOESN'T MATTER WHAT YOU ARE.
I JUST WANT YOU ALWAYS AT MY SIDE, GIVING ME THAT SAPPY SMILE...
THAT'S ENOUGH FOR ME.
...THANK YOU.

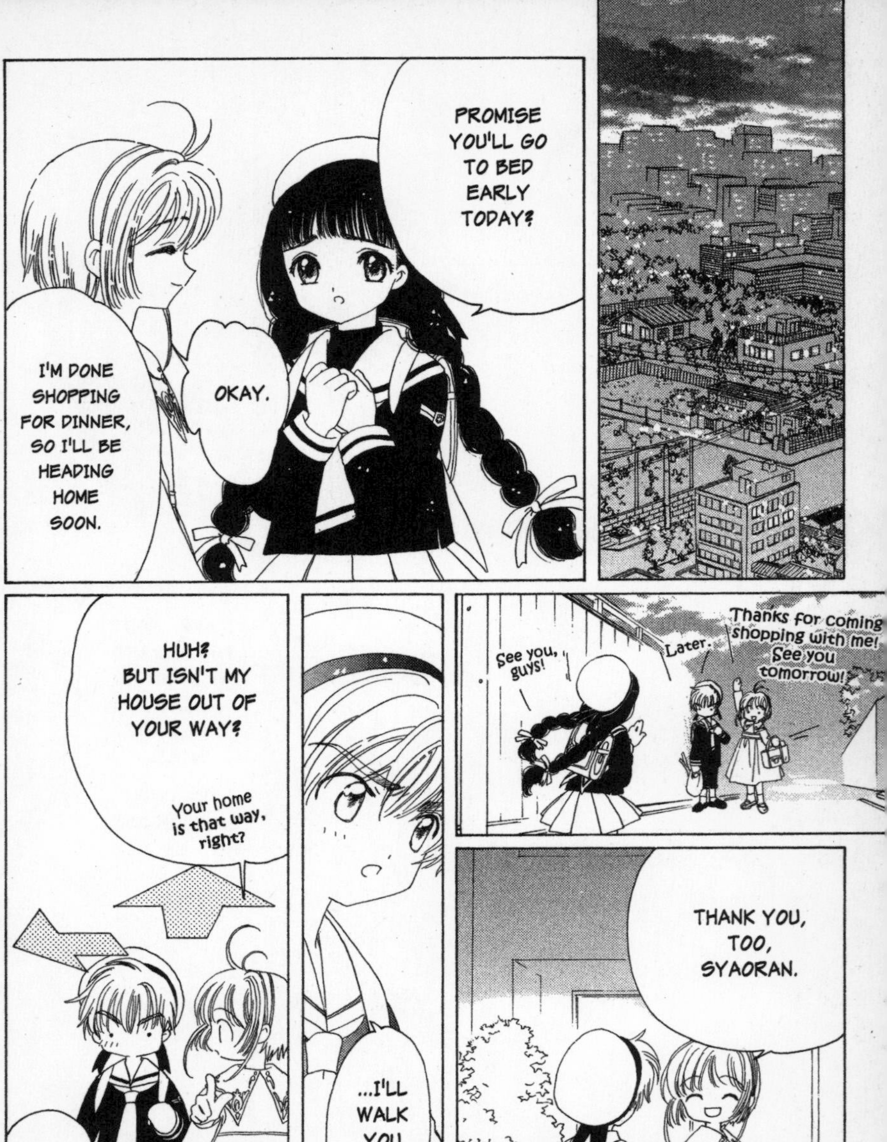
PROMISE YOU'LL GO TO BED EARLY TODAY?
OKAY.
I'M DONE SHOPPING FOR DINNER, SO I'LL BE HEADING HOME SOON.
Thanks for coming shopping with me! See you tomorrow!
Later.
See you, guys!
THANK YOU, TOO, SYAORAN.
...I'LL WALK YOU HOME.
HUH? BUT ISN'T MY HOUSE OUT OF YOUR WAY?
Your home is that way, right?
S'OKAY.

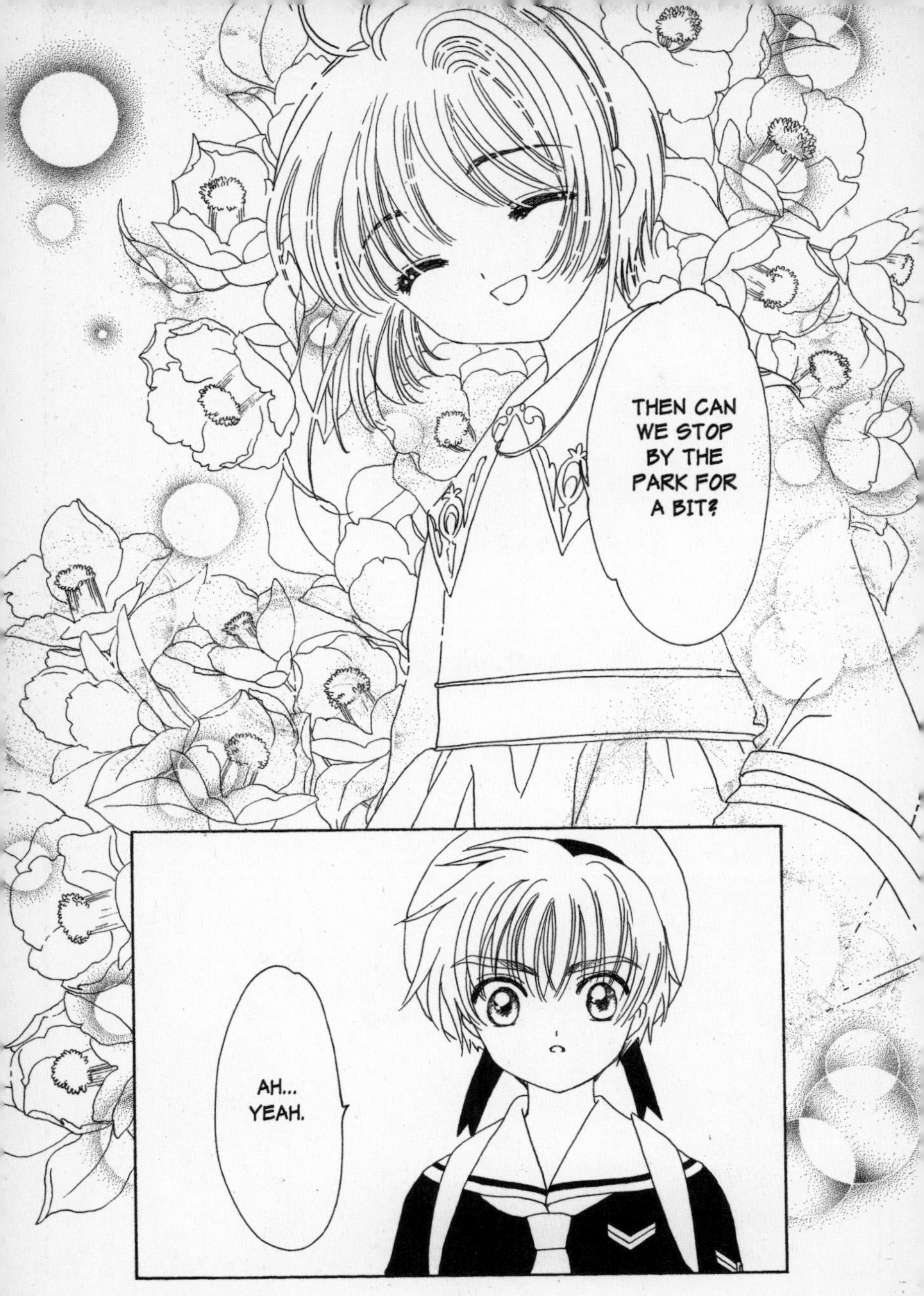
THEN CAN WE STOP BY THE PARK FOR A BIT?
AH... YEAH.

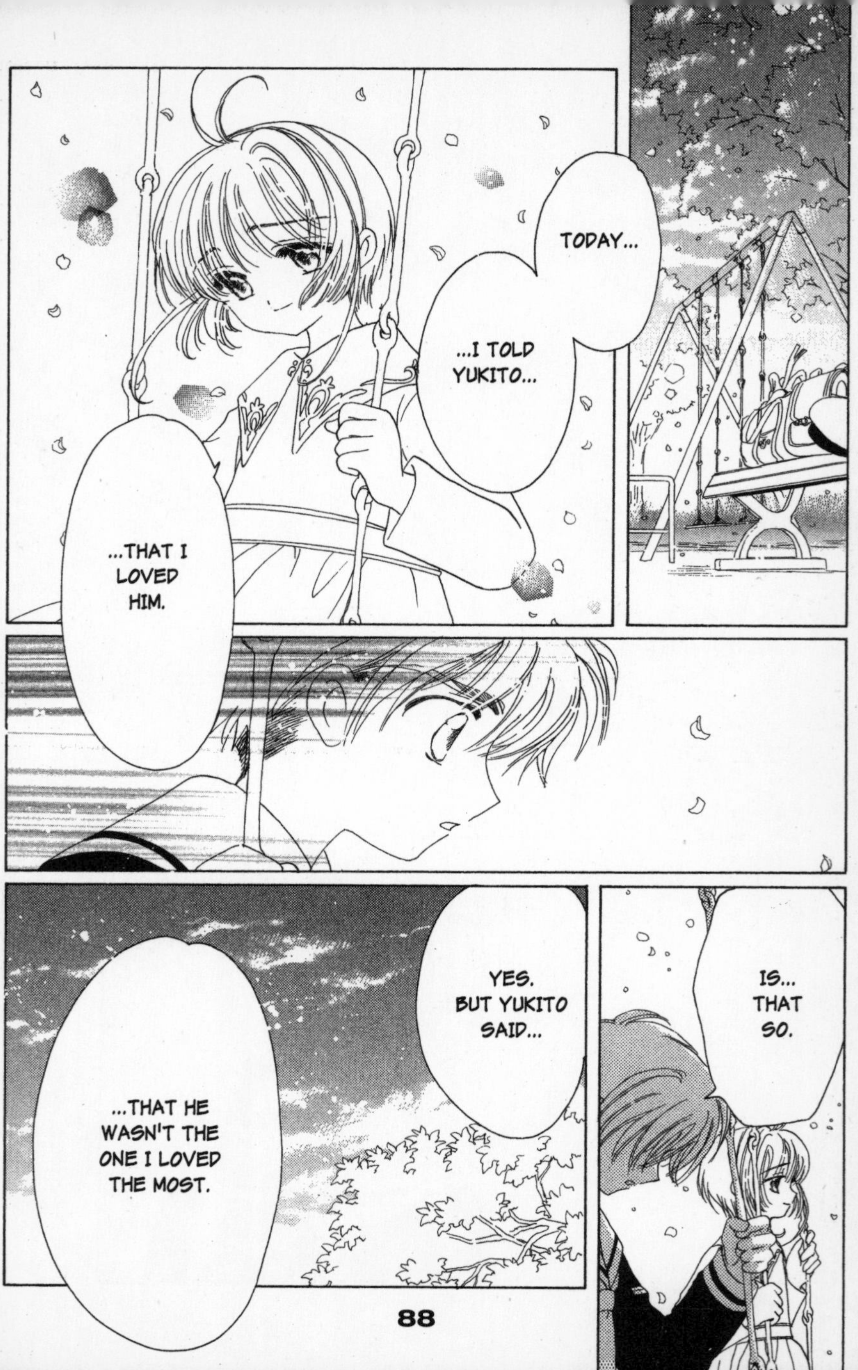
TODAY...
...I TOLD YUKITO...
...THAT I LOVED HIM.
IS... THAT SO.
YES. BUT YUKITO SAID...
...THAT HE WASN'T THE ONE I LOVED THE MOST.

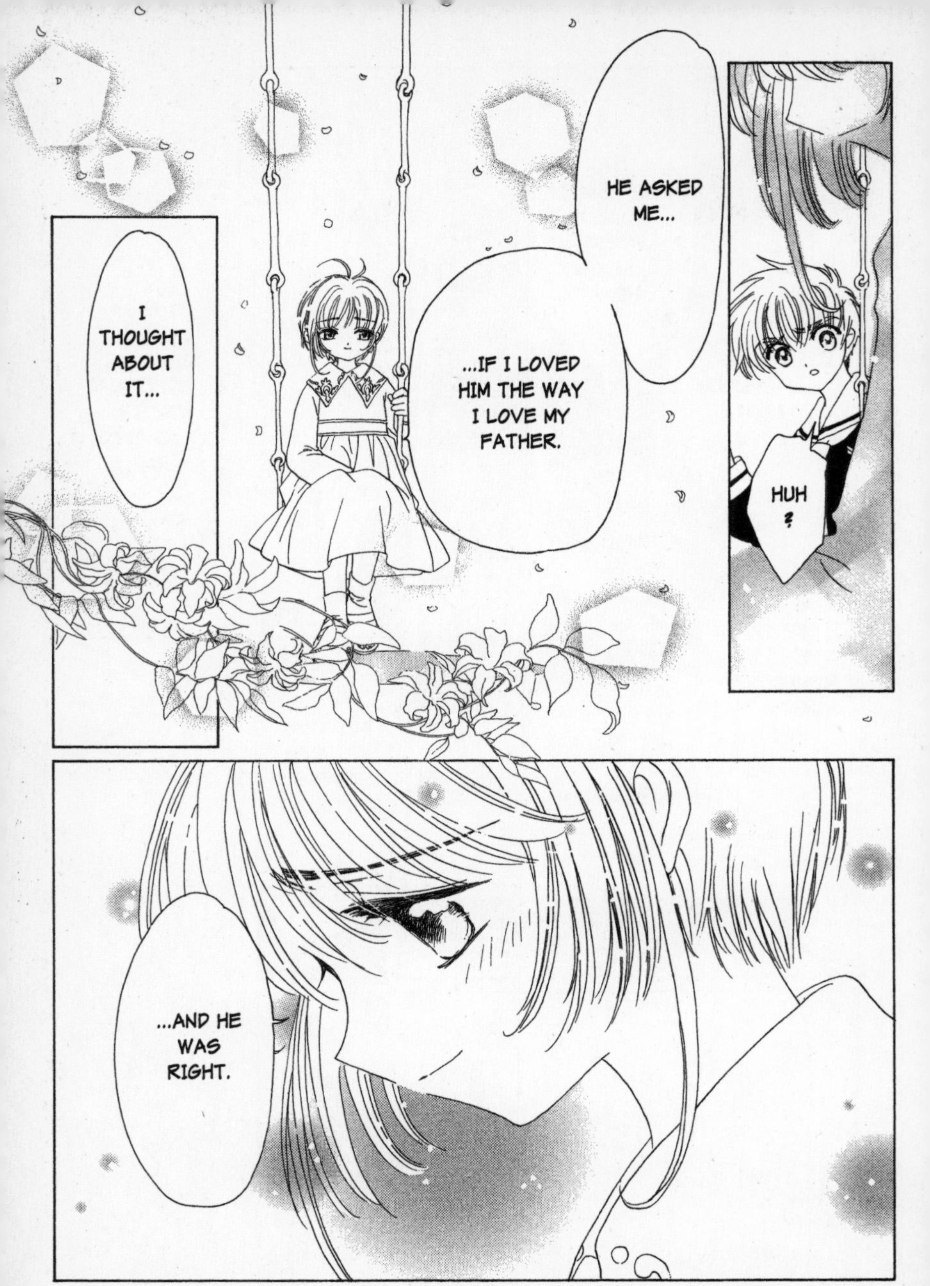
HE ASKED ME...
...IF I LOVED HIM THE WAY I LOVE MY FATHER.
HUH?
I THOUGHT ABOUT IT...
...AND HE WAS RIGHT.

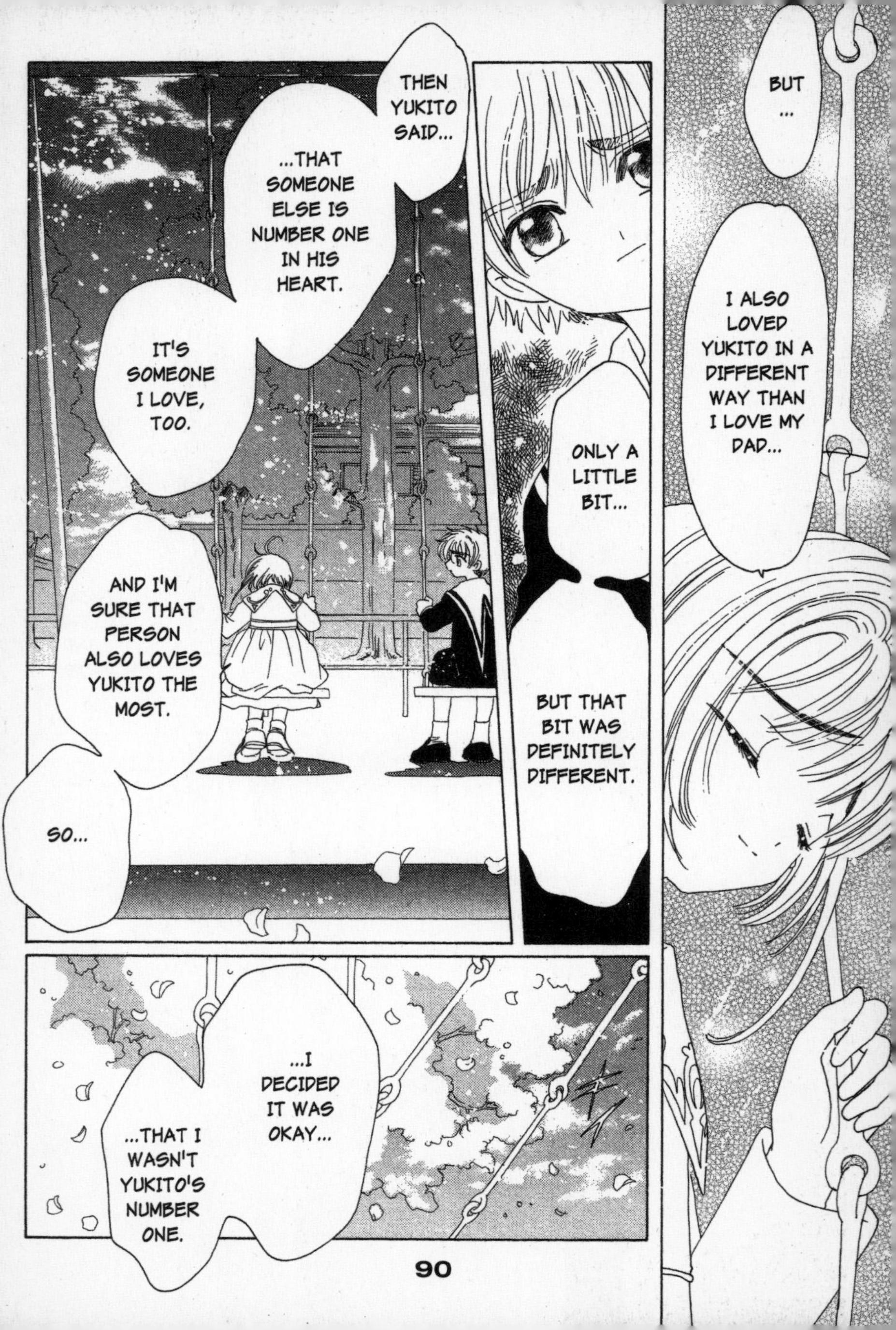
BUT ...
I ALSO LOVED YUKITO IN A DIFFERENT WAY THAN I LOVE MY DAD...
ONLY A LITTLE BIT...
BUT THAT BIT WAS DEFINITELY DIFFERENT.
THEN YUKITO SAID...
...THAT SOMEONE ELSE IS NUMBER ONE IN HIS HEART.
IT'S SOMEONE I LOVE, TOO.
AND I'M SURE THAT PERSON ALSO LOVES YUKITO THE MOST.
SO...
...I DECIDED IT WAS OKAY...
...THAT I WASN'T YUKITO'S NUMBER ONE.

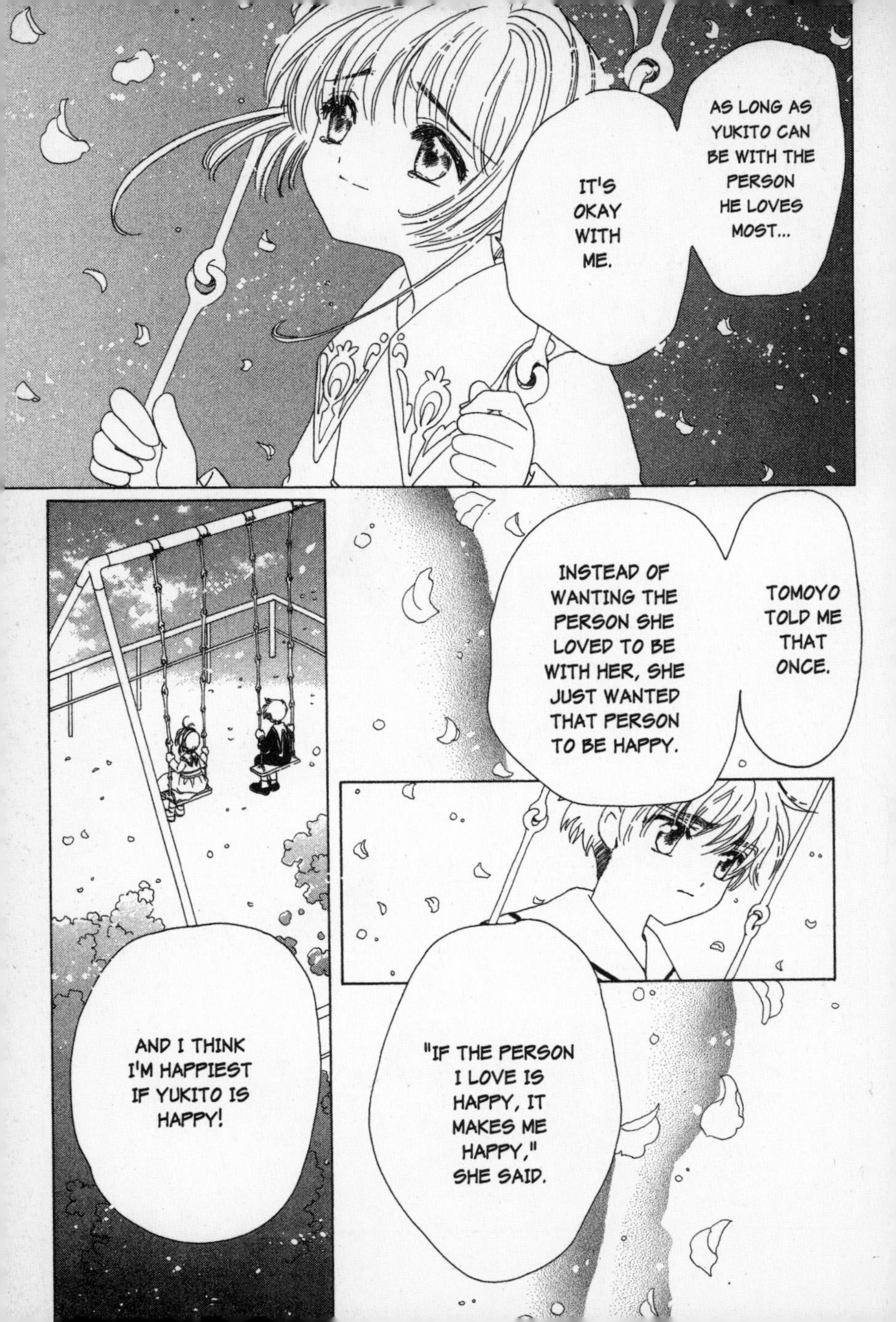
AS LONG AS YUKITO CAN BE WITH THE PERSON HE LOVES MOST...
IT'S OKAY WITH ME.
TOMOYO TOLD ME THAT ONCE.
INSTEAD OF WANTING THE PERSON SHE LOVED TO BE WITH HER, SHE JUST WANTED THAT PERSON TO BE HAPPY.
"IF THE PERSON I LOVE IS HAPPY, IT MAKES ME HAPPY," SHE SAID.
AND I THINK I'M HAPPIEST IF YUKITO IS HAPPY!

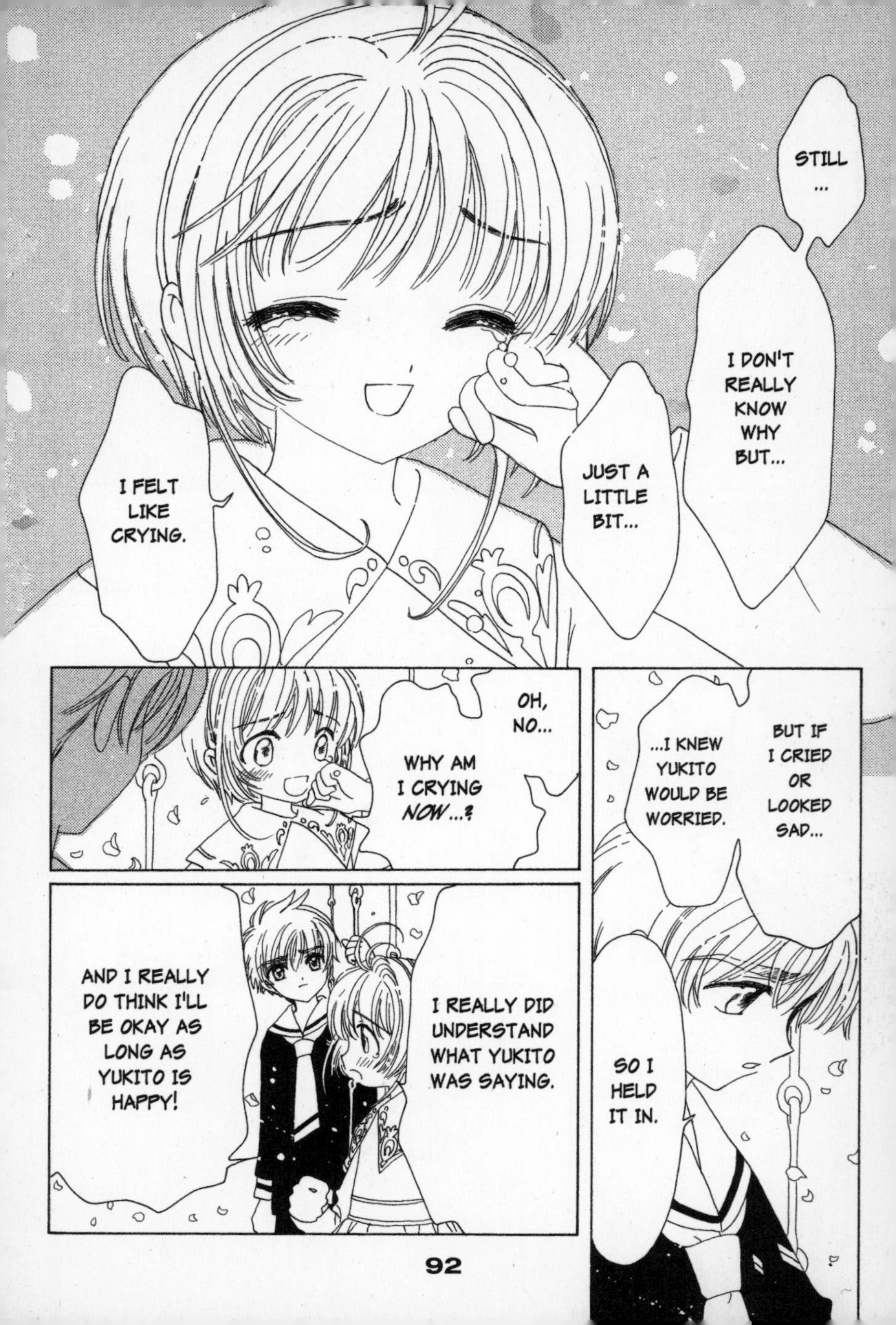
STILL ...
I DON'T REALLY KNOW WHY BUT...
JUST A LITTLE BIT...
I FELT LIKE CRYING.
BUT IF I CRIED OR LOOKED SAD...
...I KNEW YUKITO WOULD BE WORRIED.
SO I HELD IT IN.
OH, NO...
WHY AM I CRYING *NOW*...?
I REALLY DID UNDERSTAND WHAT YUKITO WAS SAYING.
AND I REALLY DO THINK I'LL BE OKAY AS LONG AS YUKITO IS HAPPY!

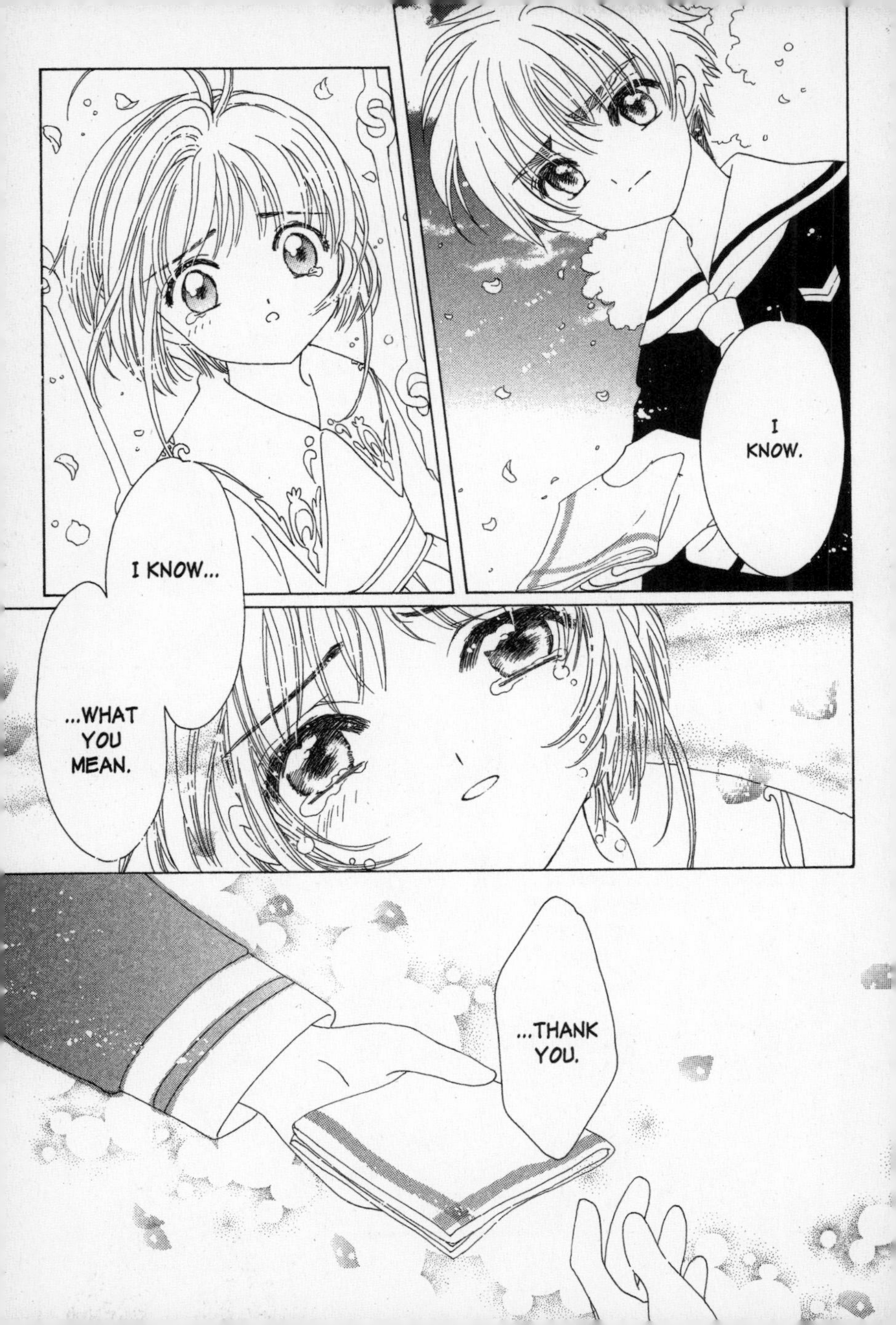
I KNOW.
I KNOW...
...WHAT YOU MEAN.
...THANK YOU.

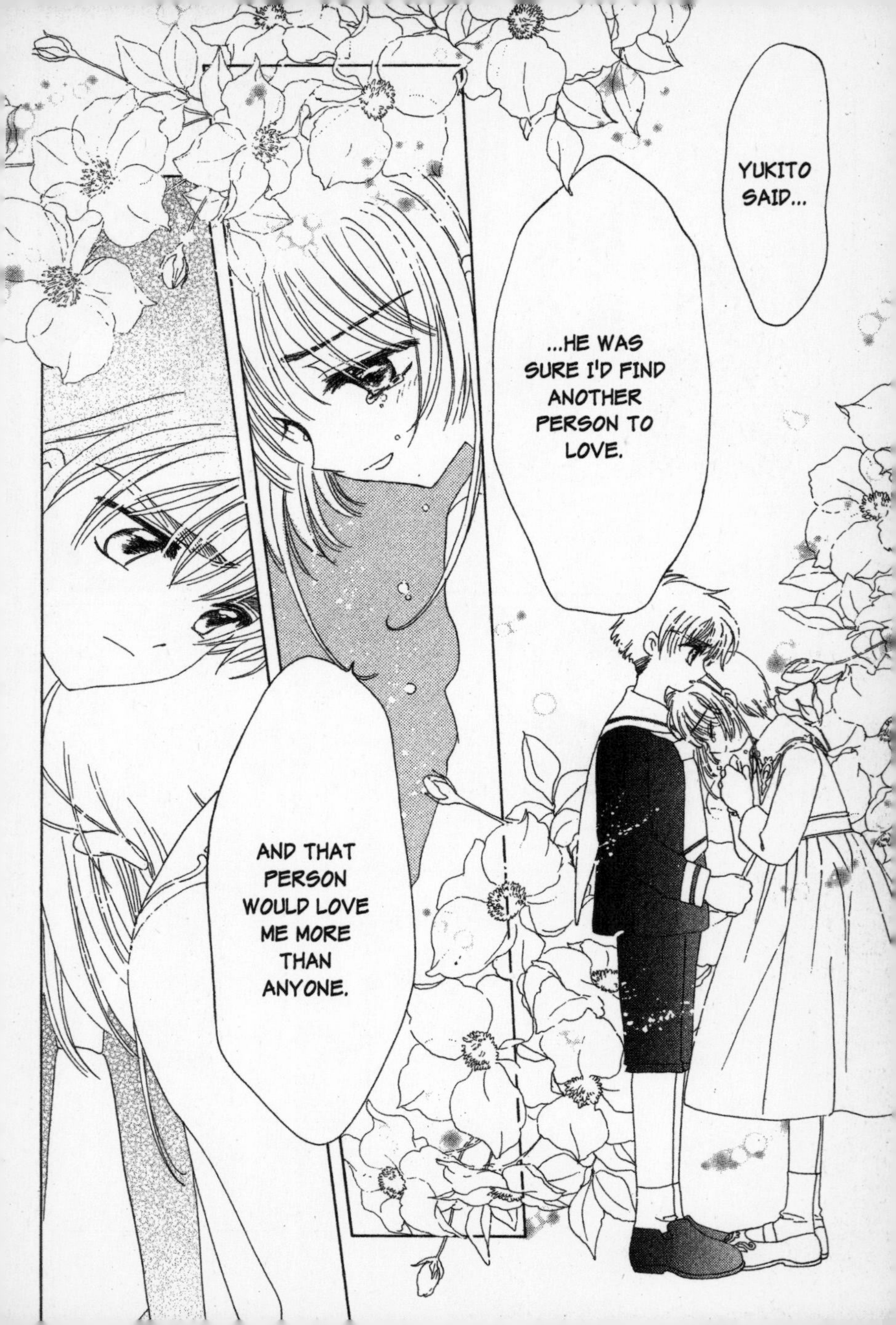
YUKITO SAID...
...HE WAS SURE I'D FIND ANOTHER PERSON TO LOVE.
AND THAT PERSON WOULD LOVE ME MORE THAN ANYONE.

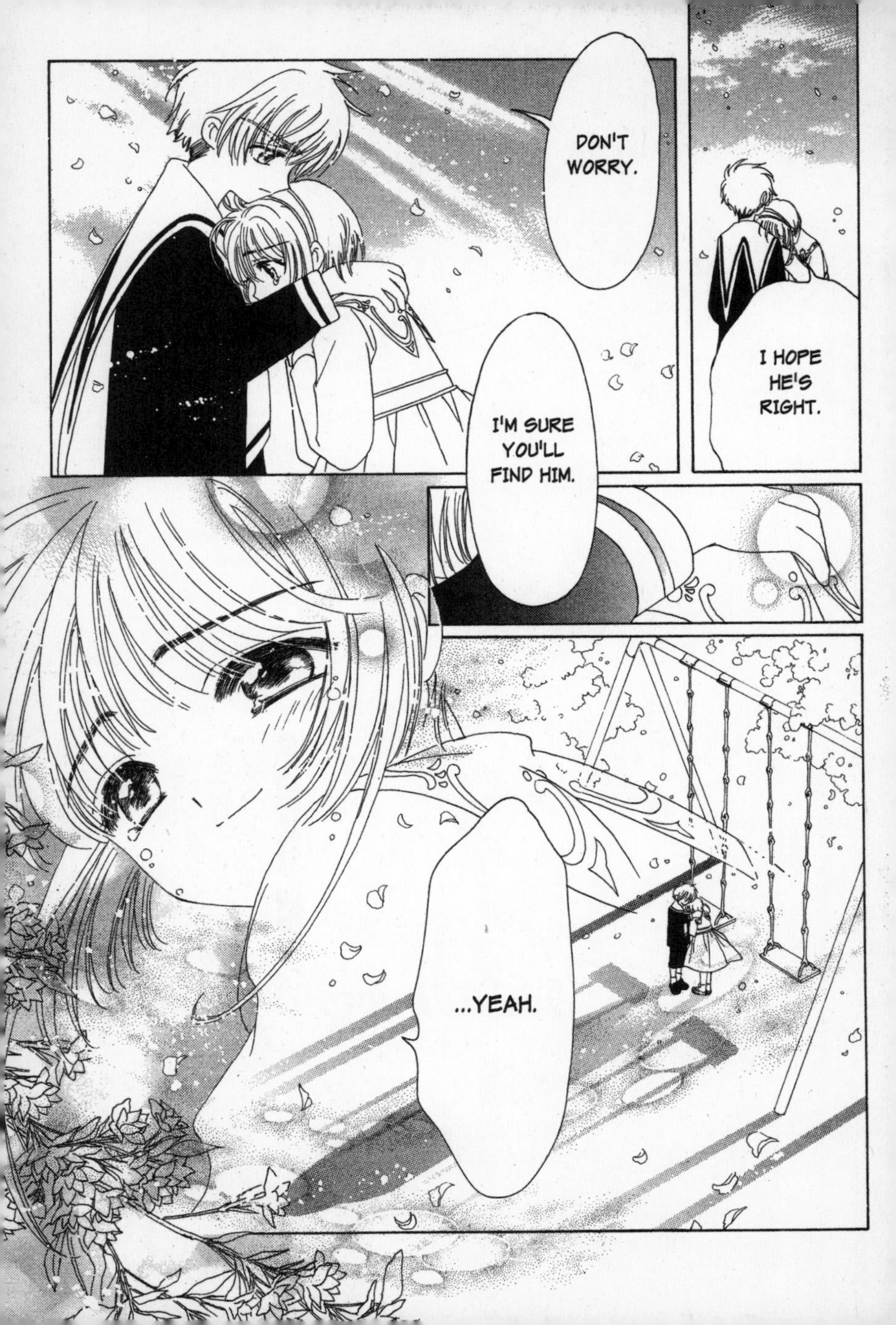
I HOPE HE'S RIGHT.
DON'T WORRY.
I'M SURE YOU'LL FIND HIM.
...YEAH.

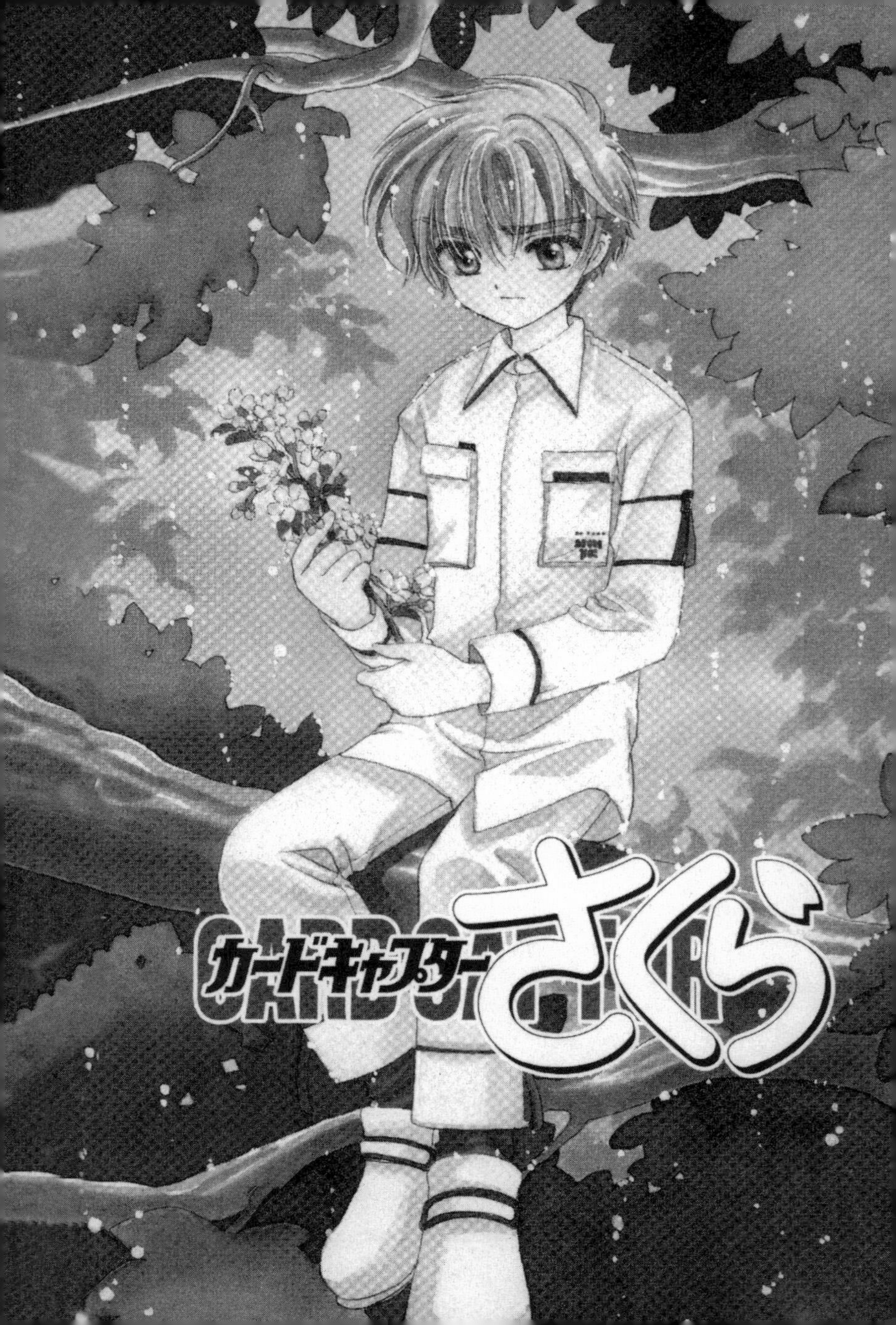
カードキャプターさくら
CARDCAPTOR

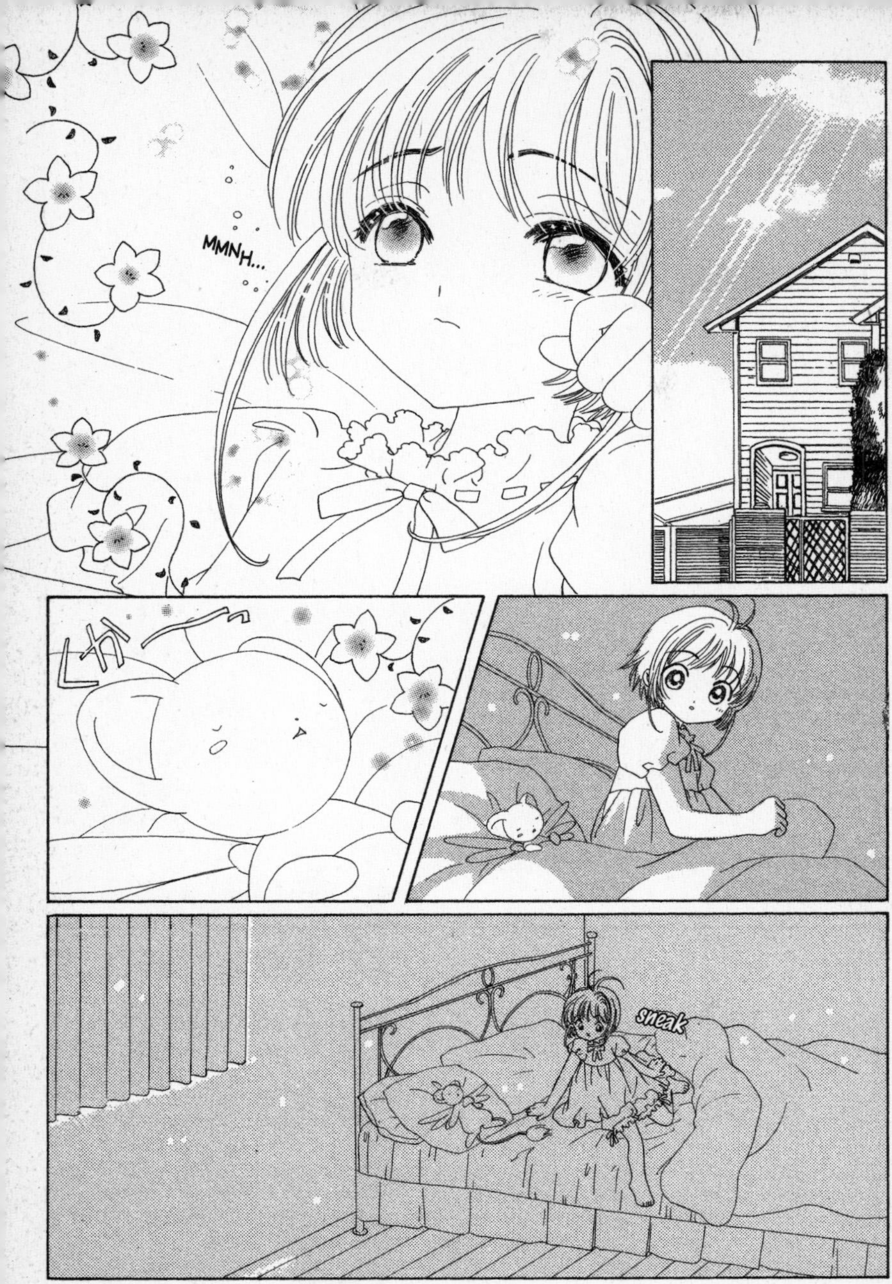
MMNH...
sneak

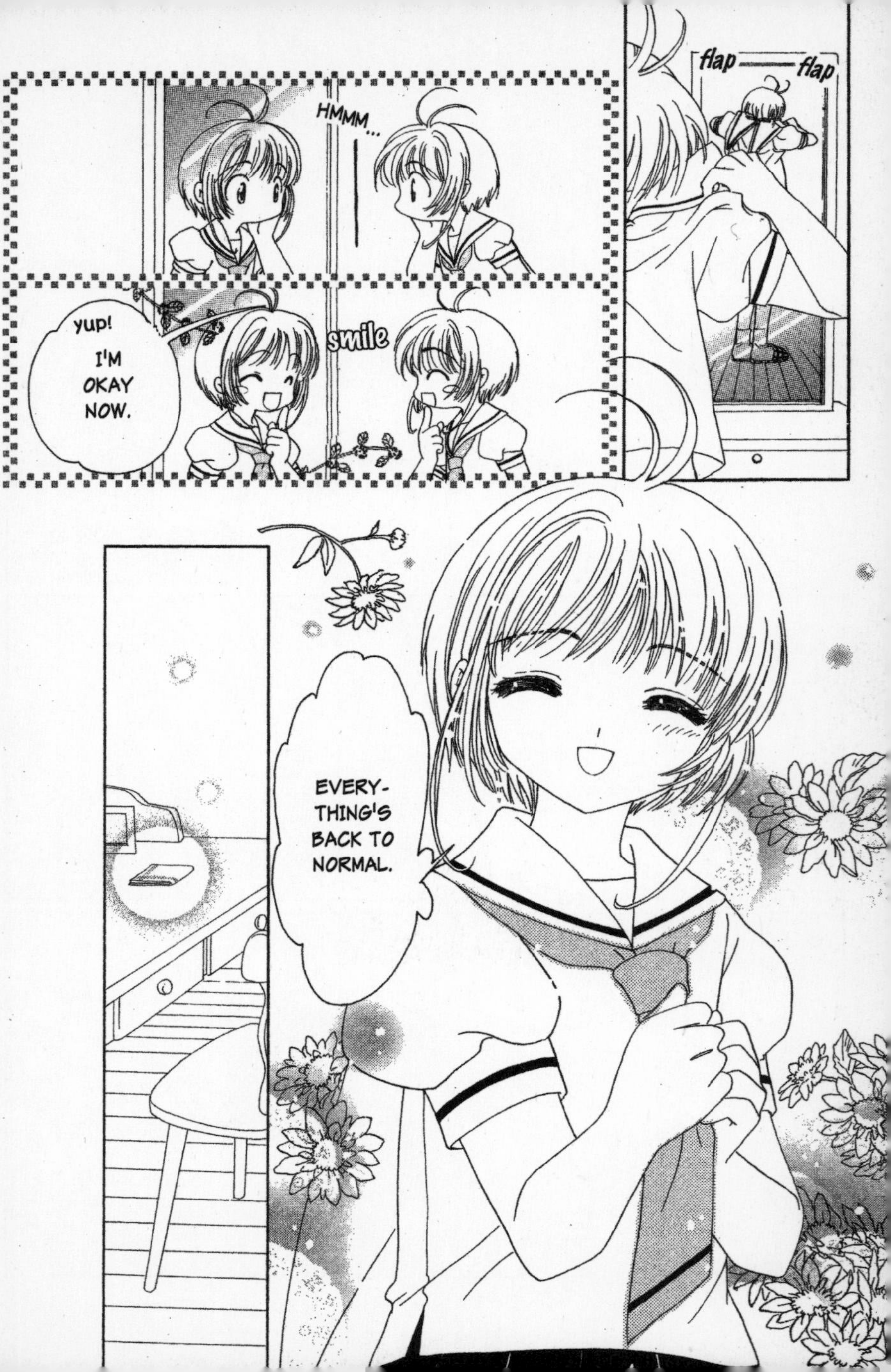
flap——flap
HMMM...
smile
yup! I'M OKAY NOW.
EVERY-THING'S BACK TO NORMAL.

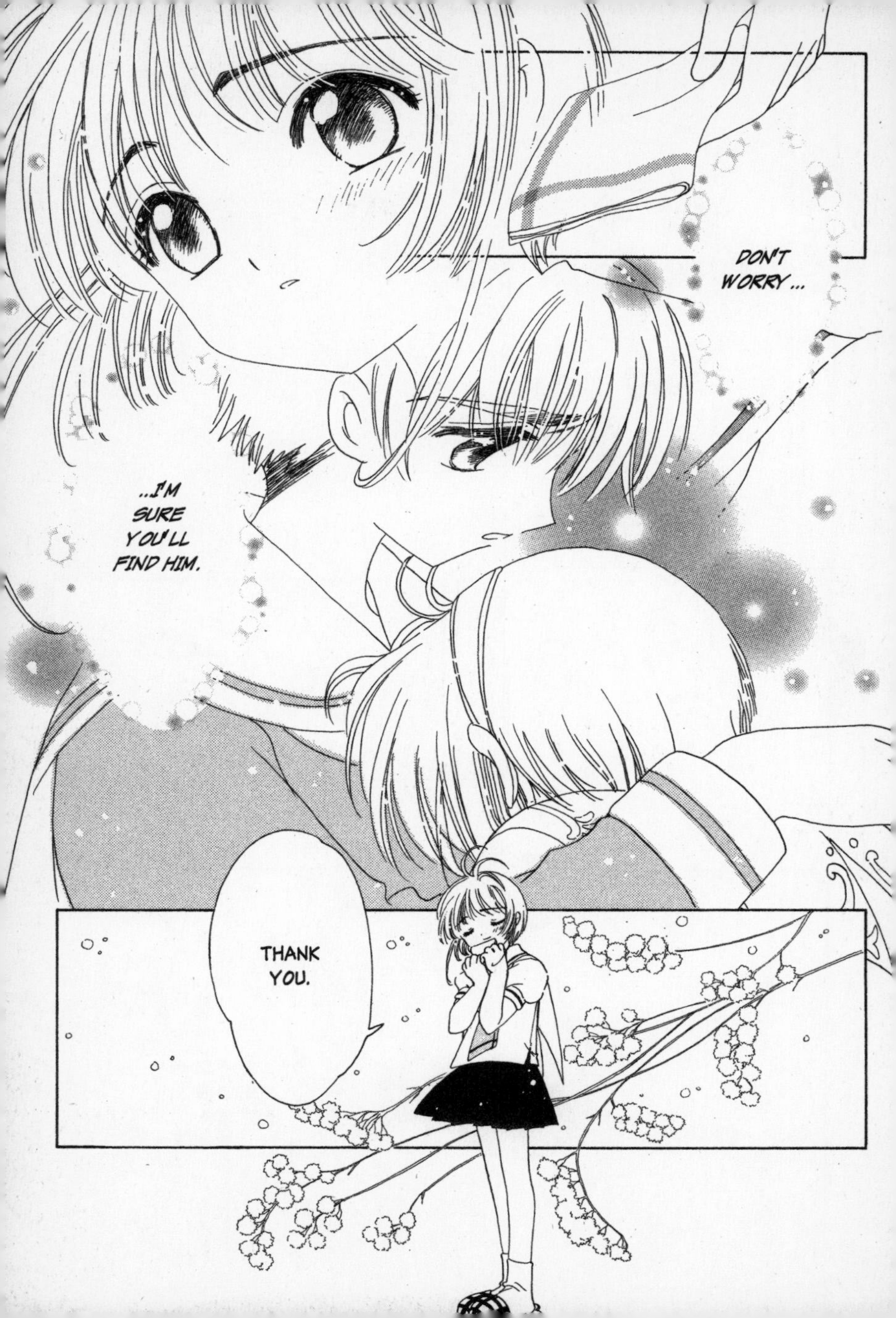
DON'T WORRY...
...I'M SURE YOU'LL FIND HIM.
THANK YOU.

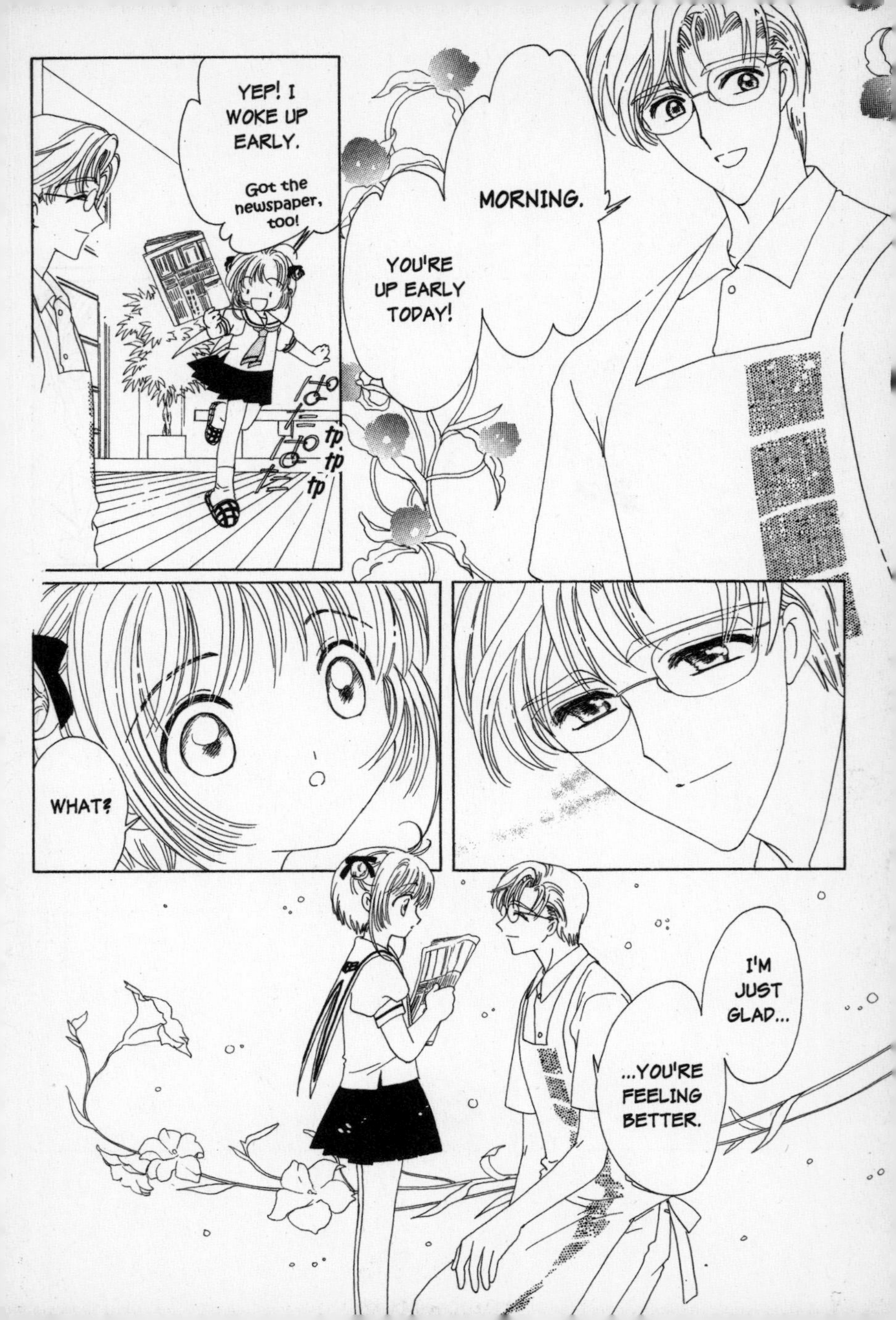
MORNING.
YOU'RE UP EARLY TODAY!
YEP! I WOKE UP EARLY.
Got the newspaper, too!
はたはた
tp tp tp
WHAT?
I'M JUST GLAD...
...YOU'RE FEELING BETTER.

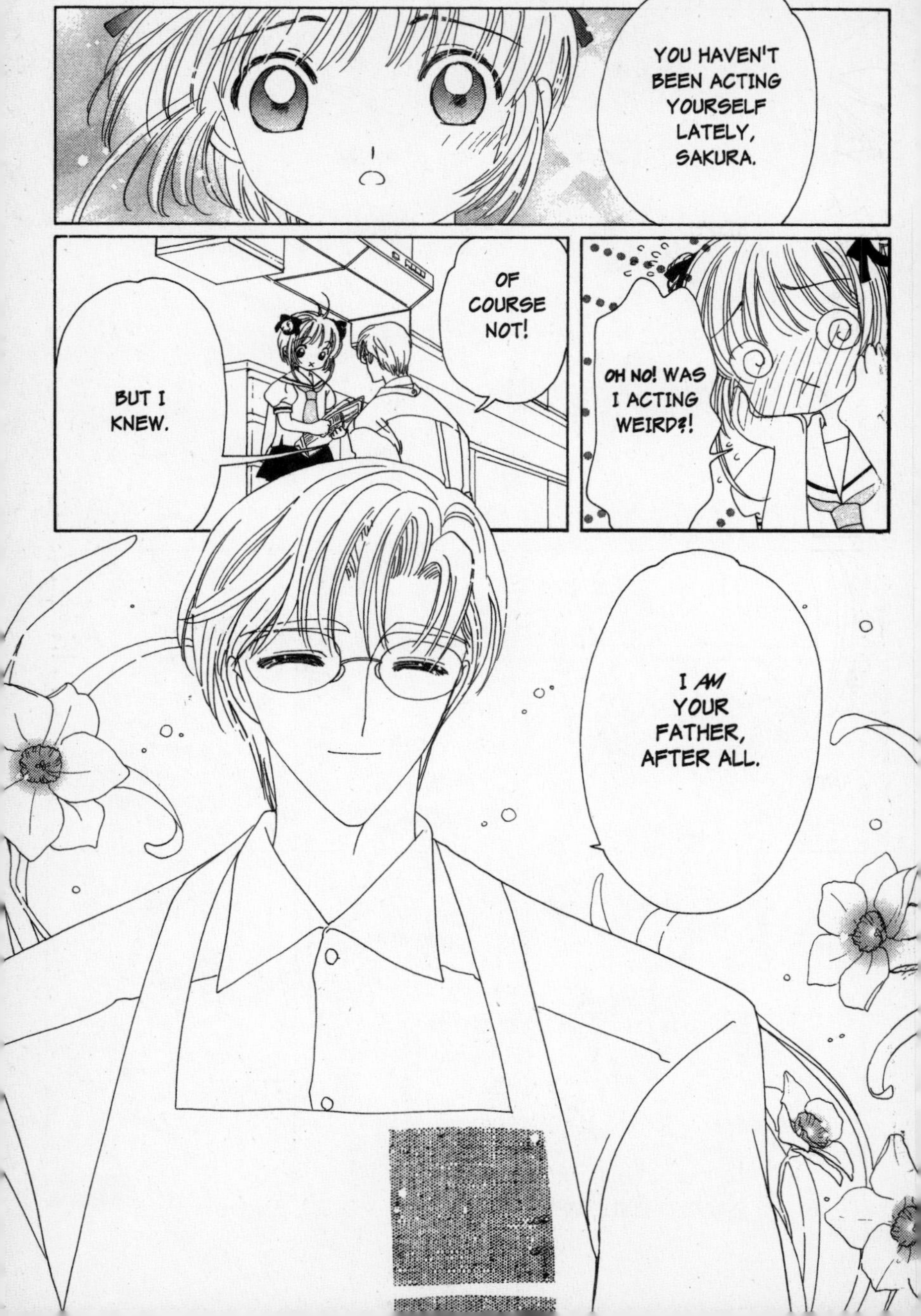
YOU HAVEN'T BEEN ACTING YOURSELF LATELY, SAKURA.
OH NO! WAS I ACTING WEIRD?!
OF COURSE NOT!
BUT I KNEW.
I *AM* YOUR FATHER, AFTER ALL.

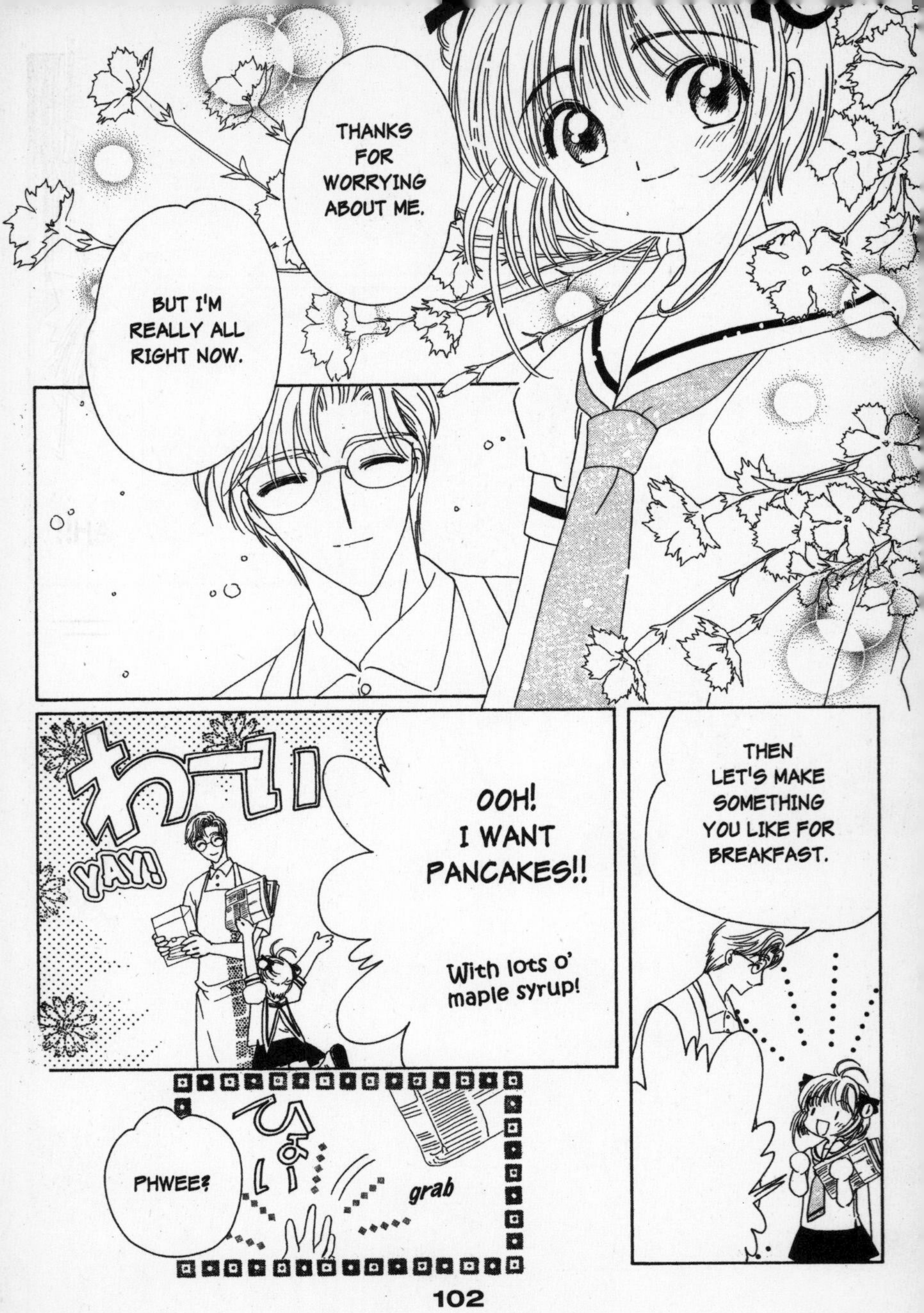
THANKS FOR WORRYING ABOUT ME.
BUT I'M REALLY ALL RIGHT NOW.
THEN LET'S MAKE SOMETHING YOU LIKE FOR BREAKFAST.
わーい
YAY!
OOH! I WANT PANCAKES!!
With lots o' maple syrup!
ひょい
PHWEE?
grab

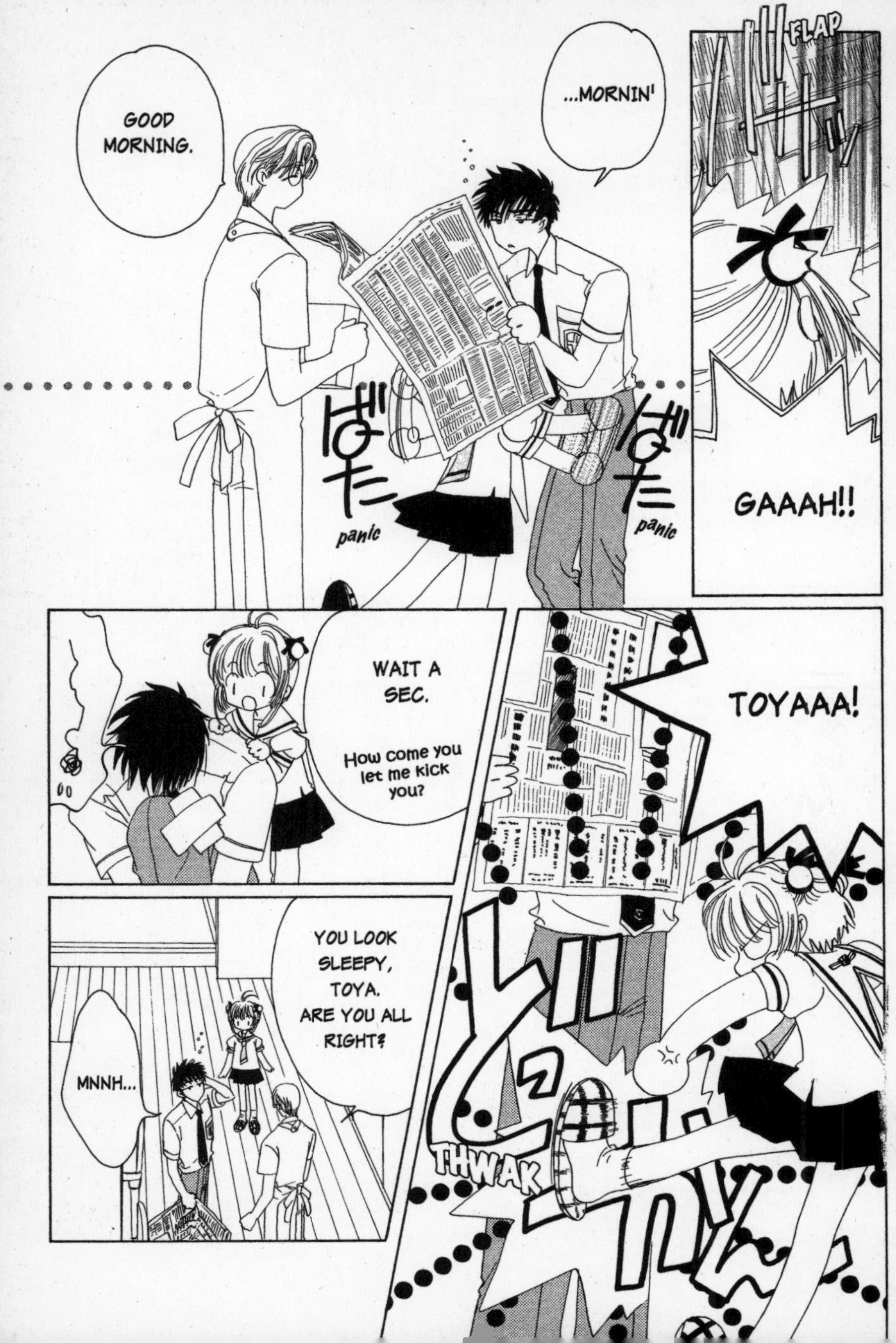
FLAP
GAAAH!!
...MORNIN'
GOOD MORNING.
ばた
panic
ばた
panic
TOYAAA!
THWAK
WAIT A SEC.
How come you let me kick you?
YOU LOOK SLEEPY, TOYA. ARE YOU ALL RIGHT?
MNNH...

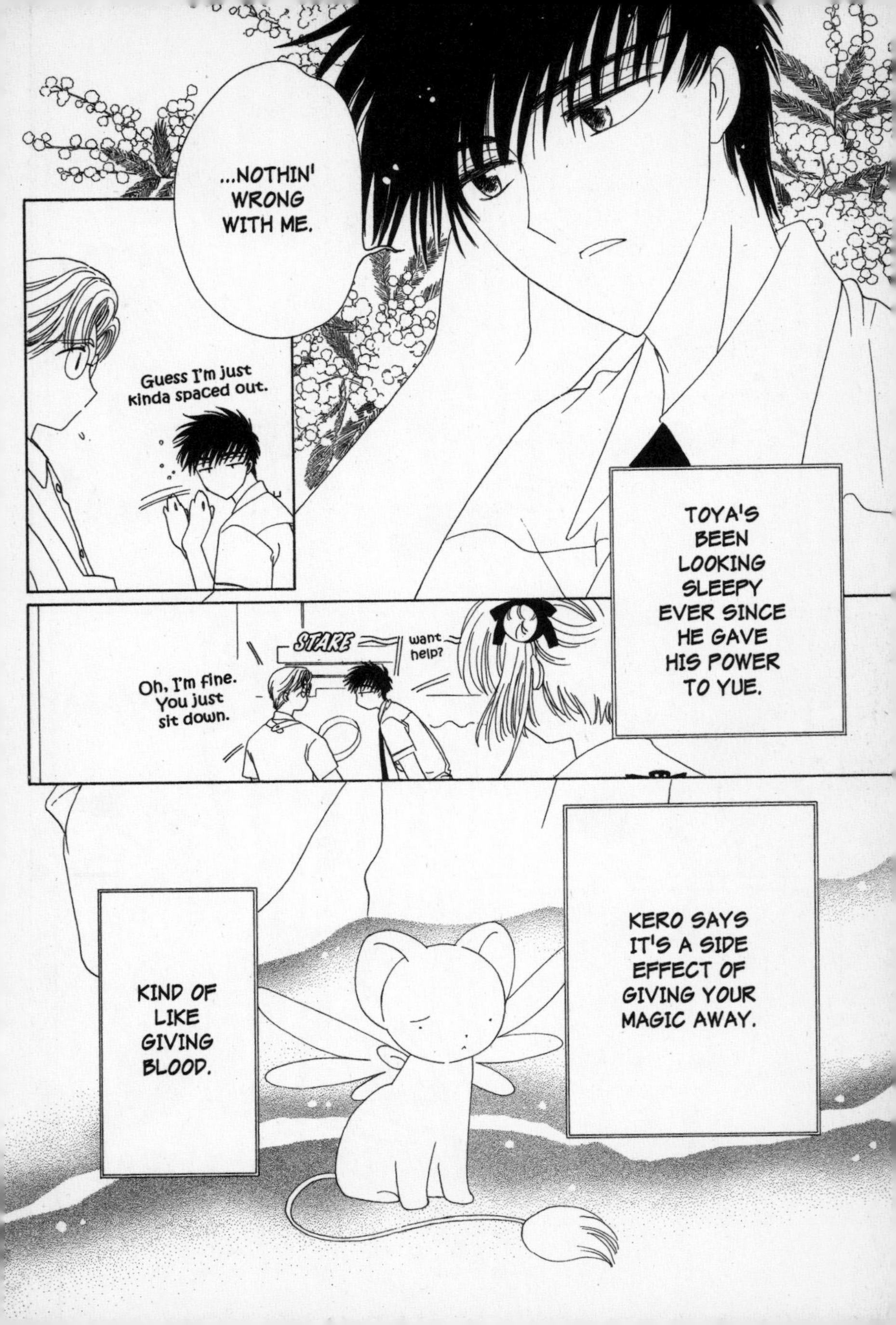
...NOTHIN' WRONG WITH ME.
Guess I'm just kinda spaced out.
STARE
want help?
Oh, I'm fine. You just sit down.
TOYA'S BEEN LOOKING SLEEPY EVER SINCE HE GAVE HIS POWER TO YUE.
KERO SAYS IT'S A SIDE EFFECT OF GIVING YOUR MAGIC AWAY.
KIND OF LIKE GIVING BLOOD.

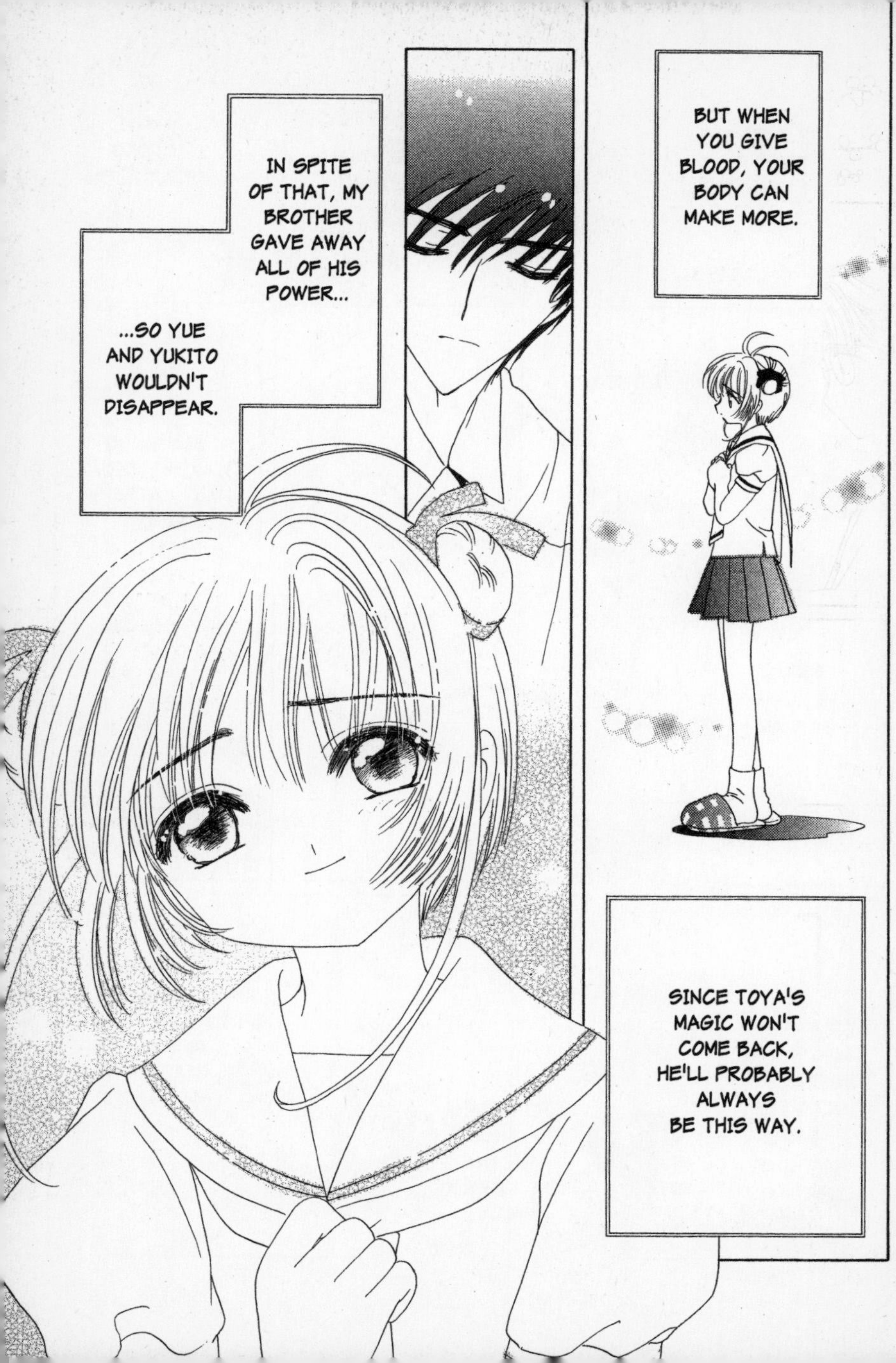
BUT WHEN YOU GIVE BLOOD, YOUR BODY CAN MAKE MORE.
SINCE TOYA'S MAGIC WON'T COME BACK, HE'LL PROBABLY ALWAYS BE THIS WAY.
IN SPITE OF THAT, MY BROTHER GAVE AWAY ALL OF HIS POWER...
...SO YUE AND YUKITO WOULDN'T DISAPPEAR.

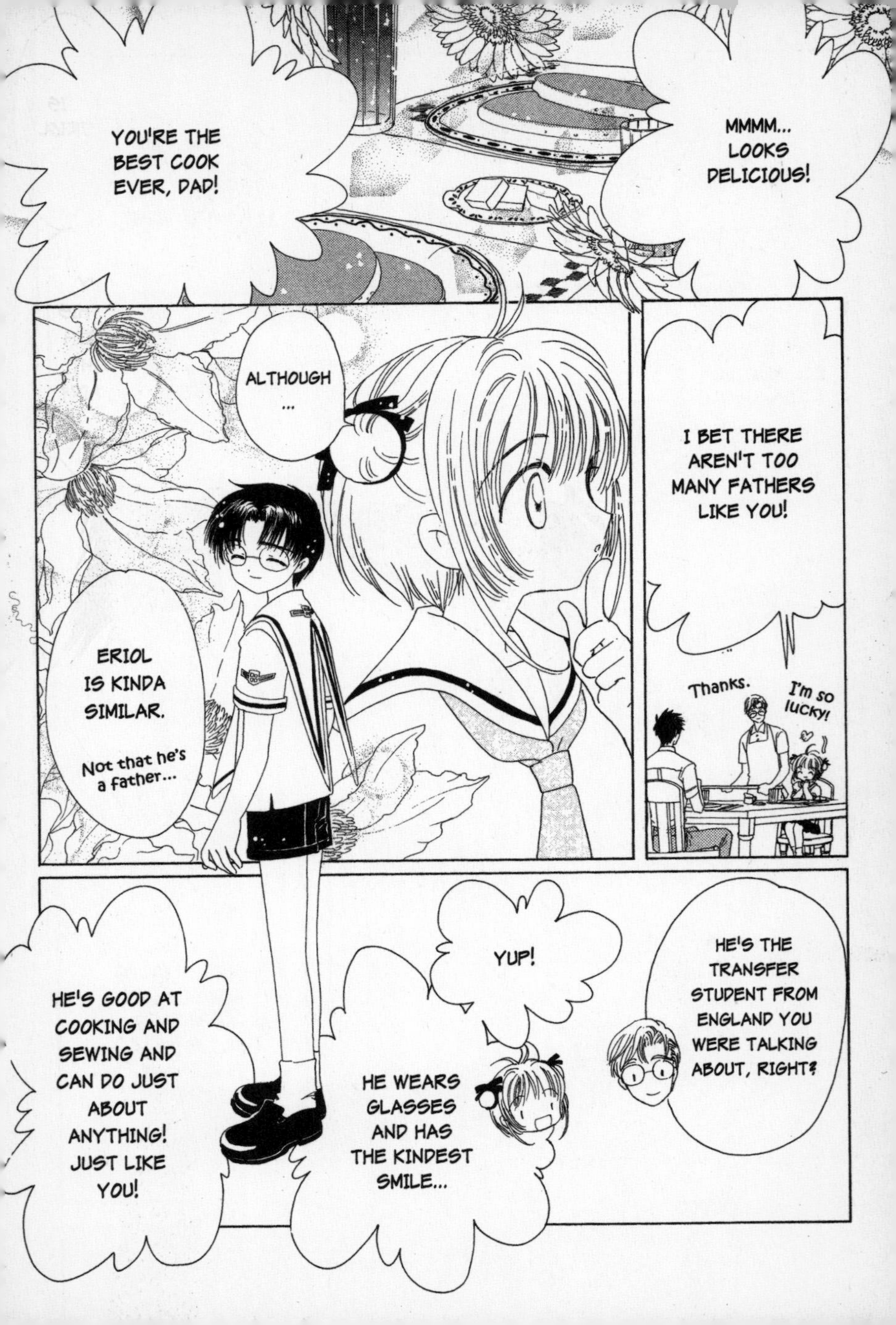
MMMM... LOOKS DELICIOUS!
YOU'RE THE BEST COOK EVER, DAD!
I BET THERE AREN'T TOO MANY FATHERS LIKE YOU!
...
Thanks.
I'm so lucky!
ALTHOUGH ...
ERIOL IS KINDA SIMILAR.
Not that he's a father...
HE'S THE TRANSFER STUDENT FROM ENGLAND YOU WERE TALKING ABOUT, RIGHT?
YUP!
HE WEARS GLASSES AND HAS THE KINDEST SMILE...
HE'S GOOD AT COOKING AND SEWING AND CAN DO JUST ABOUT ANYTHING! JUST LIKE YOU!

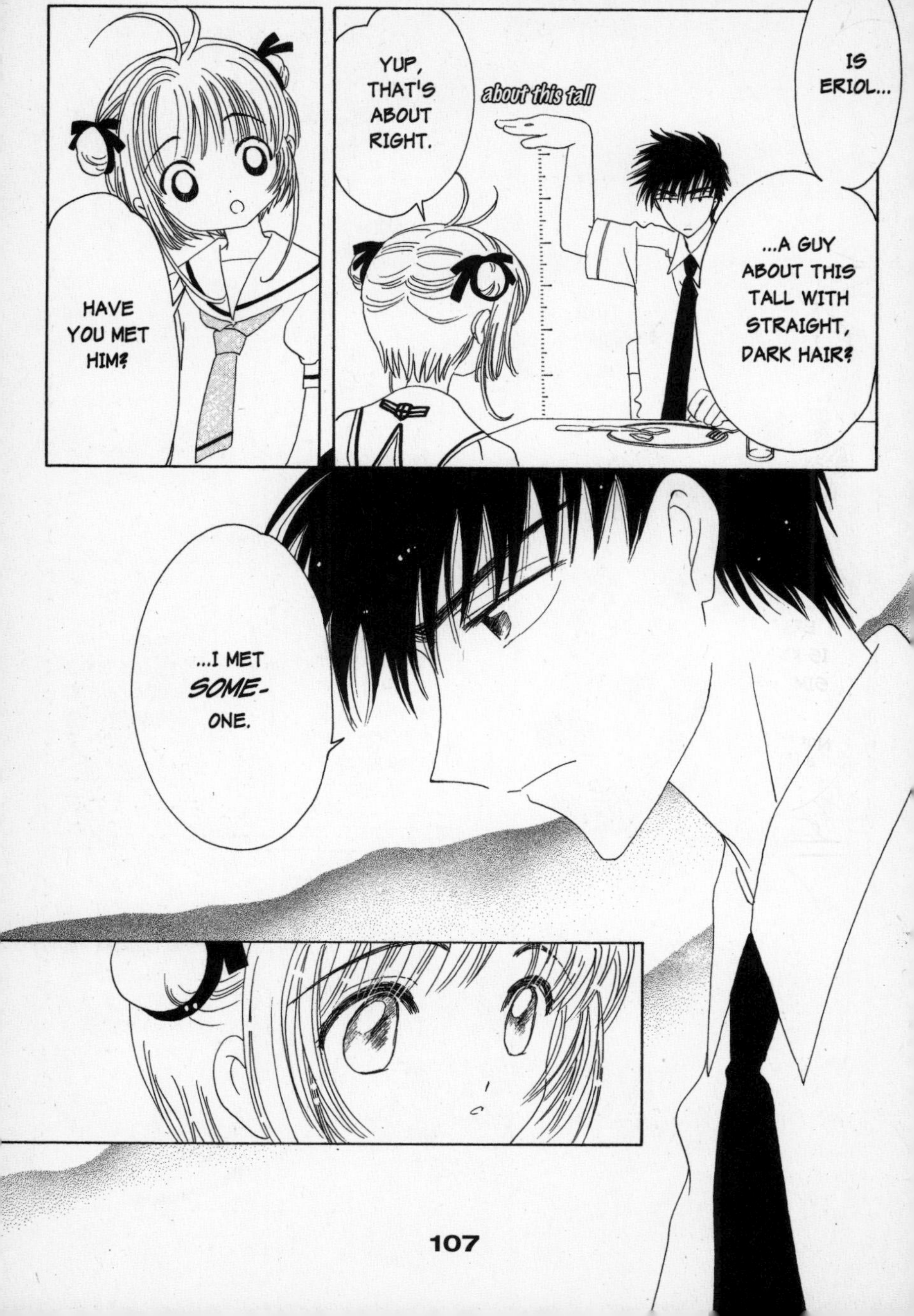
IS ERIOL...
...A GUY ABOUT THIS TALL WITH STRAIGHT, DARK HAIR?
about this tall
YUP, THAT'S ABOUT RIGHT.
HAVE YOU MET HIM?
...I MET SOME-ONE.

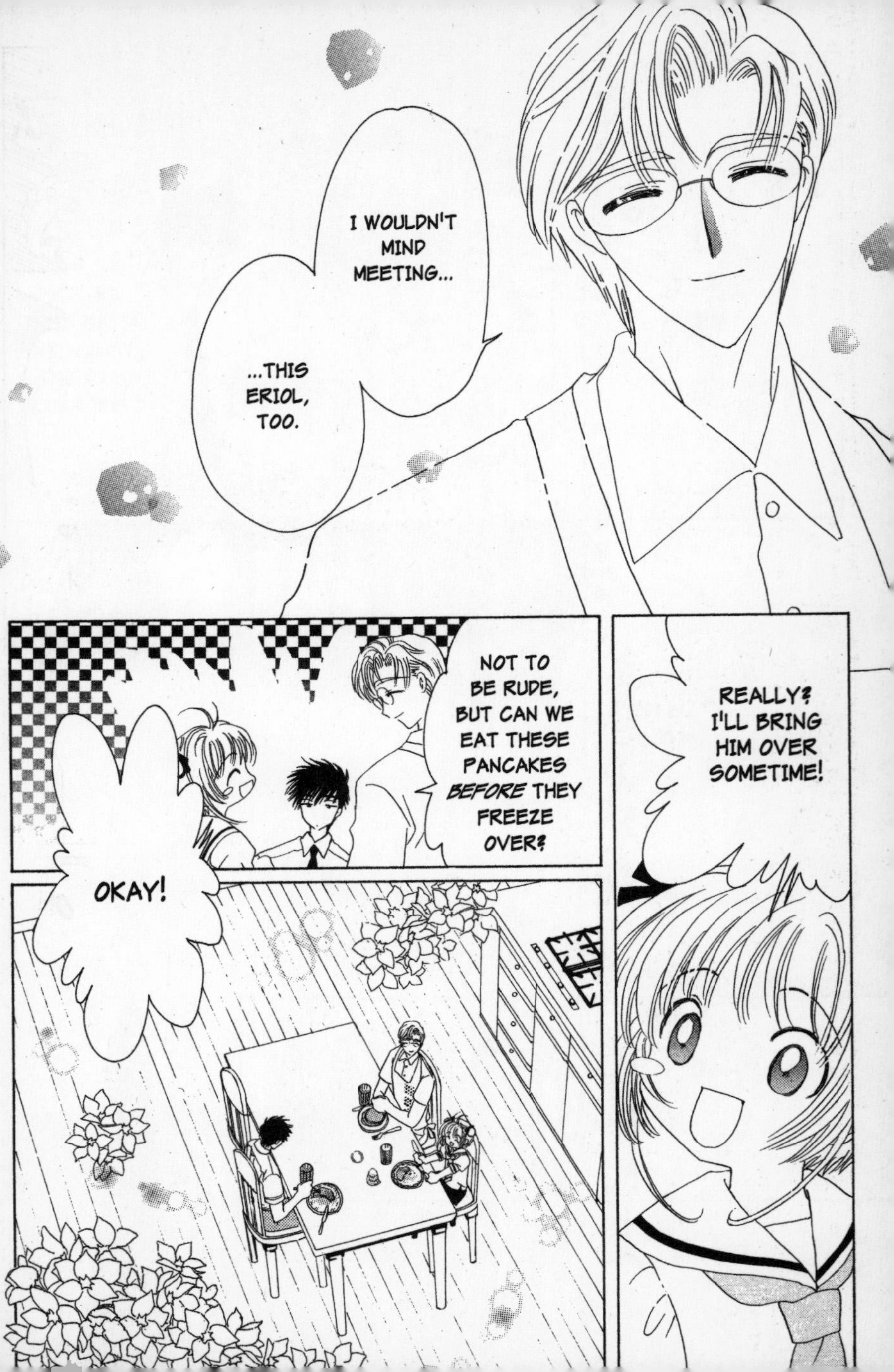
I WOULDN'T MIND MEETING...
...THIS ERIOL, TOO.
REALLY? I'LL BRING HIM OVER SOMETIME!
NOT TO BE RUDE, BUT CAN WE EAT THESE PANCAKES *BEFORE* THEY FREEZE OVER?
OKAY!

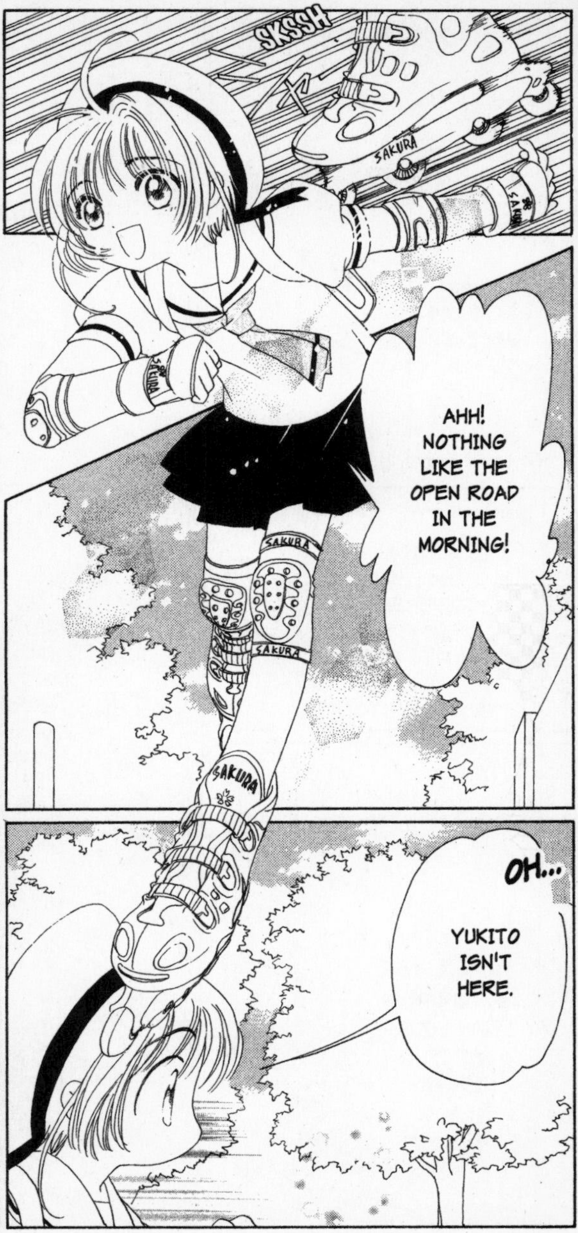
SKSSH
SAKURA
AHH! NOTHING LIKE THE OPEN ROAD IN THE MORNING!
OH...
YUKITO ISN'T HERE.

29

CLOW REED
BIRTHDAY:
UNKNOWN
JOB:
MAGICIAN
FAVORITE FOOD:
SWEET THINGS, WINE
LEAST FAVORITE FOOD:
NONE IN PARTICULAR
FAVORITE COLOR:
BLACK
FAVORITE FLOWER:
SAKURA
FAVORITE RECIPE:
ALL OF THEM
HOBBY:
SURPRISES
FAVORITE EVENT:
ANYTHING FUN
FAVORITE THING:
ANYTHING UNPREDICTABLE
WHAT HE'S THINKING:
GOOD QUESTION...

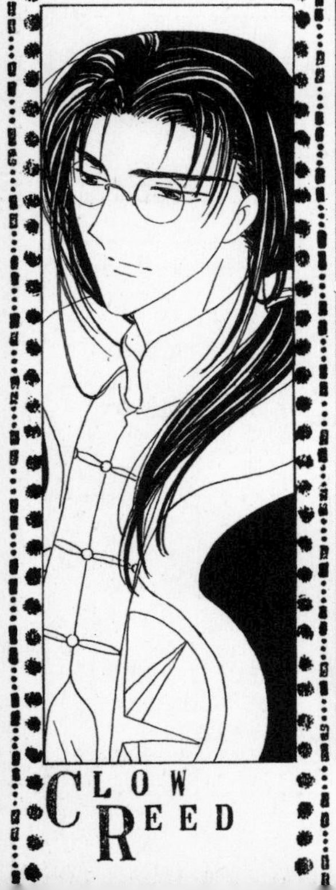

CLOW REED

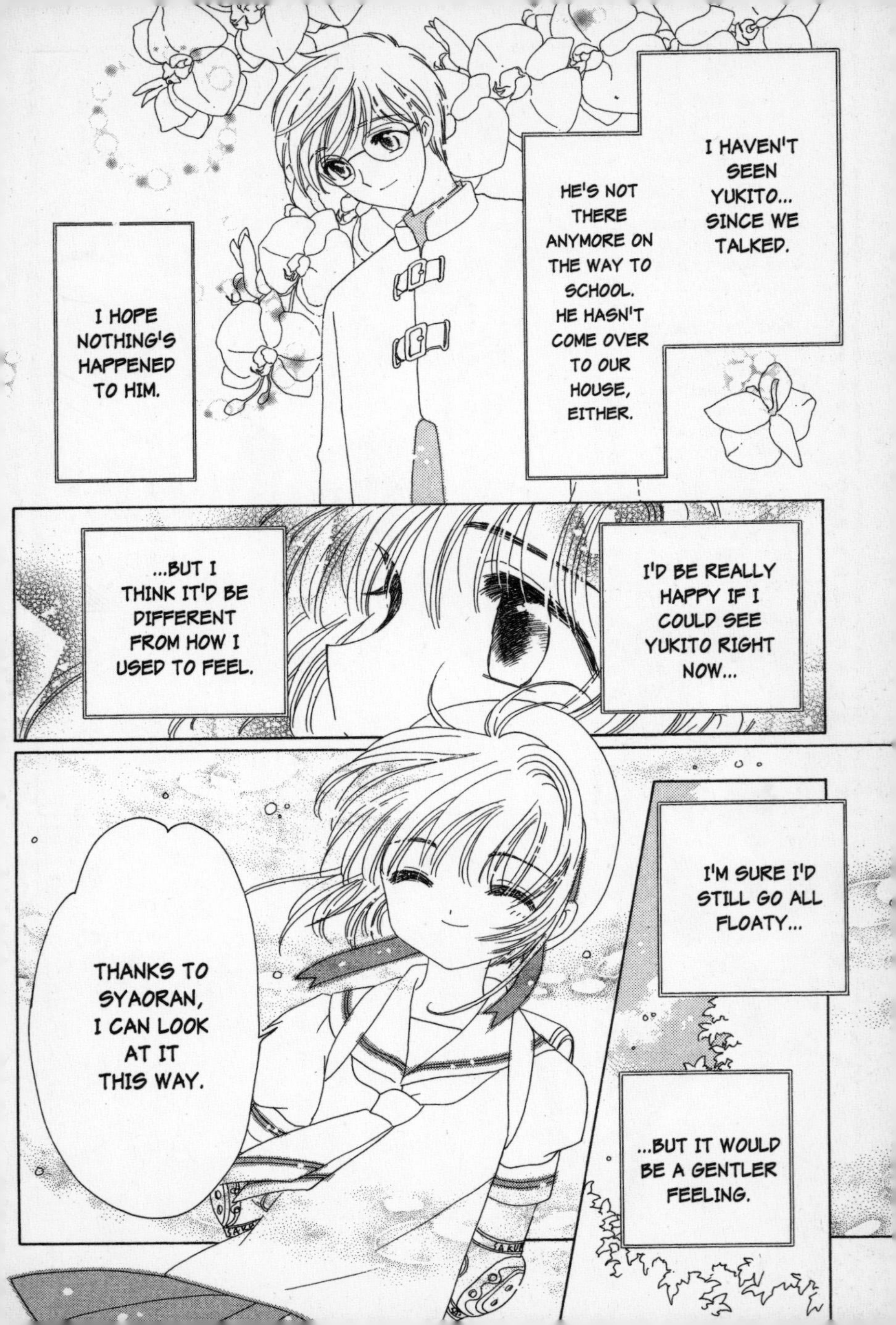
I HAVEN'T SEEN YUKITO... SINCE WE TALKED.
HE'S NOT THERE ANYMORE ON THE WAY TO SCHOOL. HE HASN'T COME OVER TO OUR HOUSE, EITHER.
I HOPE NOTHING'S HAPPENED TO HIM.
I'D BE REALLY HAPPY IF I COULD SEE YUKITO RIGHT NOW...
...BUT I THINK IT'D BE DIFFERENT FROM HOW I USED TO FEEL.
I'M SURE I'D STILL GO ALL FLOATY...
...BUT IT WOULD BE A GENTLER FEELING.
THANKS TO SYAORAN, I CAN LOOK AT IT THIS WAY.

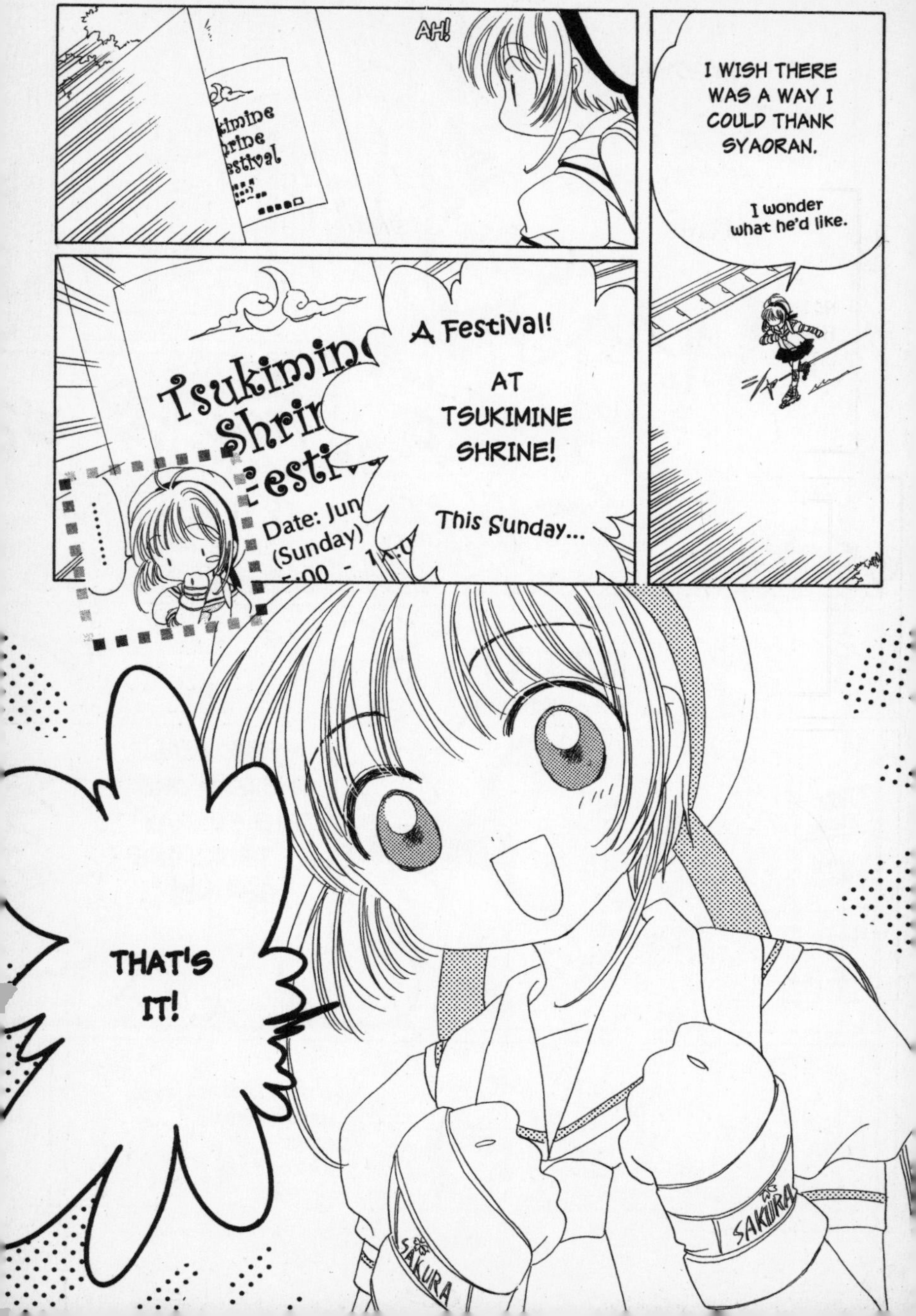
I WISH THERE WAS A WAY I COULD THANK SYAORAN.
I wonder what he'd like.
AH!
A Festival!
AT TSUKIMINE SHRINE!
This Sunday...
......
THAT'S IT!
SAKURA
SAKURA

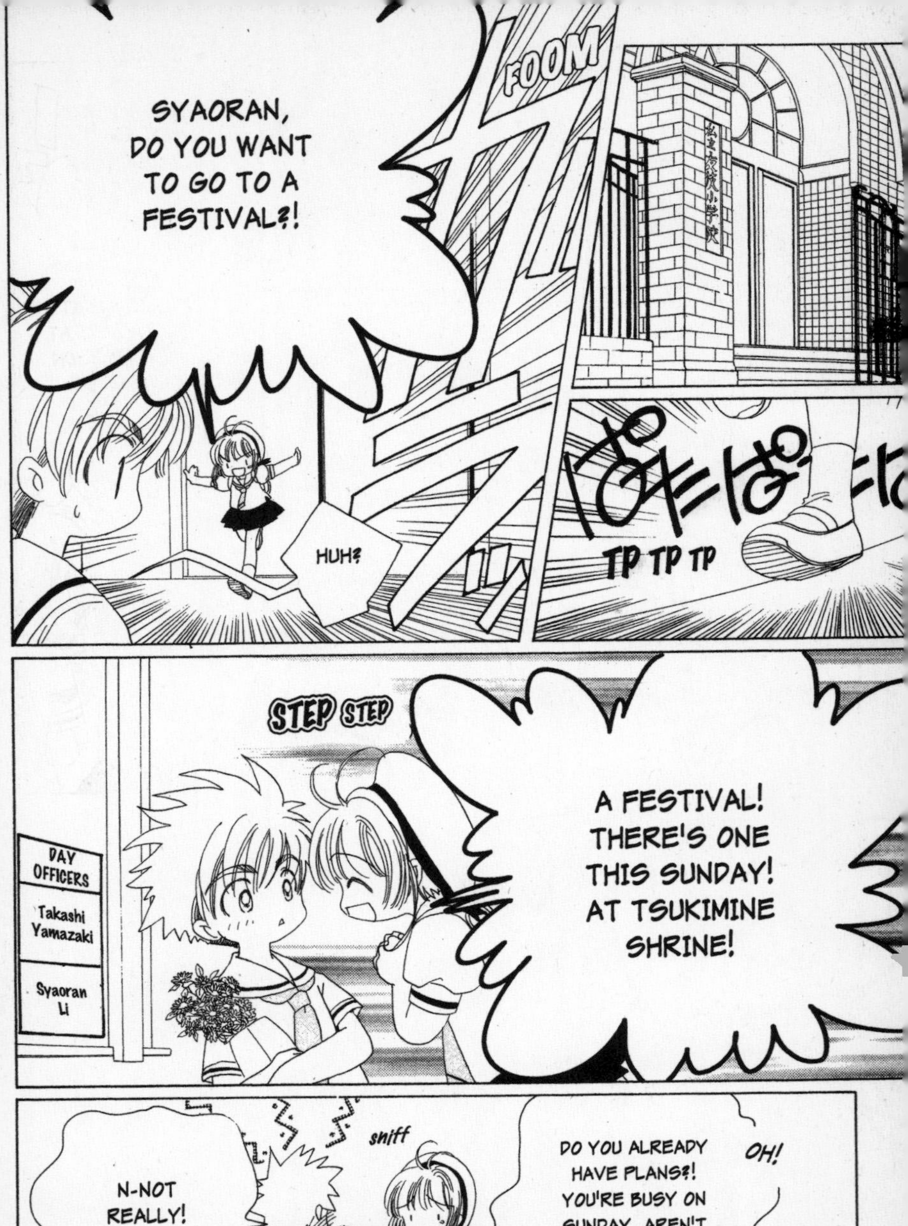
FOOM
TP TP TP
SYAORAN, DO YOU WANT TO GO TO A FESTIVAL?!
HUH?
STEP STEP
A FESTIVAL! THERE'S ONE THIS SUNDAY! AT TSUKIMINE SHRINE!
DAY OFFICERS
Takashi Yamazaki
Syaoran Li
OH!
DO YOU ALREADY HAVE PLANS?! YOU'RE BUSY ON SUNDAY, AREN'T YOU?!
sniff
N-NOT REALLY!

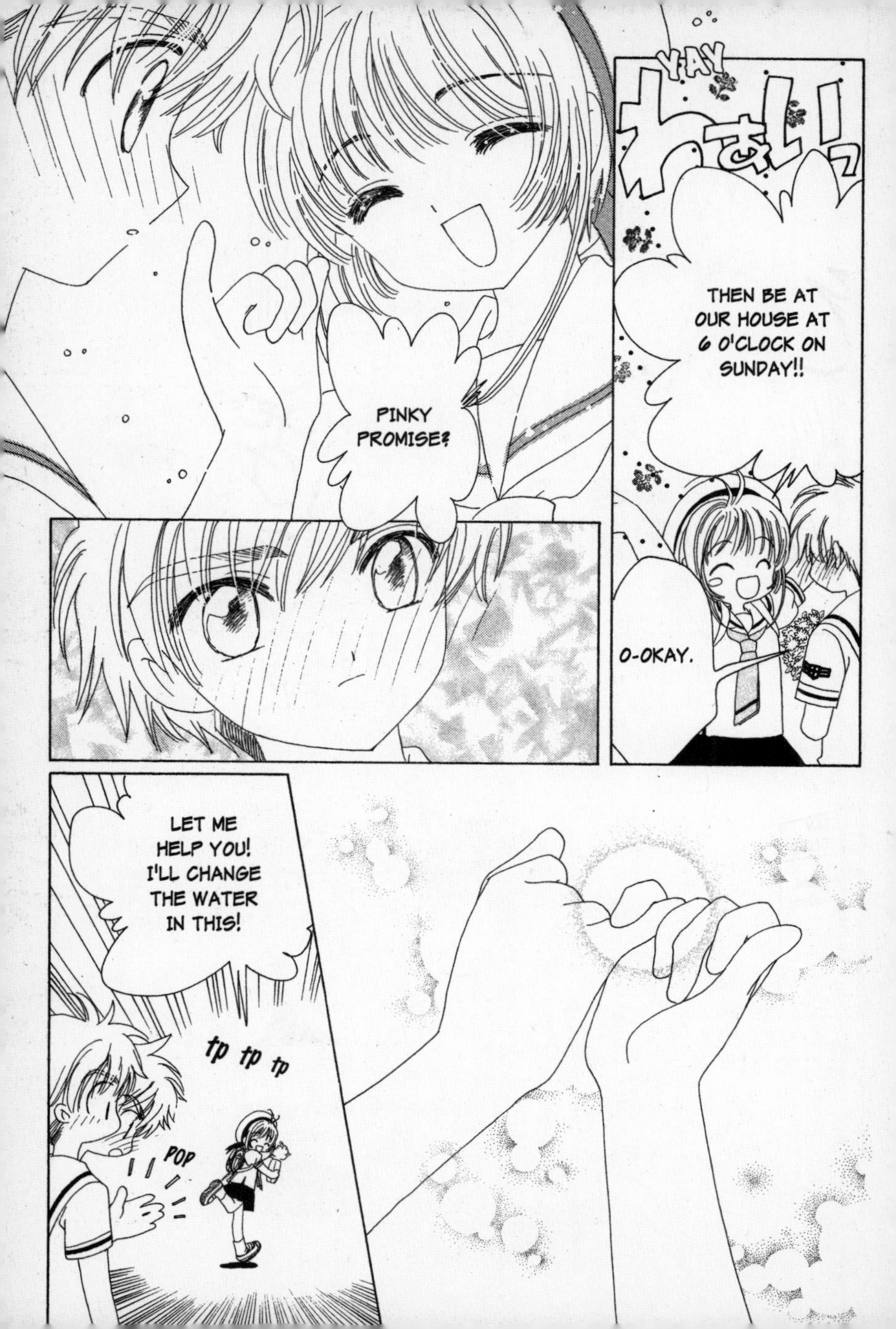
YAY
わあい
THEN BE AT OUR HOUSE AT 6 O'CLOCK ON SUNDAY!!
O-OKAY.
PINKY PROMISE?
LET ME HELP YOU! I'LL CHANGE THE WATER IN THIS!
tp tp tp
POP

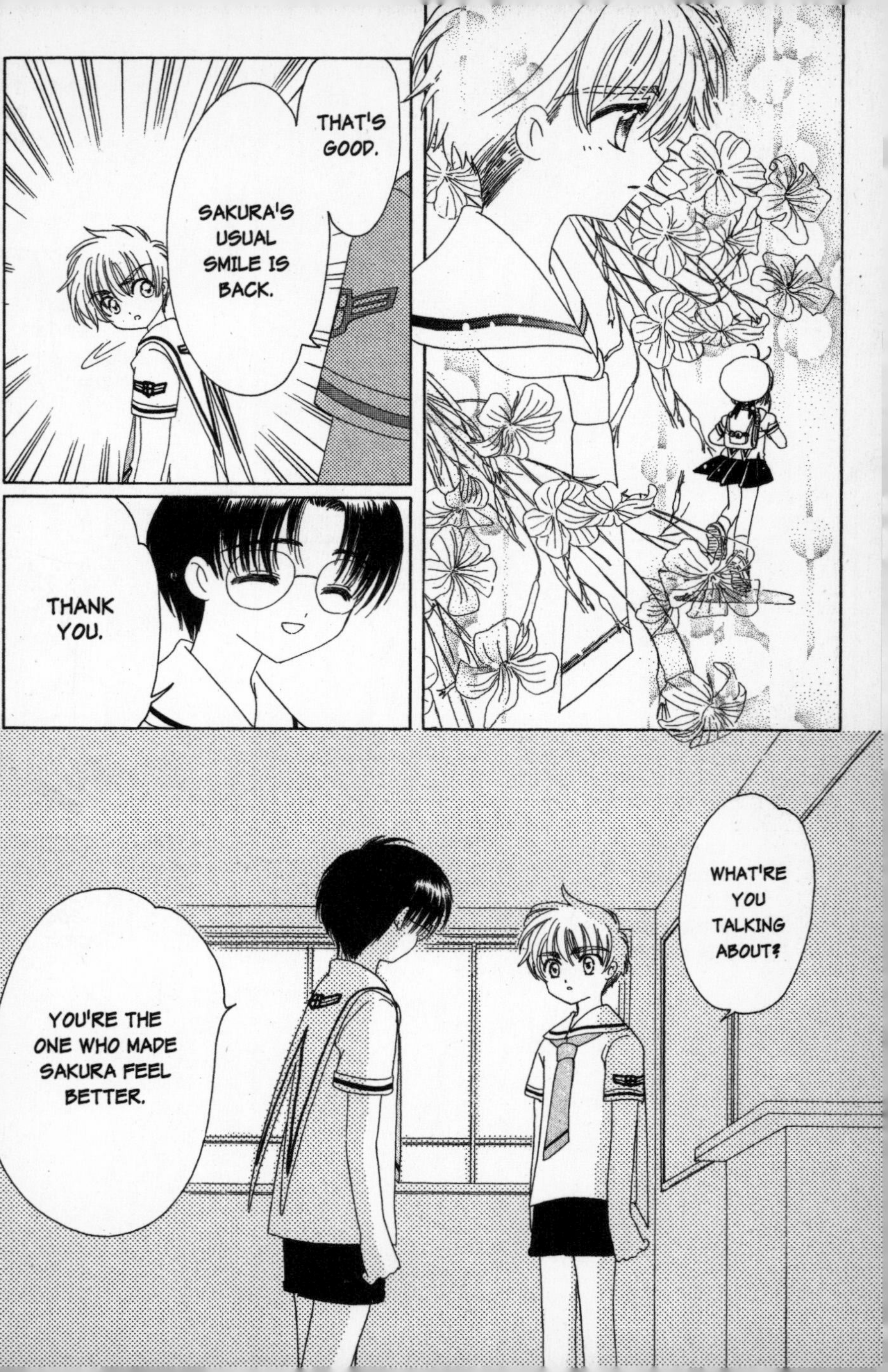
THAT'S GOOD.
SAKURA'S USUAL SMILE IS BACK.
THANK YOU.
WHAT'RE YOU TALKING ABOUT?
YOU'RE THE ONE WHO MADE SAKURA FEEL BETTER.

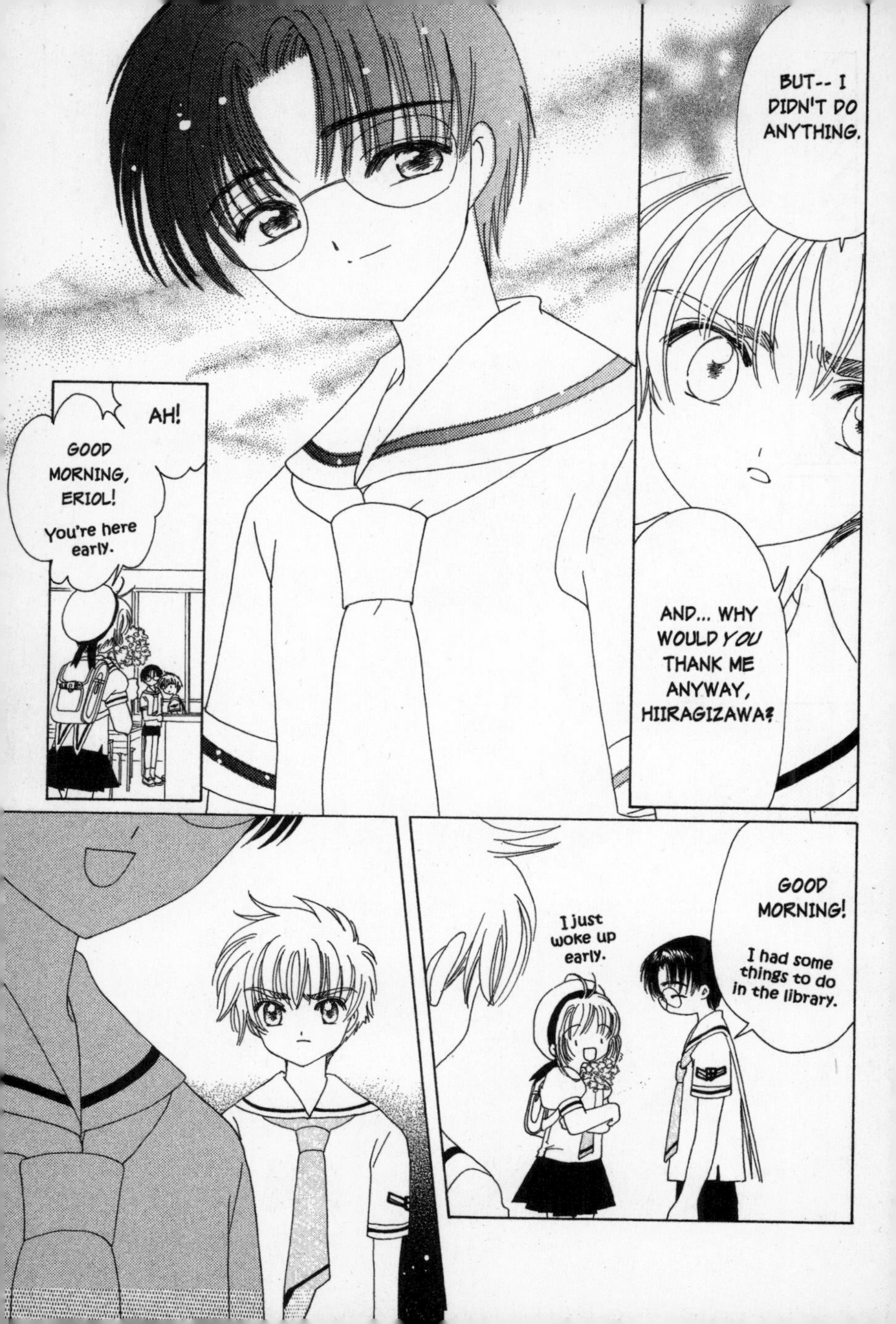
BUT-- I DIDN'T DO ANYTHING.
AND... WHY WOULD *YOU* THANK ME ANYWAY, HIIRAGIZAWA?
AH!
GOOD MORNING, ERIOL!
You're here early.
GOOD MORNING!
I had some things to do in the library.
I just woke up early.

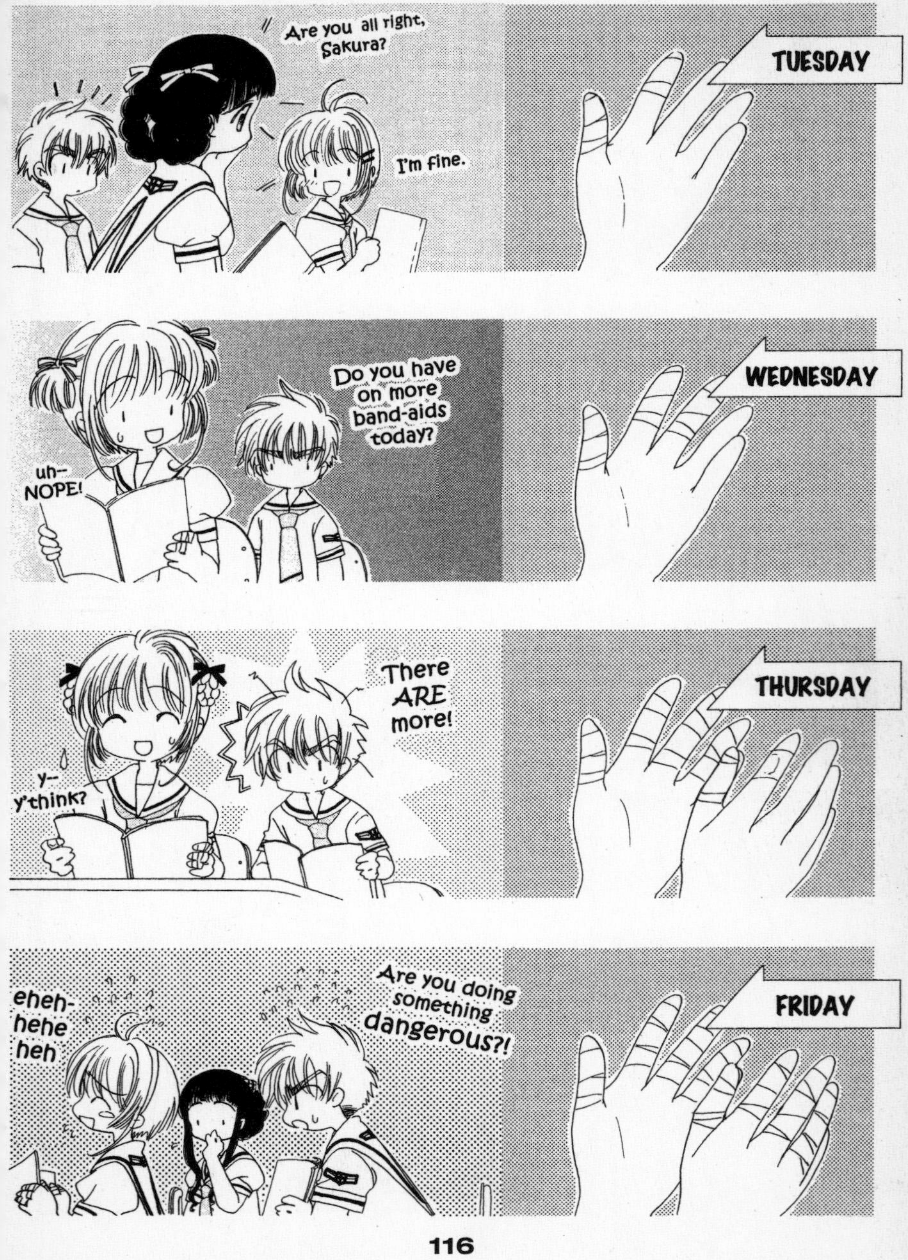
TUESDAY
Are you all right, Sakura?
I'm fine.
WEDNESDAY
Do you have on more band-aids today?
uh-- NOPE!
THURSDAY
There ARE more!
y-- y'think?
FRIDAY
Are you doing something dangerous?!
eheh-hehe heh

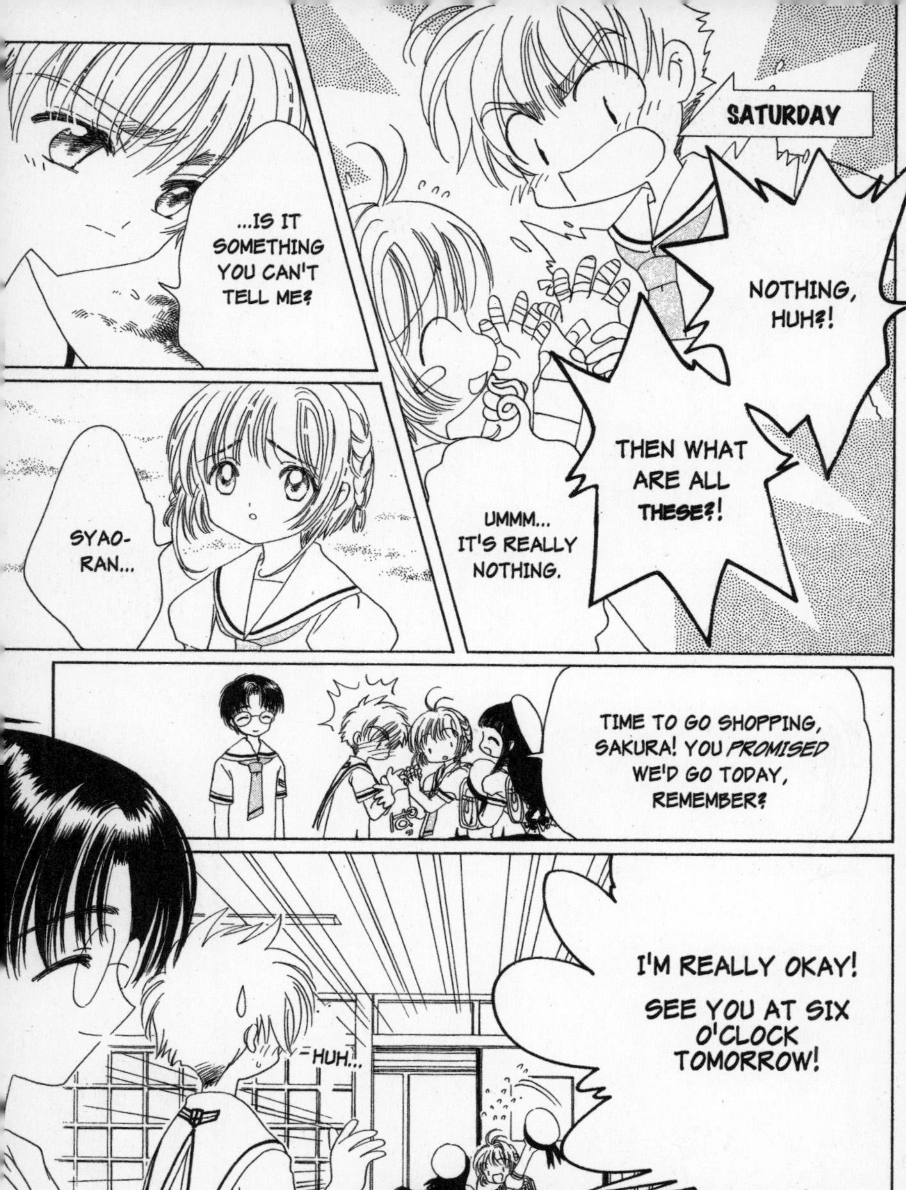
SATURDAY
NOTHING, HUH?!
THEN WHAT ARE ALL THESE?!
UMMM... IT'S REALLY NOTHING.
...IS IT SOMETHING YOU CAN'T TELL ME?
SYAO-RAN...
TIME TO GO SHOPPING, SAKURA! YOU *PROMISED* WE'D GO TODAY, REMEMBER?
I'M REALLY OKAY!
SEE YOU AT SIX O'CLOCK TOMORROW!
HUH...

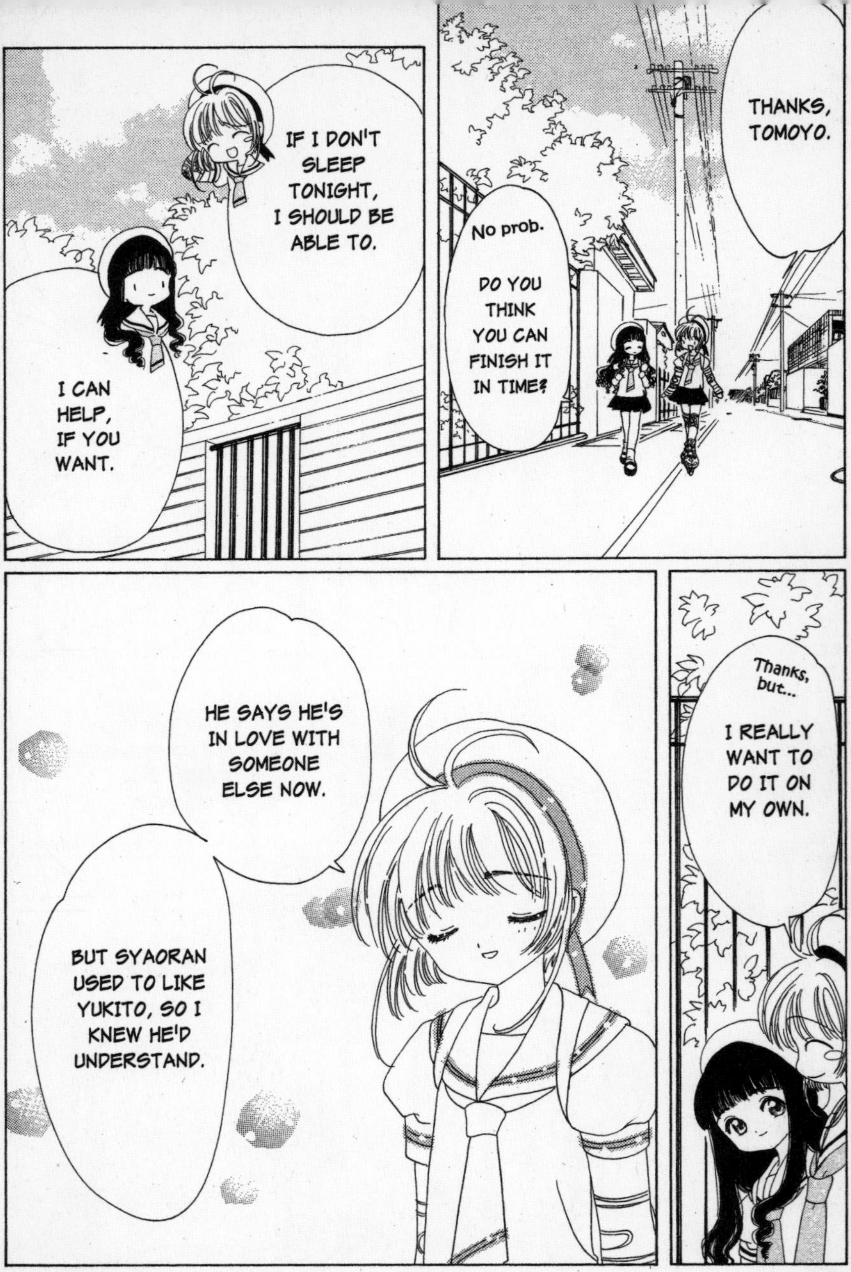
THANKS, TOMOYO.
No prob.
DO YOU THINK YOU CAN FINISH IT IN TIME?
IF I DON'T SLEEP TONIGHT, I SHOULD BE ABLE TO.
I CAN HELP, IF YOU WANT.
Thanks, but...
I REALLY WANT TO DO IT ON MY OWN.
HE SAYS HE'S IN LOVE WITH SOMEONE ELSE NOW.
BUT SYAORAN USED TO LIKE YUKITO, SO I KNEW HE'D UNDERSTAND.

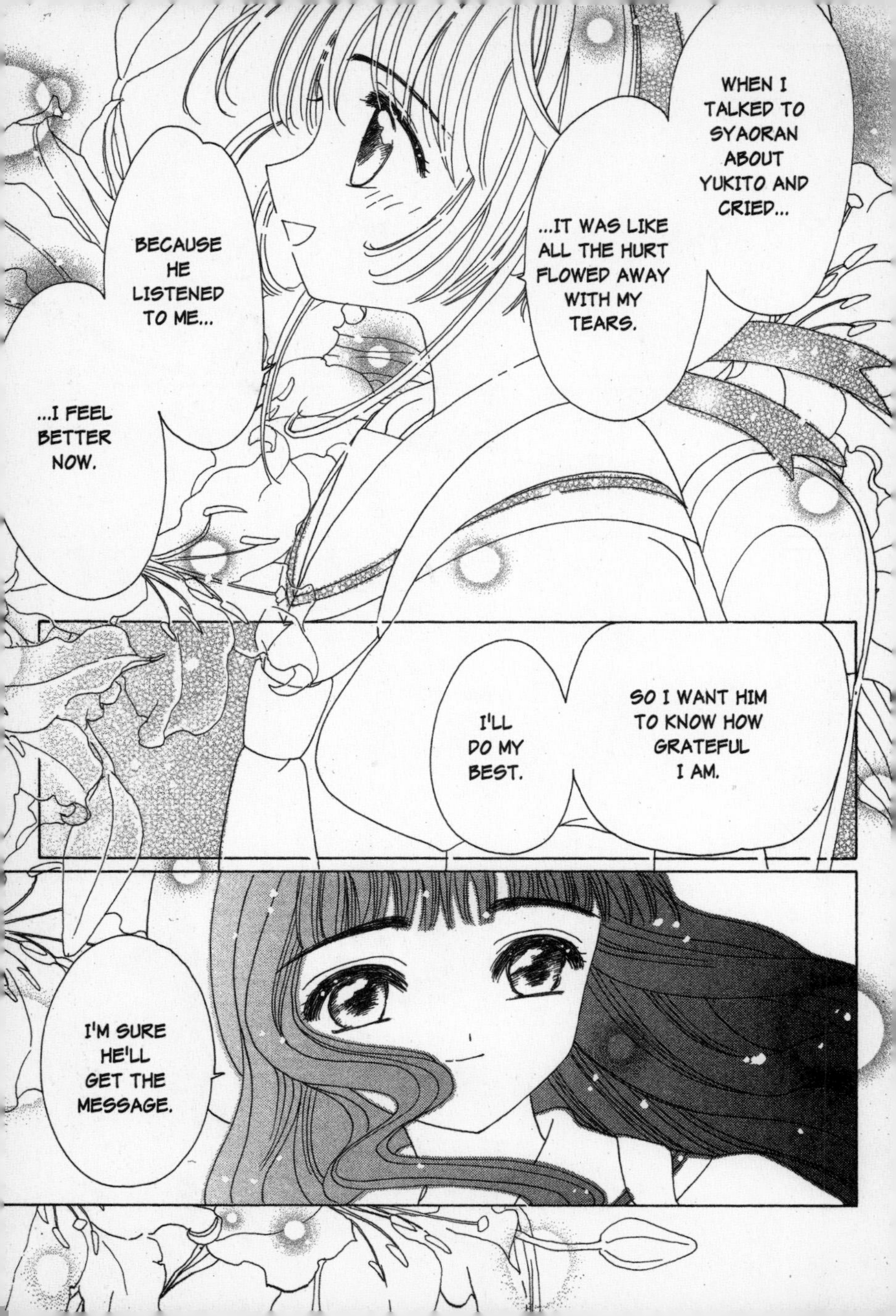
WHEN I TALKED TO SYAORAN ABOUT YUKITO AND CRIED...
...IT WAS LIKE ALL THE HURT FLOWED AWAY WITH MY TEARS.
BECAUSE HE LISTENED TO ME...
...I FEEL BETTER NOW.
SO I WANT HIM TO KNOW HOW GRATEFUL I AM.
I'LL DO MY BEST.
I'M SURE HE'LL GET THE MESSAGE.

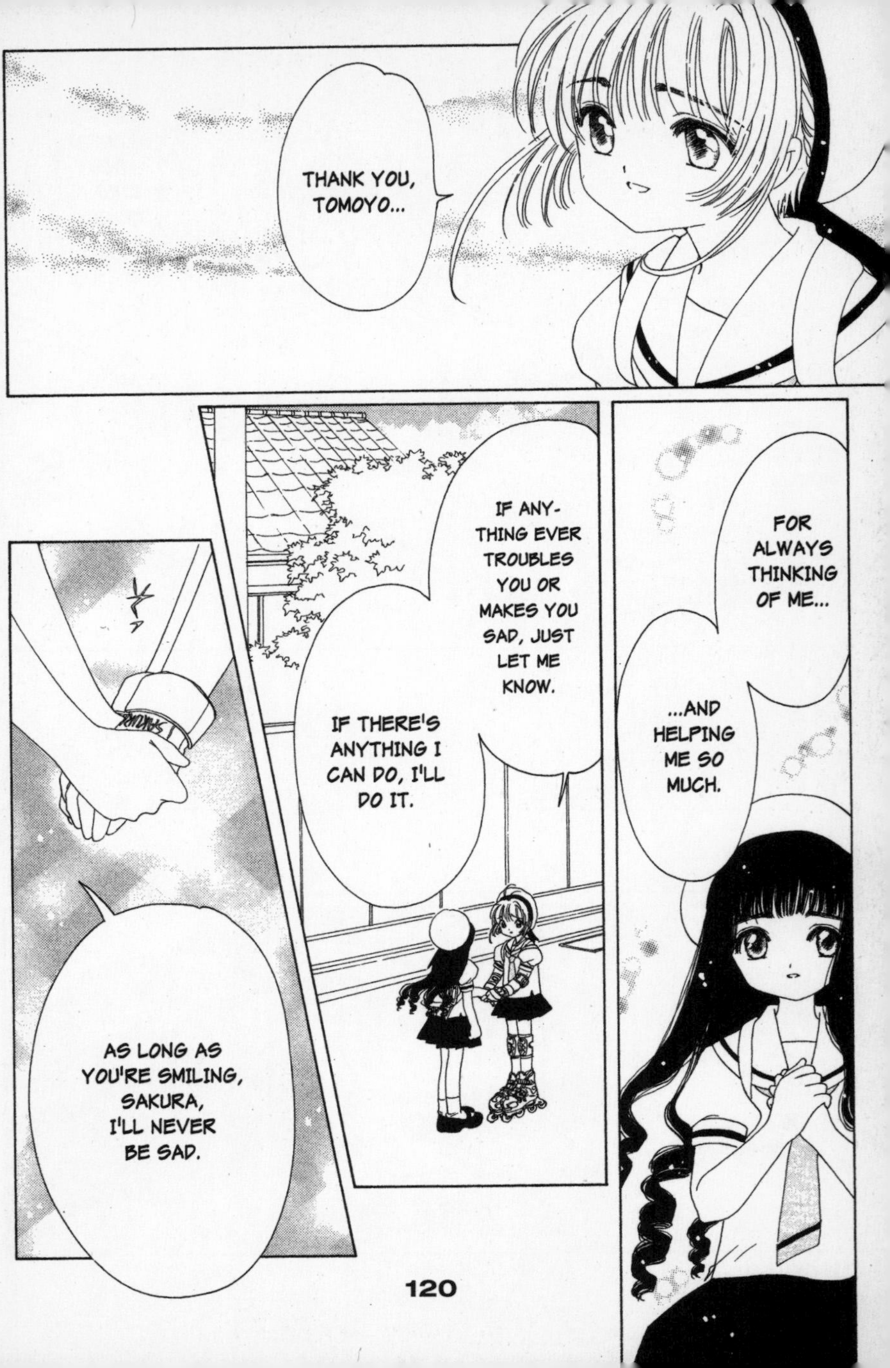
THANK YOU, TOMOYO...
FOR ALWAYS THINKING OF ME...
...AND HELPING ME SO MUCH.
IF ANY-THING EVER TROUBLES YOU OR MAKES YOU SAD, JUST LET ME KNOW.
IF THERE'S ANYTHING I CAN DO, I'LL DO IT.
AS LONG AS YOU'RE SMILING, SAKURA, I'LL NEVER BE SAD.

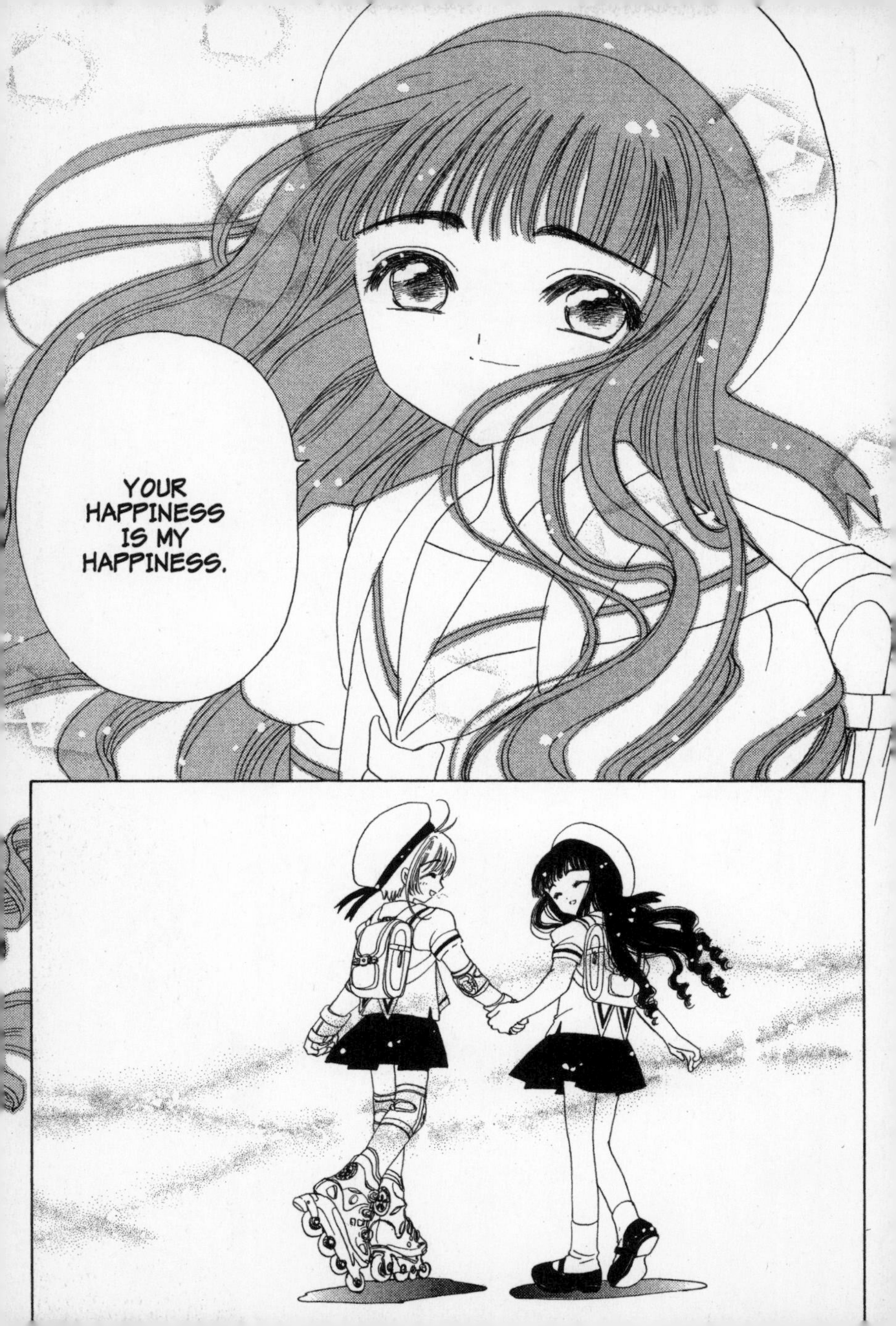
YOUR HAPPINESS IS MY HAPPINESS.

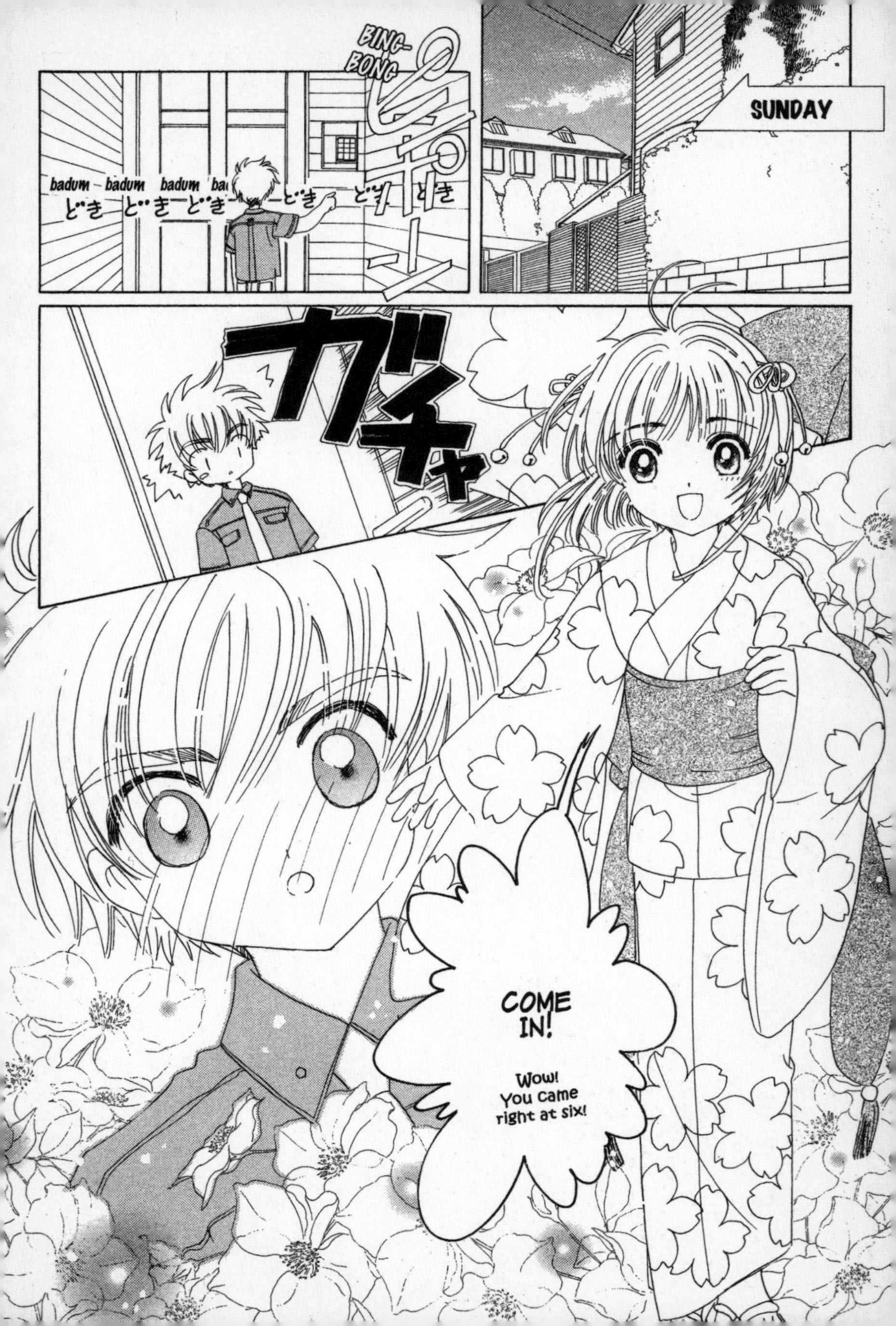
SUNDAY
BING-BONG
ピンポーン
badum badum badum ba
どき どき どき どき どき どき
ガチャ
COME IN!
Wow! You came right at six!

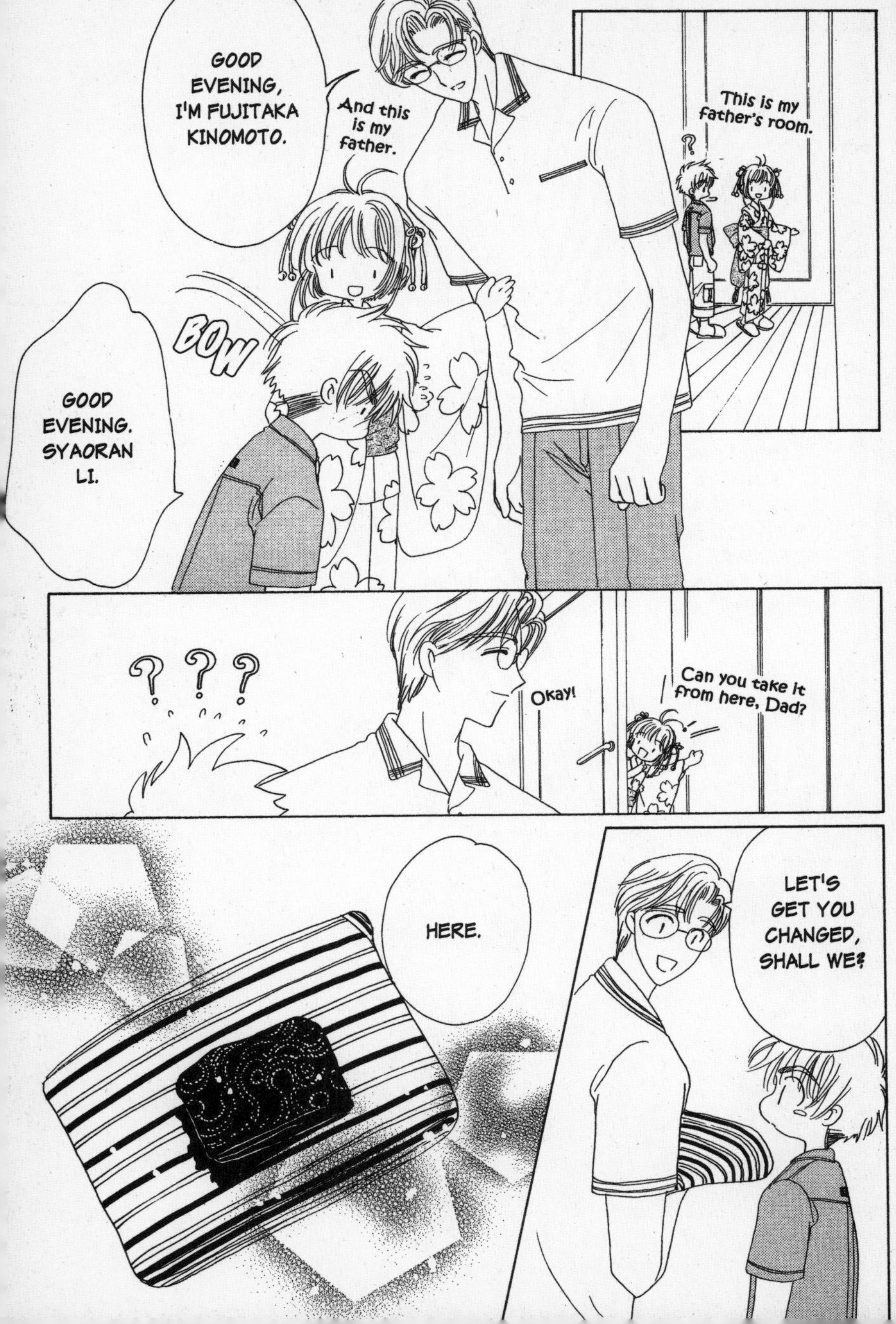
This is my father's room.
And this is my father.
GOOD EVENING, I'M FUJITAKA KINOMOTO.
BOW
GOOD EVENING. SYAORAN LI.
Can you take it from here, Dad?
Okay!
???
LET'S GET YOU CHANGED, SHALL WE?
HERE.

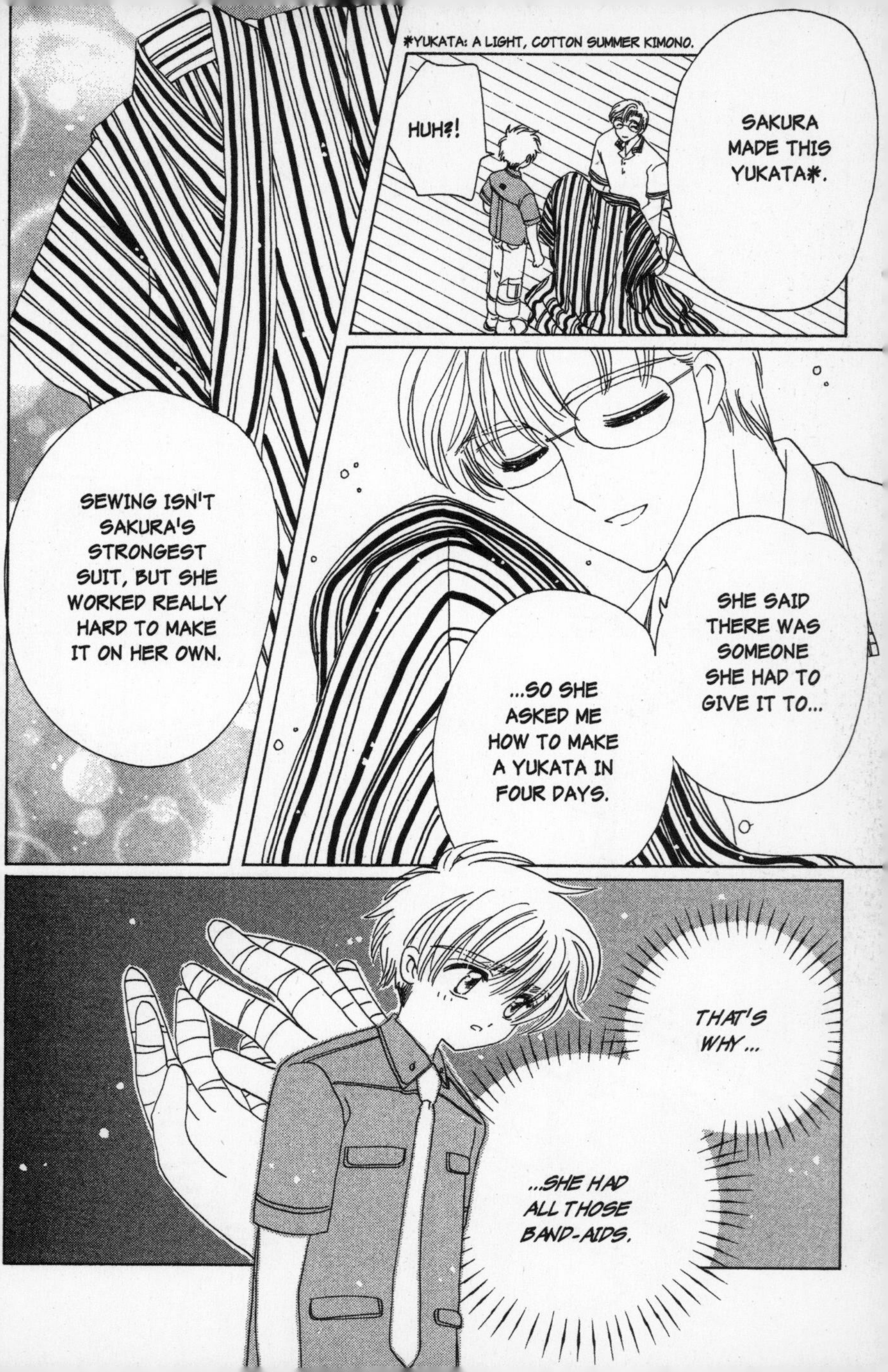
SAKURA MADE THIS YUKATA*.
HUH?!
*YUKATA: A LIGHT, COTTON SUMMER KIMONO.
SHE SAID THERE WAS SOMEONE SHE HAD TO GIVE IT TO...
...SO SHE ASKED ME HOW TO MAKE A YUKATA IN FOUR DAYS.
SEWING ISN'T SAKURA'S STRONGEST SUIT, BUT SHE WORKED REALLY HARD TO MAKE IT ON HER OWN.
THAT'S WHY...
...SHE HAD ALL THOSE BAND-AIDS.

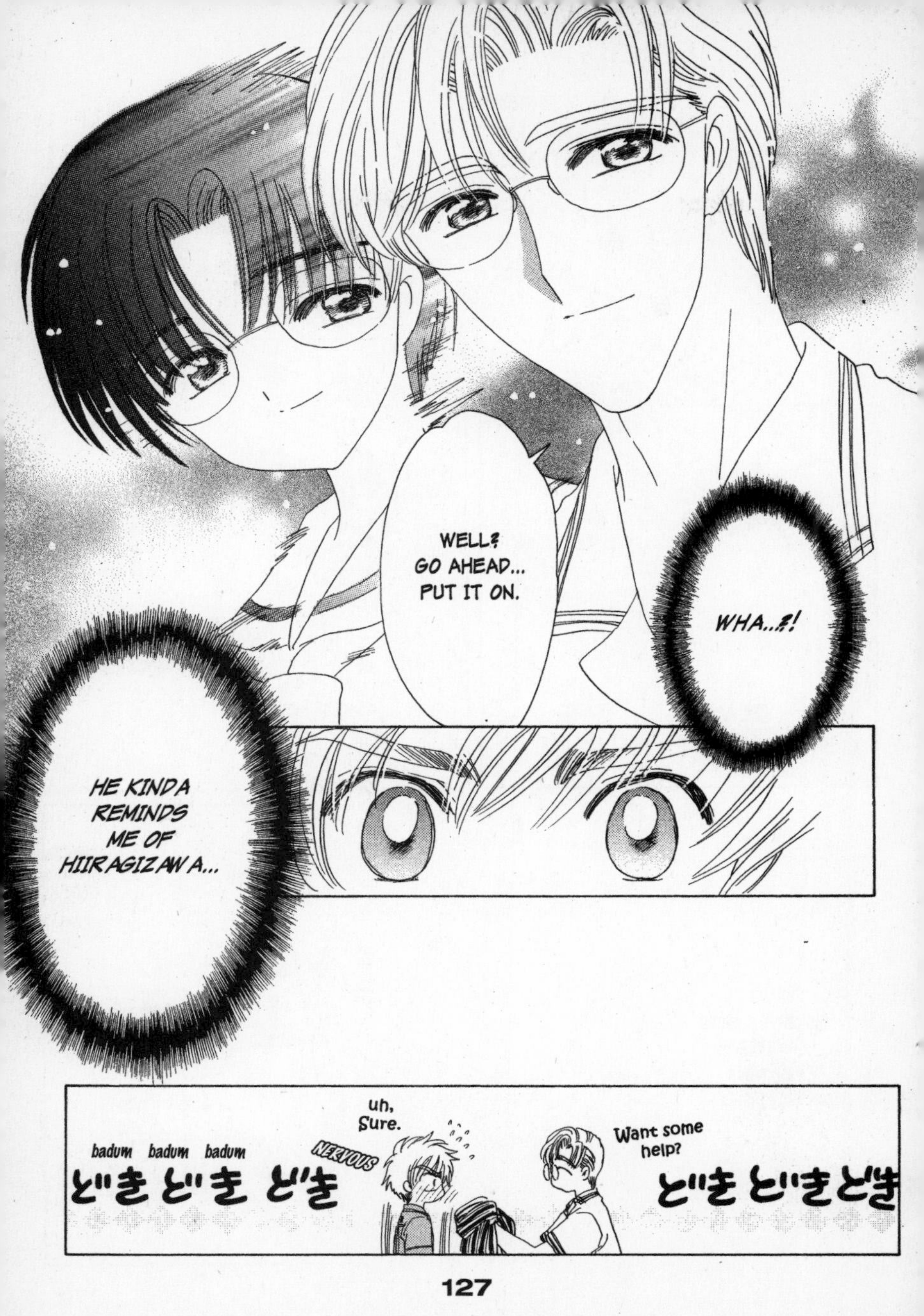
WELL? GO AHEAD... PUT IT ON.
WHA...?!
HE KINDA REMINDS ME OF HIIRAGIZAWA...
Want some help?
どきどきどき
uh, Sure.
NERVOUS
badum badum badum
どきどき どき

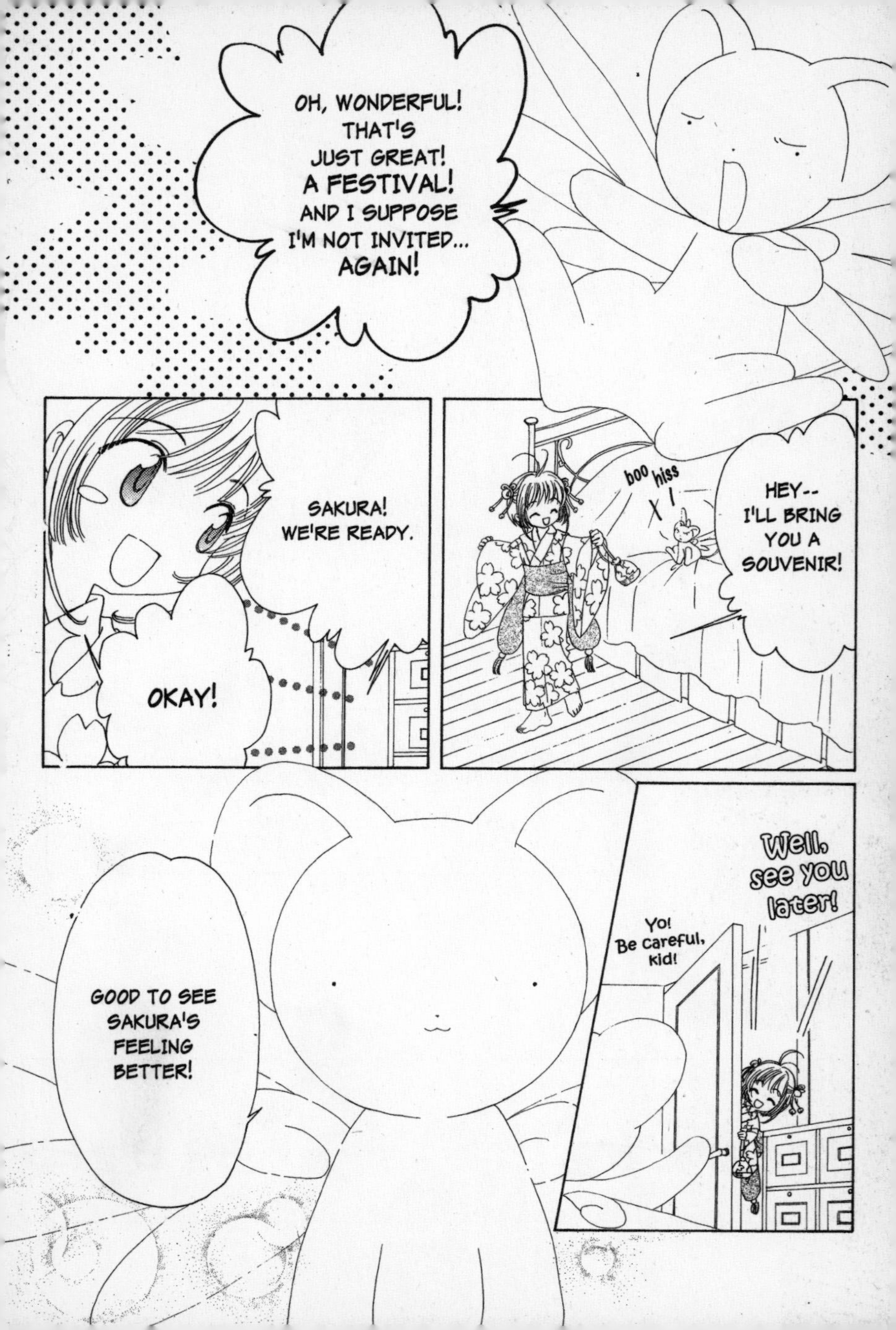
OH, WONDERFUL! THAT'S JUST GREAT! A FESTIVAL! AND I SUPPOSE I'M NOT INVITED... AGAIN!
HEY-- I'LL BRING YOU A SOUVENIR!
boo hiss
SAKURA! WE'RE READY.
OKAY!
Well, see you later!
Yo! Be careful, kid!
GOOD TO SEE SAKURA'S FEELING BETTER!

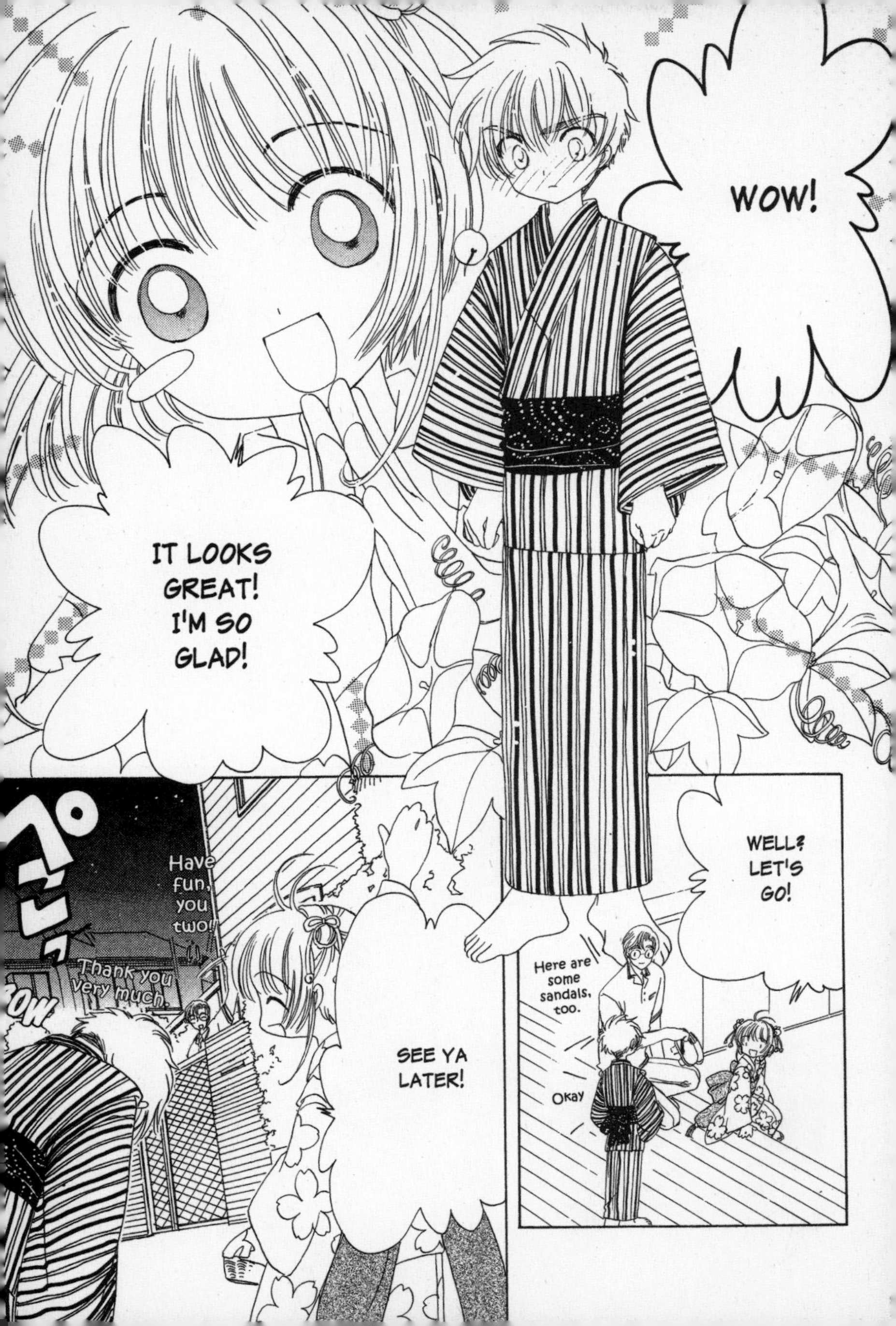
WOW!
IT LOOKS GREAT! I'M SO GLAD!
WELL? LET'S GO!
Here are some sandals, too.
Okay
SEE YA LATER!
Have fun, you two!
Thank you very much.

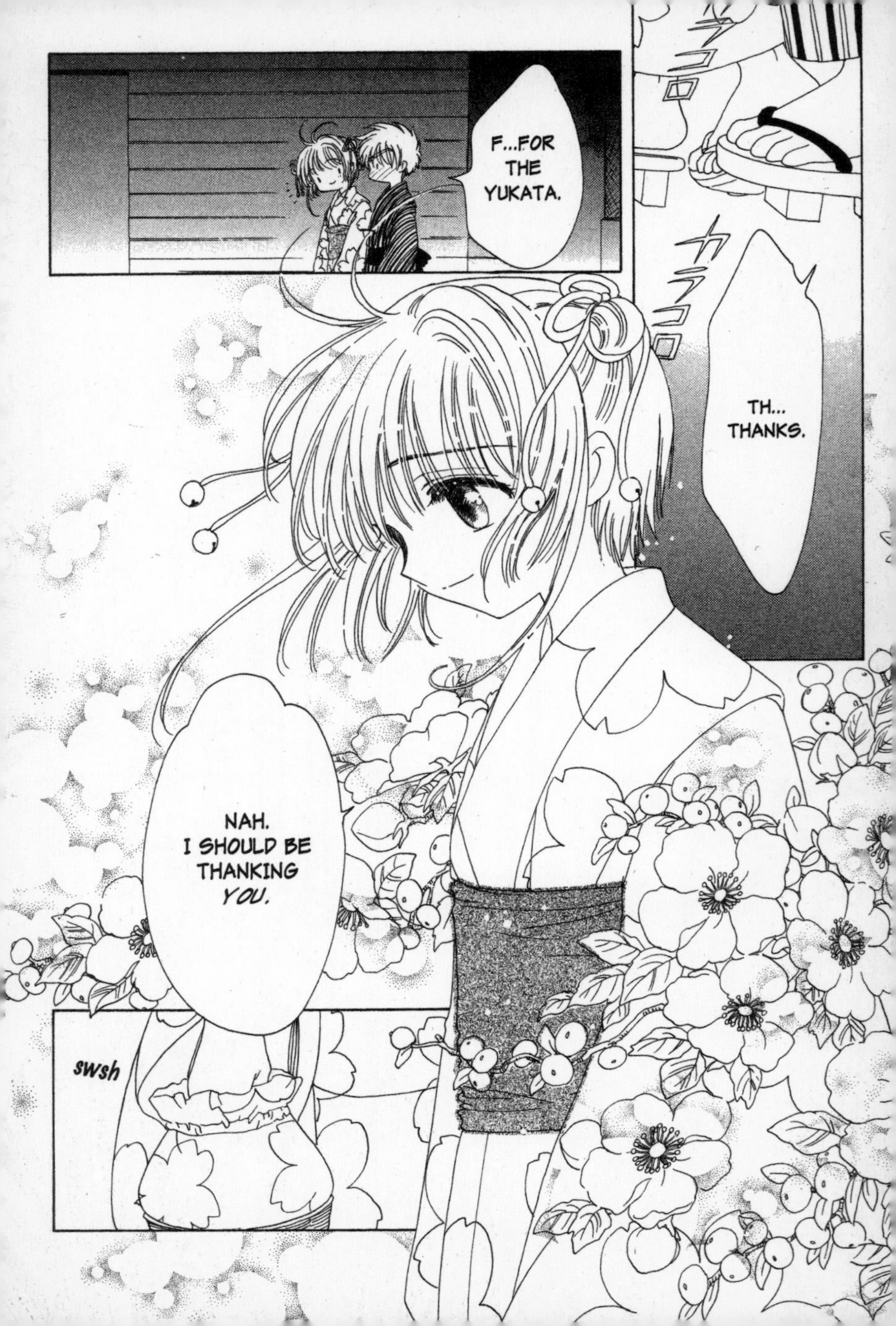
カラコロ
TH... THANKS.
F...FOR THE YUKATA.
NAH. I SHOULD BE THANKING *YOU*.
swsh

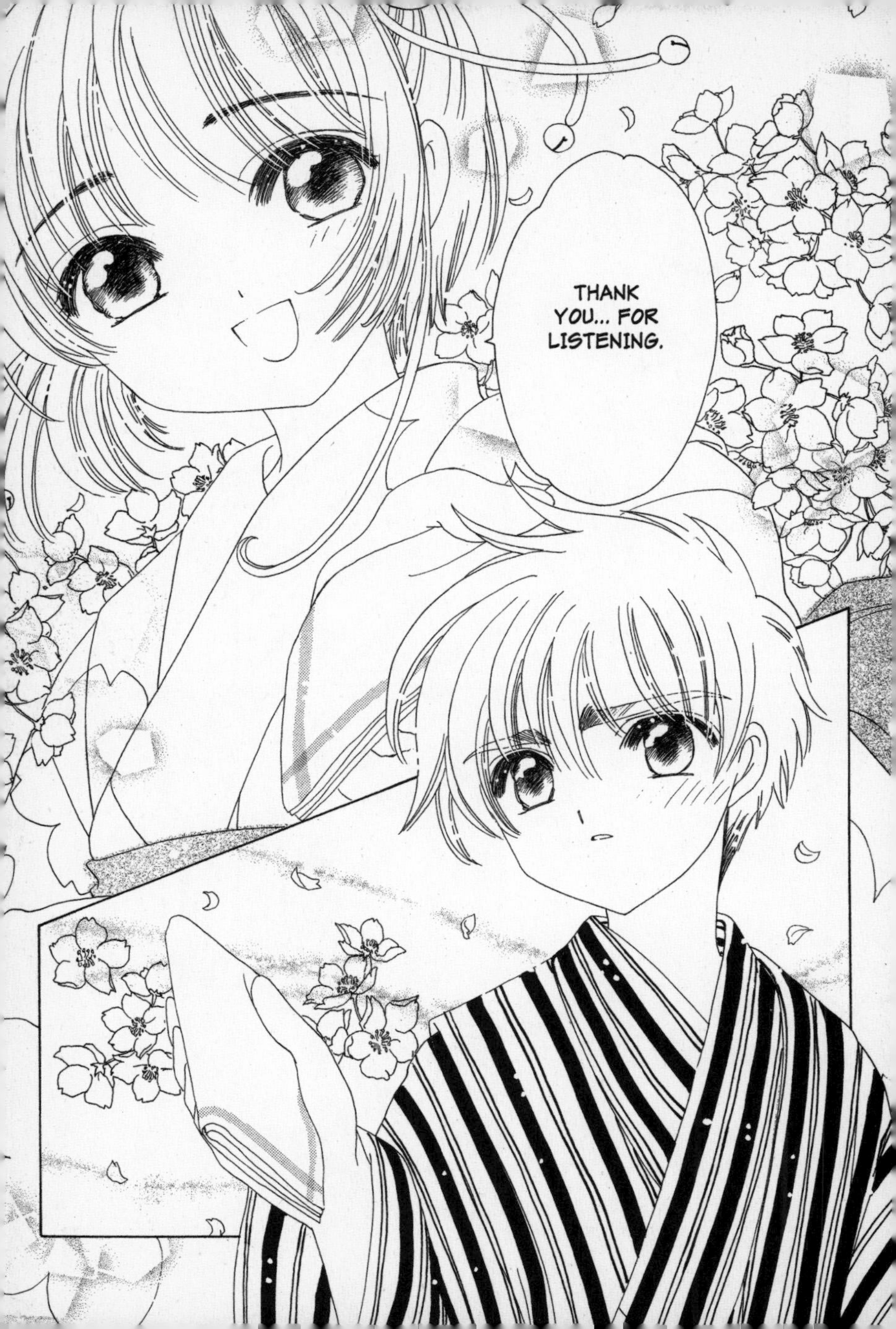
THANK YOU... FOR LISTENING.

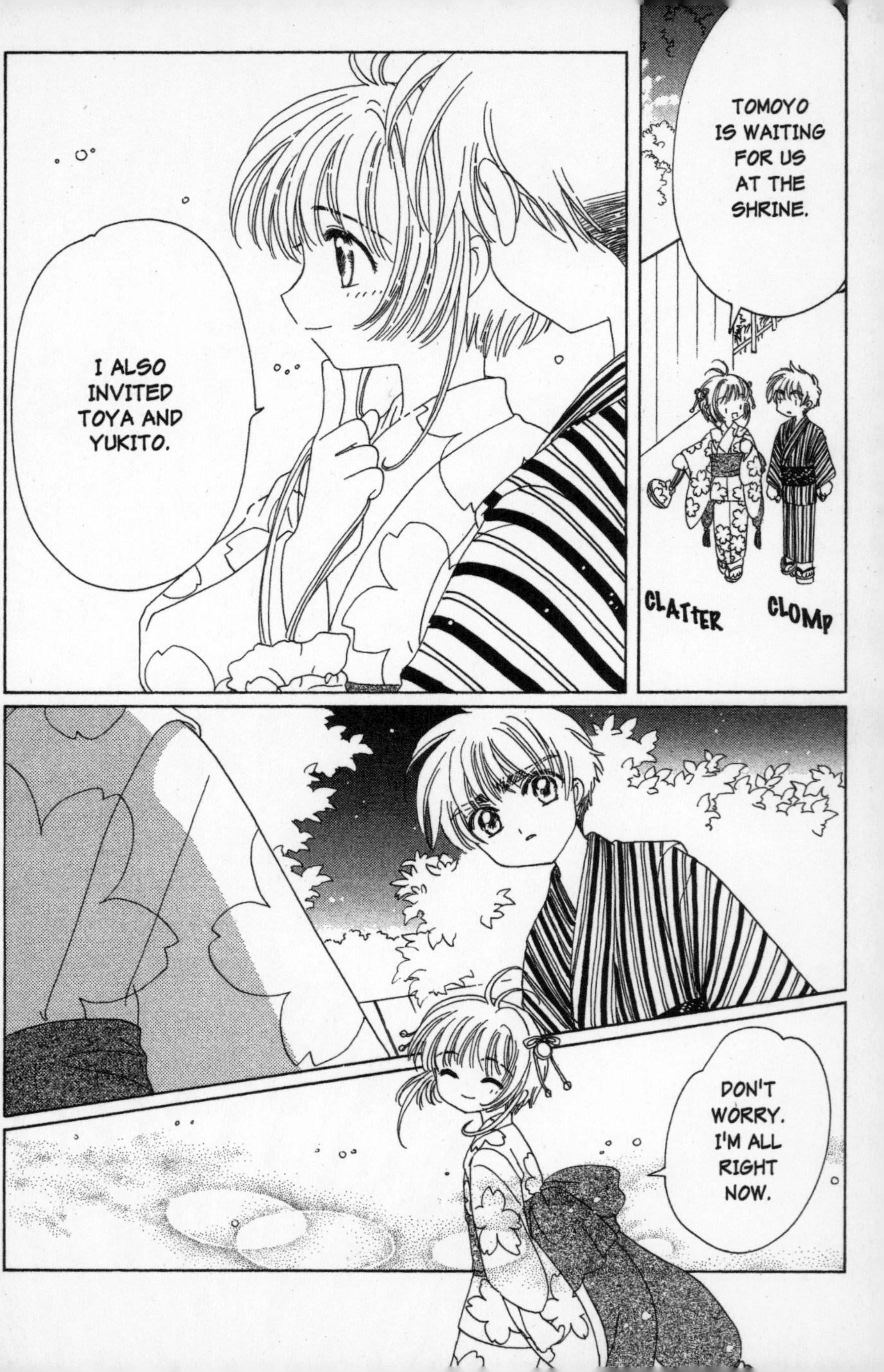
TOMOYO IS WAITING FOR US AT THE SHRINE.
CLATTER
CLOMP
I ALSO INVITED TOYA AND YUKITO.
DON'T WORRY. I'M ALL RIGHT NOW.

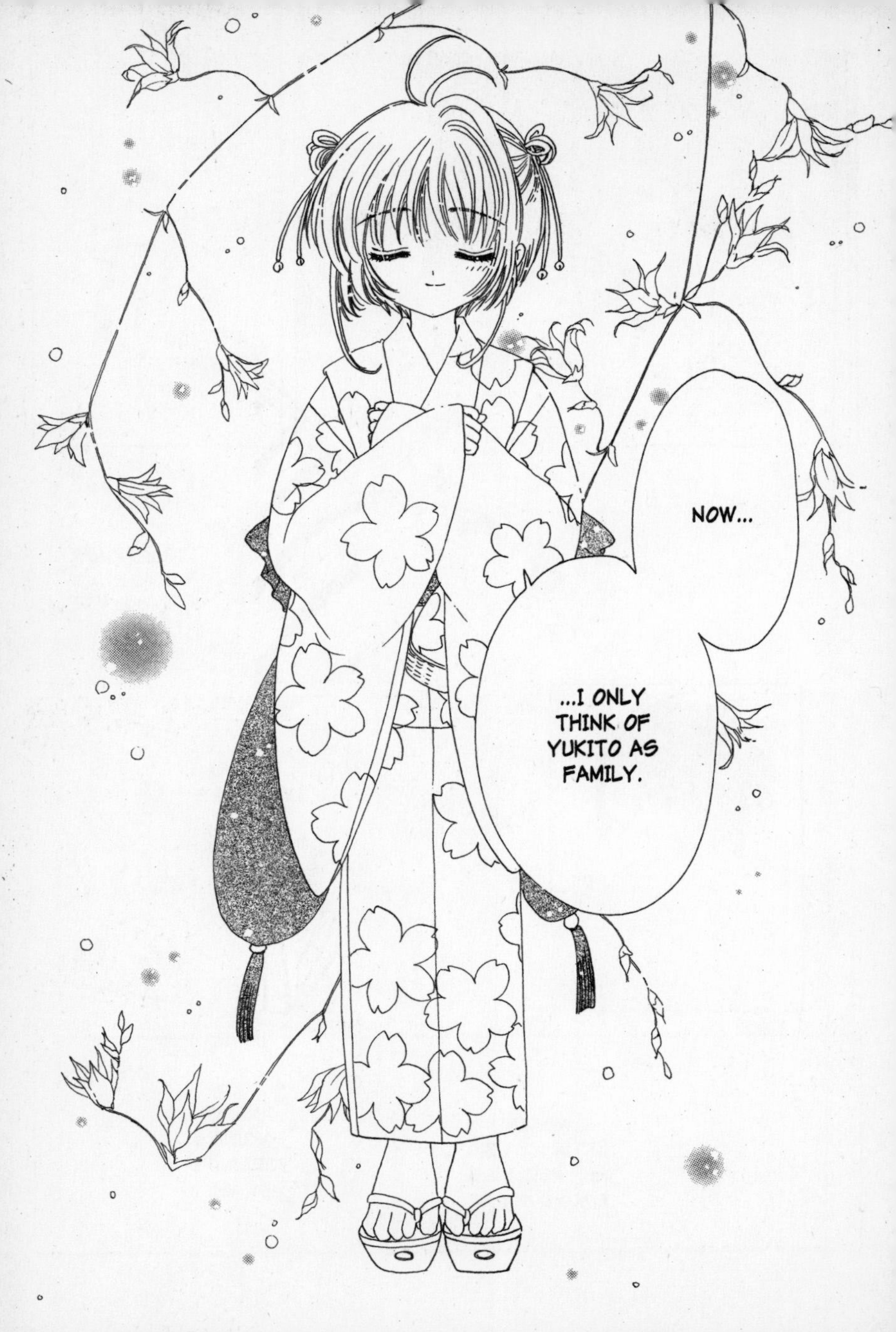
NOW...
...I ONLY THINK OF YUKITO AS FAMILY.

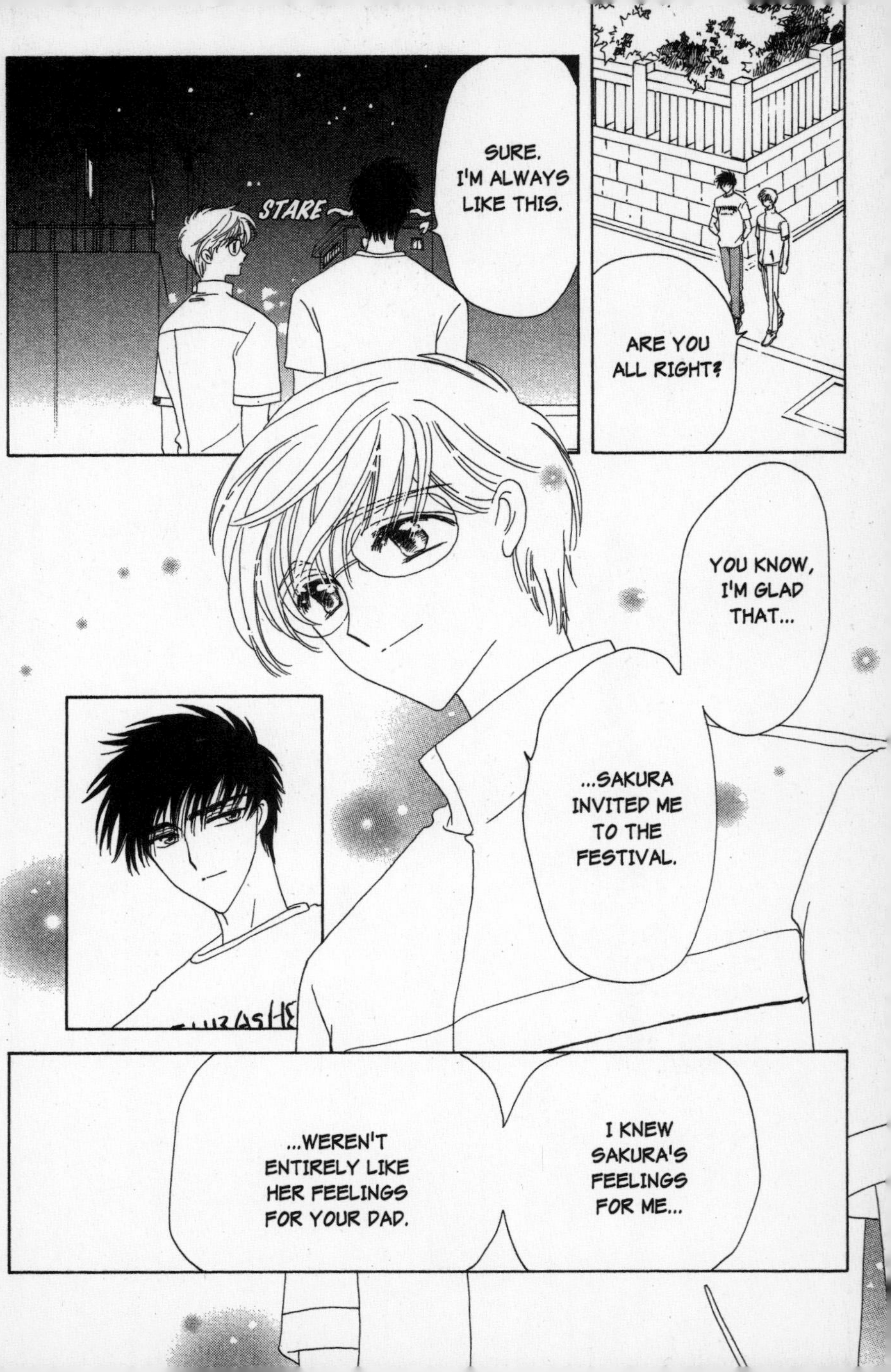

ARE YOU ALL RIGHT?
SURE. I'M ALWAYS LIKE THIS.
STARE~
YOU KNOW, I'M GLAD THAT...
...SAKURA INVITED ME TO THE FESTIVAL.
I KNEW SAKURA'S FEELINGS FOR ME...
...WEREN'T ENTIRELY LIKE HER FEELINGS FOR YOUR DAD.

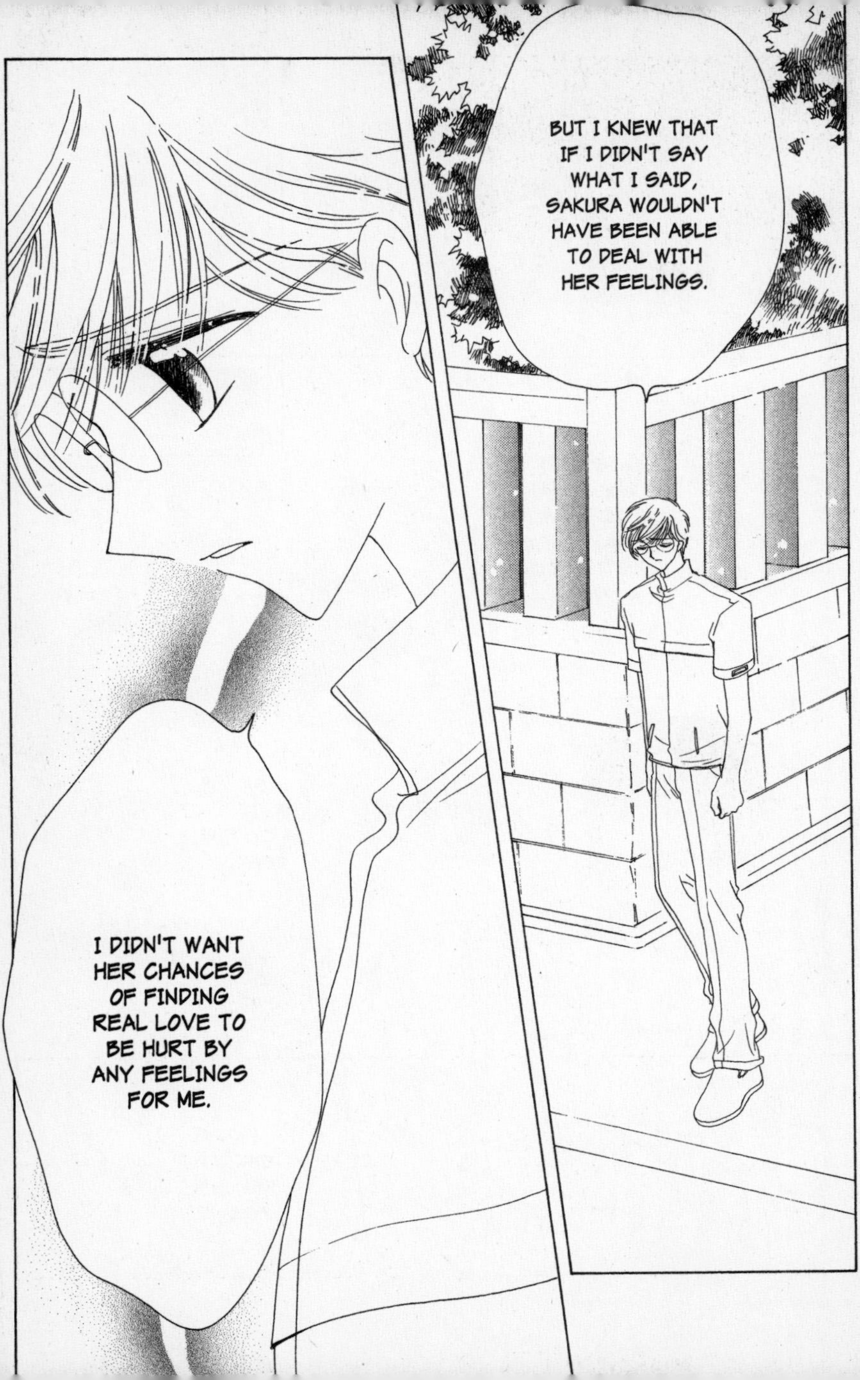
BUT I KNEW THAT IF I DIDN'T SAY WHAT I SAID, SAKURA WOULDN'T HAVE BEEN ABLE TO DEAL WITH HER FEELINGS.
I DIDN'T WANT HER CHANCES OF FINDING REAL LOVE TO BE HURT BY ANY FEELINGS FOR ME.

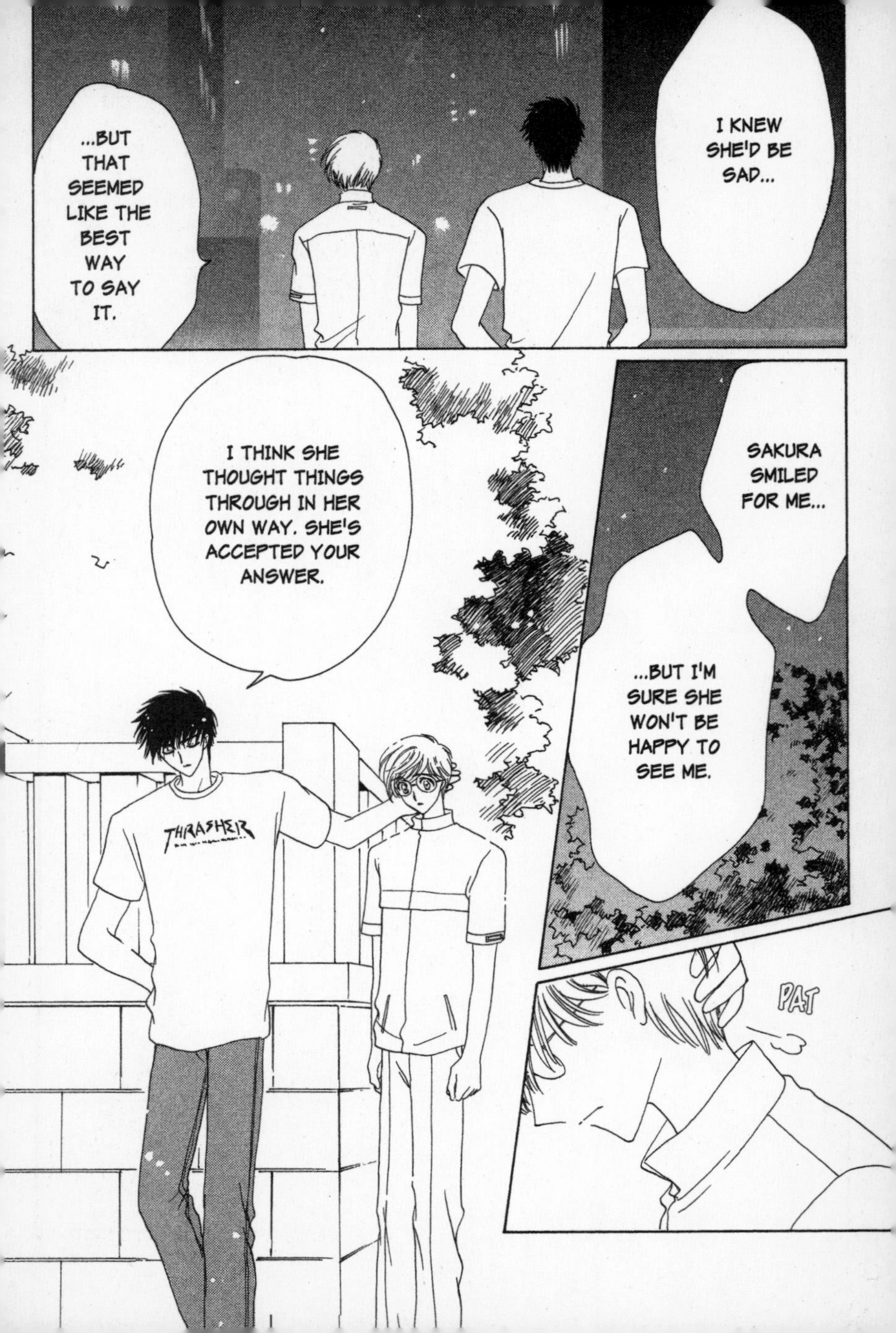
I KNEW SHE'D BE SAD...
...BUT THAT SEEMED LIKE THE BEST WAY TO SAY IT.
SAKURA SMILED FOR ME...
...BUT I'M SURE SHE WON'T BE HAPPY TO SEE ME.
PAT
I THINK SHE THOUGHT THINGS THROUGH IN HER OWN WAY. SHE'S ACCEPTED YOUR ANSWER.
THRASHER

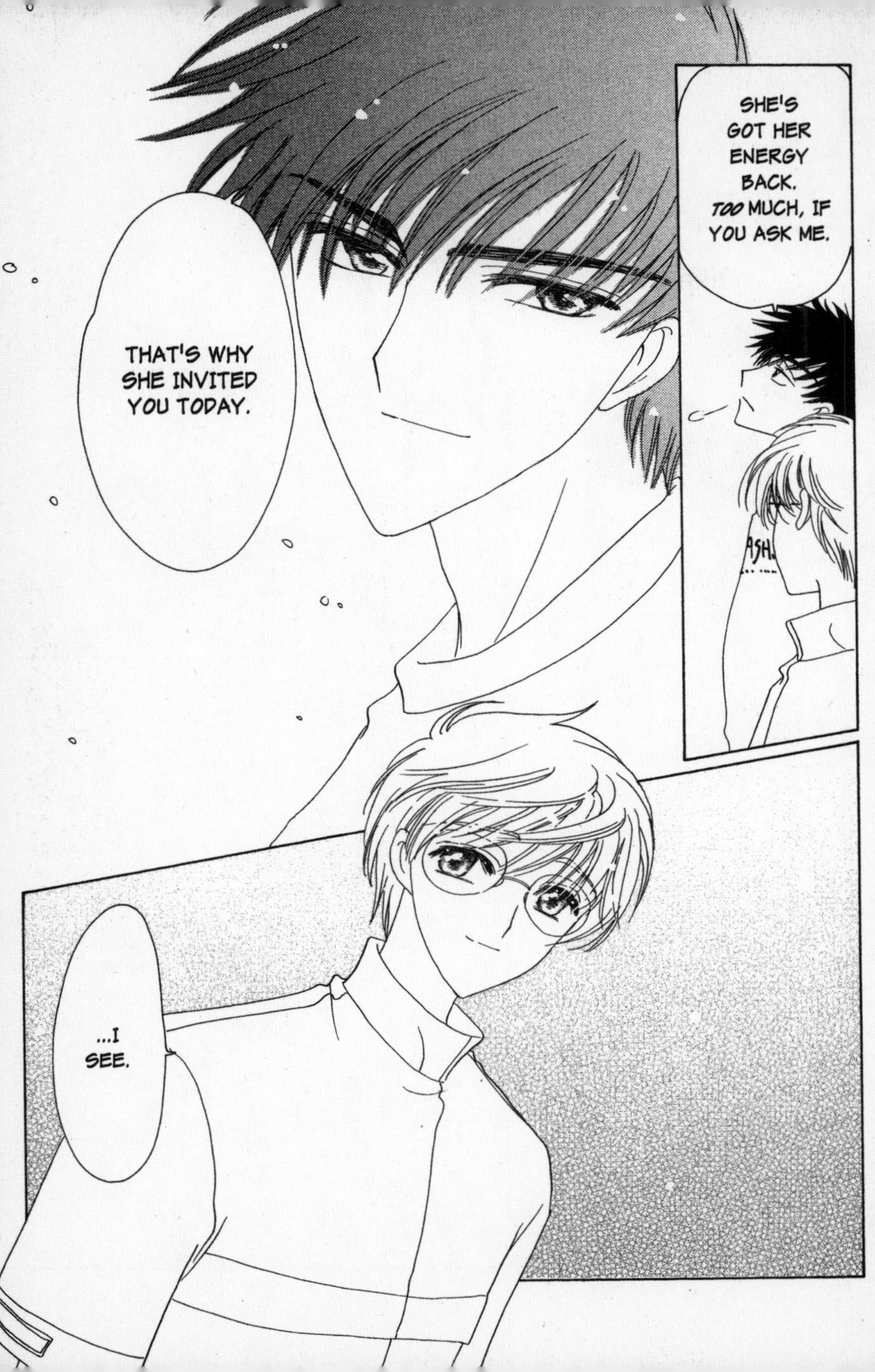
SHE'S GOT HER ENERGY BACK. TOO MUCH, IF YOU ASK ME.
THAT'S WHY SHE INVITED YOU TODAY.
...I SEE.

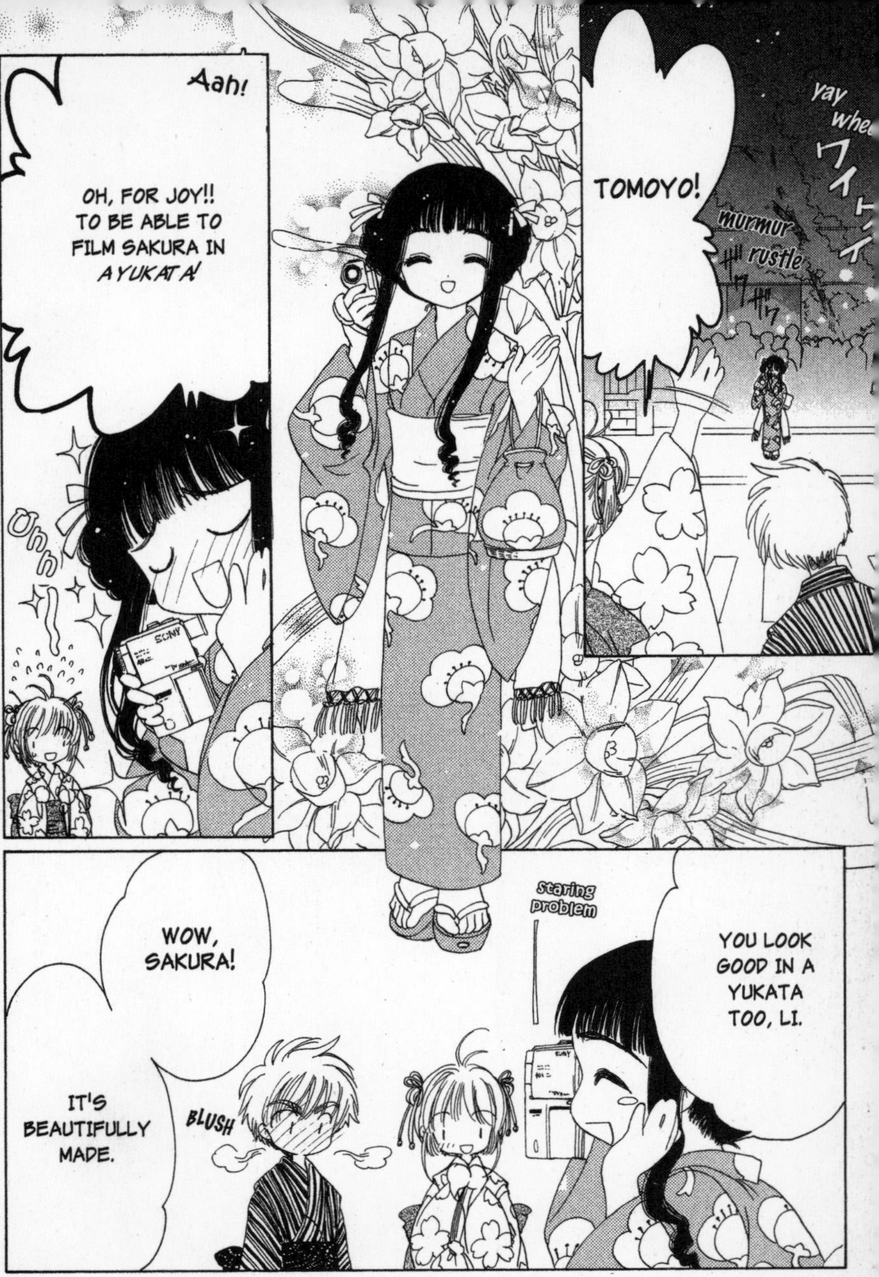

yay whee
murmur rustle
TOMOYO!
Aah!
OH, FOR JOY!! TO BE ABLE TO FILM SAKURA IN A YUKATA!
YOU LOOK GOOD IN A YUKATA TOO, LI.
staring problem
WOW, SAKURA!
IT'S BEAUTIFULLY MADE.
BLUSH

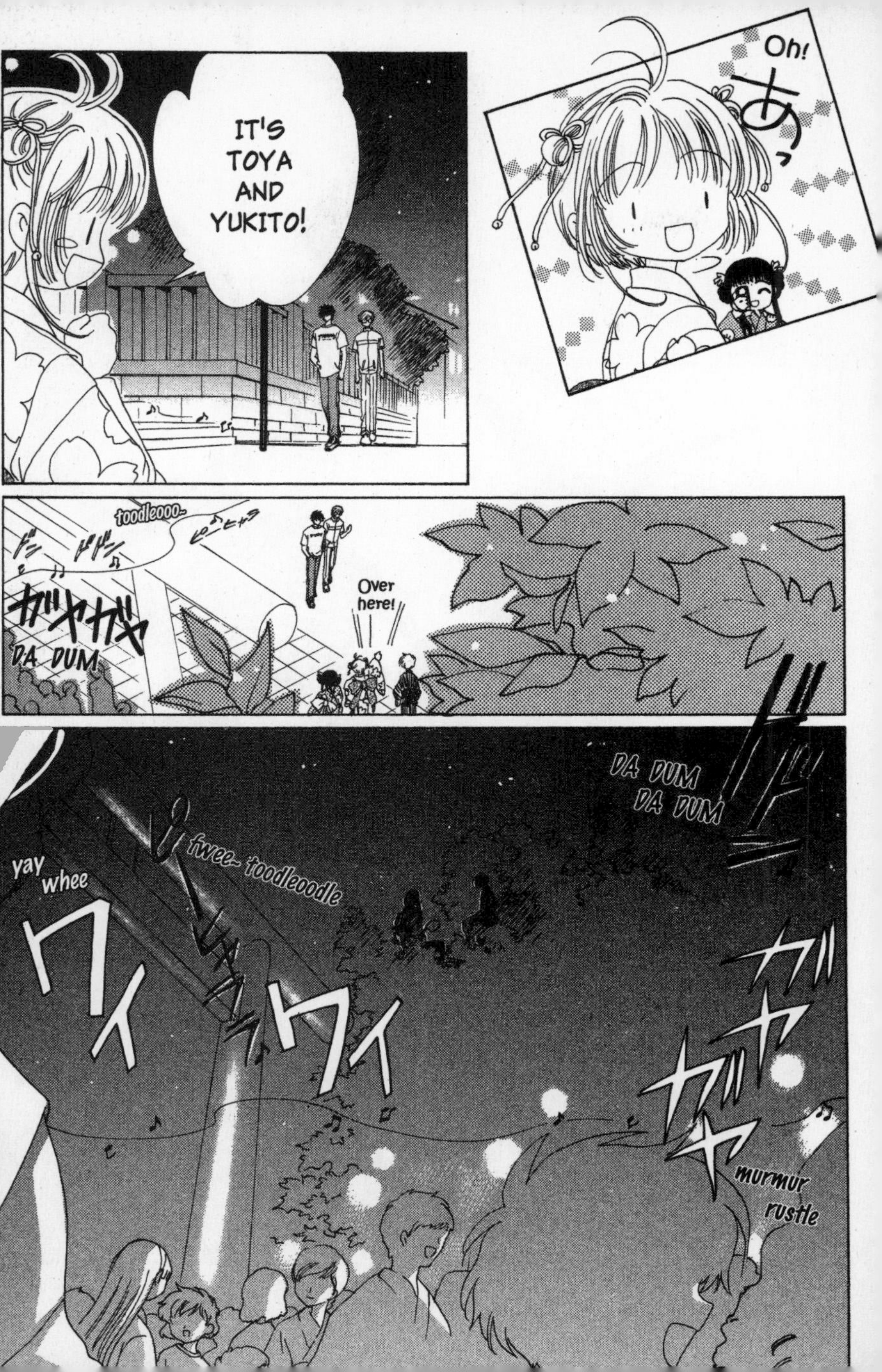
Oh!
あっ
IT'S TOYA AND YUKITO!
Over here!
toodleooo~
ガヤガヤ
DA DUM
DA DUM
DA DUM
ガヤガヤ
murmur
rustle
ワイワイ
fwee~ toodleoodle
yay whee

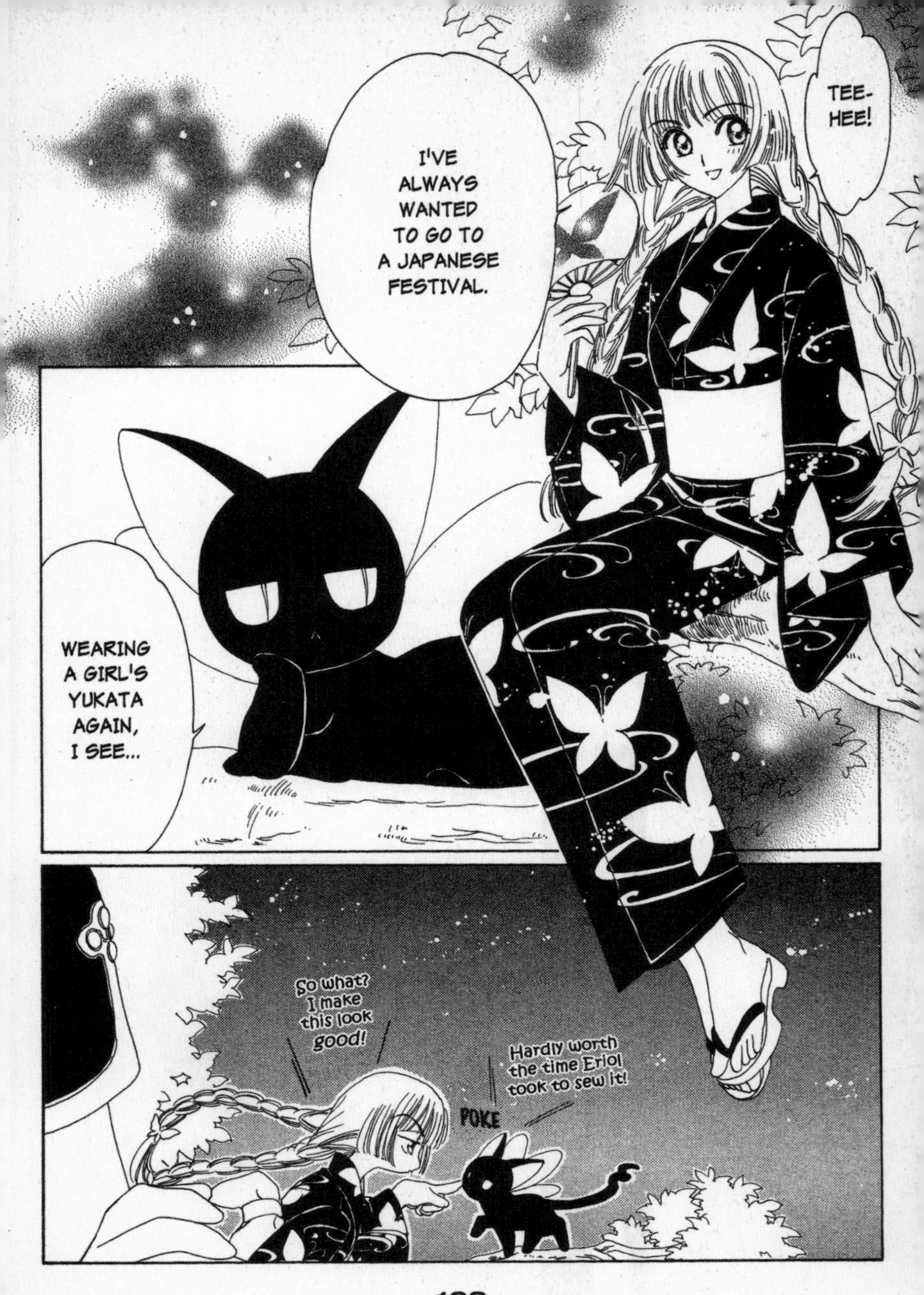
TEE-HEE!
I'VE ALWAYS WANTED TO GO TO A JAPANESE FESTIVAL.
WEARING A GIRL'S YUKATA AGAIN, I SEE...
So what? I make this look good!
Hardly worth the time Eriol took to sew it!
POKE

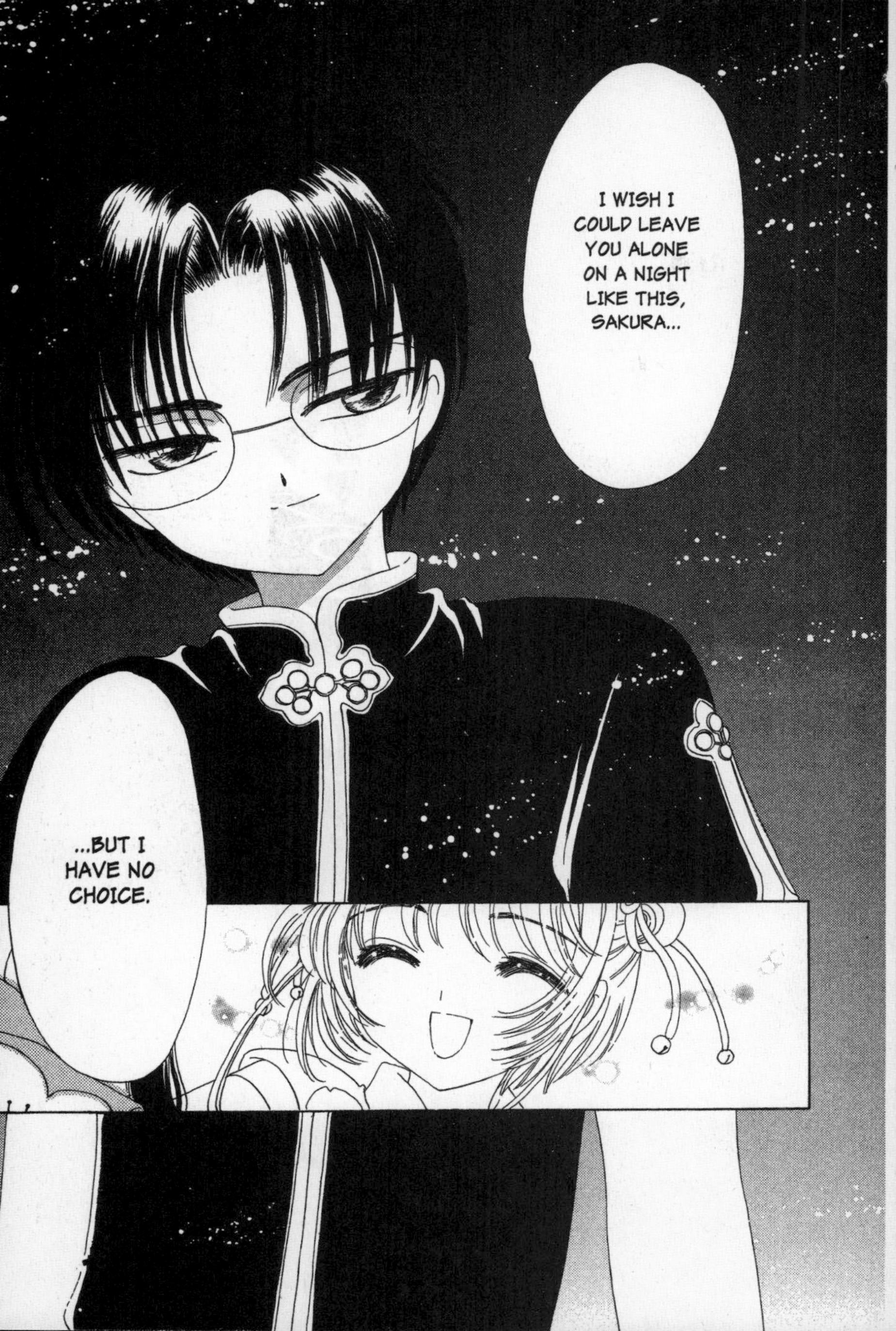
I WISH I COULD LEAVE YOU ALONE ON A NIGHT LIKE THIS, SAKURA...
...BUT I HAVE NO CHOICE.

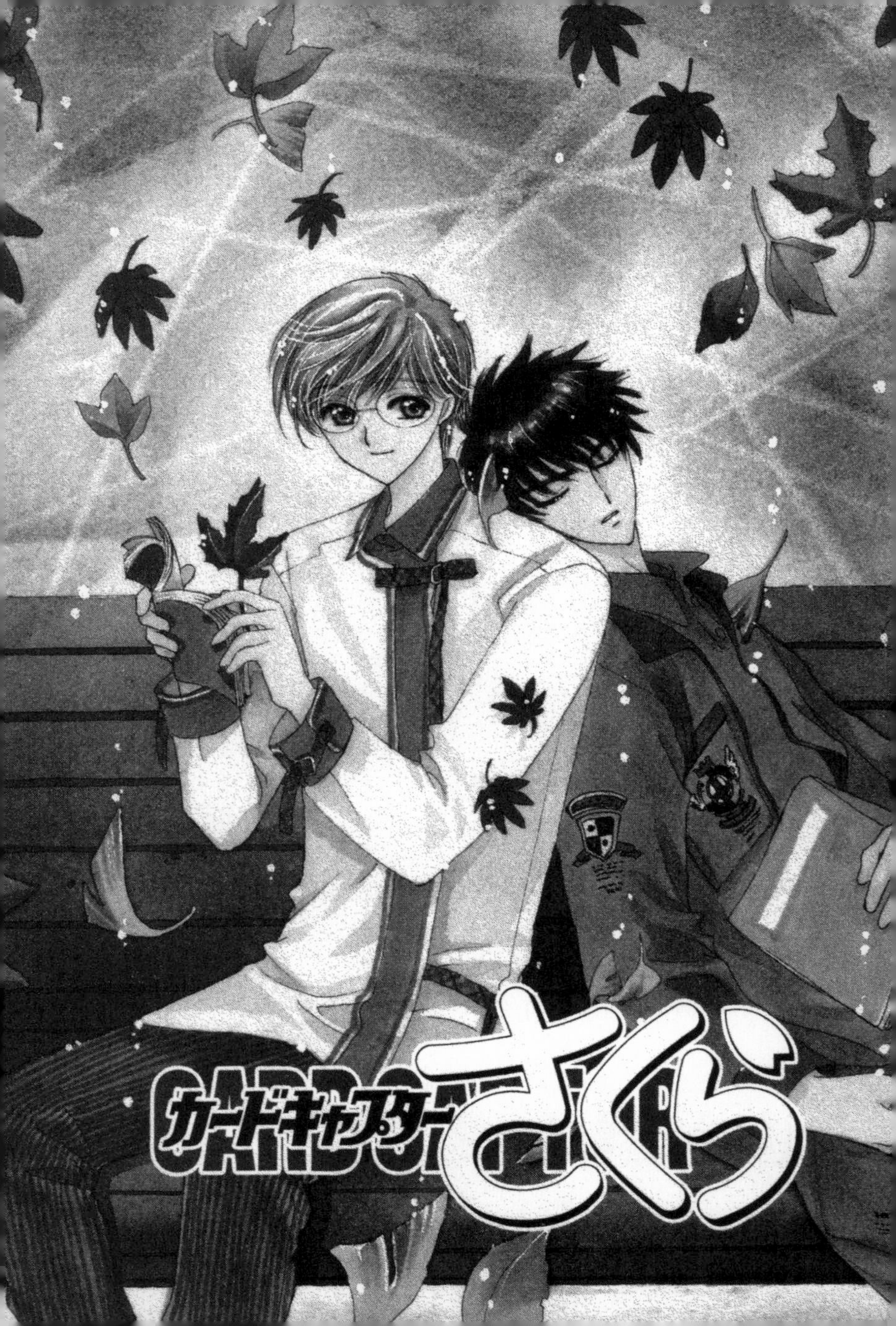
カードキャプター
さくら

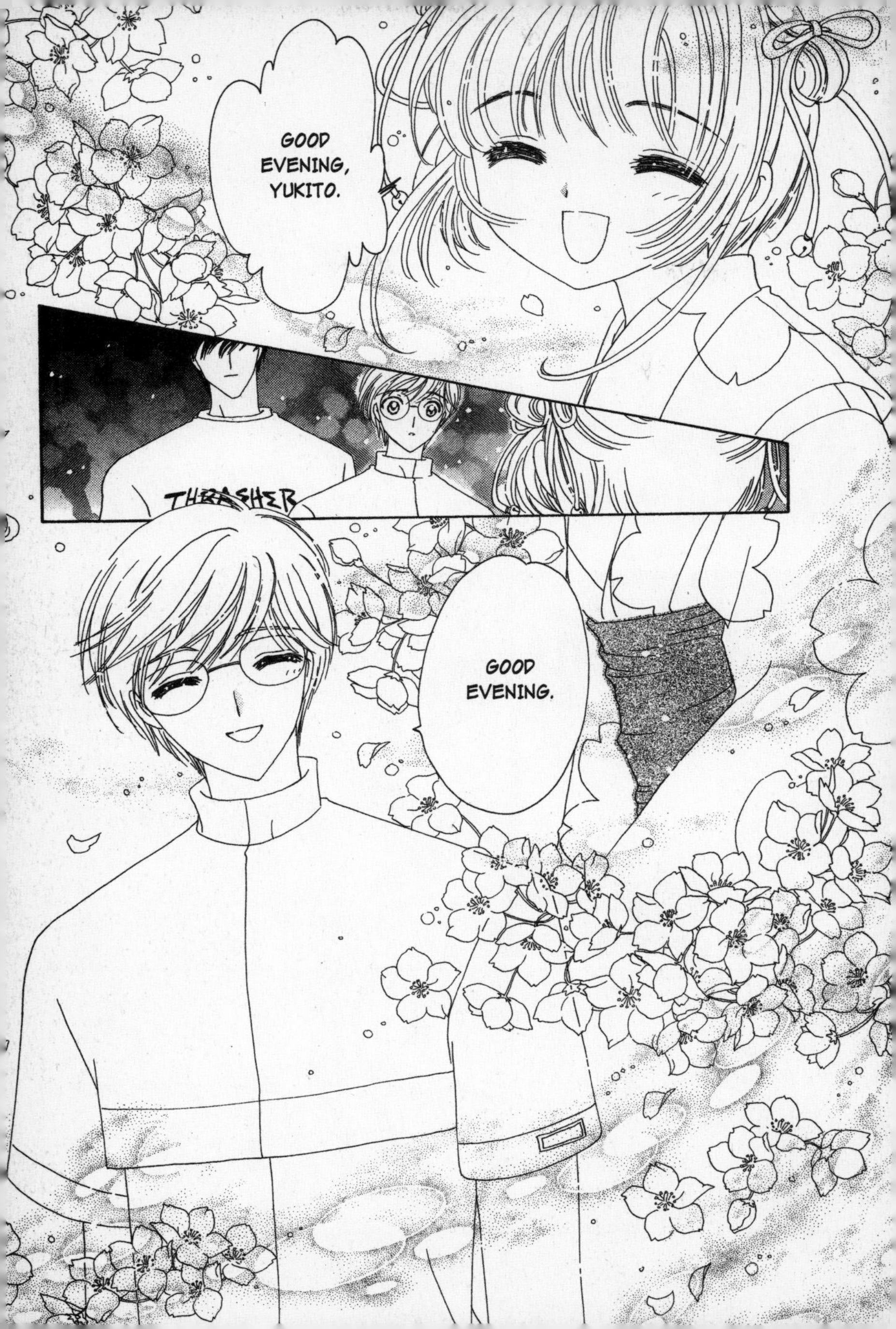
GOOD EVENING, YUKITO.
THRASHER
GOOD EVENING.

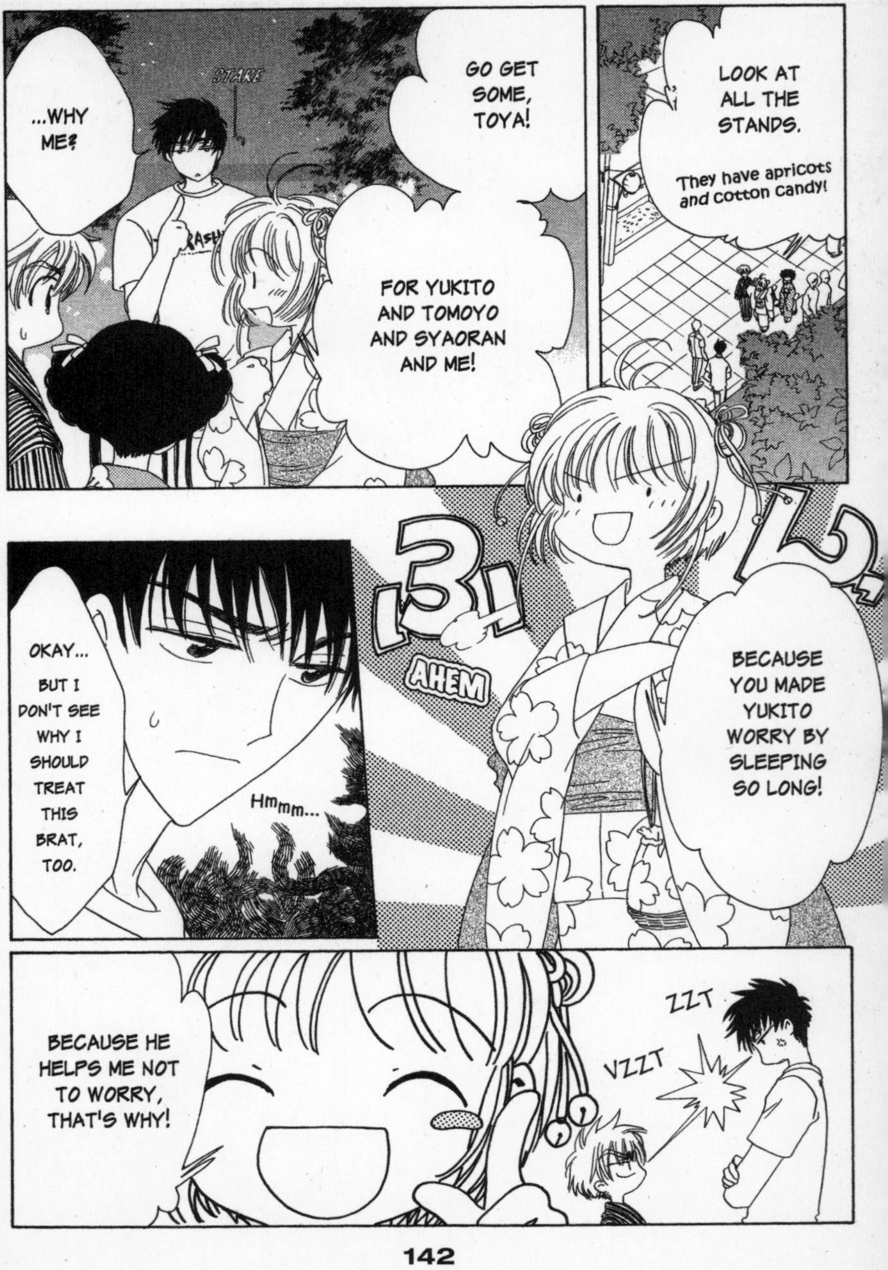
LOOK AT ALL THE STANDS.
They have apricots and cotton candy!
GO GET SOME, TOYA!
FOR YUKITO AND TOMOYO AND SYAORAN AND ME!
STARE
...WHY ME?
BECAUSE YOU MADE YUKITO WORRY BY SLEEPING SO LONG!
AHEM
OKAY...
BUT I DON'T SEE WHY I SHOULD TREAT THIS BRAT, TOO.
Hmmm...
ZZT
VZZT
BECAUSE HE HELPS ME NOT TO WORRY, THAT'S WHY!

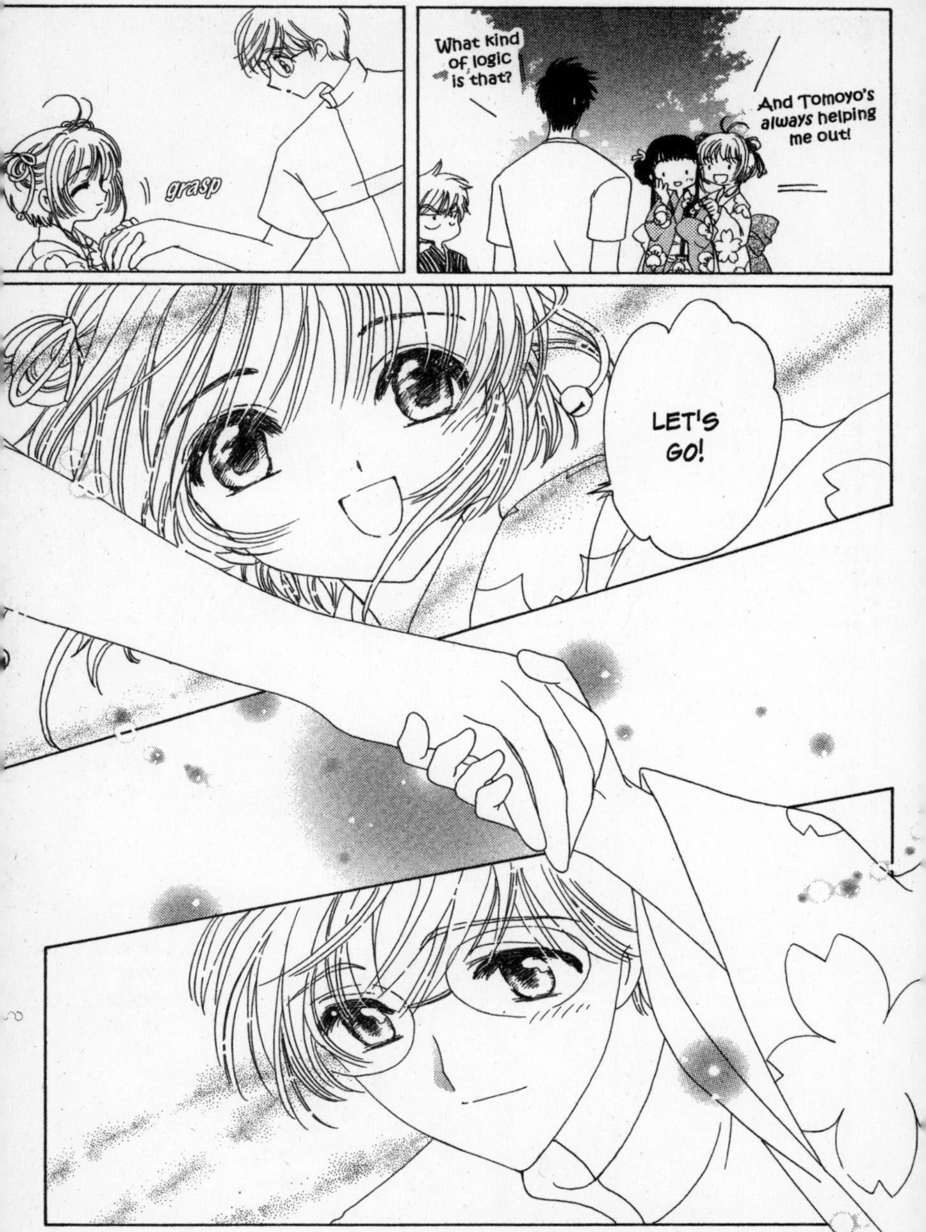
And Tomoyo's always helping me out!
What kind of logic is that?
grasp
LET'S GO!

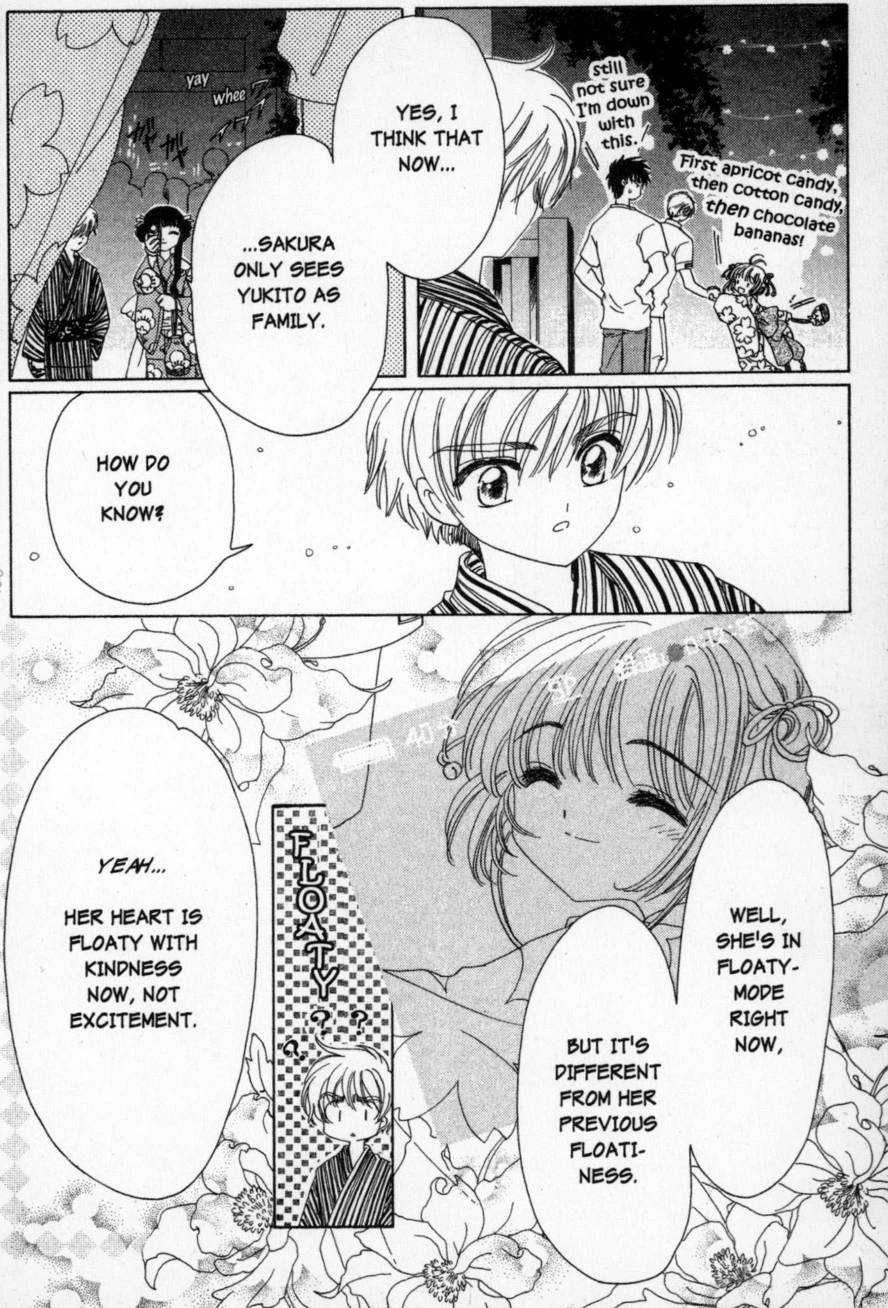
First apricot candy, then cotton candy, then chocolate bananas!
still not sure I'm down with this.
YES, I THINK THAT NOW...
...SAKURA ONLY SEES YUKITO AS FAMILY.
yay
whee
HOW DO YOU KNOW?
WELL, SHE'S IN FLOATY-MODE RIGHT NOW,
BUT IT'S DIFFERENT FROM HER PREVIOUS FLOATI-NESS.
FLOATY???
YEAH...
HER HEART IS FLOATY WITH KINDNESS NOW, NOT EXCITEMENT.

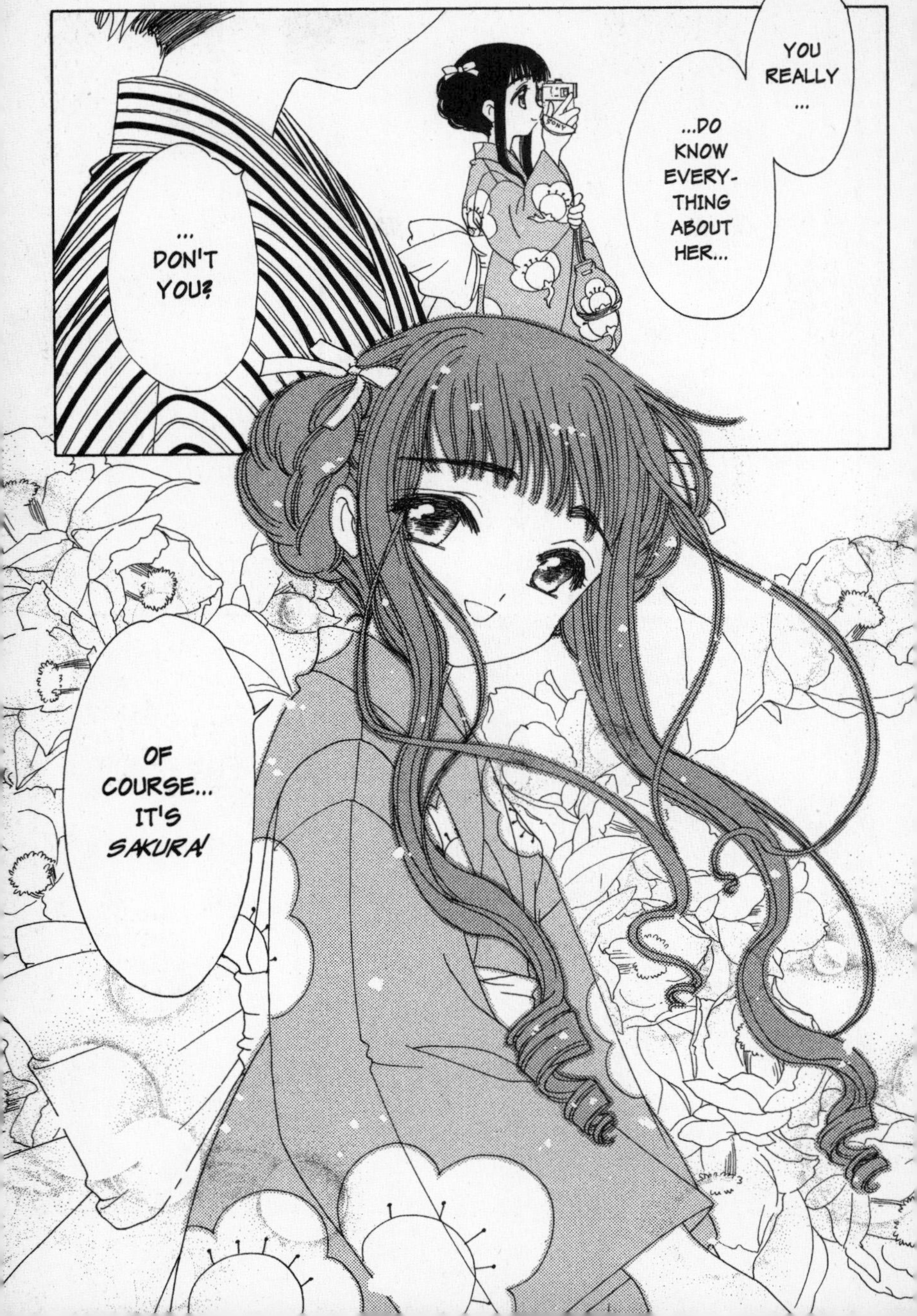
YOU REALLY ...
...DO KNOW EVERY-THING ABOUT HER...
... DON'T YOU?
OF COURSE... IT'S *SAKURA!*

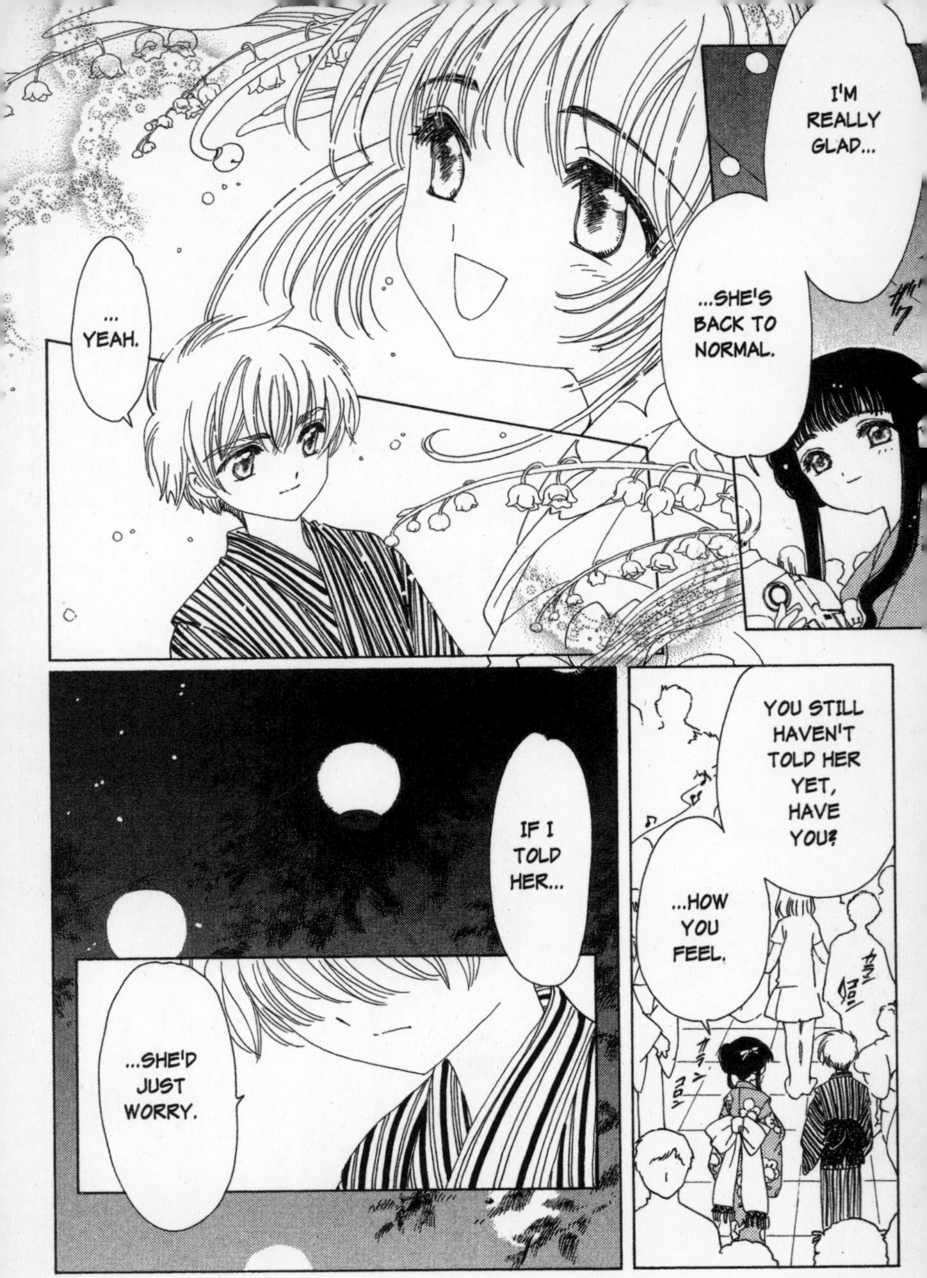
I'M REALLY GLAD...
...SHE'S BACK TO NORMAL.
... YEAH.
YOU STILL HAVEN'T TOLD HER YET, HAVE YOU?
...HOW YOU FEEL.
IF I TOLD HER...
...SHE'D JUST WORRY.

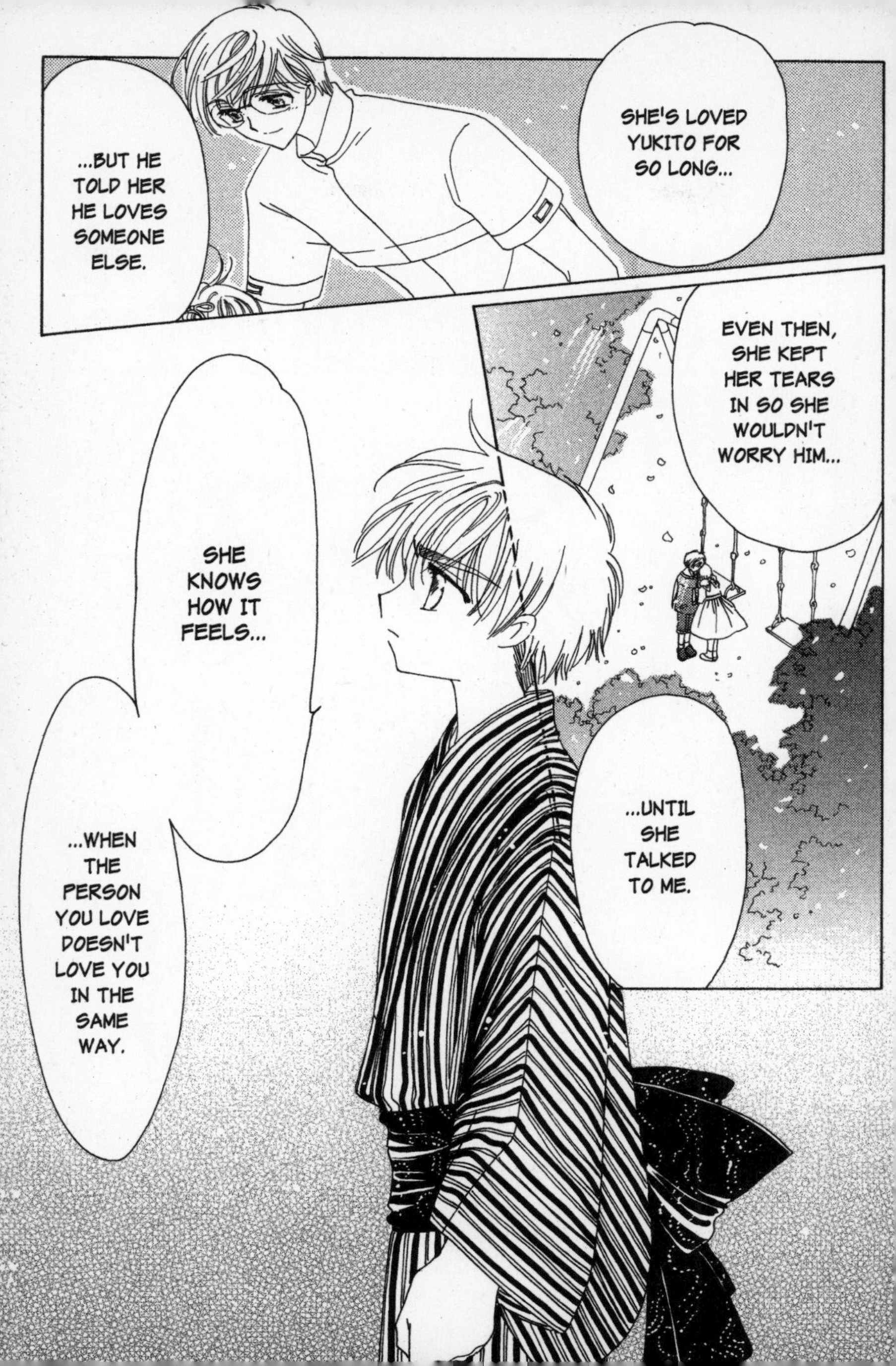
SHE'S LOVED YUKITO FOR SO LONG...
...BUT HE TOLD HER HE LOVES SOMEONE ELSE.
EVEN THEN, SHE KEPT HER TEARS IN SO SHE WOULDN'T WORRY HIM...
...UNTIL SHE TALKED TO ME.
SHE KNOWS HOW IT FEELS...
...WHEN THE PERSON YOU LOVE DOESN'T LOVE YOU IN THE SAME WAY.

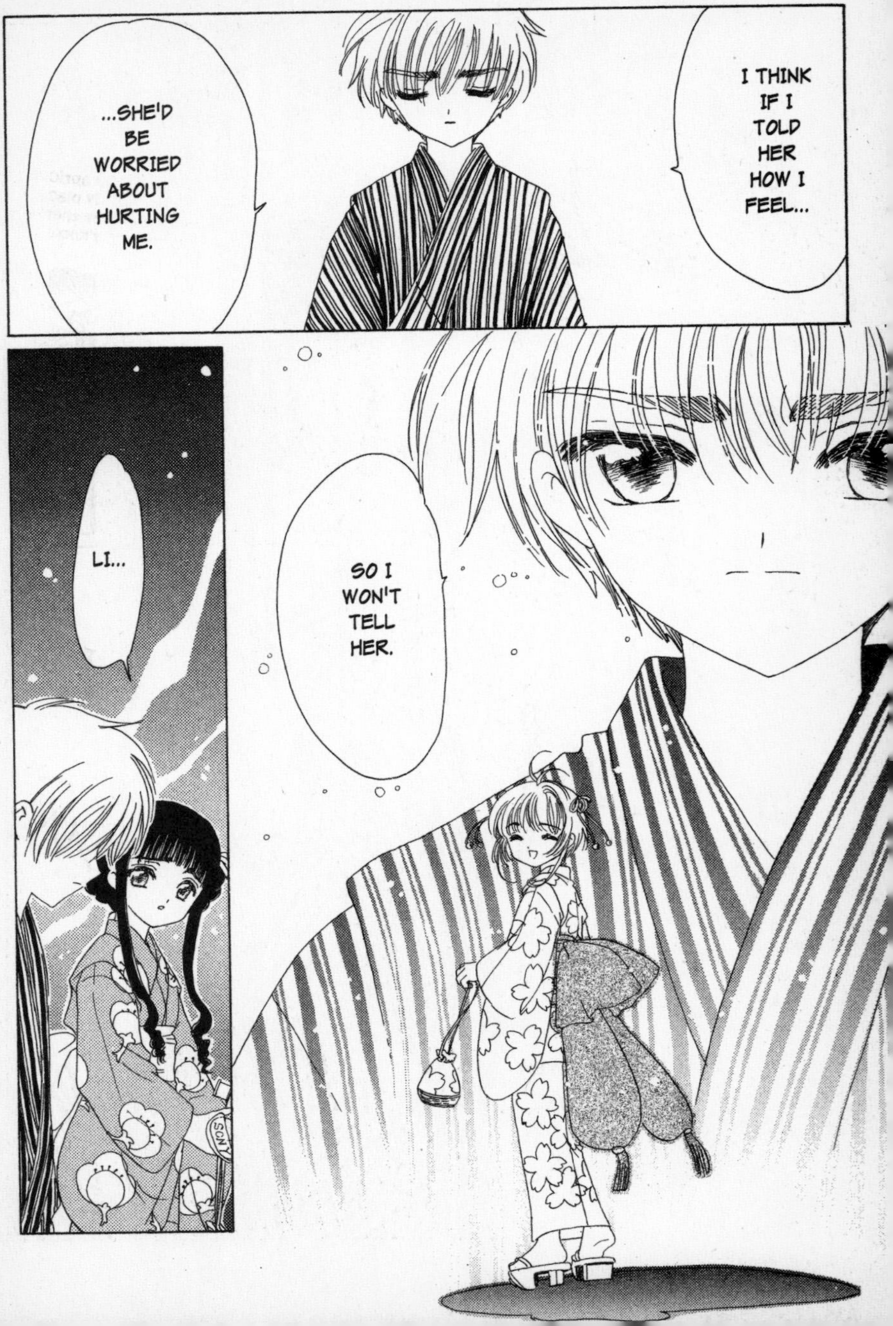
I THINK IF I TOLD HER HOW I FEEL...
...SHE'D BE WORRIED ABOUT HURTING ME.
SO I WON'T TELL HER.
LI...

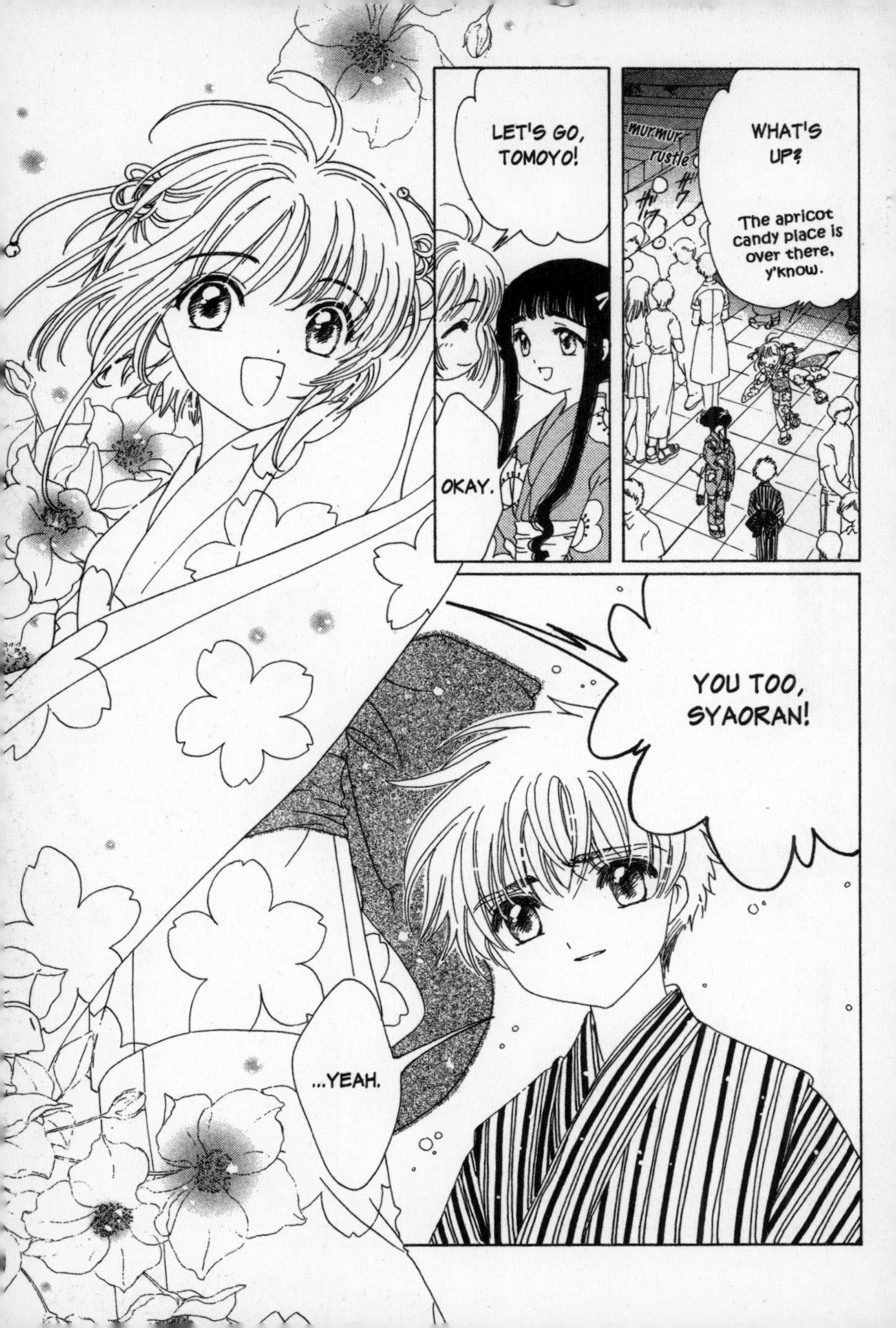
WHAT'S UP?
murmur
rustle
The apricot candy place is over there, y'know.
LET'S GO, TOMOYO!
OKAY.
YOU TOO, SYAORAN!
...YEAH.

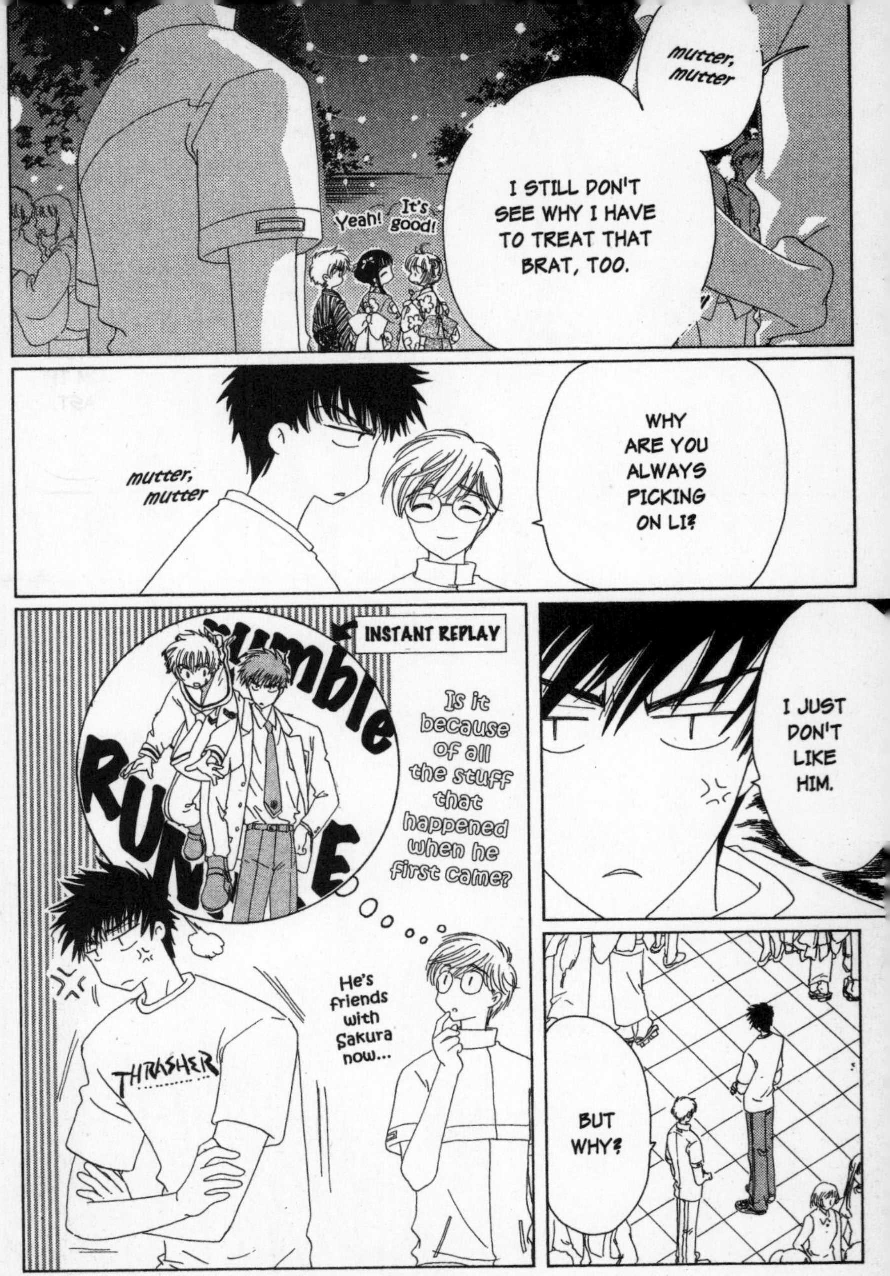
mutter, mutter
I STILL DON'T SEE WHY I HAVE TO TREAT THAT BRAT, TOO.
It's good!
Yeah!
WHY ARE YOU ALWAYS PICKING ON LI?
mutter, mutter
I JUST DON'T LIKE HIM.
BUT WHY?
INSTANT REPLAY
Is it because of all the stuff that happened when he first came?
He's friends with Sakura now...
THRASHER

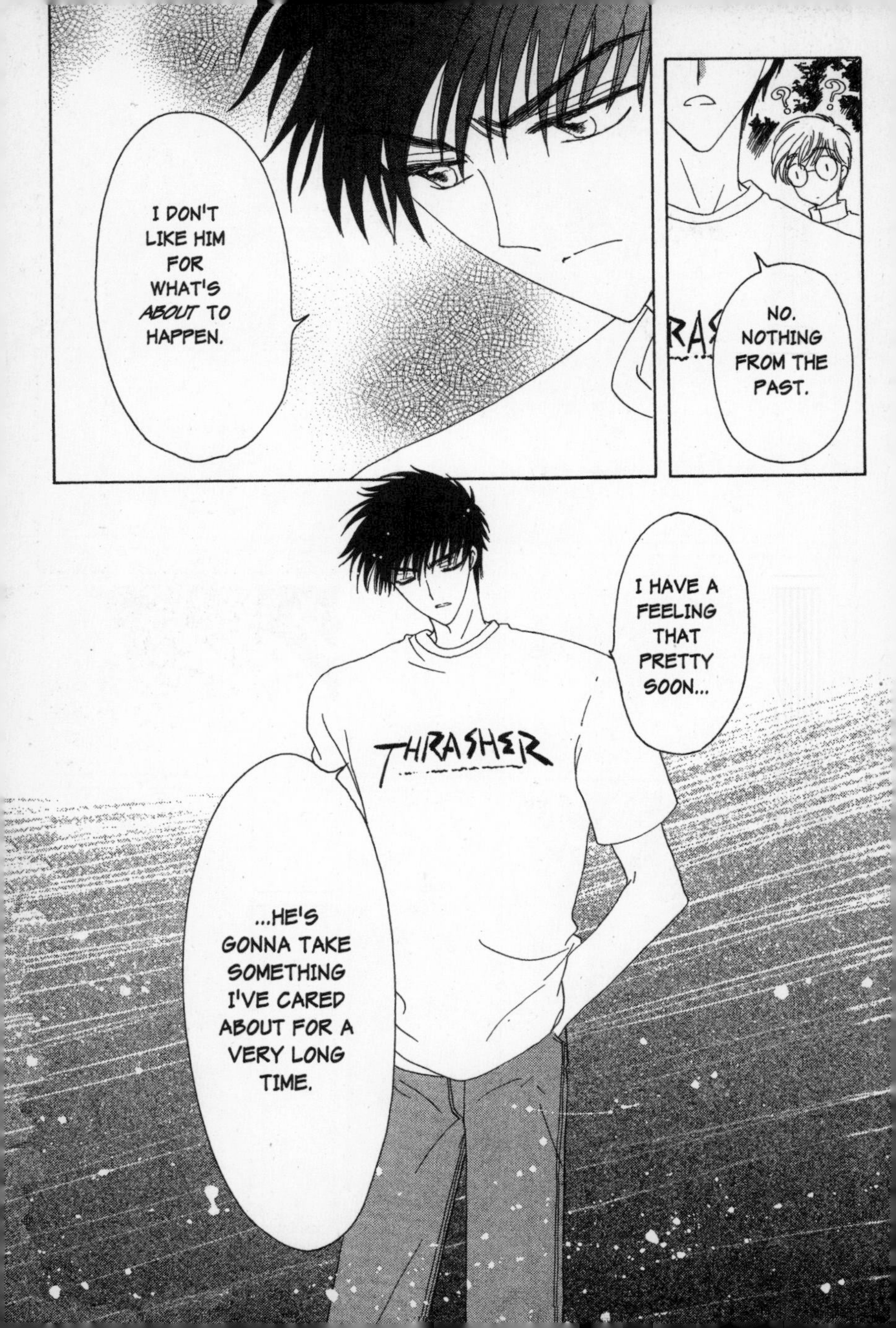
NO. NOTHING FROM THE PAST.
I DON'T LIKE HIM FOR WHAT'S *ABOUT* TO HAPPEN.
I HAVE A FEELING THAT PRETTY SOON...
THRASHER
...HE'S GONNA TAKE SOMETHING I'VE CARED ABOUT FOR A VERY LONG TIME.

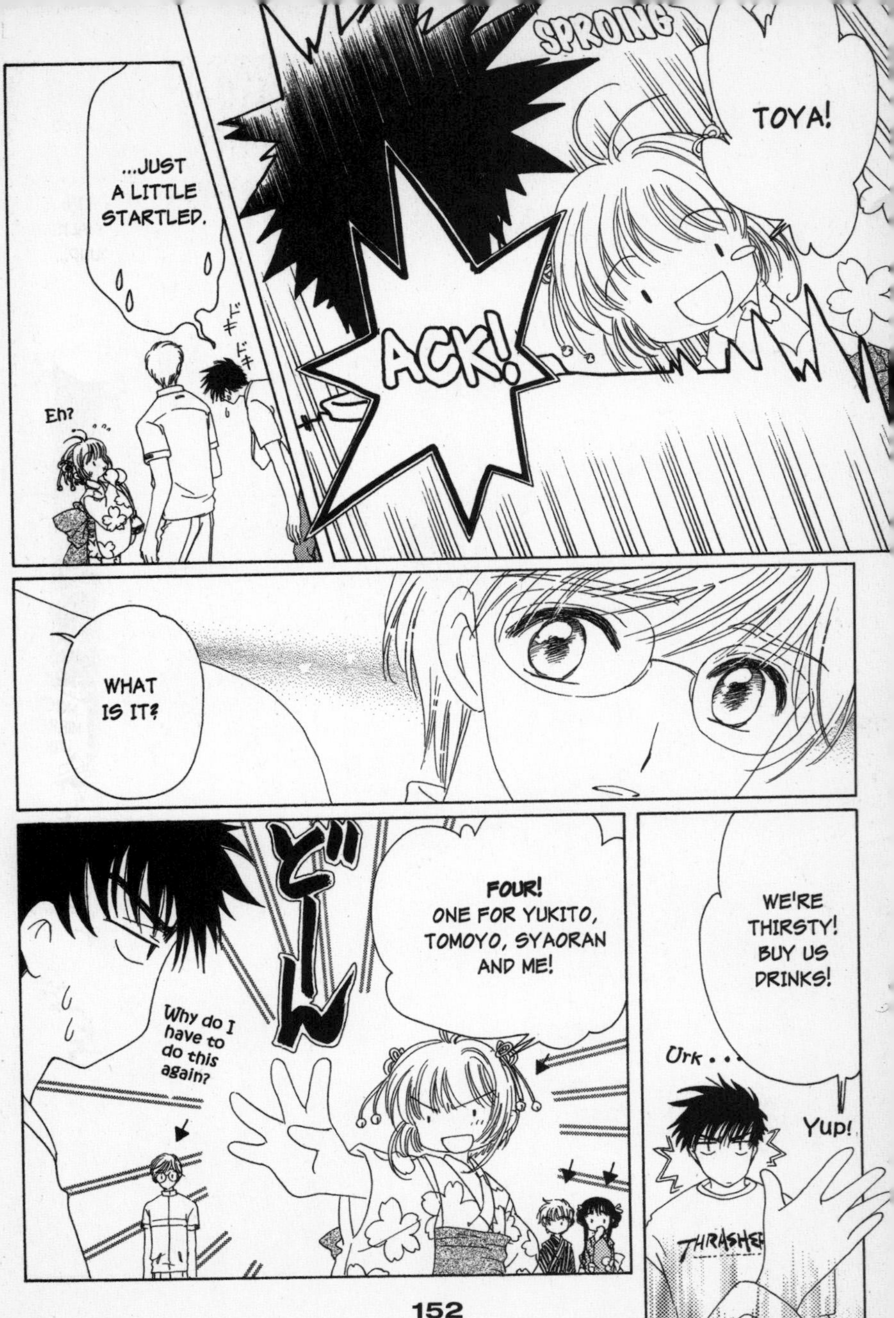

SPROING
TOYA!
ACK!
...JUST A LITTLE STARTLED.
ドキ ドキ
Eh?
WHAT IS IT?
WE'RE THIRSTY! BUY US DRINKS!
Urk . . .
Yup!
THRASHER
FOUR! ONE FOR YUKITO, TOMOYO, SYAORAN AND ME!
どーん
Why do I have to do this again?

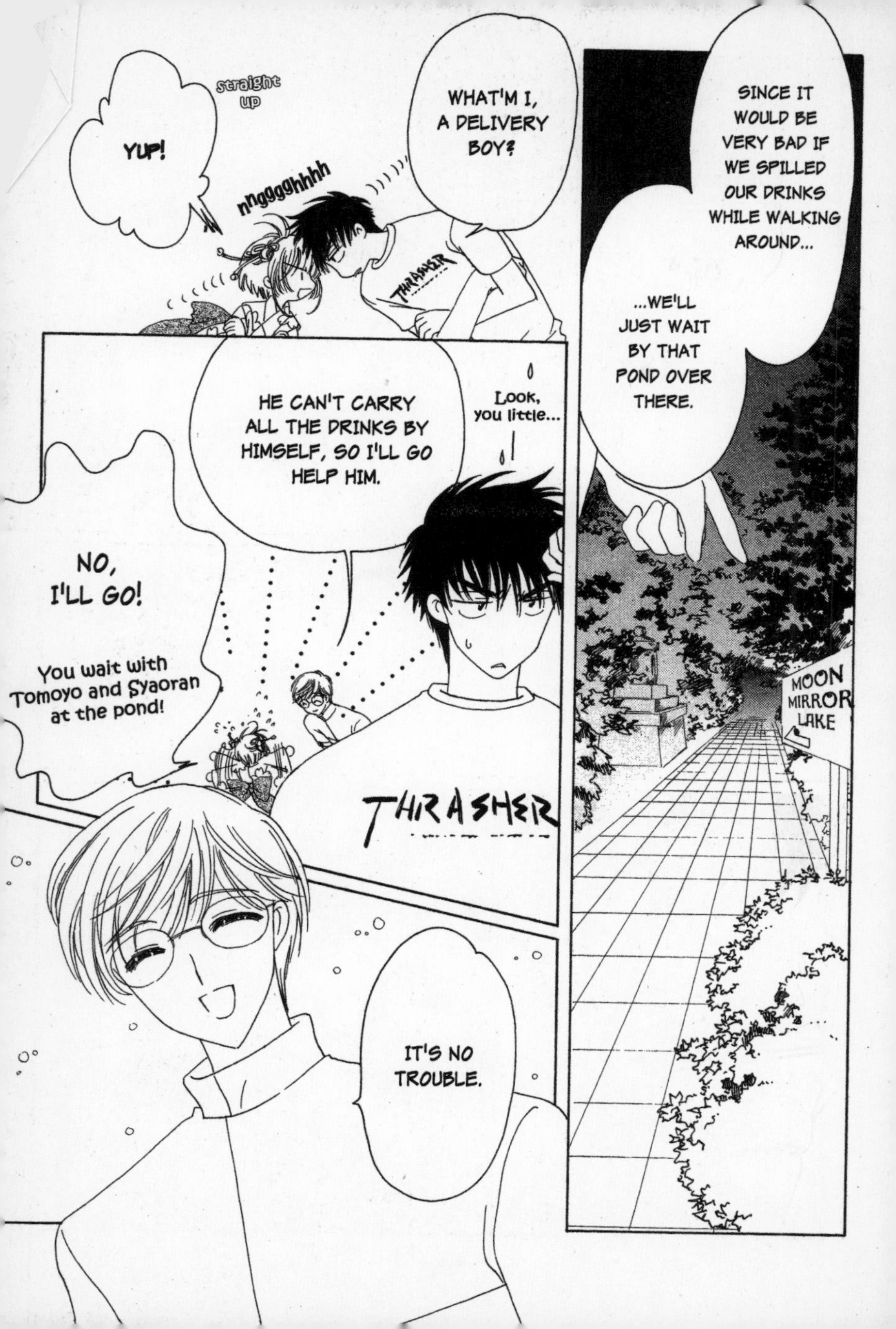
SINCE IT WOULD BE VERY BAD IF WE SPILLED OUR DRINKS WHILE WALKING AROUND...
...WE'LL JUST WAIT BY THAT POND OVER THERE.
MOON MIRROR LAKE
WHAT'M I, A DELIVERY BOY?
THRASHER
nngggghhhh
straight up
YUP!
HE CAN'T CARRY ALL THE DRINKS BY HIMSELF, SO I'LL GO HELP HIM.
Look, you little...
THRASHER
NO, I'LL GO!
You wait with Tomoyo and Syaoran at the pond!
IT'S NO TROUBLE.

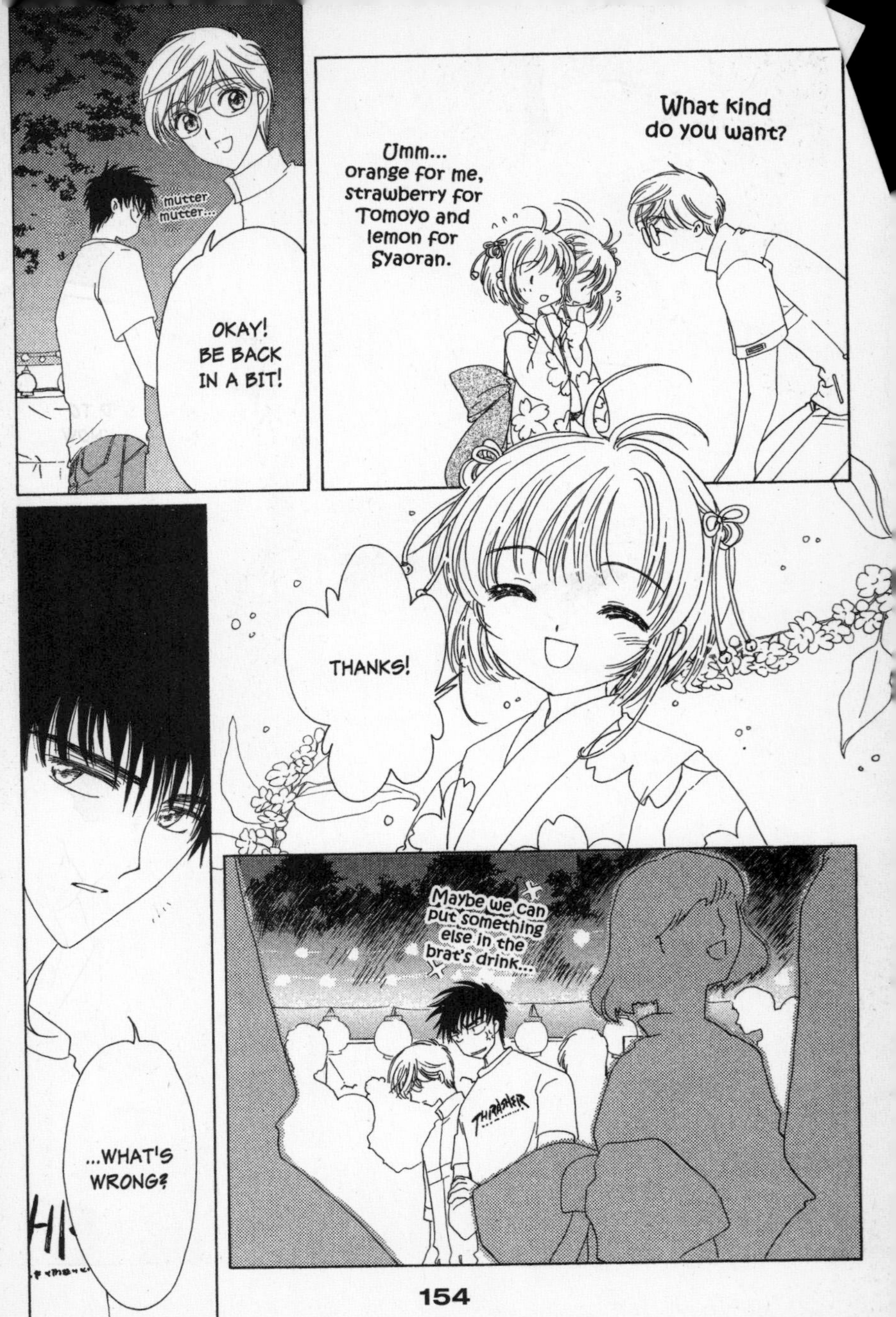
What kind do you want?
Umm... orange for me, strawberry for Tomoyo and lemon for Syaoran.
mutter mutter...
OKAY! BE BACK IN A BIT!
THANKS!
Maybe we can put something else in the brat's drink...
...WHAT'S WRONG?

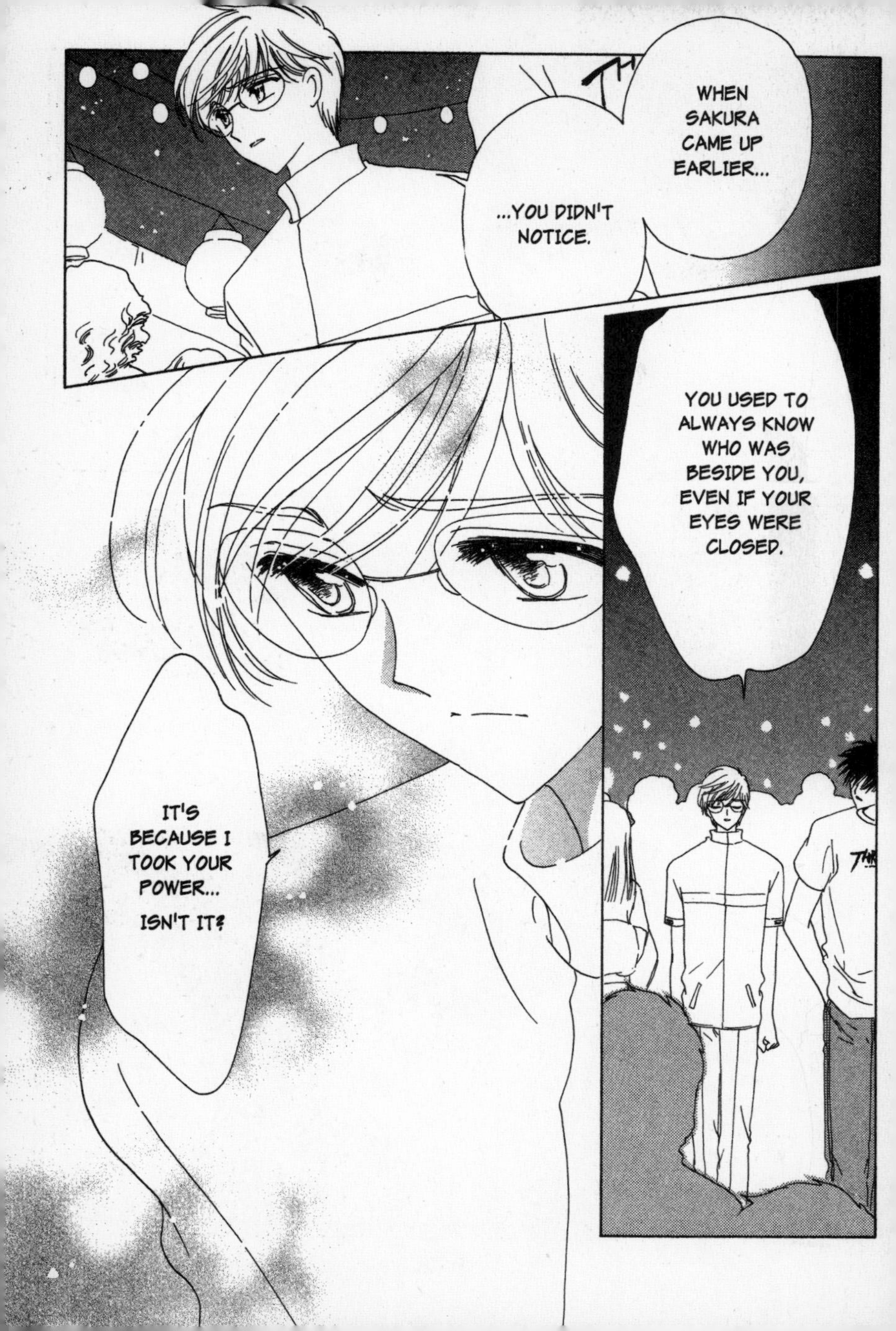
WHEN SAKURA CAME UP EARLIER...
...YOU DIDN'T NOTICE.
YOU USED TO ALWAYS KNOW WHO WAS BESIDE YOU, EVEN IF YOUR EYES WERE CLOSED.
IT'S BECAUSE I TOOK YOUR POWER...
ISN'T IT?

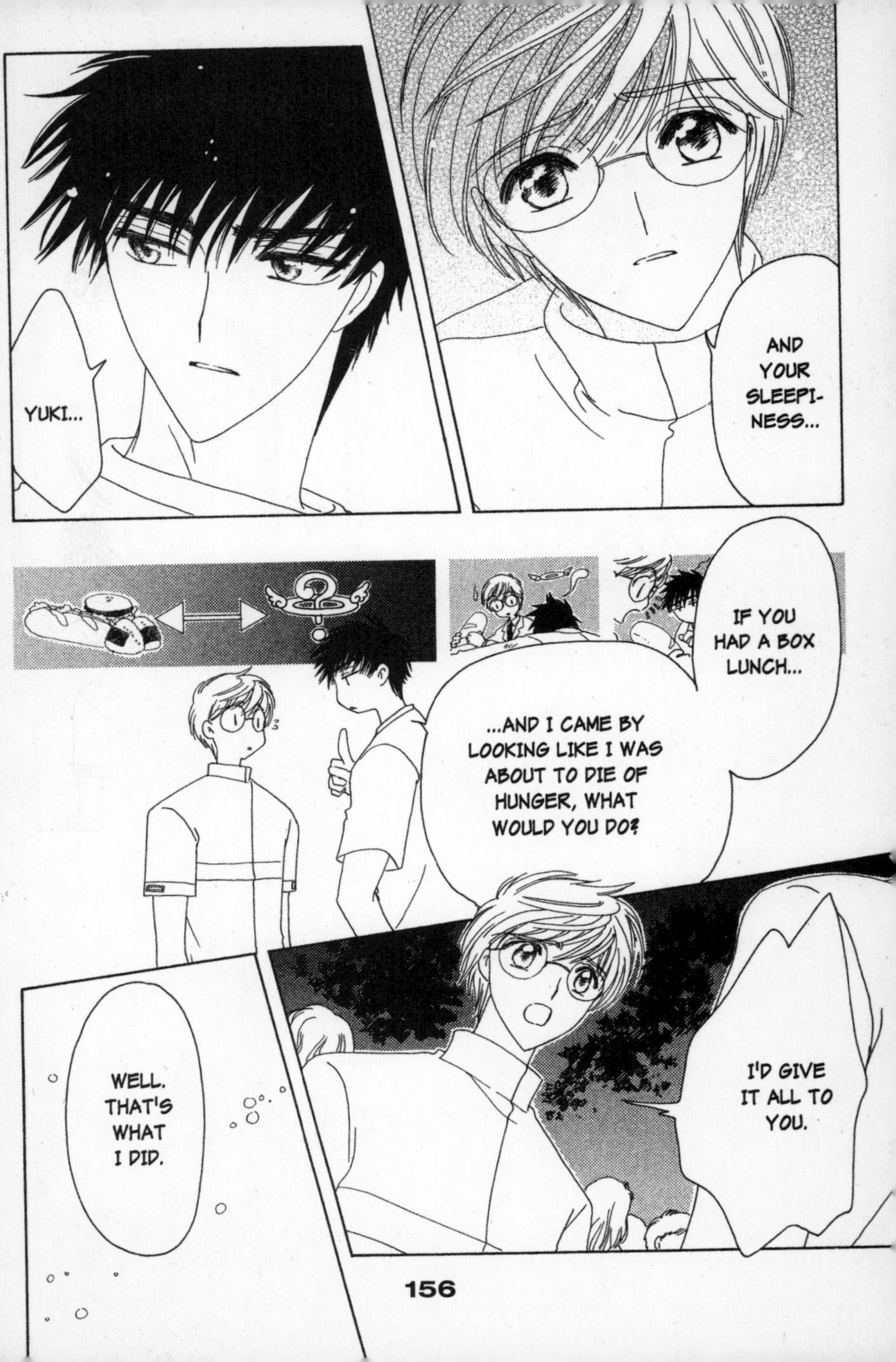
AND YOUR SLEEPI-NESS...
YUKI...
IF YOU HAD A BOX LUNCH...
...AND I CAME BY LOOKING LIKE I WAS ABOUT TO DIE OF HUNGER, WHAT WOULD YOU DO?
I'D GIVE IT ALL TO YOU.
WELL. THAT'S WHAT I DID.

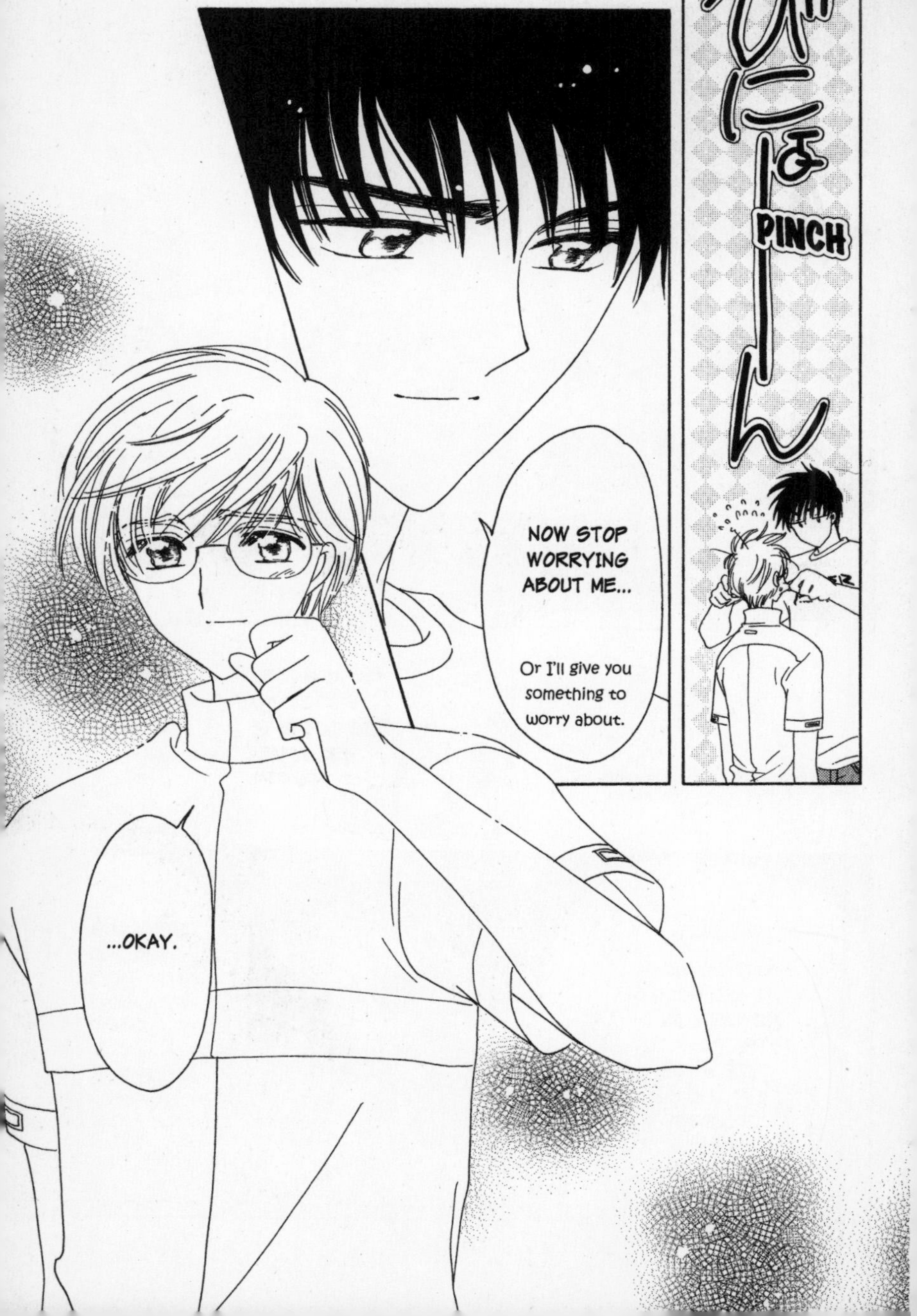
ぴにょーん
PINCH
NOW STOP WORRYING ABOUT ME...
Or I'll give you something to worry about.
...OKAY.

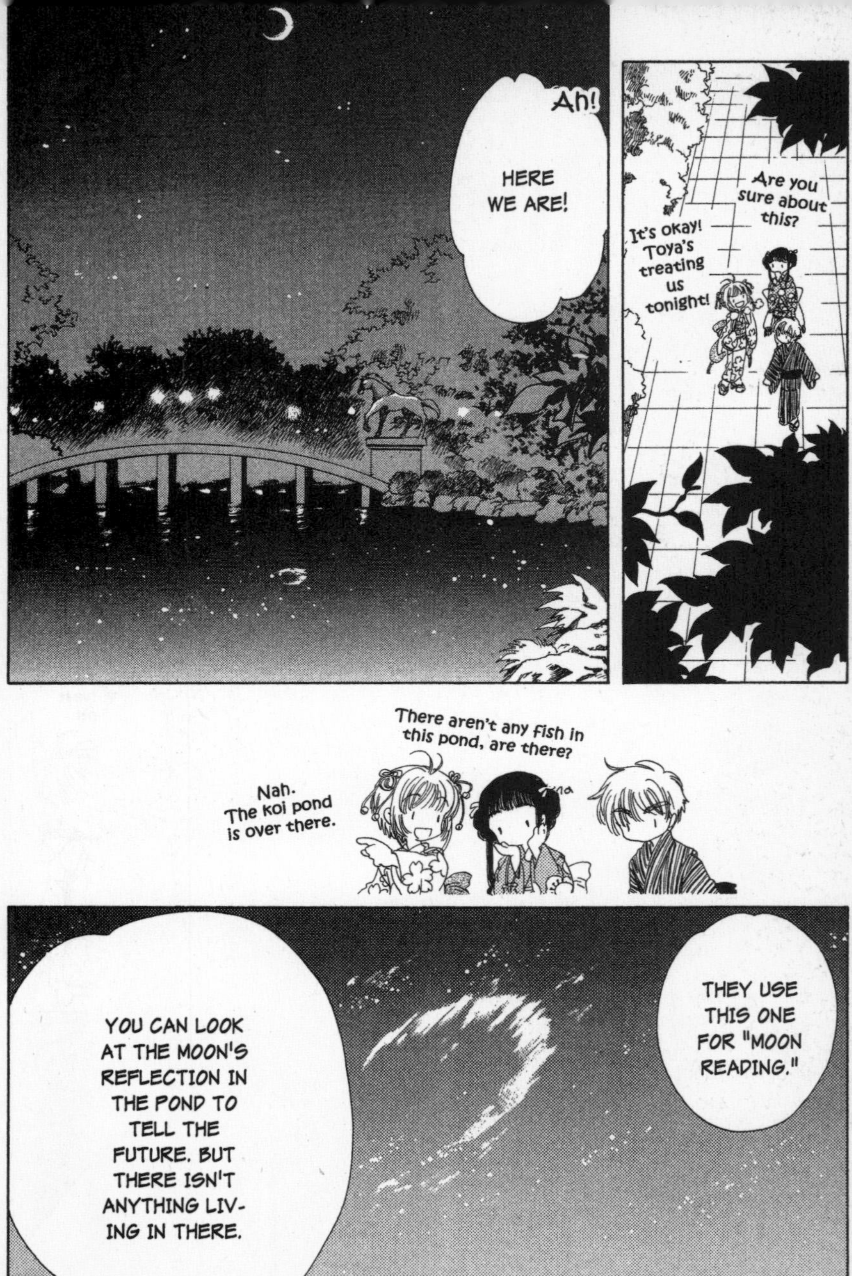
Are you sure about this?
It's okay! Toya's treating us tonight!
Ah!
HERE WE ARE!
There aren't any fish in this pond, are there?
Nah. The koi pond is over there.
THEY USE THIS ONE FOR "MOON READING."
YOU CAN LOOK AT THE MOON'S REFLECTION IN THE POND TO TELL THE FUTURE. BUT THERE ISN'T ANYTHING LIV-ING IN THERE.

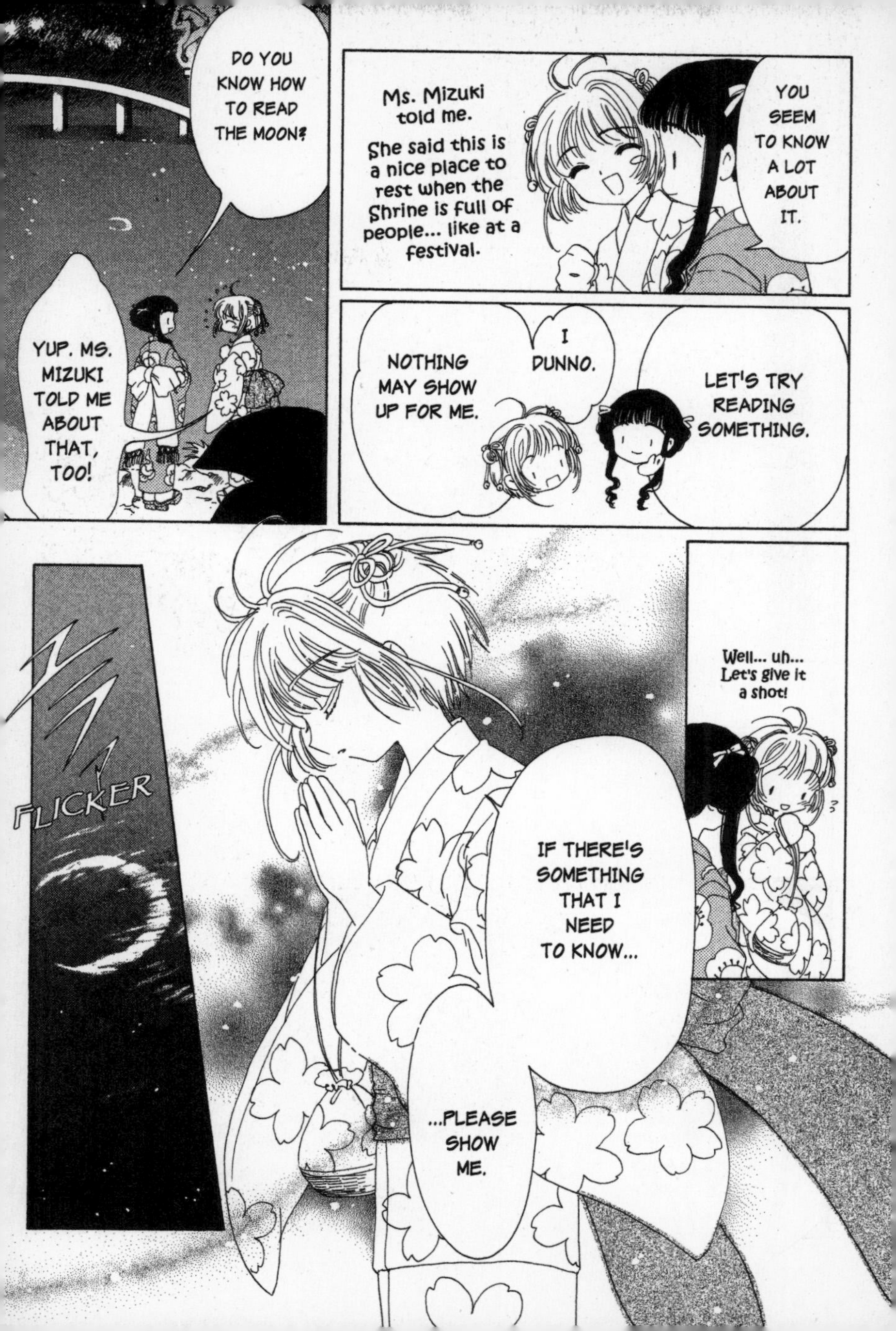
YOU SEEM TO KNOW A LOT ABOUT IT.
Ms. Mizuki told me.
She said this is a nice place to rest when the Shrine is full of people... like at a festival.
LET'S TRY READING SOMETHING.
I DUNNO.
NOTHING MAY SHOW UP FOR ME.
DO YOU KNOW HOW TO READ THE MOON?
YUP. MS. MIZUKI TOLD ME ABOUT THAT, TOO!
Well... uh... Let's give it a shot!
IF THERE'S SOMETHING THAT I NEED TO KNOW...
...PLEASE SHOW ME.
FLICKER

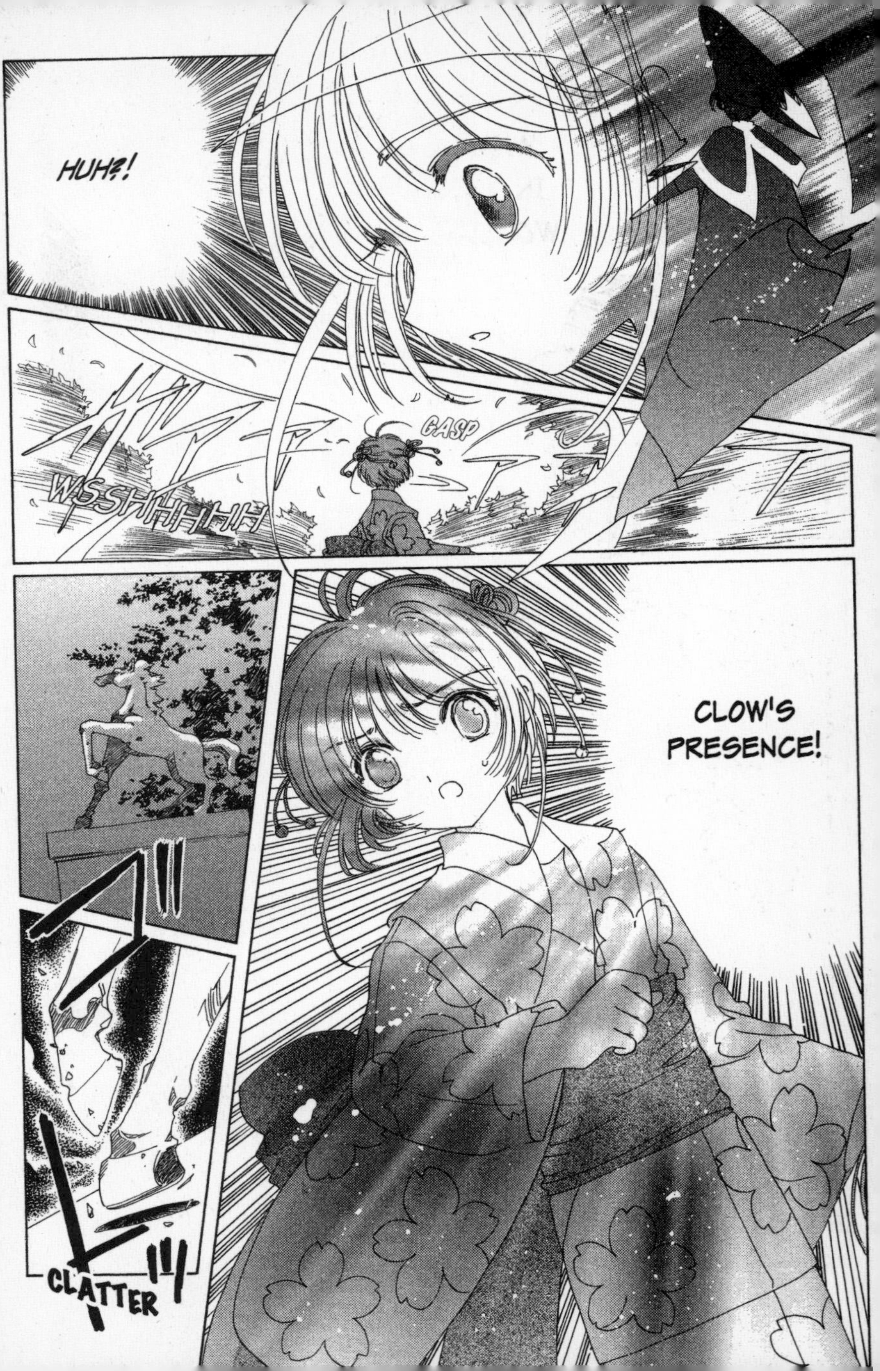
HUH?!
GASP
WSSHHHHHH
CLOW'S PRESENCE!
CLATTER

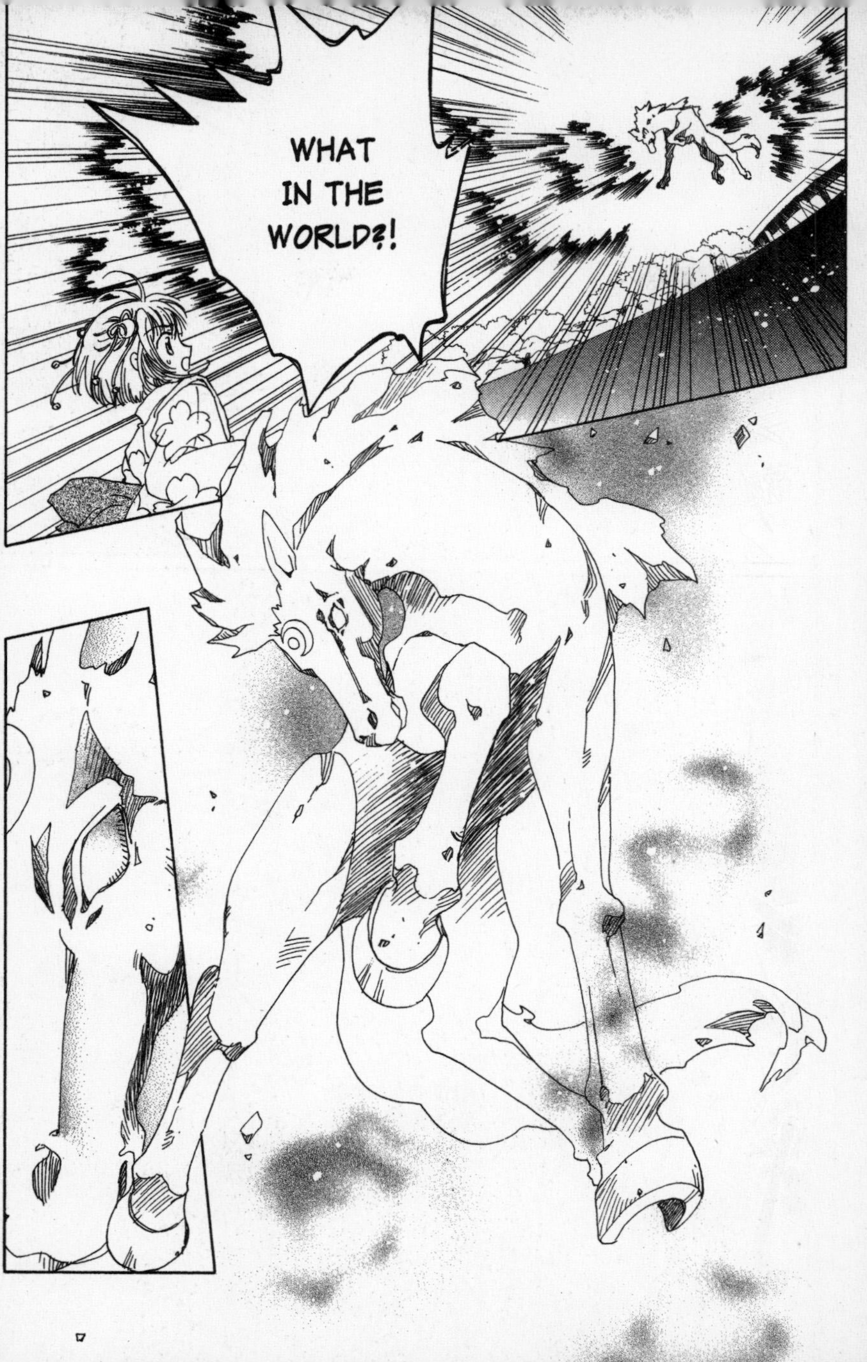
WHAT IN THE WORLD?!

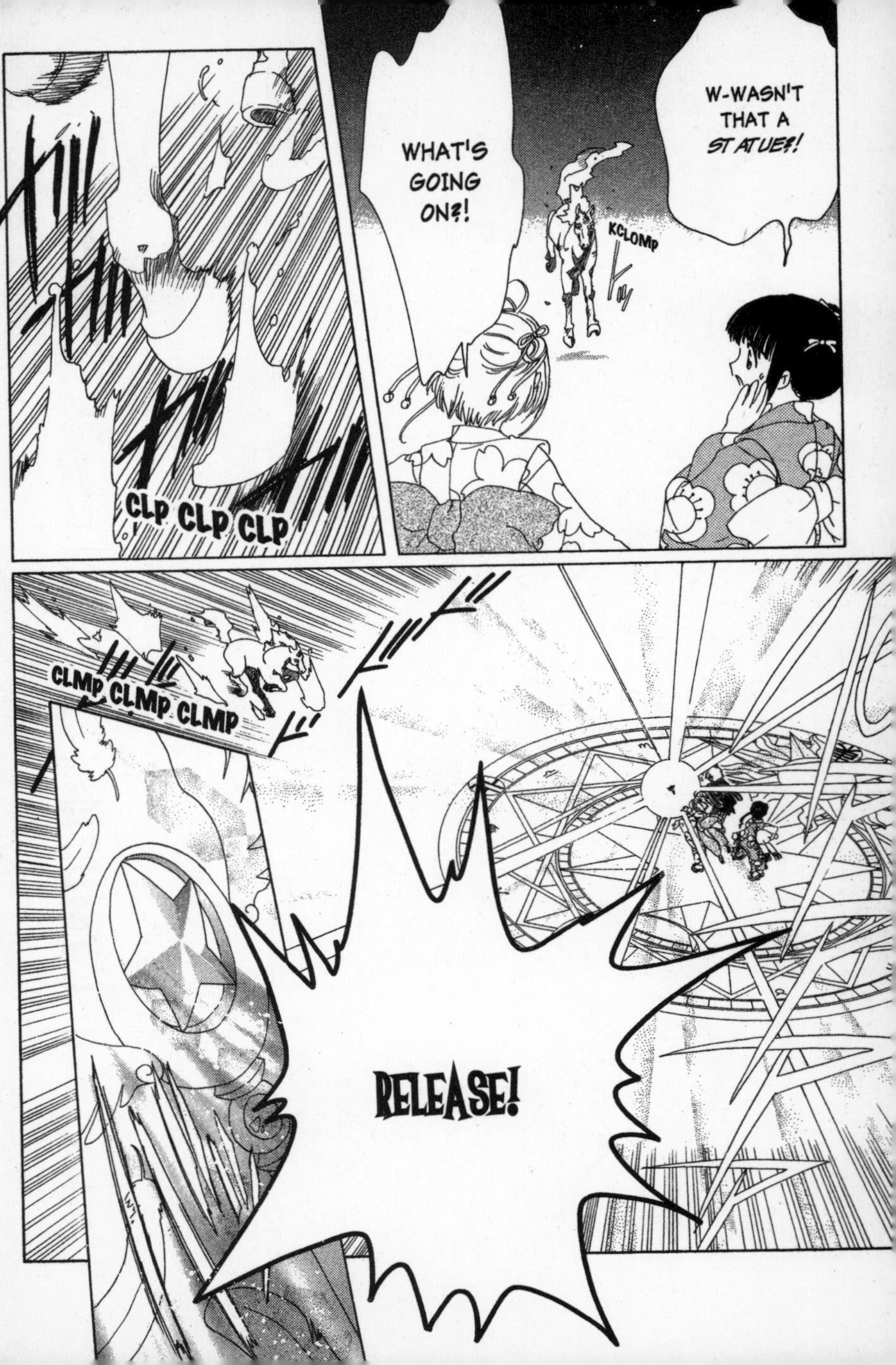
W-WASN'T THAT A STATUE?!
WHAT'S GOING ON?!
KCLOMP
CLP CLP CLP
CLMP CLMP CLMP
RELEASE!

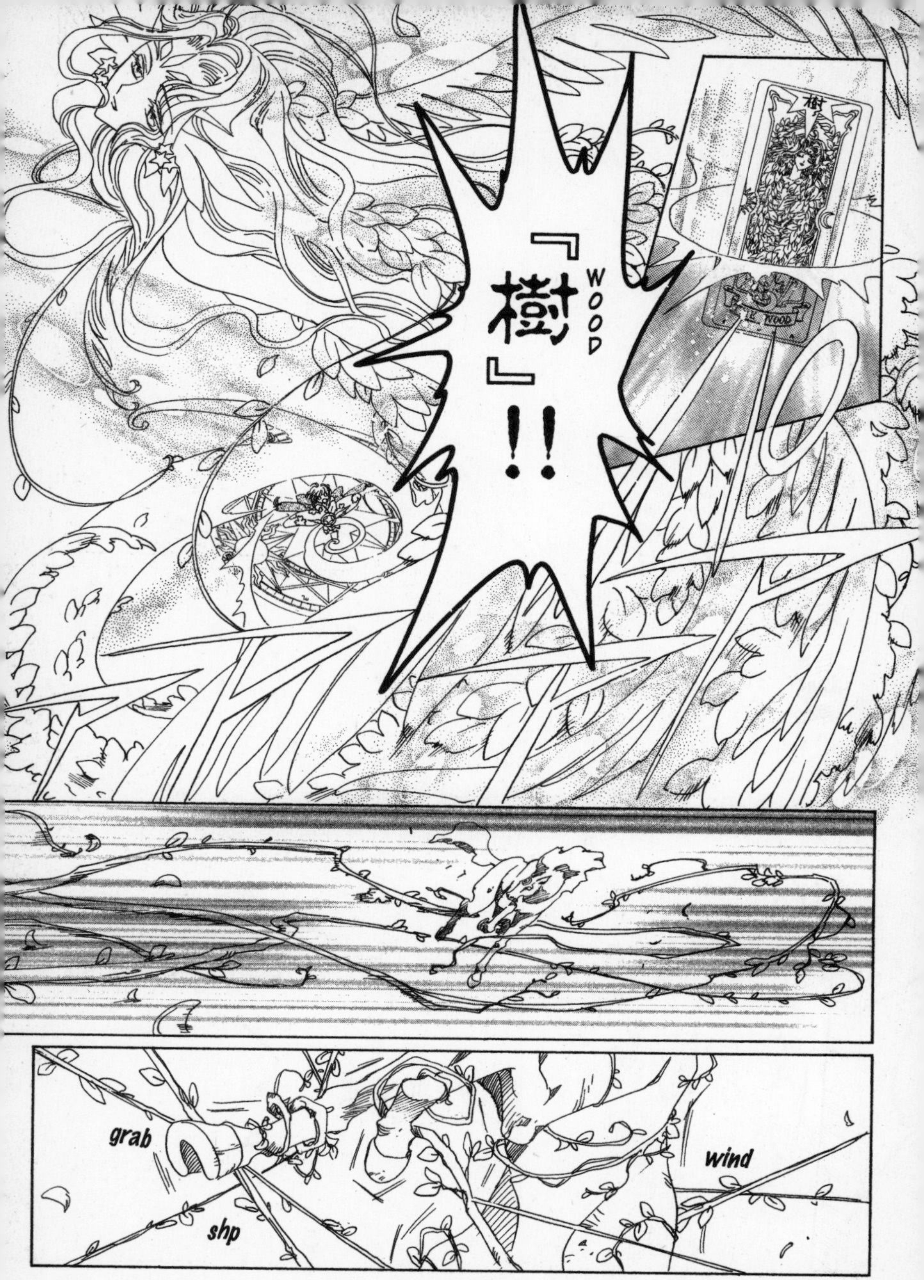
『樹』!!
WOOD
wind
grab
shp

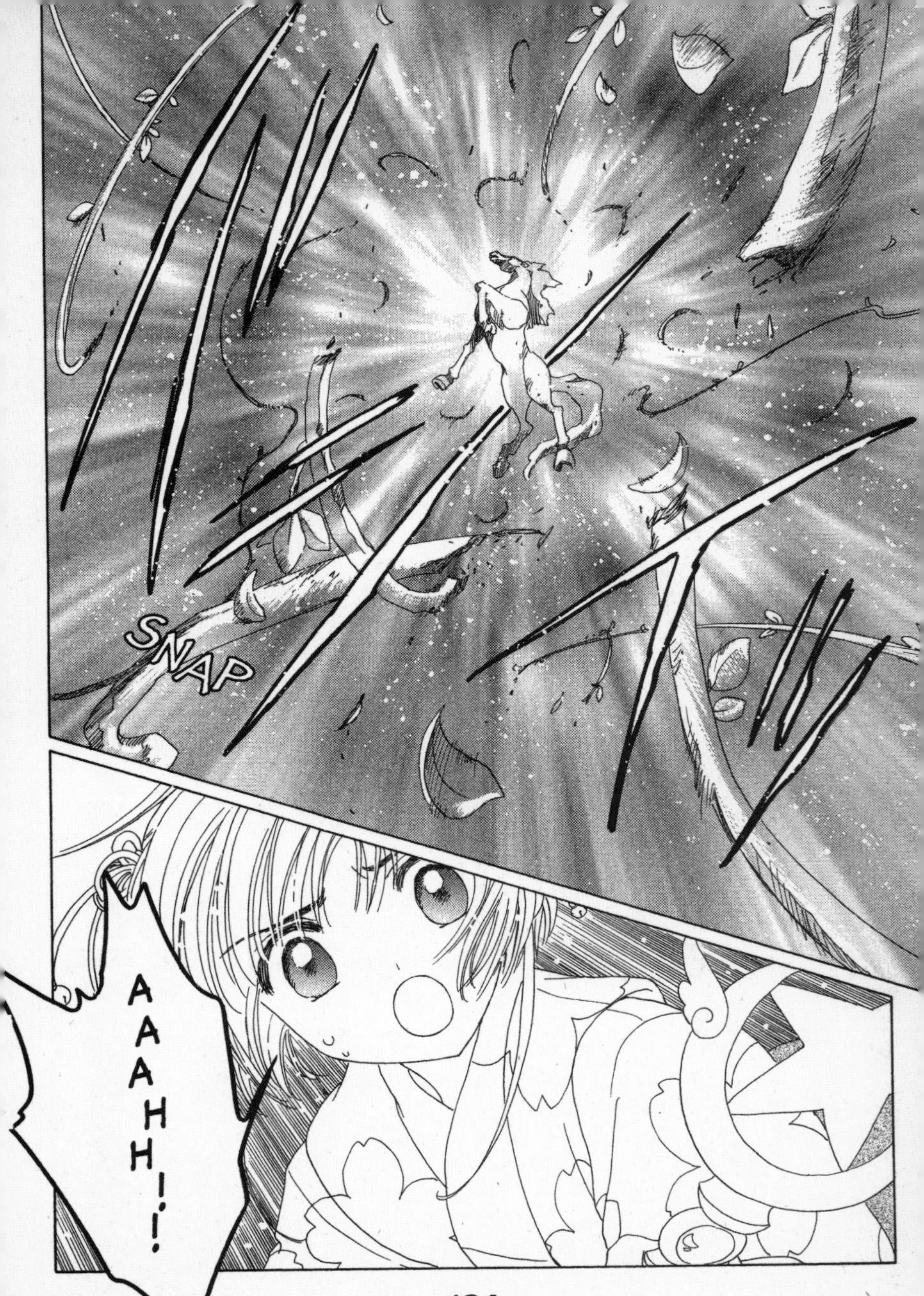
SNAP
AAAHH!!

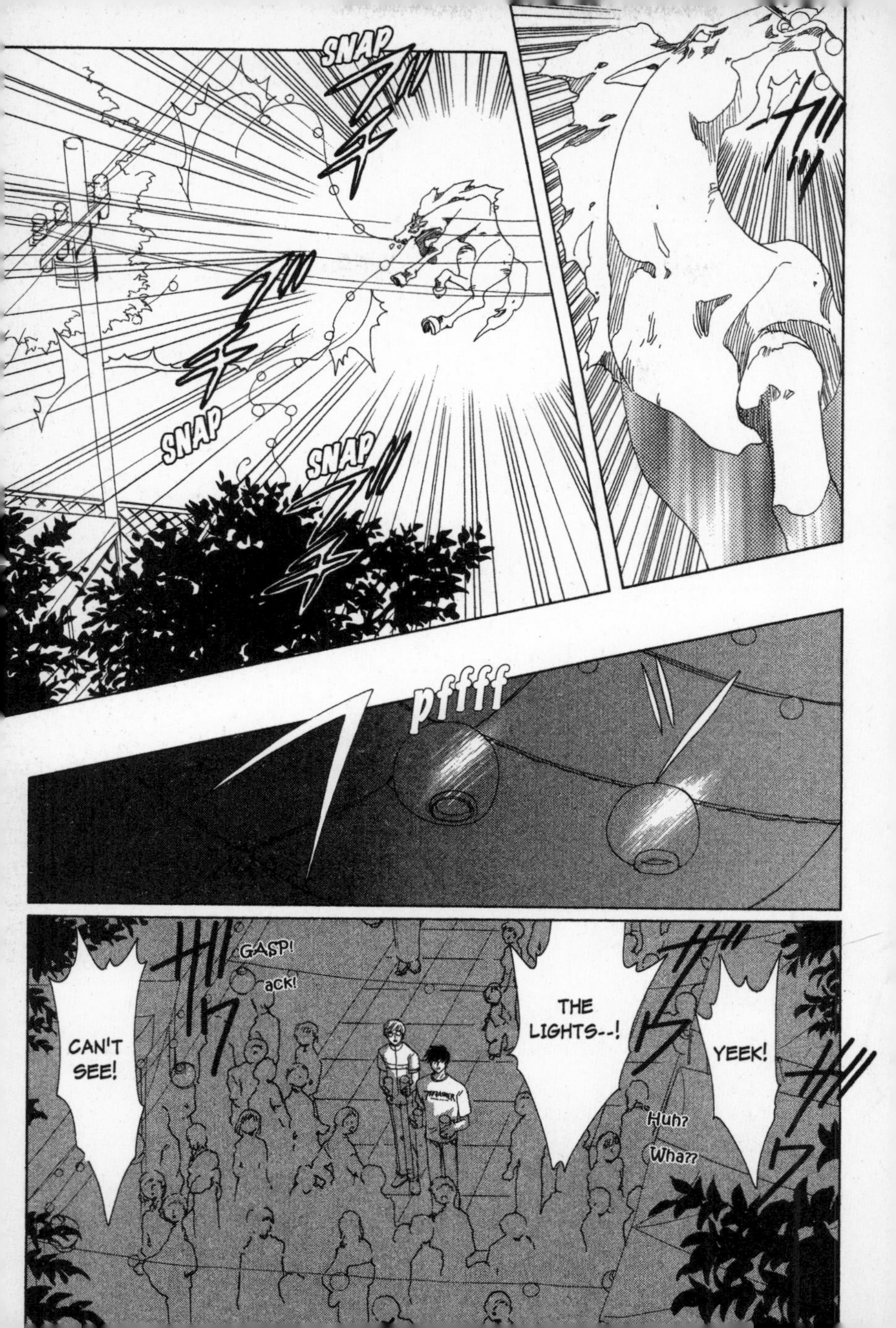
SNAP
SNAP
SNAP
pffff
YEEK!
Huh?
Wha??
THE LIGHTS--!
ack!
GASP!
CAN'T SEE!

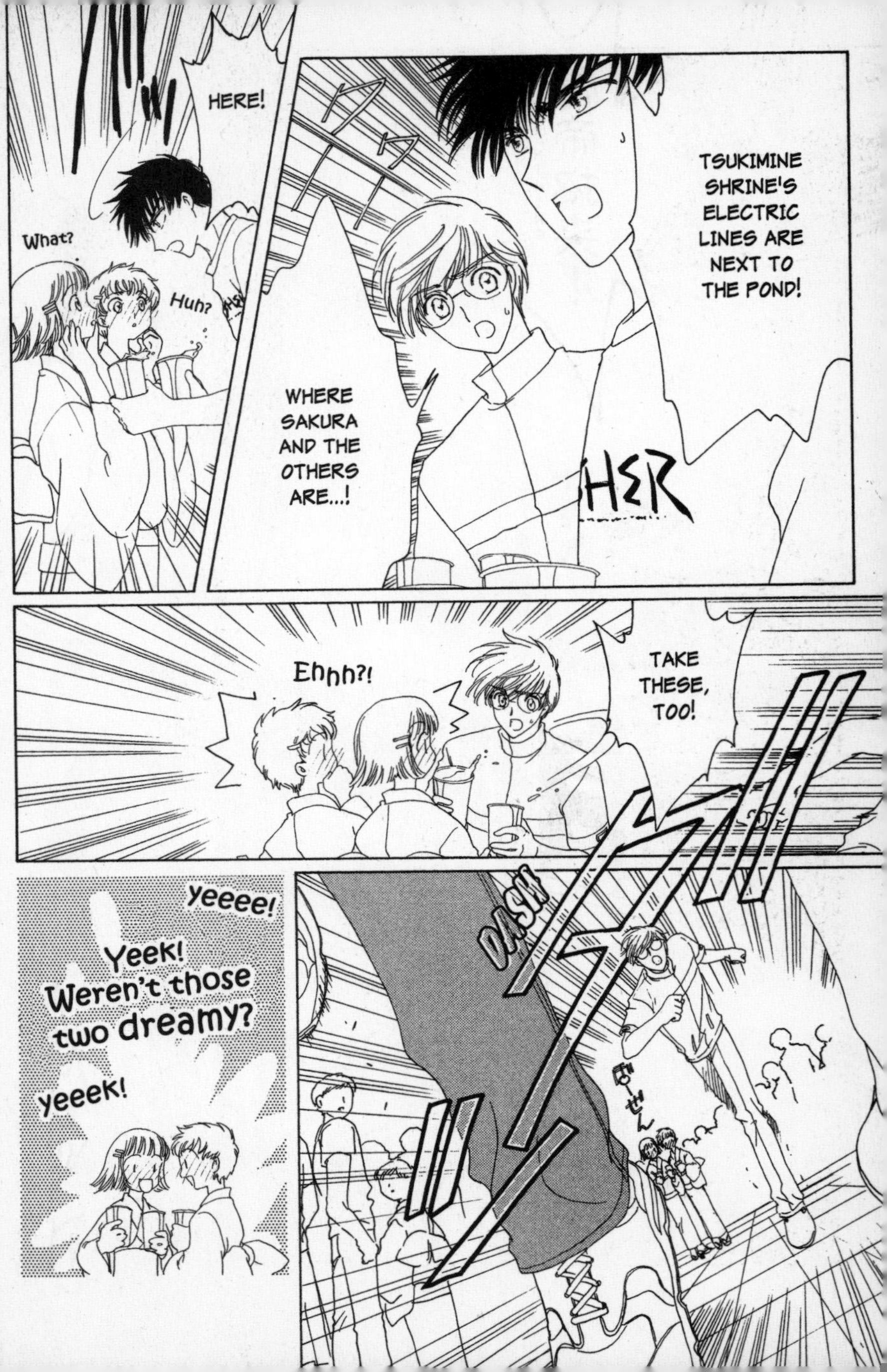
TSUKIMINE SHRINE'S ELECTRIC LINES ARE NEXT TO THE POND!
WHERE SAKURA AND THE OTHERS ARE...!
HERE!
What?
Huh?
TAKE THESE, TOO!
Ehhh?!
DASH
yeeee!
Yeek! Weren't those two dreamy?
yeeek!

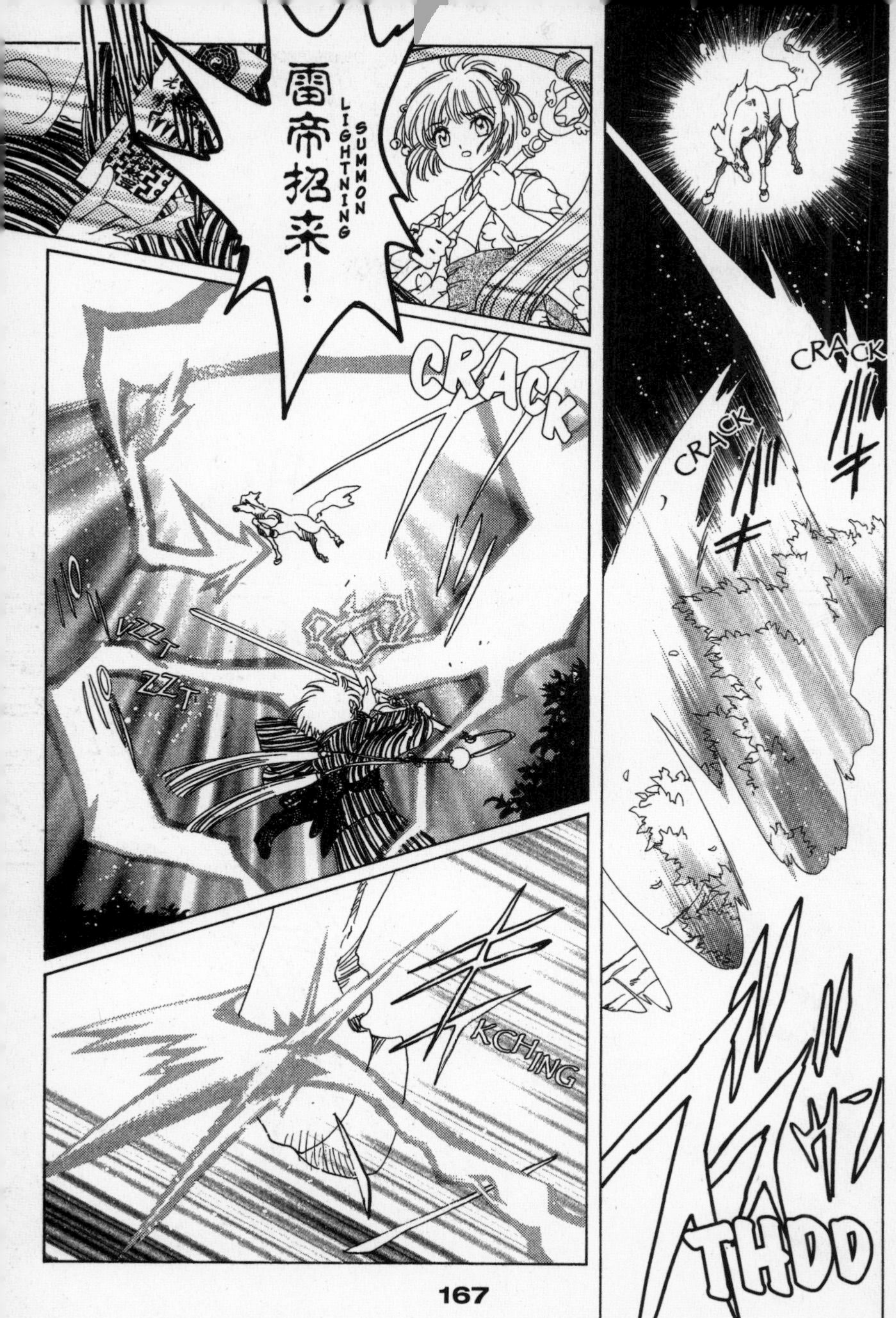
CRACK
CRACK
THDD
雷帝招来!
SUMMON LIGHTNING
CRACK
VZZZT
ZZZT
KCHING

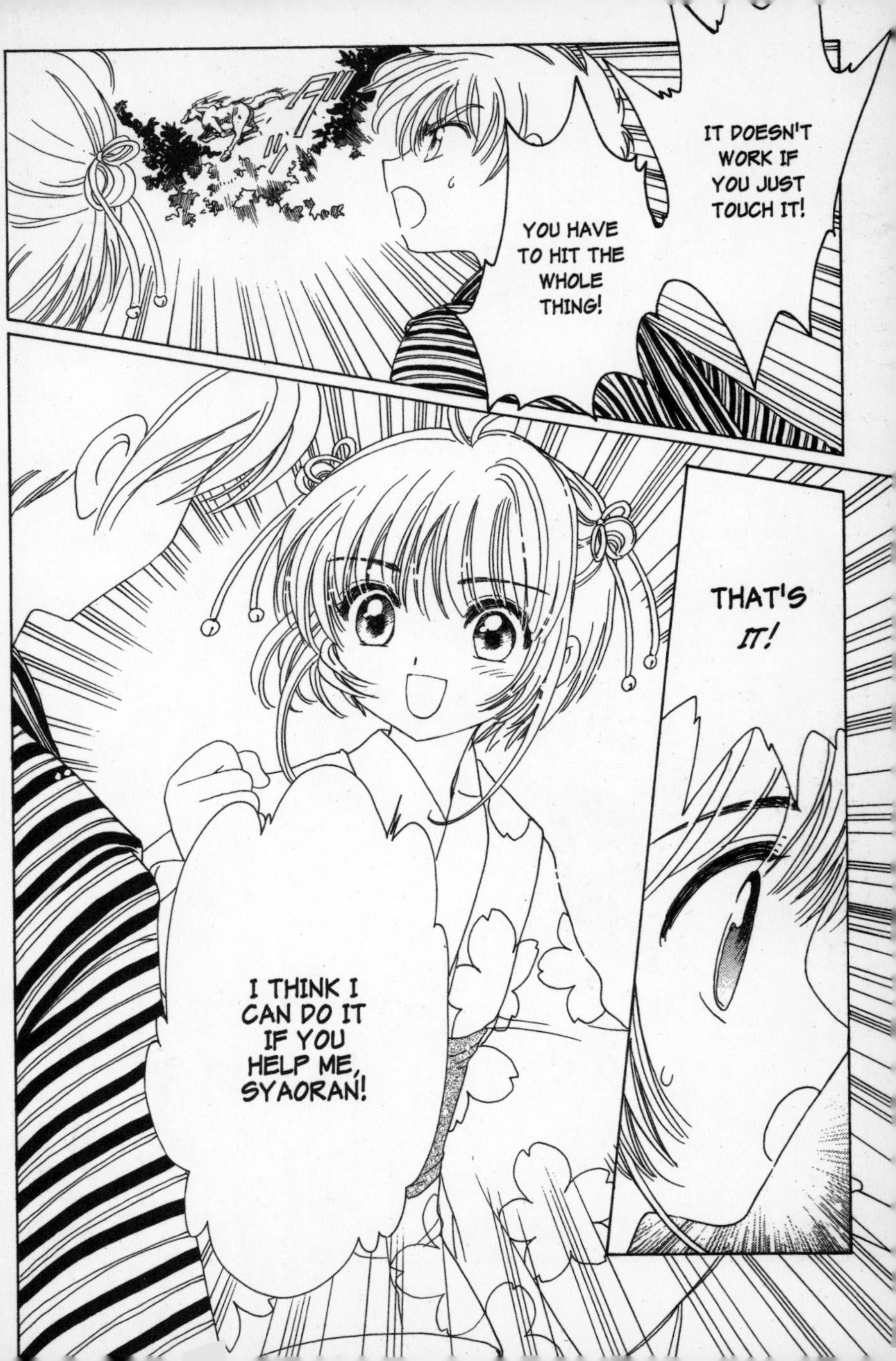
IT DOESN'T WORK IF YOU JUST TOUCH IT!
YOU HAVE TO HIT THE WHOLE THING!
THAT'S IT!
I THINK I CAN DO IT IF YOU HELP ME, SYAORAN!

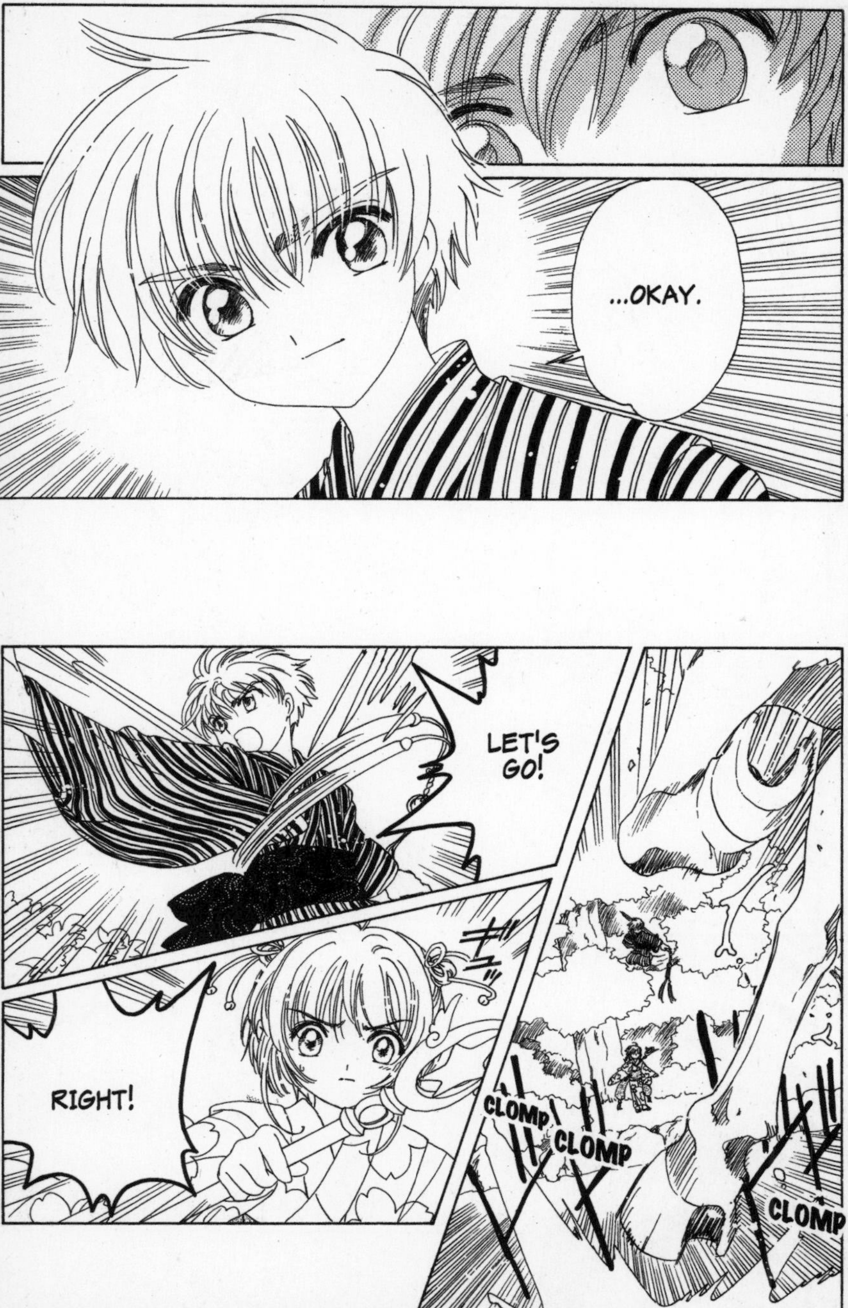
...OKAY.
CLOMP
CLOMP
CLOMP
LET'S GO!
RIGHT!

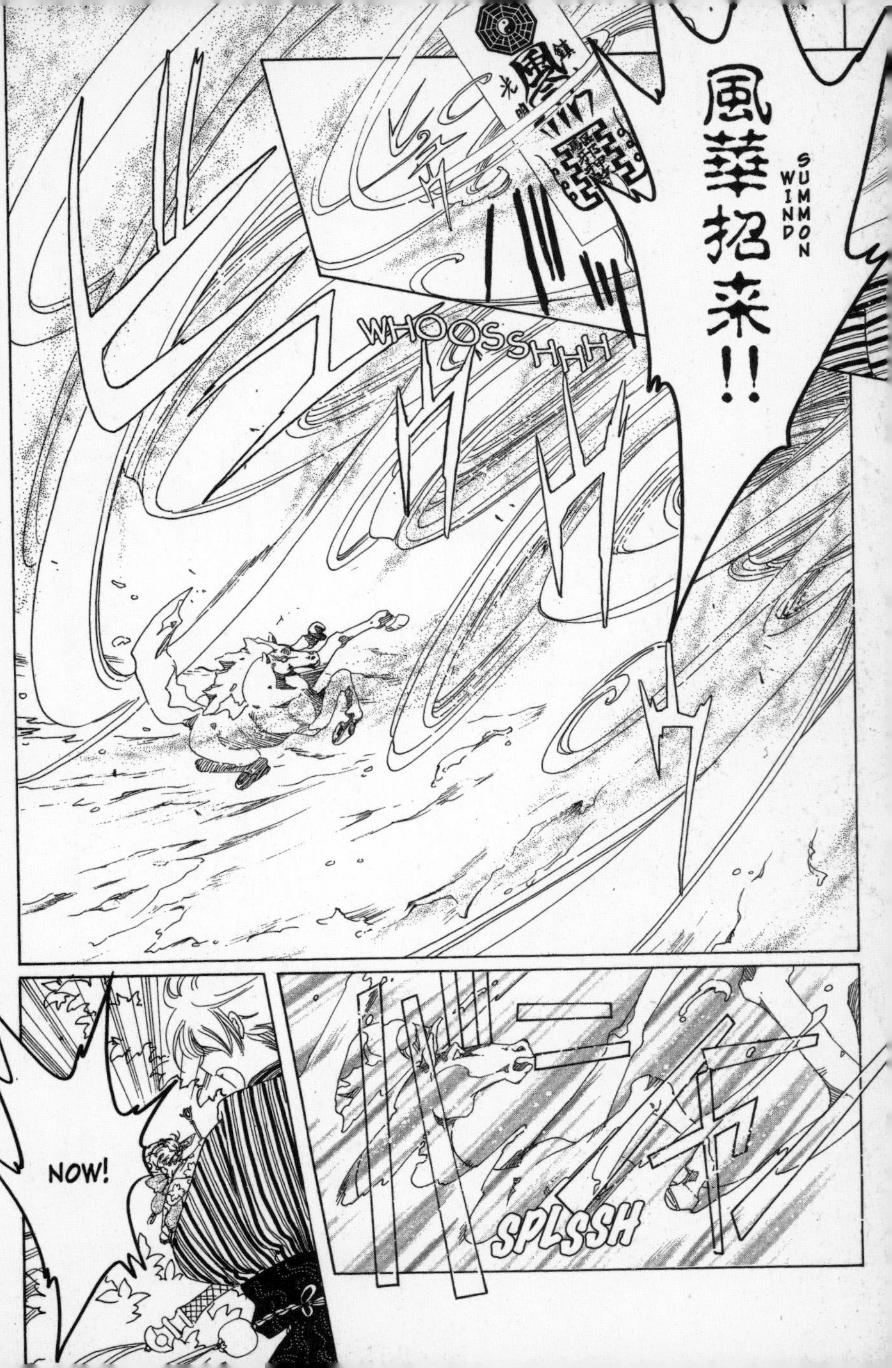
風華招来!!
SUMMON WIND
WHOOSSHHH
SPLSSH
NOW!

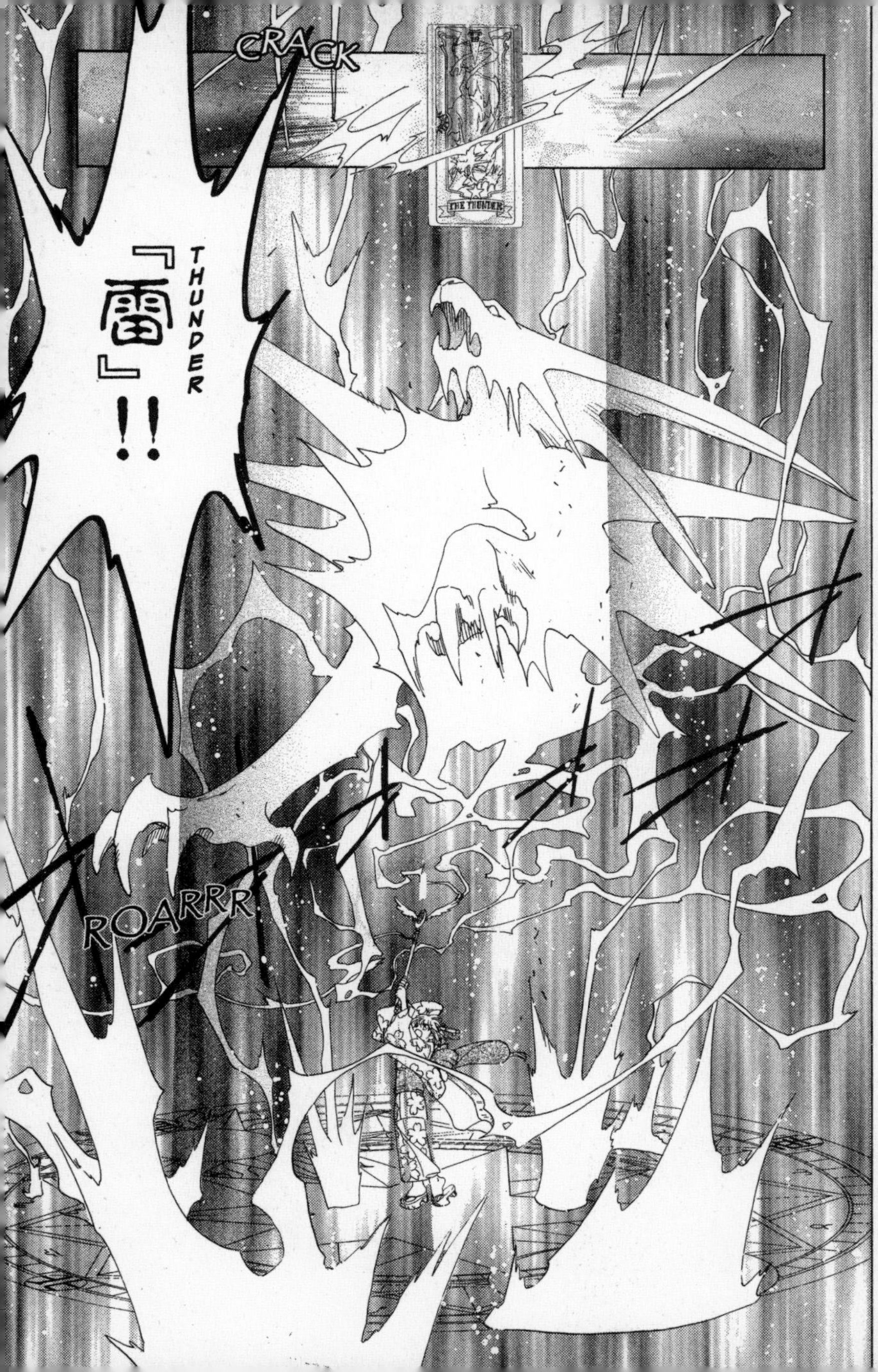
CRACK
THE THUNDER
『雷』!!
THUNDER
ROARRR

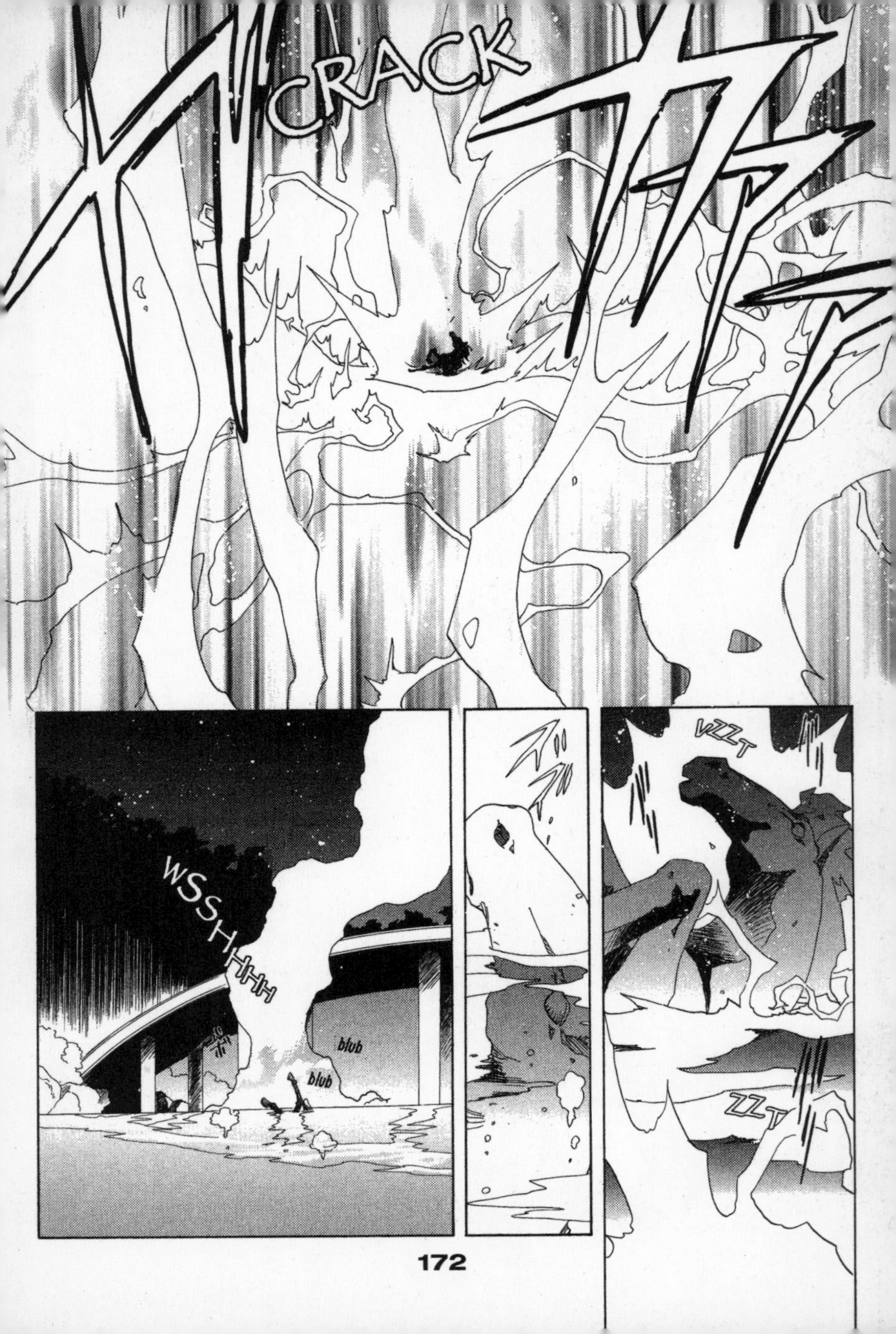
CRACK
VZZT
ZZT
WSSHHHH
blub
blub

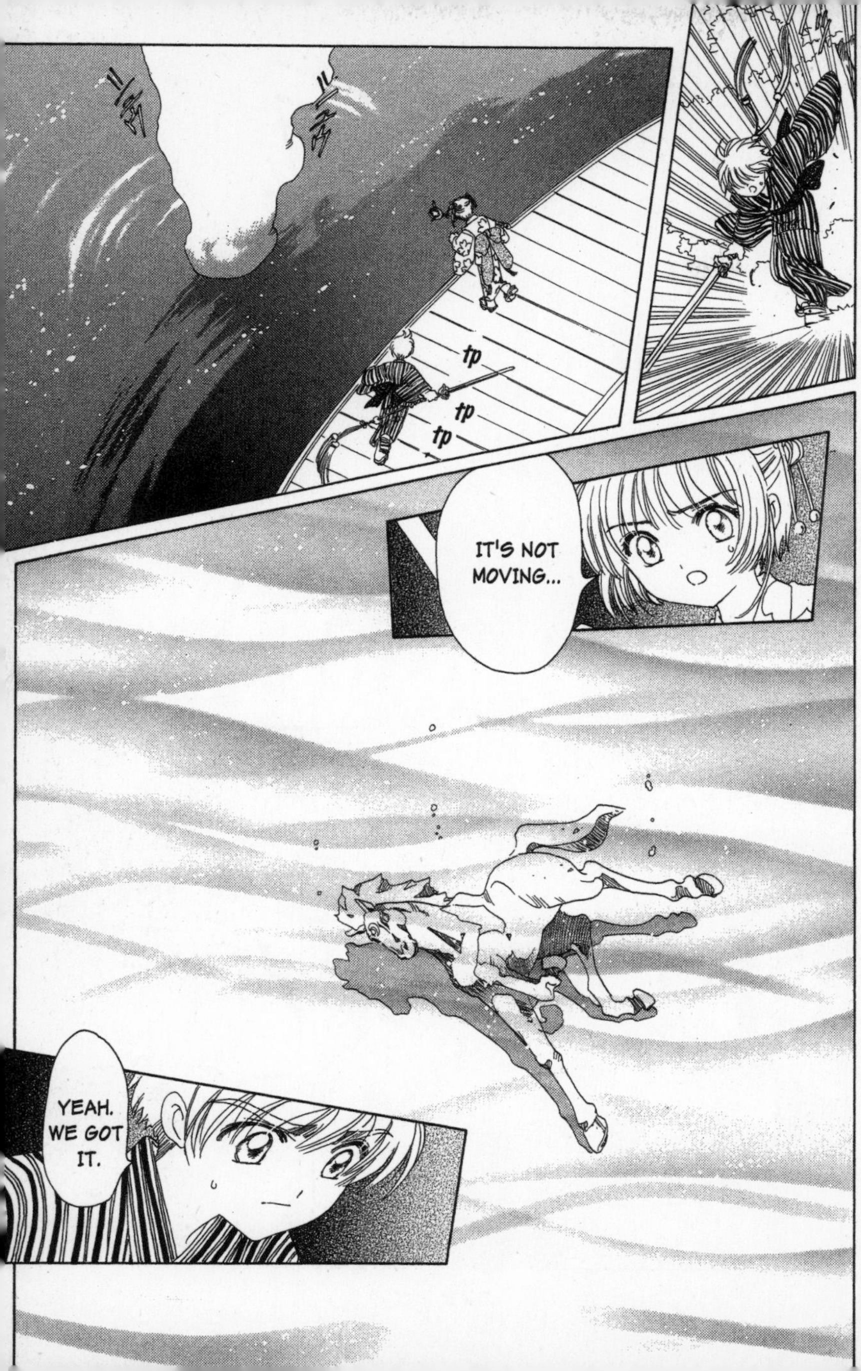
tp
tp
tp
IT'S NOT MOVING...
YEAH. WE GOT IT.

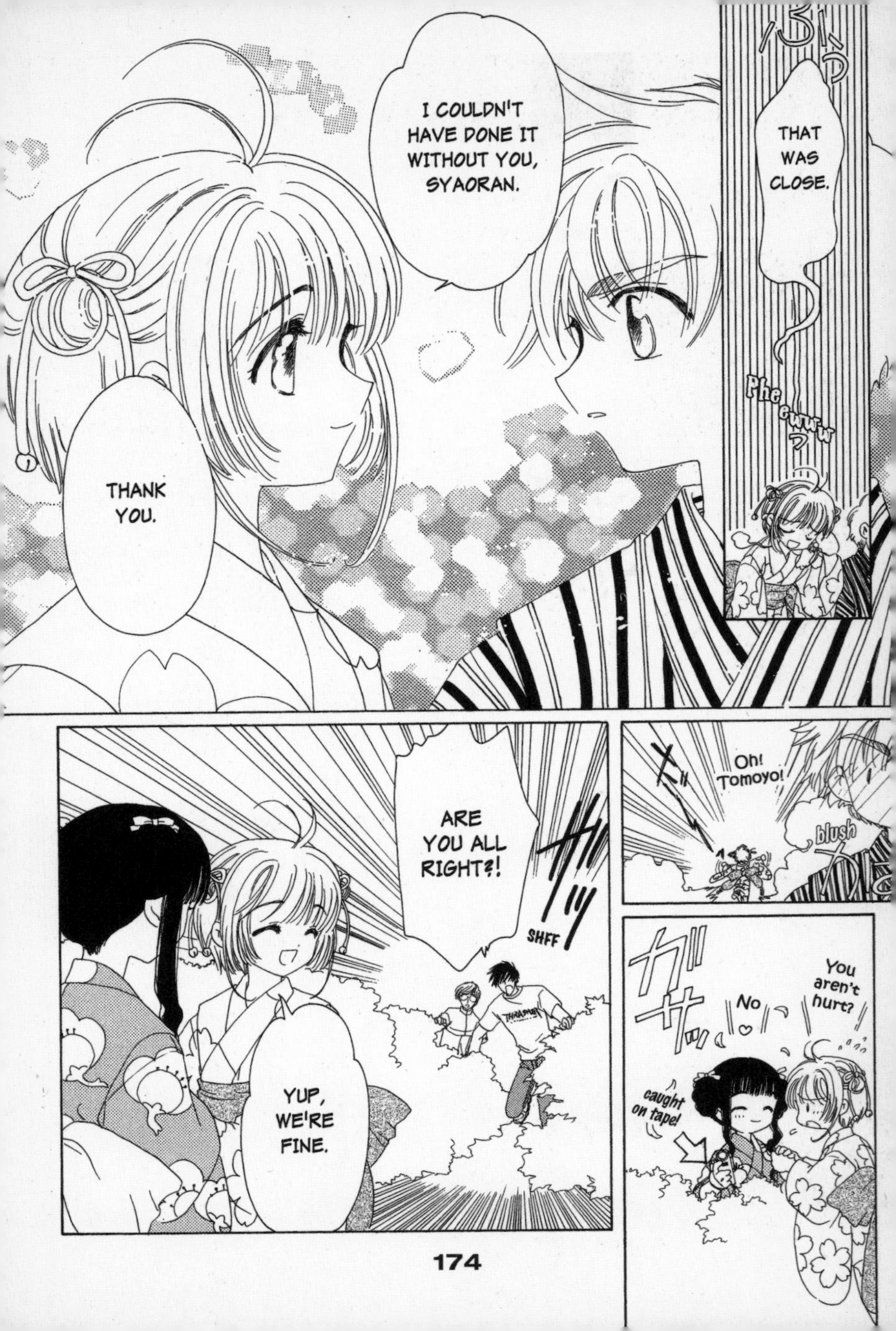
THAT WAS CLOSE.
Pheewww
I COULDN'T HAVE DONE IT WITHOUT YOU, SYAORAN.
THANK YOU.
Oh! Tomoyo!
blush
You aren't hurt?
No
caught on tape!
ARE YOU ALL RIGHT?!
SHFF
YUP, WE'RE FINE.

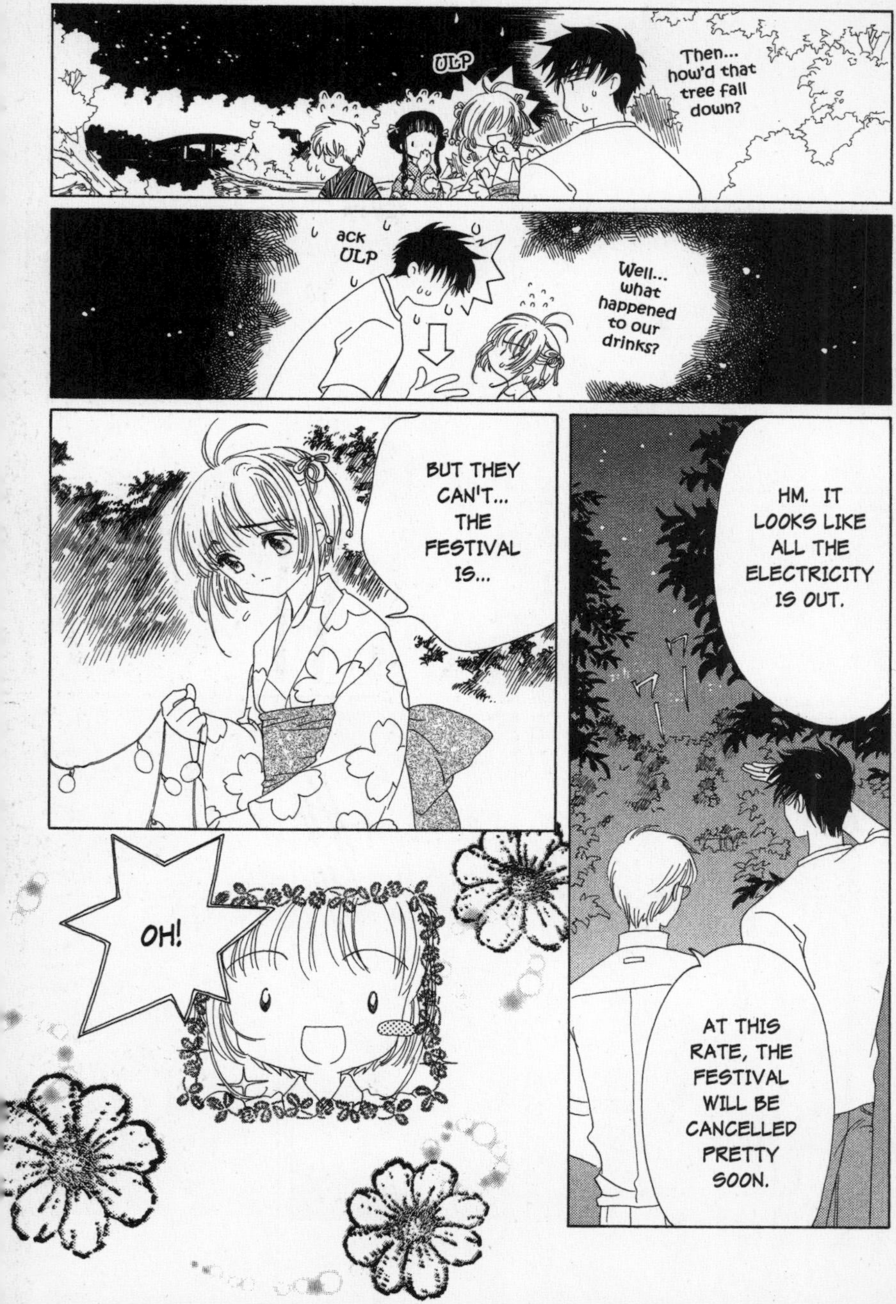
Then... how'd that tree fall down?
ULP
Well... what happened to our drinks?
ack ULP
HM. IT LOOKS LIKE ALL THE ELECTRICITY IS OUT.
AT THIS RATE, THE FESTIVAL WILL BE CANCELLED PRETTY SOON.
BUT THEY CAN'T... THE FESTIVAL IS...
OH!

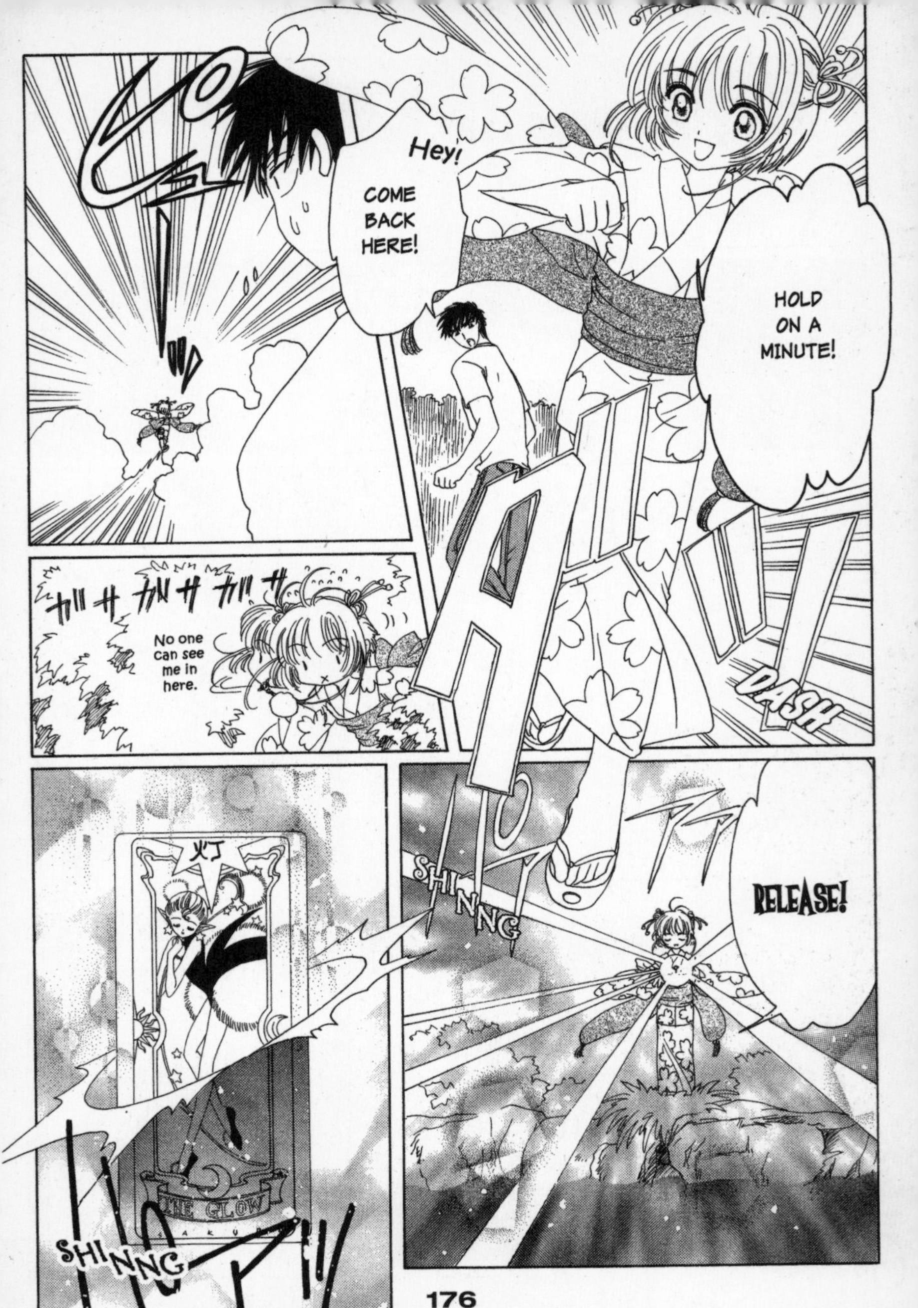
HOLD ON A MINUTE!
DASH
Hey!
COME BACK HERE!
No one can see me in here.
RELEASE!
SHINNG
THE GLOW
SHINNG

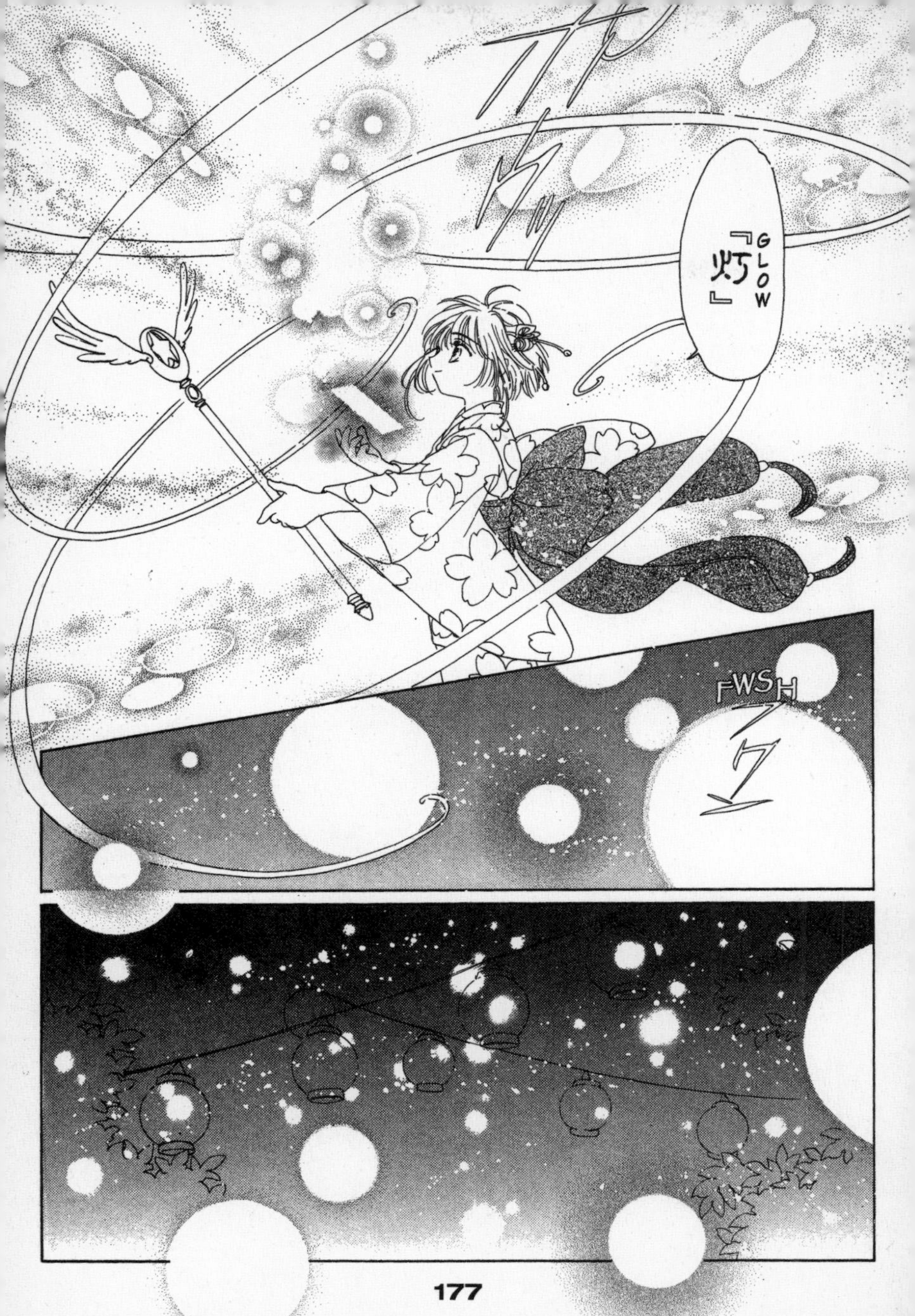
GLOW
「灯」
FWSH

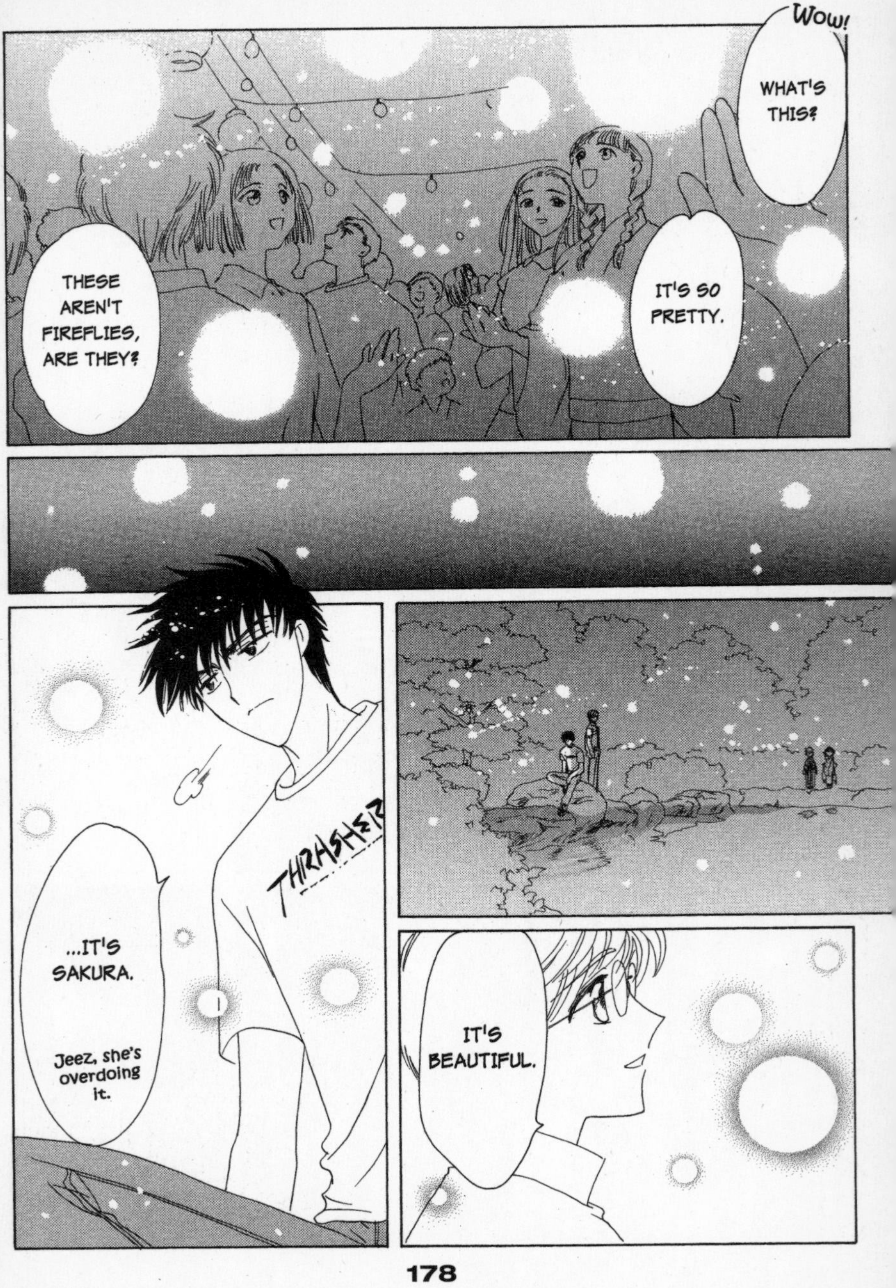
Wow!
WHAT'S THIS?
IT'S SO PRETTY.
THESE AREN'T FIREFLIES, ARE THEY?
IT'S BEAUTIFUL.
...IT'S SAKURA.
Jeez, she's overdoing it.

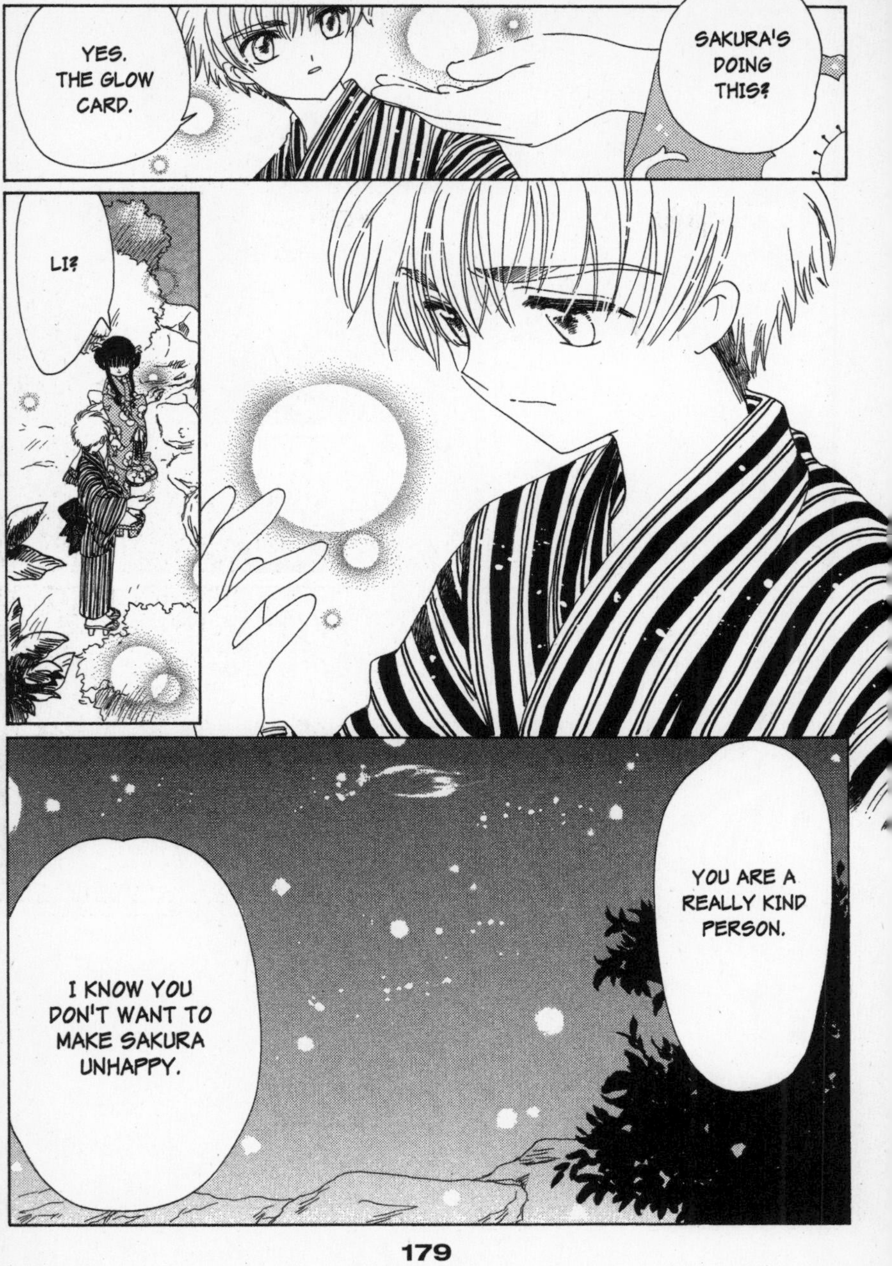
SAKURA'S DOING THIS?
YES. THE GLOW CARD.
LI?
YOU ARE A REALLY KIND PERSON.
I KNOW YOU DON'T WANT TO MAKE SAKURA UNHAPPY.

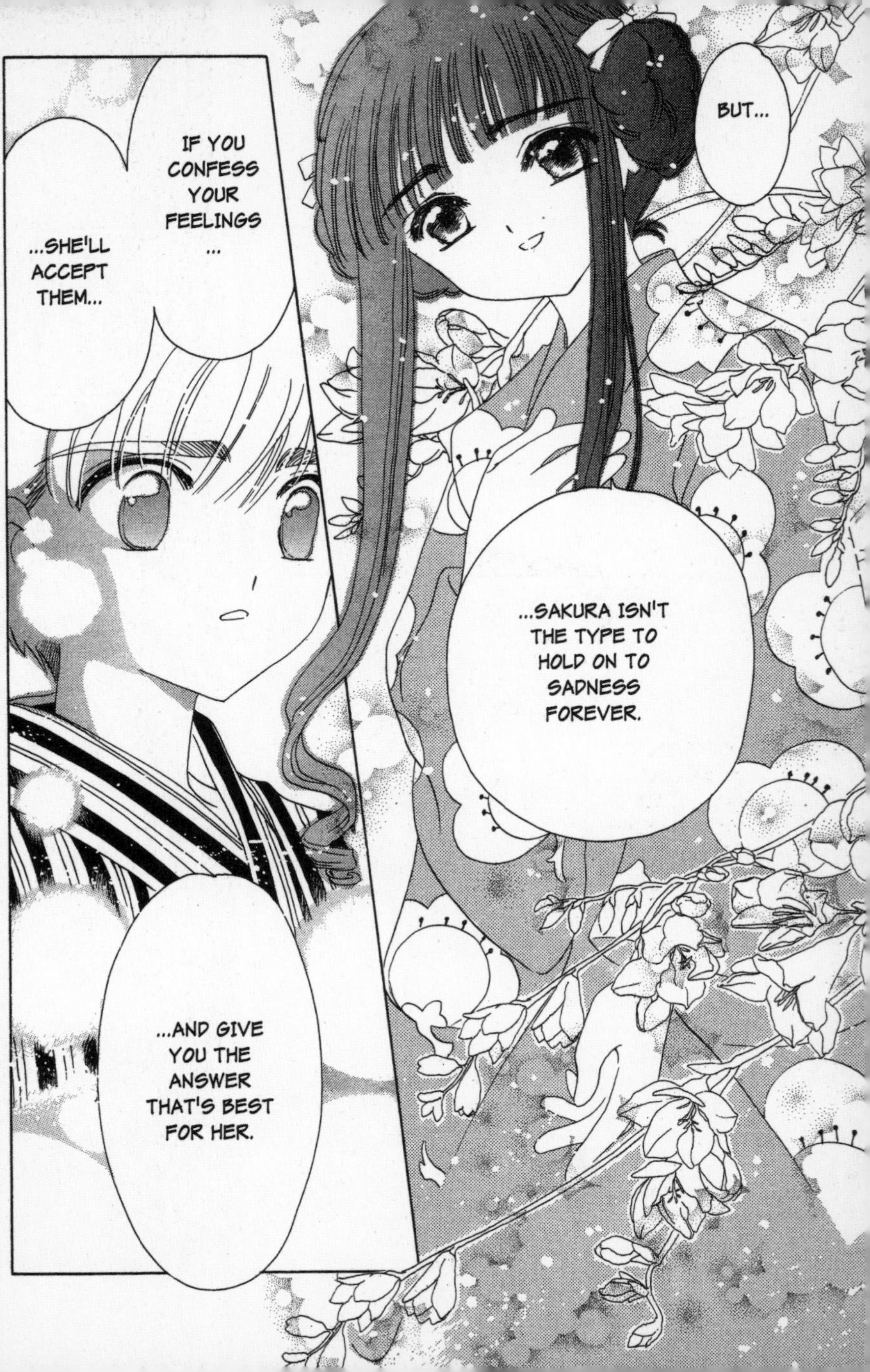
BUT...
...SAKURA ISN'T THE TYPE TO HOLD ON TO SADNESS FOREVER.
IF YOU CONFESS YOUR FEELINGS ...
...SHE'LL ACCEPT THEM...
...AND GIVE YOU THE ANSWER THAT'S BEST FOR HER.

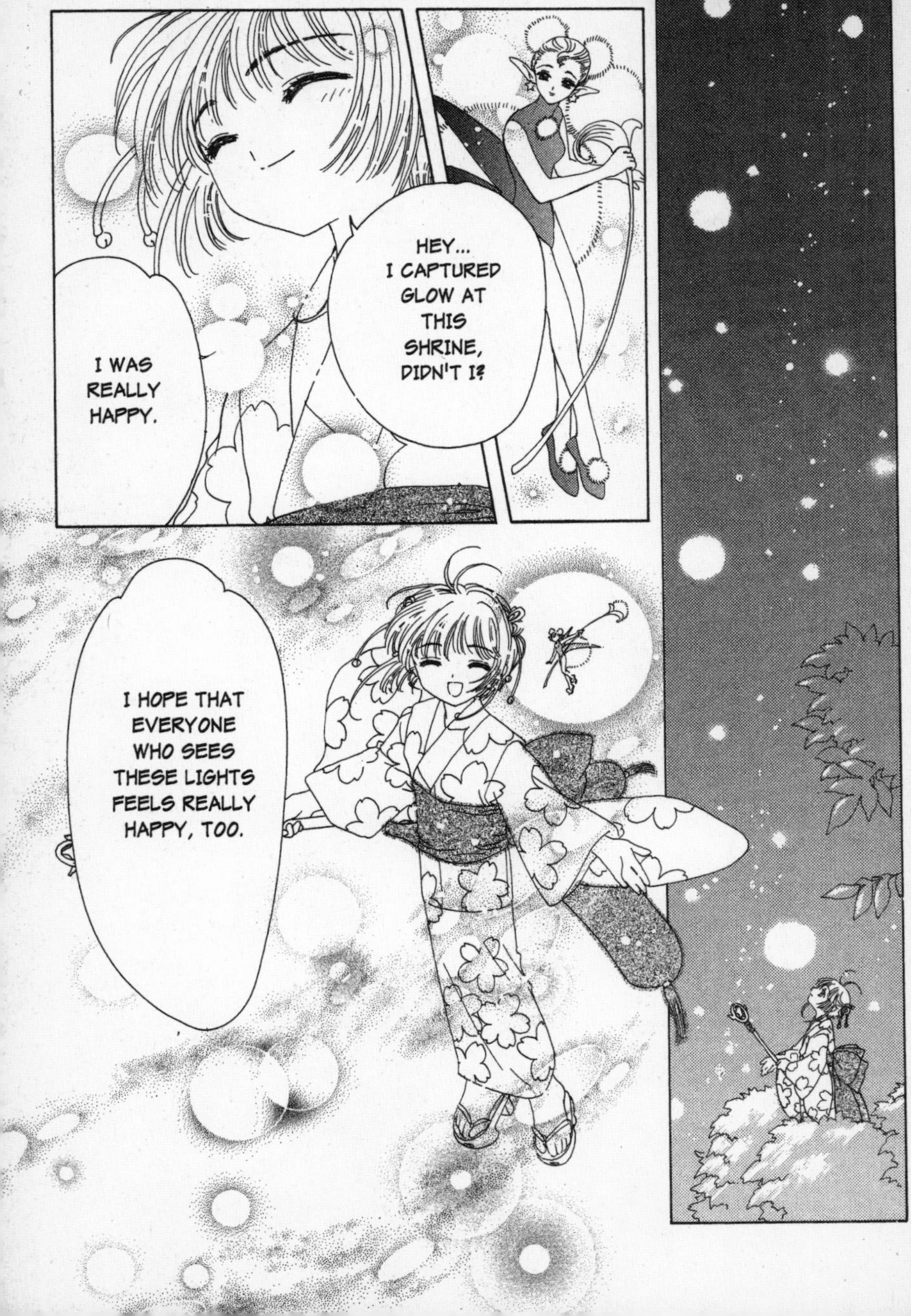
HEY... I CAPTURED GLOW AT THIS SHRINE, DIDN'T I?
I WAS REALLY HAPPY.
I HOPE THAT EVERYONE WHO SEES THESE LIGHTS FEELS REALLY HAPPY, TOO.

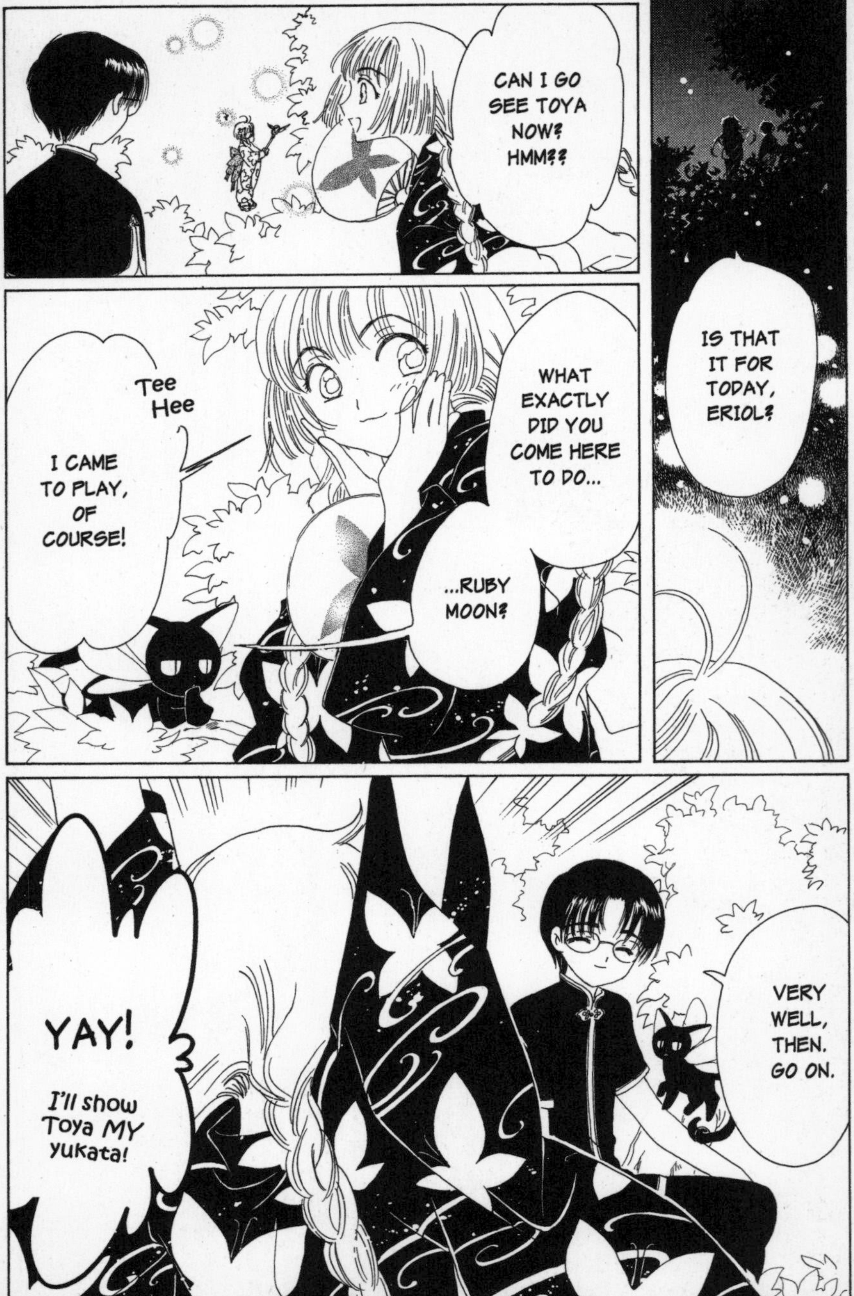
IS THAT IT FOR TODAY, ERIOL?
CAN I GO SEE TOYA NOW? HMM??
WHAT EXACTLY DID YOU COME HERE TO DO...
...RUBY MOON?
Tee Hee
I CAME TO PLAY, OF COURSE!
VERY WELL, THEN. GO ON.
YAY!
I'll show Toya MY yukata!

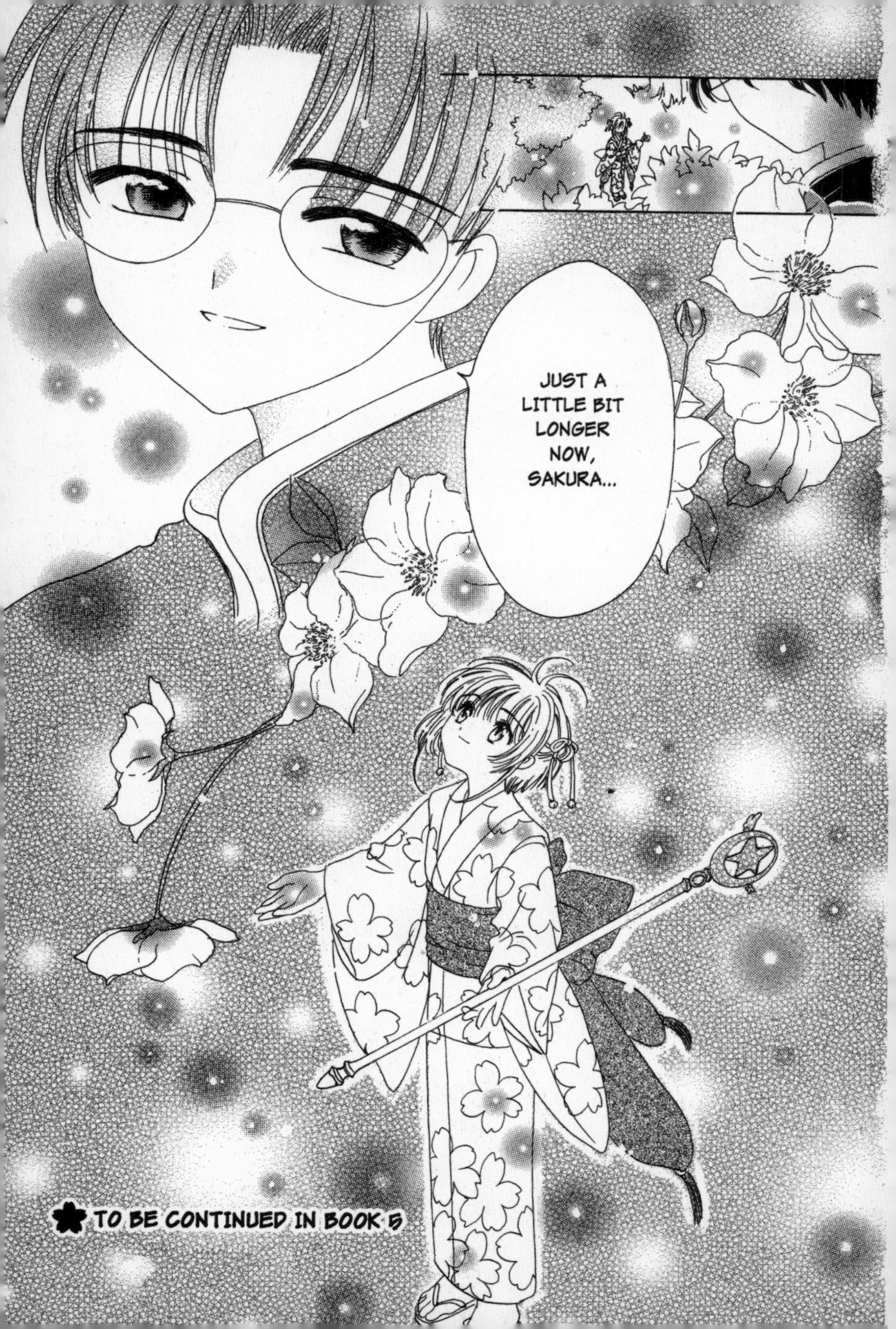
JUST A LITTLE BIT LONGER NOW, SAKURA...
TO BE CONTINUED IN BOOK 5

CARDCAPTOR SAKURA

MASTER OF THE CLOW

Part the Fifth

The magic continues June 2003

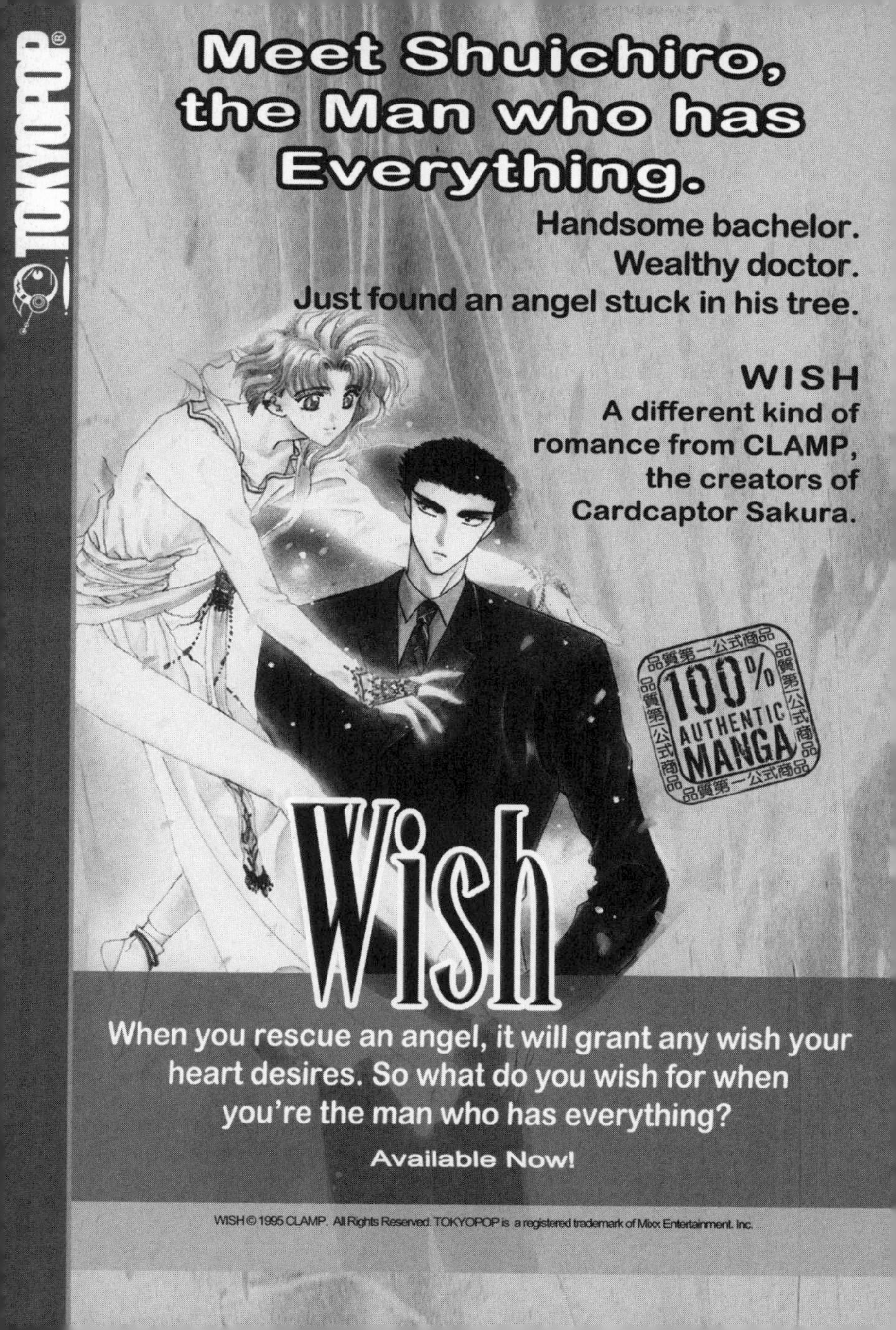
TOKYOPOP
Meet Shuichiro, the Man who has Everything.
Handsome bachelor.
Wealthy doctor.
Just found an angel stuck in his tree.
WISH
A different kind of romance from CLAMP, the creators of Cardcaptor Sakura.
100% AUTHENTIC MANGA
品質第一公式商品
Wish
When you rescue an angel, it will grant any wish your heart desires. So what do you wish for when you're the man who has everything?
Available Now!
WISH © 1995 CLAMP. All Rights Reserved. TOKYOPOP is a registered trademark of Mixx Entertainment, Inc.

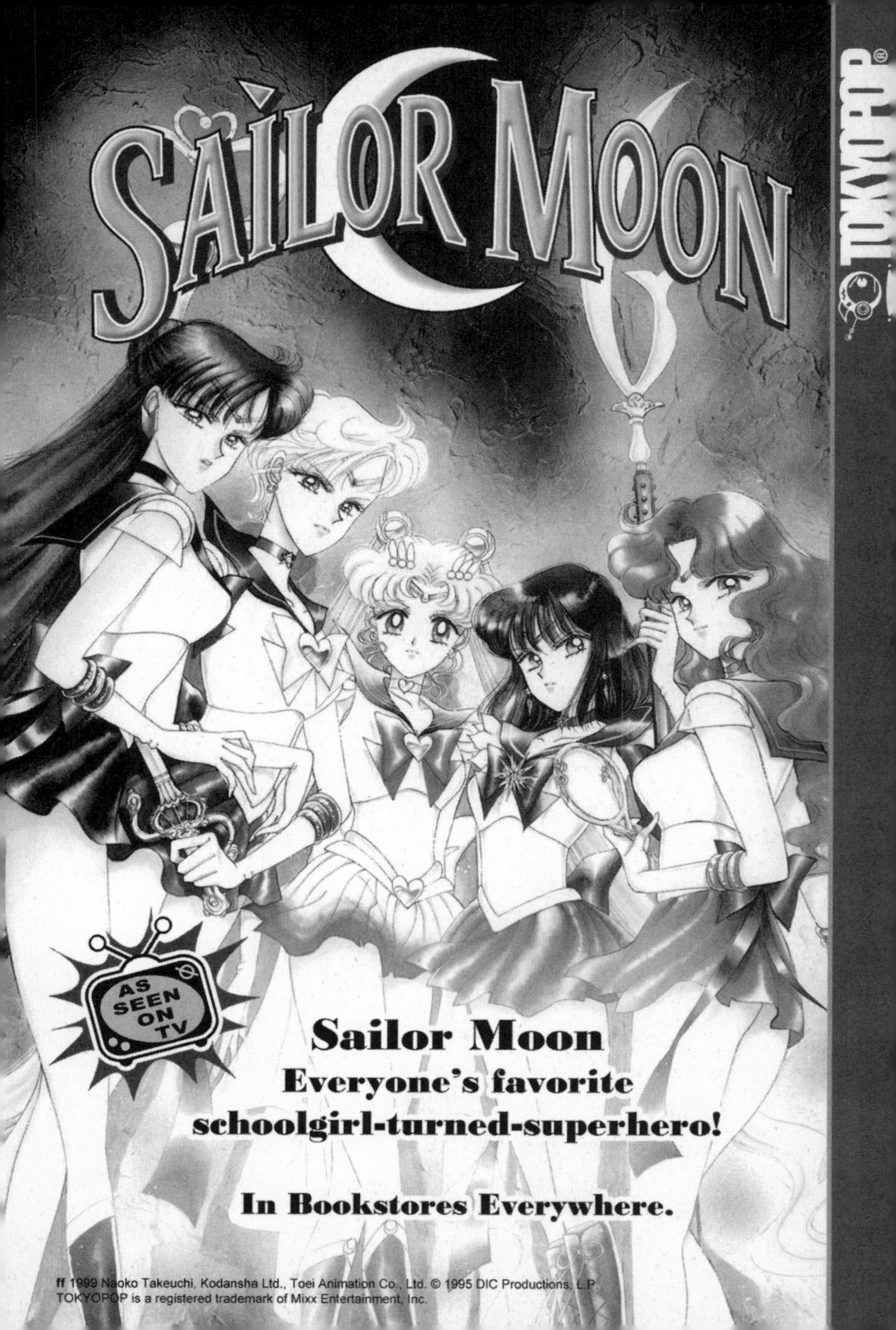
SAILOR MOON
AS SEEN ON TV
Sailor Moon
Everyone's favorite
schoolgirl-turned-superhero!
In Bookstores Everywhere.
TOKYOPOP

MARS
TOKYOPOP®
100% AUTHENTIC MANGA
A Bad Boy Can Change
A Good Girl Forever.
Authentic Right-to-Left Manga
Available Now

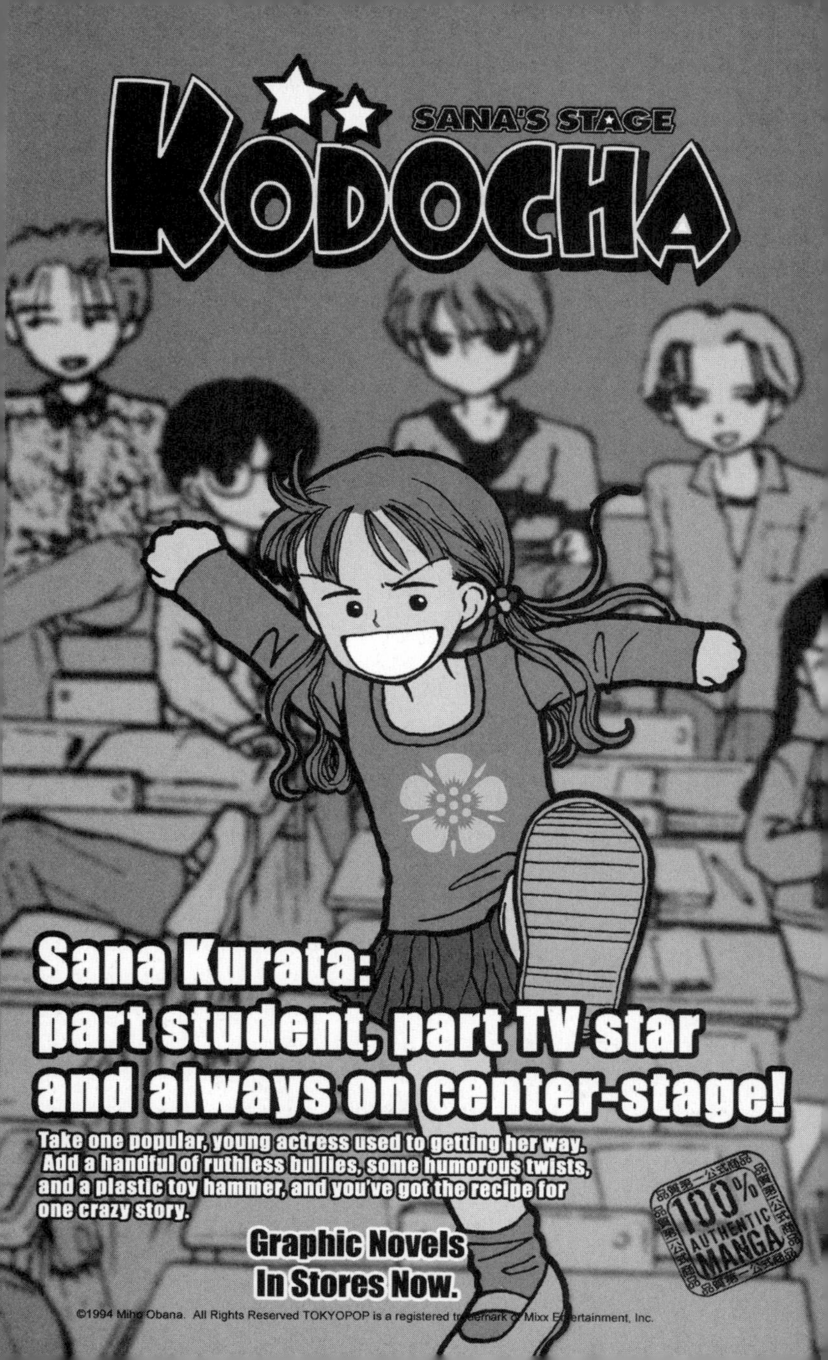
KODOCHA
SANA'S STAGE
Sana Kurata:
part student, part TV star
and always on center-stage!
Take one popular, young actress used to getting her way. Add a handful of ruthless bullies, some humorous twists, and a plastic toy hammer, and you've got the recipe for one crazy story.
100% AUTHENTIC MANGA
Graphic Novels
In Stores Now.
©1994 Miho Obana. All Rights Reserved TOKYOPOP is a registered trademark of Mixx Entertainment, Inc.

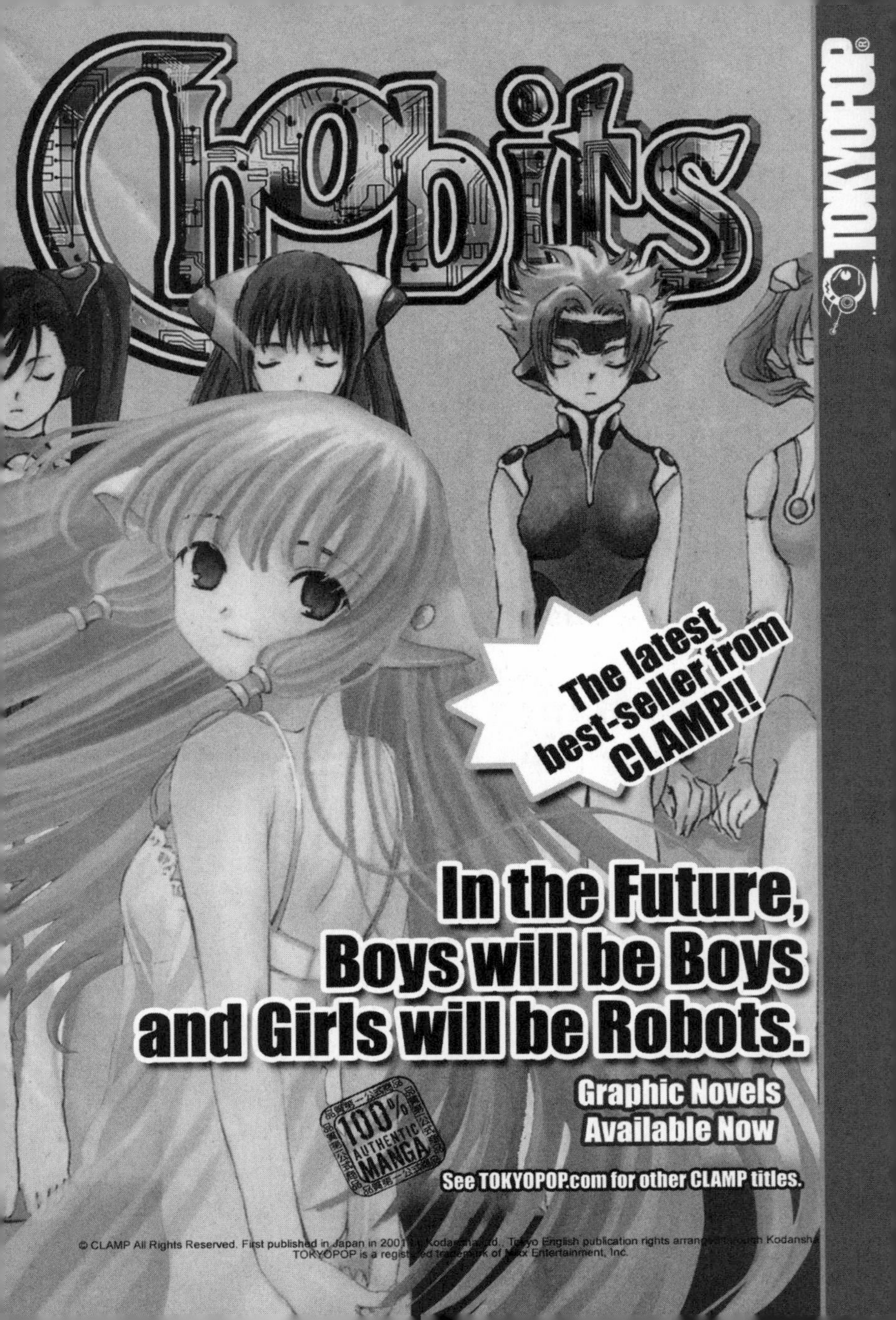
Chobits
TOKYOPOP
The latest best-seller from CLAMP!!
In the Future, Boys will be Boys and Girls will be Robots.
Graphic Novels Available Now
100% AUTHENTIC MANGA
See TOKYOPOP.com for other CLAMP titles.
© CLAMP All Rights Reserved. First published in Japan in 2001
English publication rights
Kodansha
TOKYOPOP is a regist
Entertainment, Inc.

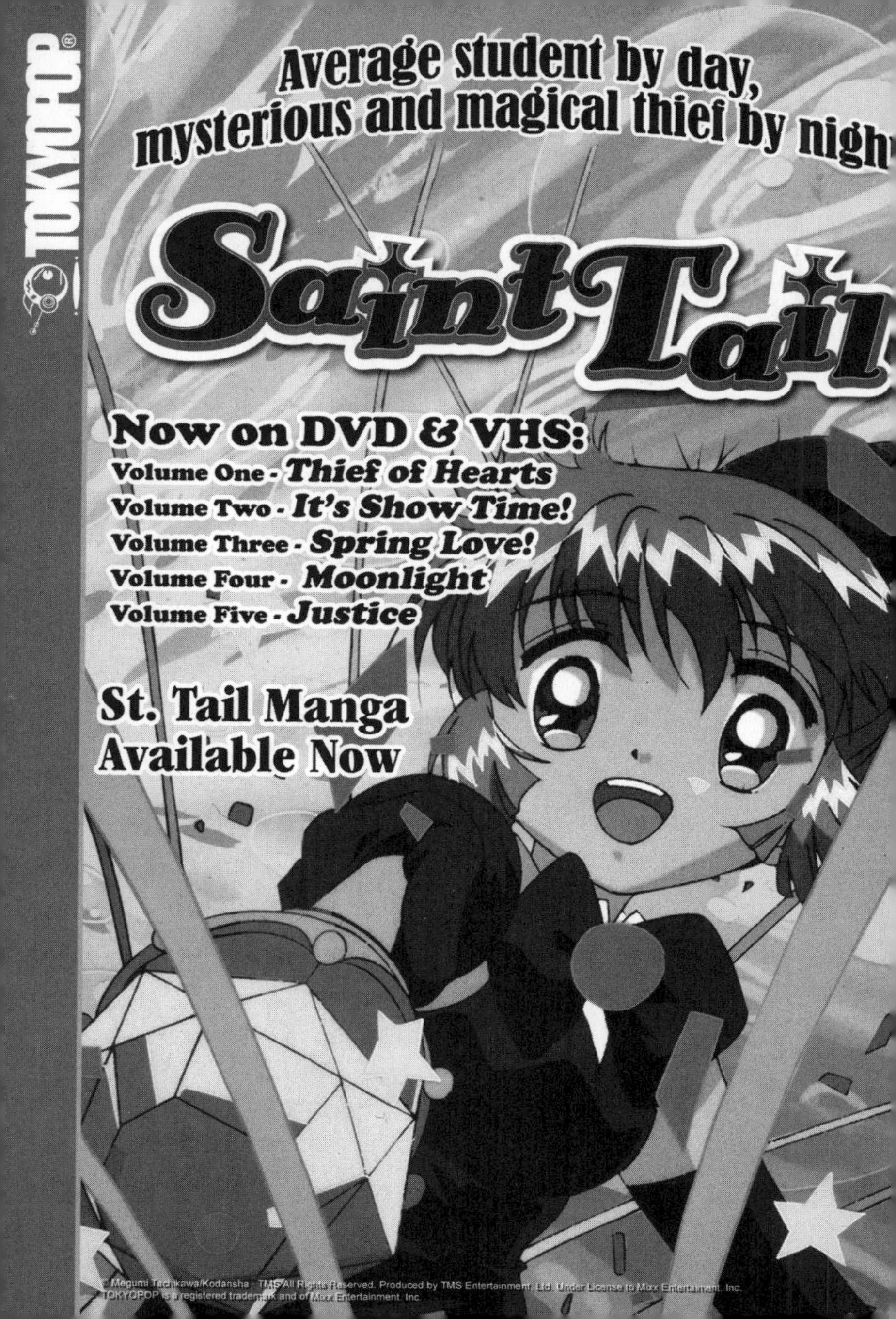
TOKYOPOP®
Average student by day,
mysterious and magical thief by nigh
Saint Tail
Now on DVD & VHS:
Volume One - Thief of Hearts
Volume Two - It's Show Time!
Volume Three - Spring Love!
Volume Four - Moonlight
Volume Five - Justice
St. Tail Manga
Available Now
© Megumi Tachikawa/Kodansha · TMS All Rights Reserved. Produced by TMS Entertainment, Ltd. Under License to Mixx Entertainment, Inc.
TOKYOPOP is a registered trademark and of Mixx Entertainment, Inc.

Meet Misaki, the Prodigy.

A lightning-fast fighting doll.
An insane mentor.
A pinky promise to be the best.

ANGELIC LAYER

The new manga from CLAMP, creators of Cardcaptor Sakura.

Available now!

STOP!

This is the back of the book.
You wouldn't want to spoil a great ending!

This book is printed "manga-style," in the authentic Japanese right-to-left format. Since none of the artwork has been flipped or altered, readers get to experience the story just as the creator intended. You've been asking for it, so TOKYOPOP® delivered: authentic, hot-off-the-press, and far more fun!

DIRECTIONS

If this is your first time reading manga-style, here's a quick guide to help you understand how it works.

It's easy... just start in the top right panel and follow the numbers. Have fun, and look for more 100% authentic manga from TOKYOPOP®!